1206   12

1206   12

GREAT
CLIMBS

ENDPAPERS: *Ascending the séracs of the Glacier des Bossons, Mont Blanc, 1861.*

PAGE 1: *Dick Renshaw leading the First Ice Cliff on Kishtwar-Shivling, with the headwall behind.*

PAGES 2–3: *The Wetterhorn in the Bernese Oberland. Its ascent in 1854 is often taken to mark the beginning of the Golden Age of Alpine Mountaineering.*

OPPOSITE: *From the summit of Mont Blanc, looking towards the Matterhorn (left) and Monte Rosa (right).*

OPPOSITE CONTENTS: *Towards the summit of the Eiger.*

OPPOSITE FOREWORD: *Ed Webster making a crucial crevasse crossing as 22,000 ft on Everest's East Face.*

GREAT CLIMBS

This edition first published in 1995 for
The Book People, Guardian House,
Borough Road, Godalming, Surrey GU7 2AE
by Mitchell Beazley,
an imprint of Reed Consumer Books Limited
Michelin House, 81 Fulham Road, London SW3 6RB
and Auckland, Melbourne, Singapore and Toronto

Executive Editor Sarah Polden
Executive Art Editor John Grain

Art Directors Tim Foster, Jacqui Small
Designers Nick Buzzard, Jessica Caws
Picture Researcher Judy Todd
Production Controller Michelle Thomas
Indexer Hilary Bird

Cartography by Philip's
Diagrams by Janos Marffy

A CIP catalogue record for this book is available from the British Library

ISBN 1 85613 2374

Typeset in Adobe/Linotype Garamond 10/11pt
and Adobe/Linotype Futura Extra Bold
Colour Reproduction by Scantrans Pte Ltd, Singapore
Produced by Mandarin Offset

Printed and bound in Hong Kong

A CELEBRATION OF WORLD MOUNTAINEERING

GREAT CLIMBS

General Editor   Editor
CHRIS BONINGTON   AUDREY SALKELD

TED SMART

Contents

Foreword

Why do people court danger? The question is often put to mountaineers, but most of us avoid the embarrassment of a serious reply. It is convenient to quote Mallory's easy answer about his ambition to climb Everest. 'Because it is there,' he said. We are aware of the urge to test our nerve and skills on steep and difficult places, but we draw back from self-analysis. Of course, the 'reasons why' may differ, at least in emphasis, between individuals, and according to their preferred kind of climbing. All climbers would agree that mountains, great and small, whether they be easy or difficult, present a challenge; at the very least, they provide a strenuous form of exercise. Where we meet difficulties, we may experience fear, which we may not enjoy, yet which we positively seek; the pleasure is likely to follow the danger, rather than accompany it.

For all but a few, I surmise, there is a sense of empathy with the whole environment in which we climb: a feeling of being at ease in the mountains. The walk to and from the crag, or mountain precipice, is the more enjoyable for its contrast with the hard way we have chosen to reach the top of the cliff, or summit. And there is a special quality of comradeship which grows from inter-dependence in difficulties and the sharing of the experience as a whole. As we grow older, this may be the most enduring of the pleasures of a pastime which some perceive as a way of life.

Such are the ingredients of the relationship between mountains and men. But they do not provide a complete answer to that inner impulse. At the lowest level, it is tempting to invite comparison between climbing and the antics of our simian ancestors. At the other end of the scale, it begs the question of what moves the human spirit. I forbear from pursuing that line of inquiry; there are others better qualified to do so.

For myself, I am content that mountains have, while climbing, walking and living among them, powerfully influenced my life. Ever since I first visited Switzerland as a child of ten, I have looked forward to the next time: to re-visit some favourite crags, or to climb on mountains further afield; to explore whenever – and in whatever mountain regions – opportunity has offered me a window. Now, I treasure my store of memories, some of them as vivid as when the events took place many years ago. And among my best memories, surprisingly perhaps, are climbs on which my companions and I did not get to the top.

So much for the passion which holds mountaineers in its thrall. But what about a host of other people who do not climb and who may have scant knowledge of the mountains, yet who derive pleasure and inspiration from climbing exploits? I have been impressed by this enthusiasm 'at second hand', which is shared by a very wide public. It creates a strong demand for mountaineering stories, through every form of communication. There is a wealth of climbing literature, which bodes well for the success of this anthology of memoirs by prominent mountaineers from a number of countries. There is, of course, the element of thrill for a sensation-hungry public. Many people, especially when they are young, choose their heroes and heroines from among the daring men and women who take risks in one way of another, in peace as well as in war. Tales of such exploits help to relieve the drabness and monotony of many peoples' lives. If climbing is likened to a drug for a climber, it can be no less a palliative against boredom for a wider range of people.

But there is something else in human nature which responds to pastimes involving dangers, some of which incur serious injuries and death. We may not fully understand what prompts some people to test themselves while sailing the seven seas, or undertaking arduous and hazardous journeys upon, above or beneath the surface of the earth, or to seek out nature's secrets in remote corners of the globe. It matters not whether the journey is undertaken for some useful purpose; or whether, in the words of a well-known French mountain guide, it is to attempt '*La Conquête de l'Inutile*'. But we do know that such enterprises elicit applause from people everywhere, in a world which is divided on many issues and conditioned by material values.

The span of experience included in this book is world-wide. It bids fair to appeal to the tastes of a wide readership, providing entertainment for many, stirring memories in others, as it does in me. For those who are intent on finding an answer to the question which I posed at the beginning of this foreword, this volume should serve as a fruitful quarry for research into the reasons why we climb.

Lord Hunt of Llanfair Waterdine, KG CBE DSO
Oxfordshire, June 1994

Introduction

This book encompasses the rich, broad spectrum of adventure that is climbing. It is something that has dominated my life and that of most of the contributors for their entire active lives. We climbers come in so many different guises, and yet I think the reader will find there are many common factors that stretch over time, age and geographical location.

For most of us, as John Hunt has stated in his Foreword, it started with an awareness of the beauty of wild country, a sense of curiosity of what is around the next corner of a valley or over the next horizon, the thrill of reaching a summit and suddenly having that panoramic view with the ground dropping away on every side. Already there is a level of exploration. It doesn't matter that others have been there before. For the individual it is the first experience, the first sight of that particular view, with a sense of wonder, that never seems to leave us. There can also be a sense of adventure. A Lakeland or Snowdon peak, the peat hags of Kinder or the featureless slopes of Ingleborough can give a sense of threat on a wild wintry day or even in summer, when enveloped by a storm with the cloud down and the rain driving in horizontal sheets. It is that element of risk, however slight, that element of the unknown, which provides the seeds of adventure. This is what led our Victorian forefathers to venture into the high peaks of the Alps and to develop mountaineering into the activity that we know today. The desire to share experience led to the formation of clubs, the first in the world being the Alpine Club. Established at a time when the British Empire was at the height of its powers, its founders, with a splendid arrogance, so typical of the times, felt that no national identification was necessary.

At the same time the early mountaineers turned to British hills to train for their summers in the Alps. They started in the reassuring embrace of deep gullies but soon ventured onto the more airy and open rock faces, and then discovered that this was a sport in itself; and so rock climbing was born. This introduced another powerful quality to the experience of climbing, the joy of physical agility, of gymnastics on rock. The same satisfaction, in essence, as that of any sporting activity but with the added spice of risk, that your life was in your hands, with a sheer drop below your feet and, in the days of hemp rope and elementary belay practice, the prospect of serious injury or death as a result of a fall.

It isn't so much a matter of doing something dangerous as being master of that danger. It is perhaps at its most elemental in rock climbing, either climbing solo or at the end of a long run out with very little protection. You reach a difficult section, pause, work out the moves, evaluate the risk, feel a tinge of fear. Maybe, there is no retreat. You can't get back down so you've no

choice but to go on. You make a tentative move, back off, try to rest, and then commit yourself, putting the planned moves into action, staying relaxed, in control, every sense sharpened, as you move upwards over the rippled rock. You've made it. There is a great sense of elation, euphoria and, at the same time, release, followed by a vast satisfaction as you bring up your second.

Your awareness of the mountains around you, of a pattern of lichen on the rock just below, the heat of the sun on your skin, are all intensified. The sensation is even stronger if it was a new route, if you have touched rock that has never felt a human hand, if you were unable to predict the outcome. This is what makes climbing so addictive.

It is very different from being out of control. I can remember my early days of climbing when I had more push than technique, of being involved in desperate, heart-wrenching struggles to stay in contact with the rock, of arriving at a stance in a panting terrified heap. At the time I accepted it as part of the process of climbing and was not deterred. It was only as I learnt my craft better and discovered how to read the rock, that I understood the difference between being in control, attuned to the environment of difficult, potentially dangerous rock, and fighting that same rock to force a way up it. That process of self-discovery, however, is an essential part of any man or woman's evolution as a climber.

The development of climbing techniques and the arguments over ethics are brought about by the need to resolve what at times can be two conflicting instincts. The use of a rope, primitive crampons, alpenstocks and even pitons enabled the early climber to attain his goal and also increased his chances of staying alive. Further advances in technique and equipment have enabled the climber to venture into ever steeper and more difficult places.

Arguments about the use of pitons on the north walls of the Alps, of the use of oxygen on Everest in the 1920s, siege-style expeditions in the seventies and the use of bolts in sport climbing in the eighties are all part of a conflict that is not solely about risk acceptance. It is also about the desire to increase the chances of success, something that is closely linked to ego, the desire to be recognized, the need to win, to be first, linked with, yet different from, the curiosity that is such an important part of the equation that makes up adventure and exploration.

Ego and competition are often seen as dirty words, were abhorred publicly and stridently in the annals of the Alpine Club between the Wars, and even today are regarded as slightly shameful. We might as well admit that most of us are competitive; it is a matter, surely, of degree; of whether a need for recognition, of winning is the dominant drive, or just one of the ingredients.

ABOVE: *The Northeast
Face of Mount Shivling,
from base camp at
Topovan, Gangotri,
India.*

LEFT: *Mark Miller
climbing Biale in the
Baltoro region of
Karakoram, Pakistan.*

RIGHT: *Nick Groves,
seen here on the Lower
Lobsang Spire, also in
the Baltoro region. The
Mustagh Tower can be
seen in the background.*

All these ingredients – a sense of wonder at the beauty and mystery of the mountains, the joy of physical prowess, the excitement of risk, the attraction of the unknown, the camaraderie and friendships, the spur of competition, gratification of ego, mixed in different proportions, are found in the make up of climbers throughout climbing history.

We have divided our collection into geographical regions to give the reader a feel for climbing activity throughout the world. The introductions to each section set the historical scene, whilst our contributors have been free to capture what they feel is important to them in their climbing experience. Through this approach we have been able to collect a mixture of reminiscences and descriptive and philosophical writings from a wide selection of mountaineers and climbers, all of whom have had a major impact on the development of climbing over the last hundred years. Together these accounts give a rich and varied mosaic of this all-encompassing activity that is so much broader than a sport, more a way of life.

Chris Bonington, CBE

Audrey Salkeld

THE ALPS

Hannibal crossed the Alps in 218 BC with some 9,000 men and mounts, not forgetting his thirty-seven elephants. The mummified body of a man found recently on the Similaun glacier near the Austro-Italian border dates back even further – 5,300 years, scientists say, though they can only speculate how he came to be in such an inhospitable place. From the earliest times, travellers and traders in mountainous areas have been forced to seek out those passes which offered the easiest passage. Surveyors and colonists regularly scaled eminent promontories to get the measure of the land. How can we tell when and where true 'mountaineering' started? If a spirit of adventure attends even an essential climb, who is to say that is not mountaineering? Certainly, where no practical purpose is served by the effort, then the spirit of mountaineering must be at work – which would make the Emperor Hadrian a mountaineer when he climbed Etna to view the sunrise in 126 BC. And Leonardo da Vinci too, whom curiosity drove part way up what must have been Monte Rosa or one of its outliers.

An ascent generally regarded as one of the earliest Alpine climbs was that of Mont Aiguille, in the Dauphiné, in 1492 by a mercenary group of some ten men (including an official ladder carrier) climbing under orders of their monarch, Charles VIII of France. But the great alpinistic breakthrough came in 1786 when, after twenty years of vain endeavour, Mont Blanc, the highest summit in the Alps, was surmounted by Dr Michel Paccard and Jacques Balmat. Both climbers came from nearby Chamonix, which was fast becoming a popular resort. Enterprising travel was all the rage among the well-to-do and, under Rousseau's influence, the universal fear of mountains as

haunts of dragons and evil spirits was rapidly evaporating. By the middle of the nineteenth century several high summits had been reached and the path to the top of Mont Blanc was becoming well-trodden, despite the assertion in Baedecker's guide that 'a large proportion of those who have made this ascent have been persons of unsound mind'.

The single event credited with ushering in this 'Golden Age' of mountaineering was an ascent of the Wetterhorn in 1854 by Alfred Wills, a barrister honeymooning in the Alps – a curiously Anglocentric vision of events since it was not the first time that mountain had been climbed. However, the following season British alpinists claimed a true first when two of the Reverend brothers Smyth clambered to the top of the Dufourspitz, the highest summit of Monte Rosa, with Charles Hudson, Charles Ainslie, John Birkbeck and the great guide, Ulrich Lauener.

The climb to receive more attention than any other – because of its attendant tragedy – was the first ascent of the Matterhorn in 1865. This beautiful obelisk of rock and ice had been taunting mountaineers for years: reconnaissances were carried out in 1858 and 1859 by British climbers with their Swiss guide, and by Italian chamois hunters who ventured as far as what is now called the 'Chimney' on the Italian ridge. More attempts followed and in 1861 the young Edward Whymper joined the fray.

He was twenty-one, a promising draughtsman and watercolourist who had come to the Alps to make illustrations for a new book, but very quickly the Matterhorn absorbed all his attention. Jean-Antoine Carrel of Val Tournanche was known to be the 'Cock of the valley', and Whymper could see that he was perhaps the only person, besides himself, to have real faith that the Matterhorn was not invincible. It is easy to see now that these two bullheaded individuals should have been working more closely together, but Carrel was determined that no outsider should snatch the prize: it was for Italian climbers to achieve, from the Italian side of the mountain, and though he made one or two tentative sallies with Whymper, Carrel did little more than string his English 'master' along, shallying on the mountain, and making promises he had no intention of keeping.

BELOW: The Alpine chain sweeps from the Mediterranean to the Eastern Alps of Austria and Slovenia, more than 600 miles end to end.

KEY TO MOUNTAINS 1 Pelvoux; 2 Mont Blanc; 3 Matterhorn; 4 Monte Rosa; 5 Ortler; 6 Wildspitz; 7 Venediger; 8 Grossglockner

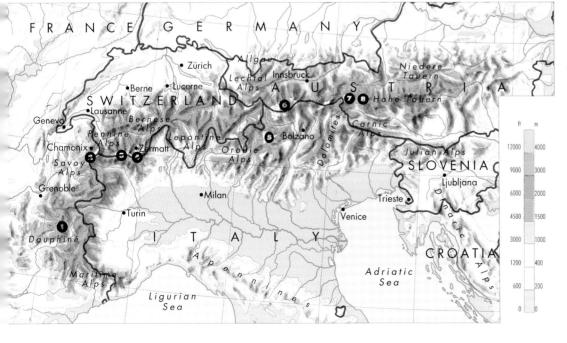

ABOVE: Alps on Alps arise. The view from the summit of Mont Blanc, highest Alp of all.

RIGHT: Horace-Bénédict de Saussure climbs Mont Blanc in August 1787, a year after the first ascent by Balmat and Paccard.

Over three summers Whymper made seven attempts on the Matterhorn with an assortment of companions. He even tackled it alone, something that nearly finished him off when he fell 200 feet from the cliffs of the Tête du Lion in a series of cartwheeling bounds, dashing himself on the rocks below. Up until 1865 Whymper had concentrated solely on the Italian ridge; now he began considering alternatives. The east face seemed promising and he sought Carrel's cooperation. Prevaricating, the Val Tournanche Cock promised to give it a try as soon as he had fulfilled a longstanding engagement, then immediately began laying stores in for a secret push of his own up the Italian route. When Whymper realized he was being 'bamboozled and humbugged', he was hellbent on revenge.

Working out that Carrel's party could not possibly ascend the mountain and return to Breuil in less than seven days calmed Whymper's temper somewhat. It permitted a slim chance of outwitting him. Even if the eastern face proved impractical, there would still be time to arrive in Breuil before Carrel's men returned from their depot-laying. 'And then, it seemed to me, as the mountain was not padlocked, one might start at the same time as the Messieurs, and yet get to the top before them.' In Zermatt he found another Matterhorn aspirant in the experienced

13

LEFT: The Matterhorn disaster of 1865. Four men died when their rope broke, coming down after the first successful climb (lithograph from a drawing by Gustave Doré).

BELOW: Relics of the fateful climb. Equipment used by Edward Whymper during his ascent of the Matterhorn.

alpinist Charles Hudson, and they joined forces for an assault on the east face. They were accompanied by a couple of teenaged mountaineers, Lord Francis Douglas and Douglas Hadow, as well as Michel Croz, a very experienced guide from Chamonix, and the Peters Taugwalder, father and son, from Zermatt. A younger Taugwalder came as porter as far as their bivouac camp at 11,000 feet.

The party left Zermatt on July 13 on a cloudless morning, reaching their camping site by midday. They spent a lazy afternoon while Croz and Young Peter scouted out the route ahead, and returned in high spirits. 'We could have gone to the summit and returned today,' they crowed. 'Easily!' And sure enough, setting out at dawn next morning, Whymper found the greater part of the east face rising for 3,000 feet like a huge natural staircase. They hugged the northeast ridge, hardly needing to employ the rope, but higher, as the going grew steeper, they crossed to the northern side of the mountain. Here, a skim of ice covered rocks and snow, demanding great caution, and young Hadow, the least experienced of the party, needed continual encouragement. In time the difficulties were passed and ahead lay only an easy unbroken snowslope. By 1.40 p.m. the world lay at their feet. Way below they could see the tiny figures of Carrel's party and understood they had beaten them by a good margin. 'We must make them hear us!' Whymper cried, but though they yelled till they were hoarse, their rivals gave no sign of having heard. 'They shall hear us!' Whymper was emphatic and, hurling down a great rock, he urged his companions to do likewise. Soon they were all prising out boulders and pouring them down the cliffs. This time there was no mistake. The Italians turned and fled under this barrage.

But glory was short-lived. Retracing their steps down the difficult section, roped together and with only one man moving at a time, Hadow slipped. He knocked against Croz, who was helping him, and as the two fell with startled cries, Hudson and Douglas were tugged off in turn. The rope between Douglas and the next in line, Old Peter Taugwalder, being thinner than the rest, snapped. Whymper and the Taugwalders could only watch in horror as their spreadeagled companions disappeared over the brow of the slope, to fall from precipice to precipice four thousand feet down the mountain.

For a century and a half, people have argued over how such a fatally thin line came to be employed and suspicion that Old Peter had deliberately used the unsuitable rope to protect himself and his son was never completely obliterated. The careers of the Taugwalders were permanently blighted and Whymper's Alpine climbing came to an abrupt end, although he later made exploratory journeys to South and North America.

To future mountaineers he left the injunction: 'Climb if you will, but remember that courage and strength are nought without prudence, and that a momentary negligence may destroy the happiness of a lifetime. Do nothing in haste; look well to each step; and from the beginning think what may be the end.' The Matterhorn tragedy checked British Alpine mountaineering for half a generation. Such was the outcry against 'the terrible and terribly silly exploits of the Alpine Club' that even many Clubmen doubted the validity of their pastime and duly resigned. British climbers ceded supremacy in the Alps to their brethren on the Continent.

With the major peaks climbed – the last to fall was the Meije in 1877 to the 20-year-old Baron Emmanuel Boileau de Castelnau, guided by the celebrated Pierre Gaspard and his son – attention turned to harder and more specialized routes. The Eastern Europeans in particular, with such climbers as the Zsigmondy brothers, Georg Winkler and, later, Paul Preuss, took rock climbing to previously unimagined levels of difficulty. Winter mountaineering became popular, and there was an all-round increase in guideless activity.

Alfred Mummery dominated the British Alpine scene, although it took traditionalists a long time to be reconciled to his bold approach. In 1879 he had made the first ascent of the Matterhorn's Zmutt Ridge and the following year mastered the Grépon, both with Alexander Burgener, a guide with whom he would climb almost

BELOW: Alexander Burgener from the Saas Valley (1845-1910), an outstanding Alpine guide who regularly climbed with Alfred Mummery.

exclusively until, in the early 1890s, confident in his own skills, he ceased to employ guides altogether. He was tall and long-limbed with considerable strength and endurance, but he suffered from a weakness of the spine which prevented him from carrying loads. In response to what could have been a great handicap, he developed lightweight equipment. He also devised a new form of boot spike. Gymnast and tactician, superb on rock and particularly so on ice, he challenged orthodoxy and improved technique, attracting around himself a group of like-minded enthusiasts. His climbs included traverses of the Charmoz and the Grépon, and in 1893 with Norman Collie, Geoffrey Hastings and Cecil Slingsby, he climbed the formidable Dent du Requin for the first time. Eleven days later, with these same men and also Lily Bristow, he traversed the Grépon again. The men went on to complete the first ascent of the west face of the Aig Plan, before rejoining Miss Bristow two days later to climb the Petit Dru. Influential as he was in life, Mummery remained no less a guiding light to subsequent generations through his book, *My Climbs in the Alps and Caucasus*. He was lost on Nanga Parbat in the Himalaya in 1895.

The years running up to World War I had seen the appearance of 'artificial' devices and rope techniques which enabled the field of action to be extended even further. In the years before World War II European climbers began vying for the big north walls of the Alps: the Matterhorn, Grandes Jorasses and, most notorious of all, the Eigerwand, which, after several years of attempts with the loss of eight lives, was finally climbed in 1938 by Anderl Heckmair, Ludwig Vörg, Heinrich Harrer and Fritz Kasparek. Social changes and easier travel brought a further climbing explosion after the War. Plum routes were plucked by young climbers of the Alpine countries and Britain. Walter Bonatti soloed the Southwest Pillar of the Dru in 1955 in a remarkable climb lasting six days, becoming the hero of a generation. Within a few years, American climbers

LEFT: 'Station Eismeer' – a poster by Emil Cardinaux for the Jungfrau railway (c. 1905).

stormed the Alps with big wall tactics developed in Yosemite. Artificial climbing reached formidable limits but then, towards the end of the sixties, having made a name for himself with some remarkable solo ascents in his native Dolomites, Reinhold Messner burst onto the greater Alpine scene. With evangelistic fervour, he set about 'cleaning up' climbing. 'Today's climber carries his courage in his rucksack, in the form of bolts and equipment,' he bewailed. Slaves of the plumb line were murdering 'The Impossible'.

He swung the tide, dominating the climbing scene for two decades. These days, with improved equipment design and lightweight materials, and above all with new physiological awareness and dedicated training, more becomes possible than ever before, enabling many strands of alpinism to coexist. Combining classic long days with swift ascents of extreme routes has produced enchainements, where several of the hardest routes are strung together, often employing other disciplines like skiing or paragliding to effect the descents in between. The 'Playground of the Alps', as it was known to our Victorian forefathers, is far from being played out.

ABOVE: The Viennese doctor, Emil Zsigmondy (1861-1885), a pioneer of guideless climbing. With his brother, Otto, he made many fine Eastern Alps ascents.

RIGHT: Mont Blanc and the magnificent Mer de Glace, the longest glacier system in the French Alps.

An Easy Day for a Lady

Well, we got to the top but saw no signs of the other party – we yodelled,

yelled and howled but heard no reply and Mr Slingsby began to be

seriously alarmed for their safety.

Montenvers, 6 August 1893
Rejoice with me, for I have done my peak – the biggest climb I have ever had or ever shall have, for there isn't one to beat it in the Alps (unless it's the traverse of the Meije, which they haven't done yet but which Fred [Alfred Mummery] doesn't believe is as good). Which you mayn't know it, but the expedition I'm referring to is the traverse of the Grépon. On the 3rd, Fred, Mr Hastings and I tracked off from here, and camped at the same place on the Nantillons Glacier where Fred and I camped before, and where we were driven back by bad weather (*n.b.* I thought that night that three people in one tent 6ft x 4ft was a tightish fit; but await the sequel). Next morning Mr Slingsby, Dr Collie and Mr Brodie joined us at the camp, having walked from Montenvers about 4.30 a.m., and soon afterwards Fred and I started so as to get the step-cutting done ready for the others when they had breakfasted. After about one-and-a-half hours' going the others caught us up, they only having to walk in our steps, and Mr Slingsby tied on to our rope, as we three were to go up the Grépon by the couloir and Fred's crack and the other three were to cross the glacier to C.P. [a rock, so called from initials carved upon it] and work up by Morse and Wicks' route – their route was easier than ours provided they could surmount one very difficult obstacle which Morse and Wicks had circumvented by rope-throwing. The two parties were to meet on the top, and we were each to descend by the route opposite to that

by which we had come. We found our couloir, however, not in the very best imaginable condition, even at that early hour of the morning, so Fred and Mr Slingsby immediately decided that the other party must be persuaded to return with us by the C.P. route. Well, it's no good trying to describe the climb; I have often felt on the climbs, that if I had sufficient knowledge and pluck I could have done it by myself, but this climb was something totally different. It was more difficult than I could ever imagine – a succession of problems each one of which was a ripping good climb in itself – you will understand well enough that in a climb of this kind there is not the slightest danger for any one except the leading man, the others merely follow in absolute safety with the rope, but certainly with vast exertion. Fred is magnificent, he has such absolute confidence, I never once had the faintest squirm about him even when he was in the most hideous places, where the least slip would have been certain death, and there were very many such situations. It is really a huge score for him to have taken me (*and* the camera) on such an expedition. I took six photographs, and have developed two, one of which is a failure. Well, we got to the top but saw no signs of the other party – we yodelled, yelled and howled but heard no reply and Mr Slingsby began to be seriously alarmed for their safety. However, we proceeded on our way along a series of summits (for the Grépon has even more peaks than the Charmoz, which as you know has five). When we got to the final

peak our shouts were at last answered from below, the other party having been stopped by the obstacle I mentioned, where Morse and Wicks threw ropes. As Dr Collie and Mr Hastings had been up before, and as it was getting late in the afternoon (about 4.30) they remained where they were, while Fred and Mr Slingsby hauled up Mr Brodie with two ropes. Then we all descended to the other two, who had got some tea and bread and butter and other luxuries ready for us – then I took some more photographs, and as the situation did not admit of setting up a tripod Mr Hastings made a support for me by wedging his head against a rock. By this time it was beginning to get dark and also heavy mists came up, which soon turned to rain. As I had been delayed by the photography, one party (Dr Collie and Messrs Slingsby and Brodie) went on, and the rest of us followed as soon as possible. Our party went on ahead, as it was rapidly getting dark and raining hard, while Mr. Slingsby's remarks drifted to us through the pauses in the wind. At last we failed to find the tracks by which the other party had ascended in the morning, so Dr Collie's party who had a lantern, went ahead and Dr C., who is a marvellous pathfinder, succeeded after about an hour in recovering the track. Everybody was wet through except myself, who was only partially so, as I was wearing Fred's short water-proof coat. We reached our camp soon after 11 p.m. and now is the sequel I mentioned. Imagine six people in a tent which had been tight for three! Sleeping-bags, tent and everything were of course sopping wet, but it was bliss and comfort after our experiences outside. Fred pulled off my boots and wormed me into a wet sleeping-bag, and I lay down in the shallowest part of the

pool and felt heavenly comfortable and warm. The other poor devils all had to sit up, as there was no room for them to lie down, and they must bave been horribly cold and wet. I actually went to sleep for a short time. We all of us got cramp more or less, and that ain't pleasant, when it is absolutely impossible to move. The wind was that rampageous that I can't imagine how the fellows managed to hold the tent down at all. As soon as it was light enough we crawled down the wet slippery rocks and traversed the bergschrund below, and I suppose we got to Montenvers about 8 a.m. faint yet pursuing. That was yesterday. I promptly went to bed after some hot milk and came to lunch with a gorgeous appetite, a very good temper, extremely sore hands, and a general feeling of gratified ambition. I am perfectly fit today, and Mares [Mary Mummery] and I are going to track round with the fellows to their *gîte*, from which place they are going to make another attempt on the Aiguille du Plan.

Montenvers, 10 August 1893

The day before yesterday we camped out for the Dru, as we have been having such perfect weather that it seemed wicked not to use our opportunities, although the gentlemen were all rather tired from their ascent of the Plan [on the previous day] – Fred, Mr Slingsby and I had the tent, and Dr Collie and Mr Hastings camped under a rock, and all passed a most comfortable night. I am getting quite swagger at sleeping on stones. As for my ankle, thanks, it is almost as good as new again. I can now walk all right on a path or a glacier; and on loose stones, one or other of the gentlemen always gives me a hand. We left our camp for the Dru about 3 a.m., it was no good starting earlier, as all the ground was fairly difficult, so it was necessary to be able to see one's way. First we went over a stretch of glacier, and then took to the rocks – Fred and I on one rope, and the other fellows together – we had none of us ever been up before, but I had been fortunate enough to spot a party coming down from the col with guides the previous evening, and had very carefully noted their route, so I had some idea of the way; this being so, Fred let me lead, which I always enjoy, it is so much more exciting. We reached the col about half-past five and breakfasted there; we had had some tea before leaving the camp. By this time we had come to much more difficult rocks, and though we remained in the same order for about half an hour, it soon became necessary for us all to go on one rope, as no one but Fred could lead up some of the places, and even he only with Mr Hastings to give him a shoulder up, so he, Mr H, came second on the rope, then I, and then Mr Slingsby and Dr Collie last. The climbing was pretty stiff, I must say, though not

RIGHT, TOP AND BOTTOM: Bessie Norton found her breath froze inside the special 'Alpine helmet' she adopted for an ascent of Mont Blanc early in 1905.

FAR RIGHT: The contemporary press was generally more interested in what women were wearing on mountains than what they climbed. Excluded from the select Alpine Club, women founded one of their own in 1907.

nearly so difficult as the Grépon, which is a real snorker. When we got to the top I was a good deal tired, so Fred put me in a safe place and I had a snooze, and when I woke the fellows gave me a lovely drink of lemons and half-melted snow. By this time I suppose it was about twelve. Going down we took a great deal longer than we ought to have done, but we were all tired; however, we got back to the camp just before dark. Dr Collie

LEFT: The Charmoz (left) and the Grépon (right) with the Aiguille Verte group behind.

and Mr Hastings had gone on ahead and had made me some tea, which revived me sufficiently for the rest of the journey. We had now some rather slabby sort of rocks to go down, and the only way we could find was along the track of a small waterfall, so we got drenched to the skin – however, in about an hour we were down the slabs, and then we had interminable moraine. I should have been quite dead, only Mr Hastings, the Hercules of the party, gave me a hand all the way, and got me along so quickly that we managed to reach the hotel by 11.30 and very glad of our victuals we were when we got them. We all feel as though we deserved some rest, so we are lazing, and talk of leaving here tomorrow for the Chalet de Lognan, a sort of little mountain pub where there are said to be three beds – I suppose the others will camp on the floor somewhere. After a couple of days there, at the outside, I expect we shall go on to Zinal; where my address will be Hotel Durand – after that we shall be at Breuil on the Italian side, and shall eventually return here for our baggage. We have just heard of the accident on the Matterhorn, Gentinetta (one of the guides here) has had a post-card from his brother at Zermatt – we get so little news here except what one picks up in that sort of way. There is a rumour, too, of an accident on the Grandes Jorasses, but I hope there is no truth in it.

If you only knew how awfully good all those fellows are in taking care of me, you would not feel the least anxiety about my safety or comfort – they all try to see who can do the most coddling, and I am even more cosseted than I used to be when I was alone with Fred. Except a wholesome sort of laziness, I am just as fit as I can be today, and my appetite is large enough to make the chef shudder – I only had my breakfast about 11 but at one o'clock I repaired to lunch with quite unabated vigour. Fred's exploits here are causing a great deal of enthusiasm. His having taken a lady up the two most difficult peaks here, without guides, in the course of one week, and having sand-wiched between these expeditions a totally new ascent of a very difficult peak [the Plan], is really worthy of some applause.

Zinal, 14 August 1893
We left Montenvers with awful pangs of regret on Saturday morning, walked down towards Argentière and then drove over the Tête Noire and La Forclaz to Martigny. It was a most delicious drive, especially the first part, where we had splendid views of the Mont Blanc range and more particularly of the Charmoz. We slept at Martigny, and next morning Mares, Fred and I came by train to Sierre and then drove to Vissoye – we all meant to have walked up from there, but Mares has not been feeling well for some days, and I think the hot air of the Rhône valley must have finished her, for soon after we left Vissoye she said she really felt too bad to walk, so Fred went back and fetched her a mule. She is better this morning, and will, I hope, be well enough to go over the Triftjoch tomorrow if the weather keeps fine. I hoped to have found a letter awaiting me here, but cannot discover any. Please write next to Poste Restante, Breuil, Italy. We shall probably reach there by Thursday, spend about a week there, and return home via Courmayeur and Montenvers, to regain our luggage, as we have only brought a very small amount with us. We expect to meet the rest of the party at either Zermatt or Breuil, as they intend travelling by the high-

RIGHT: Alfred Mummery (inset) was a technical wizard on rock and ice. The larger photograph, taken by Lily Bristow during the climb described here, shows him at work in the Mummery Crack on the Grépon and is the only surviving picture of him climbing.

level route, traversing the Grand Combin on the way. We miss them very much already.

Zinal, 15 August 1893
On Monday evening, about 9 o'clock, Fred proposed that we should go up the Rothorn next day, so we hastily made preparations and retired to bed. We got up at 1.30, but the natives were so astonished at our enterprise that, though we had ordered our breakfast beforehand, we had to wait countless ages, and only got off at a quarter to three. I had a moke [donkey] for an hour and a half up the valley, and very glad I was of it, as there was a colossal distance to traverse before we got to the peak at all. About 7 a.m. Fred told me it was quite out of the question that we could get up, that the distance was too great, but I begged and prayed in my most artful manner, and he agreed to go on a bit and see – we made all sorts of little vows – if we didn't get to the col by 10 we would turn back – at 2 o'clock we would turn back, wherever we were – and so on. As a matter of fact we didn't reach the col by ten, but I concealed the fact from Fred, and at last we triumphantly reached the top 25 minutes to two. Then we scrambled down as fast as we could, and if the old fool of a rope didn't go and knock my very superior hat and my goggles down a quite impossible slope and so completely ruin my cherished complexion! I have preserved my skin hitherto with the utmost skill, but of course, having no hat has brought my forehead up into the regulation blisters, and even the rest of my face smiles with difficulty. When we got in about 9 p.m. it was a great joke, none of the hotel people would believe we had been up the Rothorn: 'non Mademoiselle, pas possible!' They are not used to non-guided parties here and the idea that Fred and I could calmly track up their most awesome and revered peak is quite beyond them – they think we must have mistaken some grassy knoll for the Rothorn.

(First published in *The Alpine Journal*, November 1942)

John Hunt

The Meije

And suddenly, there it was! It towered above the narrow valley, 8,000

feet above our heads, its summit pyramid flaunting a pennant of cloud

in the high wind.

As a boy in my teens, who read Whymper's *Scrambles among the Alps* before beginning to climb, I was enthralled not only by the saga of the Matterhorn but also by his travels and climbs in the Dauphiné during the 1860s. His description of a savage landscape in a remote region of the Alps, isolated from the mainstream of civilization, in which life was hard and primitive and in-breeding prevalent, filled me with wonder. It seemed to me extraordinary, as a schoolboy, with limited experience in other parts of the Alps where tourism was already thriving, that such conditions could have survived in Western Europe only sixty years beforehand.

I was gripped by Whymper's account of his first crossing of the Brèche de la Meije and the daring traverse of the Écrins in 1864. I, too, wanted to travel in those parts and, above all, I was determined to scale both those peaks.

An opportunity to attempt the Meije came while on holiday with my family in the Savoie during the summer of 1927. (The Écrins had to wait another three years.) I had been climbing easy peaks accessible from the little hamlet of Val d'Isère for the past two years. Even in those days of narrow and mainly unmetalled roads, it would be no great trouble to travel to La Grave for the remainder of the school holidays. My mother agreed and my small brother had no say in the matter.

I have a vivid memory of that drive, in an open *diligence*, waiting for the moment when my dream mountain – the Meije –

BIOGRAPHY

John Hunt began his mountaineering with a traverse of Piz Palu in the Bernina when he was fifteen. His father had climbed before him, had even met Whymper, but was killed in northern France early in the First World War when Hunt was only four. It was Hunt's mother who introduced him and his younger brother to the Alps, taking them to Switzerland for their summer holidays to revisit some of the places she had enjoyed with her husband. Already moved by an earlier excursion onto the Upper Grindelwald Glacier, and 'lit up', as he puts it, by the disappearance of George Mallory and Andrew Irvine on Everest the year before, success on Piz Palu in 1925 sealed Hunt's lifelong commitment to high and lonely places. The youthful ascent of the Meije, which he describes here, followed a few years later, by which time he had made a good number of lesser climbs and traverses – some of them on ski.

would come into view. And suddenly, there it was! It towered above the narrow valley, 8,000 feet above our heads, its summit pyramid flaunting a pennant of cloud in the high wind. Here was a mountain of quite a different order from the Tsanteleina, the Sassière, the Grande Aiguille Rousse and other gentle peaks I had wandered up and down in the Savoie.

At the hotel, the proprietor, M Juge, recommended one Paul Jouffray as a guide, and I lost no time in calling on him. I had climbed with professional guides in the Engadine and, more recently, in the Savoie. Paul outstripped my limited experience of a home-bred mountaineer. He was short, solid and, despite his youth, already tending towards stoutness, a 'comfortable body'. He sported a splendid, spear-pointed moustache, a proud memento of his service as a *poilu* in the Chasseurs Alpins. Paul gave me an appraising inspection. Yes, he might take me up the Meije. But first, I must demonstrate my fitness and sureness of foot on an easy peak. He would engage a porter, a *guide aspirant*, named Georges Dode, to accompany me up the Grande Ruine, a name which was somewhat less than inspiring. I agreed. In the event, I learned that I had passed muster, at least in respect of speed and sheer enthusiasm.

So it was that, a few days later, the three of us set forth for the Meije, over the Brèche, in the footsteps of Whymper. But the weather was most disobliging. We had been told that the Muraille Castelnau was plastered with verglas and that only one ascent had been made that summer. On

LA MURAILLE CASTELNAU.

LE CHEVAL ROUGE

LE PAS DU CHAT.

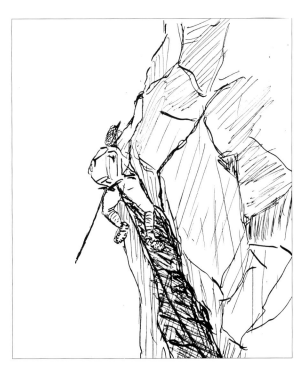

A selection of pen and ink sketches from John Hunt's 1928 journal, illustrating memorable pitches of his Meije climb.

ABOVE: John Hunt was 18 when he climbed the Meije, a solemn young man on the brink of a distinguished career which took him from soldier to diplomat and parliamentarian. He led the first successful Everest climb in 1953 and was President of the RGS from 1976-80.

arrival at the Promontoire Hut the weather was so bad that even Paul – an incorrigible optimist – proposed to go on down to La Bérarde and return to La Grave by road. But scarcely had we set foot on the Étançons Glacier than the irrepressible little man changed his mind. We would cross the Col des Chamois – itself an entertaining climb – and descend to the Refuge de l'Alpe. Disappointed though I was, I had cause to thank Jouffray, for we traversed beneath the famous Grande Muraille; my ambition was tempered with doubt whether I could climb such a daunting precipice.

There was nothing for it but to return, and in 1928, fortune smiled on my hopes. I was just 18 and had left school in July. The weather in the Dauphiné was *beau fixe*. Once again, Georges and I limbered up on the Grande Ruine. Jouffray joined us and we followed up that training climb from the Refuge Adèle Planchard with a much more serious test: the Tour Carrée de Roch Méane by its south face. 'Plus difficile que la Meije,' said Paul. It is still rated as *assez difficile* and I was duly impressed.

In continuing good weather we again crossed the Brèche de la Meije, gathering firewood for the stove at the hut from the ruined chalets of Enfetchores, on our way to the Glacier de Tabuchet. By the time we had settled in for the night, eleven other climbers had arrived from La Berarde, enough in those days to fill the little wooden cabin. For me, a dream was about to come true. I had little sleep from excitement and apprehension.

The narrative which follows may seem naive and somewhat stilted: I wrote a journal in the language of the region and my attempt to translate it into English shortly after the War has done nothing to embellish the original, if imperfect French. But I have felt it best to leave it as it is, with only minor editing, so as to convey the impressions of a romantic youngster who began to climb in that period between guided and amateur alpinism, shortly after the First World War.

*

We rose at 3.30 a.m. On the previous evening the weather had looked a bit doubtful, but now there was bright moonlight. We roped up in the hut and went out; no-one else stirred. The climbing begins at the door itself, but the moon made it easy to see the holds and, in any case, there were few problems. Most of the time, we climbed together; the rock was sound, the chimneys and slabs were interesting, without being difficult. After about three-quarters of an hour along this Promontoire ridge, we descended into the Grand Couloir, which comes down on the flank of the West Ridge, and borders the Grande Muraille. I suppose this couloir is usually snow-filled, but this fine year it

was filled with loose rock; we made quick progress and, in ten minutes, were up on the broad platform marking the junction of the Promontoire with the Grande Muraille.

As we paused to eat, I took a good look at this famous precipice immediately above us. It is crowned by the shining rim of the Glacier Carré and is stained with damp; for me it appeared as a daunting obstacle. Somewhat apprehensively, I followed Jouffray down a difficult pitch leading towards the right from the platform. The traverse continued almost horizontally, with a plunging view down to the Glacier des Etançons, several hundreds of metres below: a narrow, exposed corridor running across the face. Then we began to make height, turning back to the left. We reached the Dos d'Ane, a curious hump of smooth granite, which is not a serious obstacle. And so on to the Dalle des Autrichiens, a very steep slab, made easier by a piton fixed in its lower half. . . . Then we made a very exposed traverse to the left, with small footholds and a horizontal crack for the hands, chocked with stones. This leads to the Pas du Chat, which is definitely the hardest part of the Mur Castelnau. . . . We had reached the west edge of the wall, which has to be turned in order to reach a rib running up to the left bottom corner of the Glacier Carré. It is made possible by a big crack splitting the edge of the wall; it runs steeply up the West side, looking over the Brèche: the Pas du Chat. You have to squirm up awkwardly on your stomach, vainly groping for satisfactory holds. Round the corner, the crack leans outwards over the glacier. I had quite a struggle to support myself with my left knee, while I fumbled for holds in the crack. The remainder of the way to the glacier is not hard. We surmounted a sharp-edged slab of granite and reached a large ledge on the other side. Here we sat down to eat, and got our axes out of our waist loops.

The glacier is not altogether easy. There was no snow this year, only bare ice. We kept to the extreme left edge, near the rocks, using good steps made by a previous party. Beneath the rocks of the Pic du Glacier Carré we traversed to the right, to reach the saddle, which offered a view down to the Romanche and La Grave.

The rocks of the grand Pic are not difficult; the line is straight up, and it was seldom necessary to use our hands. The one problem is the Cheval Rouge. Here the rocks suddenly steepen, and you reach the foot of a high slab on the south side of the arête. Jouffray swarmed up it and sat astride its sharp crest, his left leg hanging over La Grave, the other one on the La Bérarde side. Then Georges installed himself behind Paul; I followed, not without difficulty. The slab is holdless and you have to rely on friction. Jouffrey then stood on the knife-edge and climbed on to the Tête du Capucin at its eastern end. After a short scramble along the final bit of ridge, we arrived on the summit of the Meije soon after 8.00 a.m.

It was a great moment, but I felt overawed by the look of the ridge running across to the Pic Central: the Doigt de Dieu. It was narrow and, of course, I had read about the problem of the Passage Zsigmondy. There was a tremendous panorama: Mont Blanc far away in the North, and the Grande Sassière, in Savoie which I had climbed last year. And there was the plateau of Mont Revard above Aix-les-Bains, from which I had seen the Meije a year ago. We looked down upon La Grave and could see the hotel *terrasse*, where tourists were probably watching us through the telescope. The day was gloriously fine and we spent a quiet hour on top before beginning the descent. For a few minutes we went down easy rocks, slightly on the south side, until they suddenly fell away towards the Brèche Zsigmondy. On our left we found a rusty iron ring. While we were uncoiling the rappel cord to negotiate this difficult and exposed pitch, we heard noises below us and saw two men evidently having some trouble in climbing the Fissure Zsigmondy. One of them was up, and they were about to haul up their sacks. We were surprised to see them, for there had been no-one ahead of us when we left the hut. Later, when we passed them on the ridge, we learned they were two Marseillais who had started the day before but, climbing slowly, had been forced to bivouac; luckily for them, it had been a fine night.

Georges went down on the rappel cord, moving towards the left above the smooth wall which drops to the Glacier du Tabuchet. He found a stance in a chimney and I followed, disliking the great exposure. After a few feet of broken rock and a short ascent we reached a kind of cave beneath an overhanging rock on our right. It is from this point that the famous ledge leads up across the north face: the Passage Zsigmondy. There had once been a stout rope along this pitch, but only some frayed ends and two iron rings remained.

We changed the order on the rope. During the ascent I had been at the end and, during the descent to the Brèche, had been put in the middle. Now I was again moved to the back for this most formidable obstacle. Jouffray started along the ledge on his stomach, using its lower edge for handholds, with his right leg on the ledge, the other one hanging out over space. The ledge is quite wide to start with, but gets progressively narrower, until you have little more purchase on the rock than your right kneee in the crack, the rest of you is out over the void. Such were my impressions as I watched Paul's progress. Then he disappeared from view. There followed an anxious pause, before Georges was signalled to follow. After what seemed a very long time, I heard a faint shout from above. I started climbing carefully along the ledge until it came to an end, with the rope running directly upwards. For a few moments I thought the next move would defeat me. Supported as I was only by my right knee, I felt most insecure and exposed. It was clear that the line lay straight up; but on my right the wall fell away vertically below a slight overhang; I felt that the slightest move would upset my balance. I dared not let go with my hands to feel for holds higher on the wall, yet I had somehow to raise my left leg to get a footing on the ledge and rise to a standing position. It took a few unsuccessful attempts before I managed it somehow and climbed up to the others on the crest of the ridge.

I won't describe the traverse in detail. This year there was no snow, just smooth slabs. We passed the Marseillais, traversed under the Central Summit and, after descending with some difficulty on its far side, began to leave the ridge. The ice slope on the north side seemed to me exceedingly steep. Jouffray established himself on a bollard of rock to safeguard our descent; I confess to having been nervous of slipping in the ice steps, but got down well enough. The slope eased off; we reached soft snow and started towards the Refuge de l'Aigle. There was a dramatic moment when Georges, in the lead, suddenly disappeared in a crevasse. Luckily he managed to get out without too much difficulty and we soon reached the hut. It was midday. We had been continuously on the move for more than three hours and it was good to rest and relax after so much exertion and anxiety.

Keeping to the edge of the glacier, we then took to the rocks running down from the Bec de l'Homme. Further down, we again set foot on the glacier and reached the last slopes above the village, where we unroped. Exuberant and with the earlier worries behind me, I hastened on. We paused only to tidy up a little before entering the village and, at 2.30 p.m. I was back at the hotel. M Juge was astonished: he had not expected us before 6.00 pm! I stood on the *terrasse*, looked up at the Meije, and wondered: Had it really happened?

Forty-two years later, in August 1970, I was back on that *terrasse*. With me were my two old friends, Paul and Georges. We were much altered in outward appearance, but it mattered little; for we were talking of those mountains of our youth, and all that had happened to the three of us in the years between. And something else had not changed: the Meije, still flaunting its banner of cloud in the wind, 8,000 feet above us. We drank a toast to that proud peak.

BELOW: Looking back. Lord Hunt with his old friend and guide Paul Jouffray, reliving the climbs of their youth.

Rob Collister

The Traverse of the Pelvoux

Much of the attraction of alpine climbing lies in the likelihood that at some point the unforeseen will occur, to delight, to terrify or to confuse.

Ian took off his pink and lilac rucksac with the rolled yellow karrimat strapped to its side and dumped it beside the path with a grunt. His orange T-shirt was dark with sweat and stuck to his back. I followed suit and, suddenly light-footed and free, scrambled down to the little stream that had been the excuse for a rest. I cupped my hands under a fall and drank and drank from the cold, clear water, then splashed it over my face, again and again, savouring the exquisite coolness on hot skin. Apart from a few stunted old larch trees, their limbs contorted by wind and the weight of winter snow, there is no shade on the path up to the Pelvoux refuge, not in the middle of the afternoon, anyway. Above us, the path zig-zagged endlessly up a steep meadow. Little figures were dotted about it, tracking their way, some to right, some to left, laboriously upwards. The hut itself was out of sight, higher yet, reached by a hidden break in seemingly inpregnable crags. All around us were flowers every bit as gaudy as ourselves – showy, orange lilies, the yellow and purple spikes of mullein, mauve and orange asters, bright pink willow-herb, the alpine variety, crimson house-leeks and many more. I pulled out the *Collins Guide to Alpine Flowers* from the lid of my sack and debated whether it was St Bernard's or St Bruno's Lily we had seen earlier. Then I lay back in the sun, arm across my eyes, and allowed body and mind to relax totally. It was a good place to be.

Much later we reached the hut. It is a solid stone-built affair, with red wooden shutters and a heli-pad in front of it.

BIOGRAPHY

'Man of culture, of peace; a renaissance man, all the good bits from the film Chariots of Fire*, arrow alpinist and as fit as a butcher's dog (a deliberately inappropriate metaphor for a vegetarian by conscience)' – so his friend John Barry introduced Rob Collister when describing a fierce new route in Alaska that the pair had pulled off with fellow climbers Roger Mear and Malcolm Campbell.*

Rob Collister has been climbing for more than a quarter of a century. He made his first expedition to the Himalaya in 1968, and since then has climbed extensively in the Himalaya, Antarctica, Greenland, Alaska, Canada, Argentina, New Zealand and Kenya. But he has never lost touch with his Alpine roots. Ice-climbing has been a perennial fascination. Many major Alpine ice lines received their first British ascent from him. For a number of years Collister worked as an instructor in the National Centre for Mountain Activities at Plas y Brenin. Now, he is a freelance mountain guide, and author of the book Lightweight Expeditions.

RIGHT: The Alps of the central Dauphiné are high and heavily glaciated, and have long been popular with climbers. Here we see Mt Pelvoux with Pic Sans Nom (left) and Ailefroide (right). The glacier is the Violettes.

ABOVE: The Alpine flower meadows of the Dauphiné were known even to the Romans, who built a small temple here. This view looks southwest from the Col du Lauteret towards the Meije massif.

Alpine huts can be delightfully sociable places, but at the height of summer they are liable to be crowded, full of people not all of whom are making an early start in the morning. Dormitories are noisy and stuffy, sleep not easily achieved. Add to that an exceedingly grumpy guardian and his equally bad-tempered alsation, both of whom I had encountered already that season, and we had every incentive to bivouac. Out of sight, out of mind seemed an adage worth heeding, so we scrambled up a rock step and contoured across the hillside until we found the perfect spot, a grassy hollow studded with spring gentians and mountain pansies, not far from a stream. A hundred yards away across the stream, four chamois stood stock-still on a snowpatch watching us. Then they were off, in a four-footed glissade down the snow and away out of sight. Near at hand, young marmots were playing quite unconcerned on the slope beneath us. Suddenly there was a strident whistle. Mama had returned and was ordering her young inside in no uncertain fashion. A second later, there was not an animal to be seen.

We had a pleasant evening. Our site kept the sun until late and we lay on our mats overlooking the valley of the Celse Nière, deep in shadow, lingering over our bread and cheese and fruit. We could not emulate Whymper who, on an early ascent of the Pelvoux in 1862, had a whole cask of wine to see him through the night, and a porter to carry it. But we did have a modest plastic bottle of *vin ordinaire*. When the sun finally set, the earth continued to radiate warmth and it was some time before we snuggled comfortably into our sleeping bags. Even then we did not sleep but chatted desultorily, watching the planets appear and light fade from the summits. I remembered W.A.B. Coolidge, the alpine historian and pedant, a man not given to flights of fancy, who had remarked of this same view: 'One of the most striking sights ever witnessed by the present writer was from a high bivouac on the S. (sic) slope of the Pelvoux when, as daylight vanished, the eye ranged over many ridges, the crest being in each case picked out by the light, though the slope was enshrouded in darkness, these ridges fading away, little by little,

towards the plains of Provence, and presenting a marvellous series of silhouettes.'

Coolidge first climbed the Pelvoux in 1870 during a season in which he made the first ascents of the Ailefroide and the central summit of the Meije, the third ascent of the Ecrins, and the second ascent of the Brenva Spur on Mont Blanc. History does not relate whether his regular climbing partners, his aunt Miss Brevoort and his mongrel dog Tchingel, were present on this occasion. However, by the time he returned to the Pelvoux in 1881 and climbed the couloir that bears his name guided by the Almers, father and son, both aunt and dog were dead and he was developing the prickly sensitivity that was to earn him the soubriquet the Hedgehog of Magdalene. Today, the Coolidge Couloir is the *voie normale*, a popular route throughout the summer. It was our goal for the morrow.

Much of the attraction of alpine climbing lies in the likelihood that at some point the unforeseen will occur, to delight, to terrify or to confuse. We fell asleep beneath a star-filled sky but we were awakened a few hours later by the light patter of raindrops on our bivi-bags. Lightning flickered on the horizon. Our little nook was sheltered from the wind, but down below a loose sheet of corrugated iron on the roof of an outbuilding clattered and banged insistently. Suddenly, from nowhere, an avalanche of rocks crashed down the stream-bed a matter of yards away. I poked my head out of my sleeping bag in time to see the sparks struck as a second avalanche roared by. We were not in the line of fire, but sleep had been well and truly dispelled. Muttering, I looked at my watch. It was three o'clock, time for us to be moving anyway.

By the time we had breakfasted and packed our bags, lights had appeared and several parties had passed not far away with a clinking of axes and a scrunching of boots. We followed them sleepily up a slope of hard-packed moraine to the edge of the little Clot de l'Homme Glacier. It was less than fifty yards across but steep enough to warrant crampons. There was a melée of stooping figures and bobbing torch beams. Whymper had problems here, too. Looking back, we could see more lights approaching. The Pelvoux was going to be busy.

Beyond the glacier, moraine, steep snow and bits of slabby rock lead soon enough to the easy-angled slopes of the Sialouze Glacier. By now dawn was breaking, albeit murkily. Suddenly, with no warning at all, there was a tremendous clap of thunder. Everybody stopped in their tracks. All over the slope, little knots of climbers formed to consider the implications. Many of them turned about and descended back the way they had come. High on a peak of nearly 4,000 metres is no place to be voluntarily in a thunderstorm. On the other hand, this was not only Ian's first big peak, but also the last day of his holiday. We were not inclined to give up just yet. The sky was overcast but the summit was still clear and the cloud did not appear to be dropping. There was no more thunder.

After waiting twenty minutes, we continued, pleased to note that the mountain was no longer crowded. Only one other pair followed us as we cramponed up névé away from the glacier proper onto the steeper slopes of the Coolidge Couloir. Towards the top, old footprints led into an icy runnel overshadowed by crumbly-looking cliffs suggesting stonefall. We chose to move slightly left, crossing sections of block scree to link up snow

RIGHT: The north face of the Pelvoux, seen from the Glacier Blanc.

LEFT: Climbing on the Meije.

patches that led eventually to the broad summit of the Pelvoux. A short walk brought us to the Pointe Puiseux (3,946 metres), the higher of the two summits and, after the Ecrins and the Meije, the highest point in the Oisans.

The panorama that greeted us was dramatic, a monochrome landscape across which grey curtains of precipitation drifted menacingly. Away to the east, the mountains were inky black, distant snowfields on the Meije and the Grande Ruine standing out a livid yellowish white, like old ivory. Thunder rumbled in the distance. A rising wind whipped up the snow at our feet, but Ian's face was glowing with pleasure in the eerie, threatening light. It was a fitting culmination to his first season.

We were about to leave when the second rope arrived. It was a French couple we had met on the path the day before, cheerful, friendly people. The man had last climbed the Pelvoux twenty-two years before, and their ascent obviously had sentimental significance for them both. We all shook hands, then we left the

summit for them to enjoy alone. They were descending the Coolidge Couloir, so we were going to have the Violettes Glacier to ourselves.

As a climb, the Coolidge Couloir is unexceptional, no more than an exercise in cramponing really, it has to be said. But the complex descent down the Violettes Glacier and back to Ailefroide, all 2,500 metres of it, makes this one of the finest traverses in Europe. At first the glacier was straightforward, but as we descended things became more exciting. There were some steeper slopes, crevasses to jump with the rope kept tight between us, a dramatic ice architecture of riven blocks and towers on either hand, and enclosing rock walls that grew higher as we lost height. Once, we had to leap ten foot down from the lip of a bergschrund: nothing unusual about that, except that a second bergschrund was yawning only feet below, waiting to snap up the clumsy or the unwary. Lower yet, we found ourselves picking a way down a rock buttress that splits the glacier. A couloir on its right flank, with a short abseil halfway down, brought us back onto the glacier at the point where it levels off briefly. Old tracks led horizontally to a brèche in the ridge beyond. It was only three hundred yards across, but threatened by huge toppling seracs and littered with avalanche debris. It was a place to suspend the imagination and run. . . .

Another short abseil and a scramble down a couloir on the far side of the brèche brought us onto a snow slope. Another rock barrier, then more snow, glissading and skating by now in slushy snow, until it ran out into ice and we took to a moraine ridge at

its side. A steep dusty path wound its way down the moraine and, almost as steeply, on down a stony meadow. The sun came out with a fierce heat, though above us the cloud had dropped, smothering the tops. We were glad to be back on terra firma. Our mouths were dry and gritty, our feet hot and sore when we finally reached alder bushes and a lovely, much-needed stream. We drank and bathed our feet and stripped down to our T-shirts for the first time since the path up to the Pelvoux hut, twenty-four hours before. We had come full circle.

However, we were not finished yet. At the point where most paths would become progressively more amenable, this one dived abruptly downwards, following a rock rake across some extremely steep ground for several hundred feet. It was not difficult, but definitely not a place to trip, and it seemed to go on and on. The only compensation was that the vertical and over-hanging rock above shielded us from the sun. It was a shock to emerge at the bottom, out of the shadow into a dry, hot world of scorched meadows and churring cicadas. The village of Ailefroide was only a few hundred yards away, but there was still a moment of excitement to come. As we picked our way through some massive fallen blocks, what should flutter away in front of us but a large, black and yellow butterfly – unmistakeably a swallowtail, a beautiful creature I had last seen over ten years before in the very different setting of Wicken Fen. And so, parched and weary, we came to the little café on the corner as you enter the village, to sit under a parasol and drink cold beer and look back with disbelief at the way we had just come.

Wanda Rutkiewicz with Ingeborga Doubrawa-Cochlin

Lionesses in Winter

For the first time women had achieved a serious Alpine face climb in winter, one which at the time was only climbed by men a handful of times each season. The wall did not become any easier simply because we had climbed it.

Four of us came to Zermatt in February 1978 with the idea of being the first all-women's team to climb the North Face of the Matterhorn in winter. We were: Anna Czerwinska, Irena Kesa, Krystyna Palmowska and myself, as leader.

Our plan was to set up a base camp in the Hörnli hut, at 3,260 metres, which was not very well equipped for winter climbing. But from there, we would take provisions higher, to the Solvay hut at 4,003 metres on the Hörnli Ridge, where we could acclimatize and make a reconnaissance climb – important since it was the way we hoped to come down after reaching the summit. All this we achieved during the period 21st to 28th February, even though conditions in the mountains were very difficult and there was great danger of avalanches after protracted periods of heavy snow. The Pennine Alps were under low pressure with winds coming in from the west. Further snowfalls were forecast, so we hung about in Zermatt for a few days. To ensure good communications from the Hörnli hut and during our climb, we borrowed a radio-telephone and arranged with the local heliport to supply us with the latest weather reports. On the 3rd March we climbed up to the Hörnli again, not expecting perfect conditions but hoping at least for settled weather.

On the 7th at three o'clock in the morning we set out from the hut, to be in position to begin climbing the icefields of the Matterhorn's North Face at dawn.

Towards the middle of the icefields a Japanese man and woman caught up with

BIOGRAPHY

More perhaps than anyone else, Wanda Rutkiewicz was responsible for the emergence of women among the ranks of world-class mountaineers. From the late 1960s and through the 1970s she dedicated herself almost exclusively to all-women expeditions, making fine Alpine and Himalayan ascents. She was a gifted and inspirational expedition leader, a climber of extraordinary resource and determination, and was particularly successful at high altitude, ascending at least eight of the demanding eight-thousanders. She was last seen high on the north side of Kangchenjunga in May 1992, bivouacked in preparation for a solo summit bid the following day.

us. They had followed our footsteps, and for a while both teams climbed together, which added to everyone's danger. As a team of two, the Japanese should have been able to overtake us, but they could not. They only pulled away towards nightfall on the second day of climbing, thanks to the assistance of another Japanese team of three men, who overtook both our parties, climbing very fast, and who were able to take the two Japanese along with them.

Once up the steep ice and snowfields of the lower part of the wall, we came to the very difficult middle section, a large rocky couloir, partly encased in ice and snow. But there was less snow than we expected, less than in summer, and the ice was very hard because temperatures were still way below zero. We set up our first bivouac after having climbed 500 metres, almost in the middle of the wall; the next one was at the end of the couloir, 250 metres higher, which we reached at night by the light of our headlamps. The third and last bivouac, and the only comfortable one, was established on the summit snowfields, about 250 metres from the top. At night we wore our down jackets, down trousers and bivouac blankets.

After the second bivouac, because the rock above the couloir was heavily iced, we chose an alternative route, more difficult technically, but shorter: an exposed traverse out to the right on very fragile rock. It was unpleasantly scary, and followed by a short vertical pitch of Grade 5. After that, the route lay across snow-covered, rocky terrain, not too difficult,

towards the Zmutt Ridge, striking it just below the summit. Unfortunately, the wind had started to blow up – just gusty at first but growing stronger as that third day wore on, until it was hurricane force. We were unable to reach the summit as we had expected. Instead, once on the Zmutt Ridge, we decided to drop down to find somewhere out of the ferocious wind. That day, and the next, the constant wind and temperatures of -10° C (14° F) caused Irena Kesa to suffer from frostbite and hypothermia. From the moment we realized her condition, the most important

problem was to find shelter where we could protect her from further deterioration and loss of body heat.

The North Face of the Matterhorn is notorious for its scarcity of places unexposed to the elements. The only spot we could find was on the Zmutt Ridge just 20 or 30 metres from the summit. Krystyna Palmowska went on to the top, while the rest of us got Irena into the bivouac and bundled her up in the exposure blankets as quickly as possible. That was early in the afternoon. Although we could not imagine any rescue attempt being

LEFT: Anna Czerwinska, one of Poland's leading mountaineers, who went on from the Matterhorn to a successful Himalayan career, mostly in partnership with Krystyna Palmowska.

RIGHT: The Matterhorn North Face in winter.

possible in those winds and the extremely poor visibility, nevertheless we had earlier called for help over the radio during a temporary halt some 80 or 100 metres from the summit. Hearing nothing further from us, the journalists back in Zermatt assumed that we had given up our attempt even though the route now lay across fairly easy ground. Despite the darkness and the 120–130km-per-hour winds, a helicopter reached us at about eight o'clock that night, piloted by the amazing Toni Loetscher. Rene Arnold and Alfons Lerjen were lowered on the rope to evacuate Irena, as well as Krystyna from the summit. Anna Czerwinska and I had hoped, in the morning, to climb down the Hörnli Ridge under our own steam, but the rescuers insisted we too should be taken off in view of the appalling conditions. Irena was whisked straight from the summit to the clinic in Visp where she stayed from 10th to 14th March. From there she spent ten days in an Innsbruck clinic which specialized in frostbite cases. Thanks to the rescuers and prompt treatment, her frostbite did not result in any amputations and she recovered completely.

This first winter climb of the Matterhorn North Face by women on their own caused tremendous interest in Switzerland and other Alpine countries. The radio, television and the press retailed all the details with great interest. Pictures had been taken throughout the ascent, whenever conditions allowed – both from a helicopter above us, as well as by photographers with their 500mm telephoto lenses far below. The helicopter rescue crew were able to correct the misunderstanding that we had aborted the climb when we radioed for help for Irena and had, indeed, reached the summit.

Headlines in the newspapers and magazines acclaimed our 'Great Victory' and the 'Magnificent enterprise by Polish Women'. The bulletin of the Zermatt section of the Swiss Alpine Club devoted an entire edition to our climb, remarking that it gave definite proof that women were capable of achieving top level success in mountaineering and of surviving the most appalling conditions. 'To the long history of Matterhorn conquest,' it said, 'from the first ascent by Whymper in 1865 and the first ascent of the North Face of the Matterhorn in the summer of 1931 by the brothers Franz and Toni Schmid, the Polish women have added a new chapter.'

It is true that there were other voices – abroad and at home – which chose to question the suitability of women for this sort of undertaking. And then of course there remains the perennial question:

ABOVE: Krystyna Palmowska was 27 when she made this climb. Later successes have included first female ascents of Rakaposhi, Broad Peak and Nanga Parbat in the Greater Himalaya.

What is the point of mountaineering at all? No-one has yet been able to provide an answer to that which totally satisfies everyone. Basically, one has to accept its validity without any real justification. In our case, the facts themselves were enough. For the first time women had achieved a serious Alpine face climb in winter, one which at the time was only climbed by men a handful of times each season. The wall did not become any easier simply because we had climbed it. In the middle of March that same year, the helicopter had to rescue a male team of Austrians from the Matterhorn North Face, and a few days later four German men died on it.

We found all the attention we received in Switzerland very rewarding. During Irena's stay in hospital, she received nothing but kindness and sympathy from wellwishers. Her first bouquet came from the Swiss pilot who had flown the rescue helicopter on what was acknowledged to be one of the most difficult rescues ever undertaken in the Alps.

*

Irena's story Irena Kesa was the youngest member of the four-girl team. At the time she was a student of physical education with strict ideas about diet. She had reduced her calorie intake by eschewing sugar and fat in favour of milk, fish and rice, and clearly this was insufficient for such an enterprise in extreme cold and wintry conditions.

She began to suffer frostbite on the second day of the climb, although there had been some signs during the reconnaissance climb on the Hörnli Ridge, when she lost her gloves in the middle of a pitch and continued without them. In the Solvay Hut she complained of lack of feeling in hands and feet and the others took turns in massaging them back to life. But she appeared all right, if a little tense, by the time the party was ready to start the main climb.

Irena has written of that feeling of tension before the climb:

'It was not that I was afraid of the Wall itself, since I had done far more technically difficult climbs, but this climb was more exhausting from the point of view of the conditions. I was afraid it would be too much for us and we would have to return to Poland empty-handed.

'The fact that we had to sit and wait about at the Hörnli, unable to do anything, and that so many people were waiting to do the climb, was a great strain and had a tremendous impact on me, although I said nothing at the time. I felt the burden of responsibility and a sense of obligation to our mission. Everything seemed to be pointing in the direction of failure, and I felt that all we would achieve was going to be one total mess.'

And in an article in the Polish magazine *Taternik*, she has told of her deterioration during the climb:

'I felt the effects of cold accumulate from the previous night's bivouac on the North Face of the Matterhorn. With great effort I attempted to control the terrifying pain in the fingers of my right hand, and only then realized that my legs were also affected. The pain in my fingers did not ease, in fact it grew worse and gradually blisters started appearing. Everything became a tremendous effort, even preparing the bivouac or brewing tea. I managed to fall asleep. In the morning, the wind had dropped a little, though it was extremely cold. We had to make a start. The others were strong and fit, but I felt worse and worse. By about midday, I could not move my legs any more. I had lost all feeling in them and in my hands, to the extent that I could not even hold my ice-axe. I had great difficulty in breathing. I felt I was slowly losing my grip on life. The girls decided to radio for help. I put all my trust in them.'

LEFT: Irena Kesa, youngest of the four-woman team, suffered badly from frostbite almost from the beginning. After her rescue, however, she made a complete recovery, going on to achieve other fine Alpine ascents with Wanda Rutkiewicz.

BELOW: Climbing the icefield – Palmowska, closest to the camera, with Czerwinska and Kesa behind. (All the photographs during the climb were taken by Rutkiewicz.)

Catherine Destivelle, introduced by Jeff Lowe

A New Route on the Dru

The route was absolutely new, and I worried to find a good way, an

original way. My line is very direct and the climbing very good.

Jeff Lowe A few years ago, at the height of success and against the well meant advice of her closest friends and advisers, Catherine Destivelle said goodbye to the world of organized climbing competitions. *Snowbird 1989* was her last event. When I spoke with her there she told me that she was out of shape for the meet because she'd been climbing all summer in the Alps. She said that she wanted to get back to the mountains, where she 'could feel more emotions' and 'have more adventure'. She'd started leading routes where she had to place her own protection, taking a small step back in terms of technical difficulty but a big step forward in commitment. Catherine confided a dream: to free-solo the Bonatti Pillar of the Petit Dru. She told me this, not to impress me but because she knew I could understand her motivation.

I invited her to attempt a free climb of the Karakoram's Nameless Tower, sensing we might make a strong team. My instincts were correct. On the Tower, Catherine was competent, courageous, cautious, calm, funny, relaxed, determined, powerful, patient, beautiful, happy and just plain excellent. She almost fiercely maintains her straightforward country-girl innocence in spite of the fact that her lifestyle is very cosmopolitan. 'I am just an average person,' she says. But the average person does not win international competitions, travel the globe regularly, keep an apartment in Paris, a house in the south of France, and a loft in Chamonix, nor is she featured regularly in the media and invited to functions at the

BIOGRAPHY
Born in 1960 in Oran, French Algeria, Catherine Destivelle's love of climbing was kindled at the age of five in the forest of Fontainebleau, near Paris. By sixteen she was leading classic routes in Chamonix, including the American Direct Route on the Petit Dru.

After training as a physiotherapist, and some film work, she began climbing competitively, winning the prestigious Bardoneccia sports climbing contest in Italy in two consecutive years, despite a near-fatal accident shortly after she won the first title. The film Seo!, *with its amazing balletic sequences on cliffs in Mali, West Africa, brought her to international recognition. She has now abandoned competition climbing for natural challenges. In March 1992 she made the first female solo ascent of the Eiger Nordwand.*

highest levels of sport, politics, society and business. A truly impressive reputation.

One month after topping out on Nameless Tower, Catherine realized her dream of free-soloing the Bonatti Pillar. She was personally satisfied with these experiences and her move into a new arena was enthusiastically reported by the press around the world. The European media, in particular, began to compare her favourably with Walter Bonatti, one of Catherine's heroes and one of the greatest alpinists of all time.

Catherine should have been content to rest on her laurels but there was something about the way the media were comparing her to Bonatti that offended her sense of perspective. This provided the impetus for her next adventure, which Catherine recounted by telephone from Chamonix the day following the completion of her new, 800 metre aid route in the French Alps.

I asked her when she first had the idea for soloing a new route on the Petit Dru, and what it was about aid climbing that had appealed to her. Even so soon after the climb, I was picking up false rumours that she'd been fed food and water from a helicopter, used an electric drill to place bolts and was helped to the top by a guided party on the nearby Bonatti route. Had she foreseen the kind of publicity the climb would generate, in particular all the malicious allegations?

And I wanted to know whether Catherine saw her climb in any way as a feminist statement.

*

Catherine Destivelle When I soloed the Bonatti Pillar, journalists compared me to Walter Bonatti: he climbed in six days and I took four hours. I thought that very unfair on Bonatti and I wanted to show what the story is when you open a route like that. So I decided to open my own route, with the idea of putting Bonatti's climb in its proper historical light. Later, the sheer enjoyment of doing something new took over. I wanted to see my reaction to such a big wall as this.

I also wanted to play with aid climbing and all the gear. I had only done one pitch of aid climbing before, a huge roof in the Verdon. It was very scary. Later, when I met you [Jeff Lowe] and asked you to show me how to climb big walls, that's when I came to the United States for two months and we climbed together. I like to learn new things. I found it interesting because you still play with the rock, but in another way. You have to think a lot, and be intelligent with the rock.

Looking at the Dru, I could see a blank place between two routes, and I hoped maybe there would be a line there. When I checked with binoculars from the couloir there was a little crack. I was not sure I could do it, but I would try.

LEFT: The Dru has held special significance for Destivelle since she climbed its American Direct Route in 1977 On this new aid route laborious sack-hauling slowed her down and the climb took ten days.

PREVIOUS PAGE: Destivelle trained for two months in the United States in preparation for her Dru climb. Here she is seen on Devil's Tower, Wyoming.

ABOVE LEFT: Cameras aboard a helicopter follow Destivelle's progress as she climbs the Southwest Pillar of the Petit Dru.

I set off at 4 a.m. on Tuesday 25 June, 1991, with 142 pounds (64 kilogrammes) of baggage and eleven days and nights of solo climbing ahead of me. I thought I might be lonely, but in fact I was very busy. Every time I finished leading a pitch, I rappeled down, took out the gear, got my rucksack and jumared. Then I pulled up the haul bag. Also I had good support from a walkie-talkie. This was important for sometimes I had no morale. At the beginning I was a little stressed, and tired, and very slow. There was a lot of snow and that had me a little worried. They told me that the weather would be better later, so I stayed.

It rained or snowed all day long for four days, but my route was very overhanging and the snow couldn't stick on the wall. There was some ice in the crack and when I put in my pitons all the water ran into my sleeves. I took a big fall on the sixth pitch, on a Bird Beak. I think I flew 10 metres because the pitons just behind came out. Four more pitons came out. This was on Sunday. I had been going far too slowly and was afraid, because I thought maybe I would never get out of this. But I remembered you taught me to be patient – and I was patient.

During the climb I lost about three or four kilos in weight. I took the same sort of food as you and I had on Trango, but I was not able to eat all those things. I ate about half as much this time, so I still had a week of food when I arrived at the top.

There were about fifteen new pitches, I think, but I didn't count them. The route was absolutely new, and I worried to find a good way, an original way. My line is

ABOVE: On North American rock – Destivelle climbs Devil's Tower (left) and in Frémont Canyon (right).

LEFT AND BELOW: First attempt at an 'eight-thousander' – although she failed to reach Makalu's summit, Destivelle was pleased with the way she shaped up to high altitude. She has plenty of plans for future projects; 'only time is missing,' she says.

LEFT: *High exposure.*
Catherine Destivelle has
learnt how to be one of
the most successful and
high-earning climbers in
the world. Darling of
the magazines, a reader
poll in France suggested

that more people there
recognized her than they
did their own Prime
Minister!

BELOW: *The hands of a*
climber.

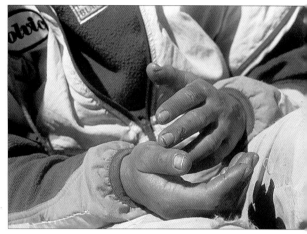

very direct and the climbing very good. There is just one pitch in common with the Bonatti route – that is, not counting the last three pitches where you can go anywhere, so I took the normal way. The rock was good all the way; the cracks were shallow, but I had no problem with danger. It was very steep and even when stones fell, they fell far out behind me, beyond harm's way. Almost all the climb was aid, probably A4. You could free climb at the top, maybe 7a or 7b in the crack, maybe even 8a, but I had too much

gear. It is possible that I climbed three or four pitches free, but not a lot.

I used only two bolts for belay anchors. I wanted to aid-climb with a third, but I broke my drill handle so I had to pendulum. I had to rappel down a little bit and run across the face to grab the new crack. I made two pendulums.

The crux came for me on the Sunday because, being without a drill, I was worried about finding a blank section after I lost the crack. I went on the left and straight on, and again on the left and

straight on, and I was stuck, couldn't move. It was very scary, and very hard aid climbing. I hesitated because I didn't know what to do. I didn't want to go down, but I couldn't go further. That was a bad day!

Now, after the climb, my hands are in a terrible state! They became swollen on the climb and a little infected. I washed them with soap on the climb, which helped a little. Now they are very sore and I can't close them. Last night I woke up and had to put my fingers in cold water, because they were so hot and swollen.

The climb was filmed, but only from a helicopter. They waited for me at the top, and filmed me in the night and the next morning. People told me to expect a lot of rumour and back-stabbing, really because a lot of people are jealous. The guide who was on the Bonatti route assured me he would tell the media the truth, that he only helped me unstick my haul bag at the very top. I was surprised at the amount of interest shown. I thought it would be something, but not like that. It was too much. But when I was on the route, mostly I didn't see the helicopter or anyone. I was at my job, just climbing, and concentrating. I forgot about all other life in the valley.

The climb was not a feminist statement; I wanted to do it for me. I don't want to be judged just as a woman in climbing.

The House of Pain

For almost two years I wore the route around my neck like a weighted chain. Andy and I both had excuses for not going up again, the same excuses I criticize others for using . . .

Andy Parkin was one of the world's best alpinists of the late 1970s and early 1980s, having soloed the Droites by several lines, the Walker Spur alone in winter (in 19 hours), the serious Boivin-Vallencant on the Aiguille Sans Nom, and in Pakistan he climbed Broad Peak and attempted K2 in alpine style. But a groundfall nearly killed him in 1984. It left his hip in thirteen pieces, many of his organs displaced inside his torso, and his left arm shattered along with his future. Today, both the hip and elbow are fused into immobility, but despite doctors' predictions to the contrary, Andy has climbed again, and climbed well. In the late 1980s, early 1990s he put up five big routes (all of which are unrepeated) in the Mont Blanc range, attempted Makalu and Everest, and climbed Shivling. He consistently climbs 5.11 and gets in the occasional waterfall routes when his career as a painter and sculptor allows him the time. Andy is one of the most gifted climbers on mixed terrain that I have ever had the pleasure to climb with. His determination, experience and willingness to risk it all propelled him up three new, modern alpine routes in the Chamonix Aiguilles in the winter of 1991-2. Beyond Good and Evil (on the Aiguille des Pèlerins) is the most serious and difficult of these climbs.

*

The Aiguille des Pèlerins' pitiless north face is an austere, monochromatic wall. Its shades of oppressive, life-threatening grey lighten as the sun passes over, but they never warm to red. Great men have left little trace of their presence on this face,

BIOGRAPHY

In 1984 Marc Twight surprised the mountain world when he soloed a number of test-piece climbs in the Alps during a 3-week visit. The following year he was back, succeeding on the famed Eigerwand and a host of serious ice climbs. These caught the attention of the American alpinist Jeff Lowe who invited him to climb in the Himalaya in 1986. On that expedition Marc climbed new routes on Lobuche and Kangtega with Alison Hargreaves and attempted the South Pillar of Nuptse with Jeff Lowe – a climb which eluded the pair then and when they tried it again that winter.

In the Alps the following year Marc seized the first solo ascent of the Marsigny Route on Les Droites, while adventures in Alaska and the Canadian Rockies included what Vertical *magazine hailed as the most difficult ice climb in the world, the first Grade 7 frozen waterfall route – The Reality Bath on the north face of White Pyramid. Solo climbs in the Pamir Mountains of Tadjikistan have included a new route, Suicidal Misfit, on Pic Vorobyova and the overall second ascent of the Czech route on the north face of Pic Communism.*

Marc Twight has established more fresh routes on peaks in the Everest area of Nepal, but his hardest new climb to date is the one described here, Beyond Good and Evil on the Aiguille des Pèlerins above Chamonix and climbed with Andy Parkin.

having accounted for three (seldom repeated) routes. It is a cathartic place, attracting only those few who want to test themselves, to throw the dice, to beat their heads against it. All efforts undertaken in moderation count for nothing up there, every movement the heart does not believe in, every word the hand does not write in blood is wasted effort, squandered without reason. I was beaten on this wall. I spent my blood and my energy for nothing up there. I tried to build a monument to my efforts and I failed, littering

the rock with a few fixed pins and my tears. The climbing left a scar that time wouldn't heal and I vowed to return and acquit myself. I could see the face from the gym where I train and it tortured me to think that all the weights I lifted and the hills I sprinted up meant very little on that great north wall.

Andy and I had twice tried to climb a new route on the Aiguille des Pèlerins, but were stopped once by technical difficulty – and how slowly we made progress against it – and the second time by variations on the same and a turn of the weather. Our first attempt was back in November of 1989 when the days were criminally short and the belays interminable and cold. I took a 25-foot upside-down fall out of the big corner on the fifth pitch. We were demoralized by the difficulty and the relentless

approach of the fourteen-hour night and unknown terrain waiting above us. We retreated from the top of the sixth pitch, turned our backs and snowshoed away.

For almost two years I wore the route around my neck like a weighted chain. Andy and I both had excuses for not going up again, the same excuses I criticize others for using; it never really comes into condition, the weather forecast is no good, our work is in the way and the cable car is still closed. We recited the usual list of rationalizations, substituting them for fear and laziness and lack of motivation. Neither of us were ready to give what we knew the wall was going to take. Finally, in April of 1992, we clicked and meshed and started up again. It hadn't become any easier in the interim; conditions were not ideal and the aid went slowly. We managed to climb seven 60-metre pitches (the long rope was our latest secret weapon) to get a look at the upper wall before the clouds moved in and snow forced us down.

With failure stuck sideways in my throat and sickness in my heart I wrote copy for a catalogue (that didn't need to be written) for the following nine days before Andy called and said he was free. I dropped everything and filed my ice tools into lethal instruments. For this, the real thing, we decided to get on the wall and stay on it until we finished it. We took bivvy gear and a pair of jumars so the second could follow carrying it. We loaded up the packs with metal and rope because experience dictated a rack of hardware larger than anything I had ever taken in the mountains (except for the South Pillar of Nuptse). Nine Camalots, 13 nuts, 13 pitons, two screws and I don't know how many karabiners was a huge judgement against our ability and confidence, but previous attempts proved this to be the minimum. I was quite embarrassed to be seen by my friends as I boarded the cable car with such a huge pack. It was a decidedly un-French affair, but if we succeeded (and then managed to sandbag some poor soul into trying to repeat the line) we could tell them all to go to hell. I knew I was right, for me, and I wasn't about to subscribe to the current 'do-it-in-a-day' fashion as it would only result in yet another washout.

Jumars made the whole thing reasonable since the passage of the leader often left nothing for the second to climb on. But the seventh pitch started with some unreasonable aid climbing off copperheads and tied-off pins directly above the belay. Pulling out of the étriers into a 70° corner stuffed with just enough ice to mask the crack, I slowed down to face the music. The corner was capped with an overhang. Andy said that (on the last attempt) he'd found a place for an upside-down $^3/_4$-inch angle but the latest storm had plastered a huge snow mushroom under the roof and I was afraid to touch it. My imagination had me tapping it and then as it broke loose hugging it like a pillow as I sailed thirty airy feet, trying to keep the cushion between myself and the wall hoping it might break my fall a little. Instead, I dry-tooled out left onto a slab with my right calf shaking uncontrollably and my frontpoints dancing a psychotic, carnival step against the granite. I torqued the shaft of my tool in a wide, flaring crack and locked off low enough on it that I could hook a thin flake with the pick of my other tool. Gingerly weighting it, I leg-humped an arête and tried to rest. The only hope for gear was a slot for a wide Leeper; I hand-placed the pin halfway and beat the life out of it, fixing it for the next generation. The pin gave me just enough confidence to reach a small shelf and good ice. 'Resting' on the six inch ledge, I drove a long Bugaboo and equalized it to a nut, backed it up with a Camalot and my heart slowed down little by little.

Two exciting pitches higher I made the evening radio call to get the weather report while we dug out a bivvy ledge.

Everything was working in our favour; the bivouac was large enough for two to curl up on and the stormy forecast had been modified to call for a few snowflakes caused by thunderstorms forming elsewhere. We slept as well as one does in these places and woke to broken, timorous clouds with the promise of amelioration during the morning.

After Andy holstered his hammer following the tenth pitch he heard a noise and turned quickly to see it tumbling down the wall. Removing pins with the adze of a Barracuda was fairly ridiculous

LEFT: The British climber Andy Parkin is seen here on the fourth pitch of Beyond Good and Evil, on the Pèlerins. He and his partner, American climber Marc Twight, had twice before failed to force a route up this austere north face. Success was finally theirs in April 1992.

ABOVE: The fifth pitch, where their first attempt came to grief when Twight took a 25-ft upsidedown fall. 'For almost two years I wore the route around my neck like a weighted chain,' he says.

ABOVE: Andy Parkin on Pitch 6 of the climb.

RIGHT: Aiguille des Pèlerins. The Twight/Parkin route, Beyond Good and Evil, takes a line up the centre of the north face.

but placing them was worse and he couldn't get them in very far. He fell fifteen feet onto the belay as he started the thirteenth pitch; of course it had to be the thirteenth, and the belay was suspect and I had one hand in the pack searching for some food when his pin popped. I mistakenly gave him a dynamic belay but it's probably what saved us from going to the ground. He finished the pitch and I followed it warily, eyeing the heinous slot clogged with big, loose blocks that gave access to the Col des Pèlerins and the end of the climb. The only belay anchors were directly beneath this deadly cavity and it was too steep to avoid pulling on the flakes and teetering bricks. I was quite happy to be absorbed in the process of leading rather than waiting for the sky to fall on me. I fought with every ounce of self-control that remained after thirteen hair-raising pitches; I pulled gently, and pushed resolutely down and inwards on the creaking mess. Tunnelling through the cornice well above my last piece of protection I felt the familiar greasy fear-sweat running freely from my armpits and the small of my back. It cooled rapidly as I belayed Andy up and relished the world's greatest remedy (victory) and my second nightfall route-finish of the year.

The snow was hideous: a light crust over heavy wet glop that often sucked us in to the waist. We rappelled and downclimbed the west side of the col and began the long march back to the cable car midstation where there was a small hut in which we could spend the night. My newly-scarred watch showed 2.30 a.m. when we reached its drifted-in doorway. We'd been on the mountain for about 45 hours and spent 26 of them actually climbing. My hands were smashed-up and bleeding, I was dehydrated and wasted as badly as I ever have been, and the knee I'd broken several years before was inflamed and pulsing dully. I swung gently at the end of my rope and had just enough energy to force the hut door open and collapse inside. I kept my pain to myself because what I felt was certainly trivial in comparison to what Andy must have been going through. I admired his drive and commitment to the ideal.

> 'Only great pain is, as the teacher of *great suspicion*, the ultimate liberator of the spirit . . . it is only great pain, that slow protracted pain which takes its time and in which we are as it were burned with green wood, that compels us philosophers to descend into our ultimate depths and put from us all trust, all that is good-hearted, palliated, gentle, average, wherein perhaps our humanity previously reposed. I doubt whether such pain "improves" us – but I do know it deepens us . . . '
>
> Friedrich Nietzsche

And we are chained together in the house of pain searching for our truths – beyond good and evil.

Destroyed Myths, Dead Heroes

*I wanted to climb this inaccessible mountain by the de Ville Route –
nowadays secured with metal wires and pegs – so that I could
understand what drove people of the Renaissance to climb.*

*RIGHT: Mont Aiguille,
one of the Seven
Wonders of the
Dauphiné. Known in
the Middle Ages as Mont
Inaccessible its isolated
summit was nevertheless
stormed by king's
mercenaries in 1492,
and Alpinism was born.*

'It is one of the most terrible and grue-some paths which I or any member of our party has ever trodden. We had to climb up on ladders for half a mile, then continue for another mile. But the summit is the most wonderful place one could imagine. To give you a vivid picture of the mountain, I should tell you that the summit area measures a quarter of a mile in length and an arrow shot in width. It consists of wonderful pasture land. Here we encountered a sizeable herd of chamois which is destined to stay here for eternity. Among them were new-born kids of the same day's litter, of which we killed one, but this was by acci-dent. We would never have touched one on purpose without knowing the King's intentions.

'I am writing this on 28 June on the Aiguille. I have now been up here for 3 days with more than 10 people and a royal ladder carrier. I shall not descend until I receive word from you so that you can send out people who will confirm our presence on the summit, should you so wish. I have baptized the mountain in the name of the Father, the Son and the Holy Ghost and named it Saint-Charlemagne, in honour of the King. I have also arranged for the reading of a mass and for the erection of three big crosses at the corners of the summit area.'

These words were written by the mercenary leader Antoine de Ville, after reaching the summit plateau of Mont Aiguille by order of Charles VIII, King of France. This table mountain, 2,086 metres high, whose walls

BIOGRAPHY

The most famous and influential climber in the world today, Reinhold Messner has been climbing since he was five years old. He grew up in Villnöss in the St Magdalena valley of South Tyrol, which he has described as a childhood paradise. Reinhold and his younger brother Günther would share a helmet on their increasingly adventurous rock climbing forays.

By the age of twenty, he had climbed most of the hardest routes in the Dolomites and the Western Alps and had begun to formulate his philosophy of clean climbing. Despite Günther's death on their first visit to the Himalaya, Reinhold has seen no cause to compromise his dedication to lightweight alpine-style mountaineering. In succession he made a swift two-man ascent of an eight-thousander (Hidden Peak with Peter Habeler, described later), an oxygen-free ascent of Everest, then solo ascents of both Nanga Parbat and Everest. He was the first man to climb all fourteen eight-thousanders, but considers the first traverse of two of these in a single expedition – Gasherbrums I and II, with Hans Kammerlander in 1984 – as his supreme Himalayan achievement. In recent years Reinhold Messner has become absorbed with lightweight polar expeditions, but here he reflects on the heroes of Alpine mountaineering.

rise vertically on all sides, was regarded as one of the seven wonders of the Dauphiné and its summit invincible. Now, a group of men, among them the royal chamberlain Julien de Beaupré and two priests, had destroyed the myth of invincibility and sent news of their victory by messenger to the Parliament in Grenoble.

This was 1492, the year Columbus discovered America. The beginning of the New Age, therefore, signals the beginning of the history of vertical ascent. It was to develop into a history of continuous improvement, like a spiral of increasingly eccentric goals combined with increasingly refined techniques. But it is also a history of destroyed myths. The fact that fifty per cent of those obsessed met death on the mountain, those 'heroes' who followed Antoine de Ville into vertical ascent and determined the history of climbing, corresponds to the law of probability. As long as gravity prevails, the game on the edge of human capability, high on the wall, will be a game with death. The half who survived were no better than those who had fallen, just luckier. At the same time they were unlucky, for 'true heroes die young'! Winkler, Preuss, Buhl would not be legendary figures today if they had died in bed as old men, or indeed were still alive.

Five hundred years after this first ascent I was drawn to Mont Aiguille in the Vercors group of the Dauphiné by that same curiosity which, next to my ambition, had always been my main motive for climbing on vertical rock. I was curious, too, about the history of climbing. I wanted to climb this inaccessible mountain by the de Ville

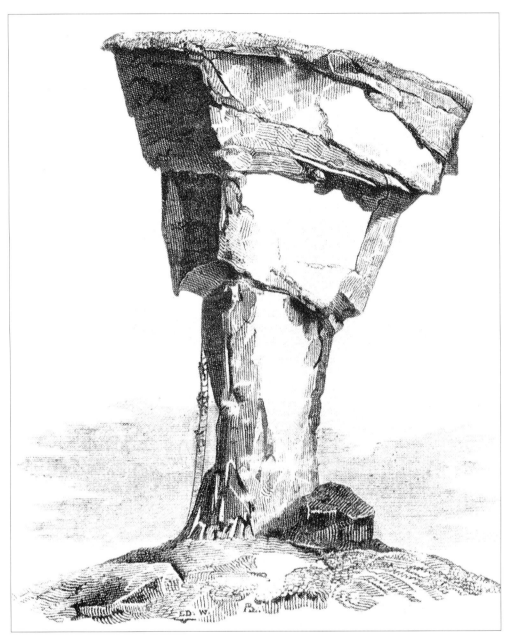

been his impulse, nor the exploration of the mountain, nor the opening of access to it. Only conquest, in its own right. Nothing else. The ascent as the holy deed was the battle. It is therefore no surprise that a second ascent of Mont Aiguille was not com-pleted until 1834, when a shepherd, Jean Liotend, climbed the peak allegedly in search of lost lambs.

Although the route of the first climbers is nowadays marked, and in places has lost its edge, it still remains difficult. Left of the deep gully I climbed over steep rock before clambering diagonally to the right. After a number of vertical stretches and two more traverses, exposed at times, I reached the bottom of a high chimney, smooth and in places overhanging. My respect for the first climbers grew as I asked myself how on earth they fixed their ladder!

As a lad of twelve I climbed many of the classic routes in my native Geislerspitzen, where I began climbing at the age of five. At first, my father took me on easy routes. Then, as a teenager, I became fascinated by vertical rock. It soon dominated all other interests: family, school, friends in the village, even girls. In 1966 I failed my Abitur exams. My ambition grew yearly. By now I had repeated the most difficult routes in the Dolomites and on my first ascents I was keen to eliminate points of aid. The Abitur successfully repeated, I went on to study engineering in Padua, but it was a half-hearted affair. During those years I climbed more than ever and more extremely than any of my partners. It was not just that I was filled with a desire for continuous advancement, but life in the vertical had become a necessity for me, a

Route – nowadays secured with metal wires and pegs – so that I could understand what drove people of the Renaissance to climb.

The sight of Mont Aiguille from the east is impressive. All the other mountains surrounding it seem climbable, so why did King Charles VIII, who was on his way to Italy, order his men to attempt this particular pile of rock? Was it just a whim? Surely not. Curiosity? But then he would have climbed it himself. A lust for conquest? Perhaps. At the beginning of the New Age the idea of conquest spread like wildfire in the Occident. Man wanted to rule the earth once and for all: the philosophy was perceived as a reli-gious mission by Europeans. De Ville's report does not exude such traces of joy as might have filled Petrarca or Leonardo da Vinci during the ascent. Here was a conqueror, a taboo-breaker, a hero. Even though Antoine de Ville had been assigned his role as 'first climber' by accident, he played it to the full. Like a star pupil. Despite the physical effort, the climbing difficulties (which at the time were extreme), the problems within his team, he surmounted all obstacles and reached his goal. In doing so, discovery had not

predestination even. The excitement before the route, the days of climbing between sky and scree, the view back from the valley were the substance of my everyday life. Increasingly, I grew preoc-cupied with my predecessors. The first explorers of the routes I climbed became familiar to me, even though many of them were dead. I felt the development of the art of climbing in my finger-tips. For me, the true act of climbing was the ascent of a vertical wall: without rope or natural holds, 500 metres or 1,000 metres of climbing. It was a wonderful time. The best time of my life.

If only it had not been for those bourgeois concerns: the doubts about my professional future and the morality of alpine clubs which attributed to climbing the very same ideals fascism had preached twenty years before. For me, climbing was an end in itself. Any thought of 'conquest' I regarded as suspect. Neither was I an explorer. If I climbed within the traces of alpine history, as now on Mont Aiguille, it was because I was curious about the activities of alpinists, 500, 100, ten years ago. Later, I also devel-oped a desire to penetrate the psyche of my predecessors, to

comprehend their contradictions. Questioning everything had become as important as climbing everything.

*

The sky above Mont Aiguille, clouds upon clouds, almost touched the earth. Everything hung low, so that only a narrow band was left between the clouds and the unblemished hills of this mountain country all around. The atmosphere was similar to that preceding a change of weather. Quiet villages here and there. A landscape of infinity. Mass tourism had not invaded this area.

Anthoine de Ville must have felt sublime. . . . To be first up there, elevated high above the lowland. In his report, man is sublime, not nature. Those first ascentionists will have felt like heroes, having subjected a part of the most inaccessible world to man's will, as commanded by the Bible. An enemy had been defeated. Edward Whymper expressed similar feelings four centuries later when, in 1865, he returned to the valley from the tragic first ascent of the Matterhorn:

> 'So the traditional invincibility of the Matterhorn was vanquished, and was replaced by legends of a more real character. Others will essay to scale its proud cliffs, but to none will it be the mountain it

was to its early explorers. Others may tread its summit-snows, but none will ever know the feelings of those who first gazed upon its marvellous panorama; and none, I trust, will ever be compelled to tell of joy turned into grief, and of laughter into mourning. It proved to be a stubborn foe; it resisted long, and gave many a hard blow; it was defeated at last with an ease that none could have anticipated, but, like a relentless enemy – conquered but not crushed – it took terrible vengeance.'

Almost 1,000 years before, just 500 years before Antoine de Ville climbed Mont Aiguille, the Yogi Milarepa (1040–1123) is said to have reached the summit of Mount Kailash, riding on the sun's rays, as one legend recounts. This did not mean that he discovered the Theory of Relativity like Einstein, nor that he intended to occupy the summit of the holiest of all mountains. He touched it, merely, preserving all its secrets. From its base, Mount Kailash rises vertically on all the sides. Above, a snow pyramid thrusts into the mostly blue sky like a crystal, a symbol of purity, which should be protected from any human scars. All modern climbers – Mummery as the promulgator of 'by fair means' not excepted – used iron pegs, wooden wedges, rope-techniques in order to

44

ascend and then descend the steepest mountains. The aids they carried were driven into fissures and holes, to be held on to, or lowered off from. Later they drilled into the rock to place safe belay pegs. Already by 1881, Albert Frederick Mummery and his mountain guide Alexander Burgener looked to place wooden wedges on the Aiguille des Charmoz in the Mont Blanc area, as they were abseiling down a doubled rope to the ridge below the summit:

> 'All went merrily till we reached the ice couloir. Here Burgener tried to fix one of our wooden wedges; but do what he would, it persisted in evading its duties, wobbling first to one side and then to another, so that the rope slipped over the top. We all had a try, driving it into cracks that struck our fancy, and even endeavouring to prop it up with ingenious arrangements of small stones. Someone then mooted the point whether wedges were not a sort of bending the knee to Baal, and might not be the first step on those paths of ruin where the art of mountaineering becomes lost in that of the steeplejack. Whereupon we unanimously declared that Charmoz should be desecrated by no fixed wedges.'

Only because the wood wouldn't hold, Mummery remembered his sporting spirit. In 1887, Georg Winkler, the boldest of all solo climbers in the last century, did not hesitate to place an iron claw in order to climb the peak which nowadays carries his name. His report on climbing the smallest of the three Towers of Vajolet (approximately 2,660 metres) reads like the training schedule of a modern sportsman:

'17 September. Up 6.15; start climbing 7.30; through a system of narrow chimneys to the foot of the last pinnacle, and this over some walls. 9.50, summit cairn; view clear but obviously restricted; 10.30 down; a block cut my rope almost completely so that it was only held by a few fibres. The block had hit the rope which was lying on a firm rock and cut through it; finished climbing 1.30; the tower offers a magnificent sight from its base and is the finest summit formation I have ever seen. Huts in Sojal 2.45, down 3.07; down to Mouzon over the Bridge (4.15) to the road. ¼ hr rest. Campitello 5.45; "Al Molino".'

Only half a human life later, in 1924, Fritz Rigele discovered the ice piton. With the use of this tool, vertical ice pitches were now accessible. Willo Welzenbach describes the mood before the attempt to climb through the Northwest Face of the Wiesbachhorn:

ABOVE: The astonishing Mont Aiguille, seen here from the east, remains a difficult climb 500 years after its first ascent.

> 'The longer the eye was fixed on the wall, the more accustomed it grew to its perspectives and the less frightening the image appeared. Slowly the initial response of "impossible" gave way to a dubious "perhaps".'

The vertical had lost its myth long ago and the best alpinists competed to solve the last big wall problems in the Dolomites, Kaisergebirge, in the Alps. Emil Solleder, writing in 1925 of the North Face of the Furchetta in the Geisler group, tells how, before the War, as one wall after another lost its nimbus of unclimbability, there were already some who were countenancing an ascent of the Furchetta by its terrifying north face:

> 'Over the years, the most select rock climbers tried their skills on this sunless, featureless, steep rock face and soon it had become the most significant problem in climbing circles. Many a young climber, in quiet hours of reflection, would sit on the summit-roof of the Furchetta, looking down its vertical flank to the scree where the most gigantic blocks of rock blended indiscernibly with the stream of boulders.'

Luis Trenker, aspirant guide from the Grödner valley, more than anyone kept trying to convince himself it would be possible to find a way up. Shortly before the War he finally attempted the hostile face with Hans Dülfer, the best rock climber of the day. In a cairn high on the face they found maps by Dibona, the Mayer brothers and Rizzi, who had retreated from this spot, declaring it to be 'hopeless!' Zig-zagging their way up, the two, however, pushed on to the last rest point on the face, the so-called 'Dülfer Pulpit', below an outcropping white triangular plate. To the right it looked impossible, but to the left, a promising edge soared upwards which could perhaps be reached over some red, brittle rock.

ABOVE: Emil Solleder (1889-1931), a prime mover of big wall climbs in the 1920s.

Solleder tells how two rusty pegs bore witness to the traverse which was started from this point. But stonefall and approaching night forced a return. Solleder attempted the face himself in the summer of 1925, with Fritz Wiessner. At the Trenker/Dülfer highpoint, he peered up over the edge into the yellow, overhanging rocks. There was no way up to the left. With the help of a few pegs, he climbed over the brittle, vertical rock up to the summit roof. Where Dülfer and the genial Angelo Dibona had failed, Solleder and Wiessner forged a way.

During the years of my youth, the North Face of the Furchetta was for me like a silent lover. She stood high above the Gschmagenhart pasture where I had spent ten summers, so perfect in form, so provocative that I was compelled to go up. It was a trail of the heart.

Five years later, when I climbed the face again, it was for the first winter ascent. I had been gripped by the obsession of 'ever higher, ever steeper, ever harder', an obsession which would last twenty years. I was not yet aware that each goal achieved is also a dream destroyed. I also lived according to the values of a classic mountaineer, who idolizes the brotherhood of the rope, self-sacrifice and the courage to die, and for whom progressive advancement is the only adequate outlet of energy – with a shot of romance, the suppression of fear and self-doubt.

When the Schmid brothers climbed the North Face of the Matterhorn in 1931, it sounded like a hero's song. Toni Schmid:

> 'The goal which seemed so remote only days ago has now been reached. Courage, the determination to win and a lot of luck – these were our travelling companions. The mountain of mountains has been robbed of its best secrets. Always, however, it will stand in all its powerful magnitude, as an eternal symbol of courage and strength and as a landmark of alpinism.'

Not long afterwards Toni Schmid's good luck abandoned him. He fell to his death on the Northwest Face of the Wiesbachhorn, victim of another attempt to destroy myths. Likewise before him, Mummery on Nanga Parbat, Winkler on the Weisshorn, Paul Preuss, and so on, and so on. Solleder was to fall in the year of the first ascent of the North Face of the Matterhorn and Welzenbach died three years later.

*

You may think my examples false and my quotes chosen maliciously. No, alpine literature is full of clichés, values which glorify 'team spirit on the rope', 'summit conquest', 'national pride' (all reminiscent of First World War military jingoism). Emilio Comici, the first to climb the North Face of the Cima Grande, was fond of empty phrases like these. Only Giusto Gervasutti, who narrowly missed climbing the Eiger and Walker Spur, placed individual creativity above such mighty '-isms' as idealism, nationalism and moralism:

ABOVE: Heroes of the Eigerwand, left to right: Heinrich Harrer, Fritz Kasparek, Anderl Heckmair and Ludwig Vörg – after their successful climb in 1938.

LEFT: Toni and Franz Schmid received Olympic Gold medals for their daring ascent of the Matterhorn North Face in 1931.

ABOVE: Willo Welzenbach, one of the most experienced mountaineers of all time and the father of modern ice climbing. He perished in the German Nanga Parbat disaster of 1934.

> 'After the North Face of the Eiger and the Walker Spur fell in the same year, climbing in the Western Alps reached a turning point. Five nations had competed for these two big problems, resulting in one win for the Germans (in partnership with the Austrians) and one for the Italians. There did not appear to be any other wall which would present a challenge big enough to warrant competition on such a nationalistic scale. Climbing could therefore become a personal affair once more, and a new route the private creation of the individual climber.'

After the Second World War, not only did the use of artificial aids to overcome the abyss continue, but so did the national jealousies. 'Beyond the vertical', the purely technical climbing style which was practiced and defended by George Livanos in the Dolomites and Guido Magnone on the Drus, began to catch on. Magnone:

> 'For a long time rock pitons and foot slings have been used in impressive numbers on many routes in the Dolomites and the Tyrol. But until now it seemed that only in the Eastern Alps we should be permitted long pitches of artificial climbing. However, several Italian teams managed to drive a wedge into this general belief by succeeding on the East Face of the Grand Capucin du Tacul. It was the first great "artificial" route over granite rock and the victory was acclaimed as a major success of the 1951 season by everyone – including the monthly review of the Italian Alpine Club. Yet, the same magazine, in its chronicle of the 1952 season, commented that our success on the West Face of the Dru was "really nothing more than a first-rate gymnastic exercise transferred to another place", which demonstrates a remarkable lack of objectivity.'

The lack of objectivity which had been lamented by Paul Preuss in relation to the dispute over rock pegs in 1911 continued to dominate the climbing scene for successive generations. As soon as the actors had their feet back on the ground, they would often forget that the debate was not about people but issues, about the game in the vertical realm. Frequently, those heroes preached about an idealistic world which did not seem to correspond to their character. The gulf between preaching and practice was often deeper than that between Dru and Walker Spur. The psychological disturbances resulting from this struggle were sublimated by action – with devastating consequences: the last vertical dreams were pegged up and those who did not lose their lives retired in time not to lose their hero image. From the safety of the armchair, alpinism was swiftly declared sick, its protagonists corrupt. Philistines and club moles would applaud. Yet it is not climbing that is sick but a few individuals: those who suffer by the existence of others and those who have to put everything and everyone on trial. It is not the sponsored climber that is corrupt but the men backing him – people who want to divert the attention away from the 'doers' to their own weary egos. Even the criticism of heroes provides a good living and a share of the limelight.

The era of climbing heroes has thus happily come to an end, helped by the shrinking of new territory. They have been replaced by sportsmen. Walter Bonatti deserves the last laurel for all the heroic deeds he accomplished on rock, with or without pegs, with or without preparation. He is the Achilles of alpinism. And he survived – in contrast to Herman Buhl and Lionel Terray. If he had remained silent like Milarepa and Dibona before him, he would be counted a sage.

Thirty years ago, the art of climbing received a new lease of life. This new impulse came from the paradise of rock, Yosemite Valley, from Britain, from a few climbing anarchists in the Alps who were looking for their own way through vertical climbing and for their own morality. Reinhard Karl was one such:

'On the third day we reach the big roof which had always blocked our view of the summit. Richard leads this. Then follows the Headwall with the overhanging crack, snaking through the granite wave which crashes over our heads, and which ends somewhere in the sky. Once again, a dream born of a photograph turns into reality. This time I am stronger, more open than that time on the "Nose" [of El Capitan]. But I can't say I'm happy just because I am here and able to photograph a dream myself. Compared with the real images the view through the lens is nothing. What can two dimensions express, even in Kodachrome? Richard has reached the belay above the roof and is ready to haul up the sack. Wumm! It swings in space like a pendulum. Richard is hovering 50 metres above me, a tiny spot on the belay, suspended in space.

'This can only be experienced in three dimensions. Neither photograph nor even writing – perhaps the best chance of conveying feelings – will do justice. What can you say anyway? That the wall is

LEFT: The charismatic Reinhard Karl forged his own path, becoming a cult figure to a new generation of mountain climbers. The first German up Everest, he lost his life in an avalanche on Cho Oyu in 1982.

1,000 metres high and that we are now 900 metres above the ground? That sounds ridiculously prosaic. That it is one of the most beautiful pitches in the world? What does that mean? To climb up this pitch and this crack, that is an art and we are the artists. That's also rubbish! We are climbers who are working their way up by technical means and who are happy not to take a fall. All these things are fine, but they are merely a tiny fraction of the whole set of experiences which is called "Salathé". The Headwall is a fantastic place and somehow we are very happy to be here. To be suspended so far in space and still belong to the earth. To reach such a point does not happen very often in one's life. This is a rare chance, a climax, when you suddenly realize that you own something very precious. Something you have always wanted.'

In the meantime, we climbers have long been overtaken, yet again, by the hunt for ever higher goals. Only now we are not destroying myths but breaking records. Whilst world climbing championships take place inside a hall and are pure sport, adventure on rock is more than ever comparable to an existential struggle. Climbing in this context is only possible, not necessary. Jean-Marc Boivin, the most diverse climber of my generation, became the victim of this cycle of acquisition in 1990, after he had introduced a new variant to advancement in 1981, the linking of several different routes in one day:

'By chance in the spring of 1980, I met Patrick Bérhault at the house of a common friend, and as is usual among climbers our conversations revolved around climbing. Patrick was preparing for an expedition to Nanga Parbat, I planning an ambitious objective on the Matterhorn. Both of us have more or less the same motives when it comes to climbing. In all our ventures, the joy and fun of climbing is always in the foreground. Out of the blue Patrick asked whether I thought it possible to climb the South Face of the Fou, hang-glide over to the Dru and finish off with the American Direct. This crazy notion had come to him from an article in a French magazine in which the author, elaborating on fast climbing times, suggested to anyone who wanted to be even better, that they should climb both these routes in a single day. The idea caught my imagination and immediately I started to work out the details – the hang-glider, the difference in altitude, the distance, the jump. Finally, I was convinced that it wasn't actually as impossible as it sounded.'

*

For a long time I sat on the summit plateau of the Mont Aiguille, absorbing the view. Suddenly, in a daydream, I saw myself again on the last third of the East Face of the Fanis Tower. Angelo Dibona must have had angel's wings when he first overcame this 80 metre-high rock precipice. Or maybe he was imbued with a confidence which reached deep into the roots of his hair, into the tips of his fingers and the very ends of his toes. A trust negating any fright or fear, perhaps even gravity. Today, Dibona is my climbing star. He never took a fall, he never destroyed any myths. He did leave a few behind.

To quote Milarepa, the mad sage who advises us in his *One Hundred Thousand Songs*:

'If you are frightened by the cycle of existence, you only have to give up the eight worldly delusions. Let us, brother and sister, move to the snowy heights of Mount Lachi.'

Audrey Salkeld

EUROPE BEYOND THE ALPS

Although the Alps provided the main cradle of mountaineering and remain an important crucible for development, there can be few peaks and crags anywhere in Europe that have not been investigated by climbers. The Caucasus, on the border with Asia and the loftiest range of all, with a dozen summits higher than Mont Blanc, attracted sporting mountaineers as long ago as 1866. Even those pioneers found that soldiers and explorers had preceded them, one of the summits of Elbruz possibly having been climbed as far back as 1829. The position was much the same in the Pyrenees, that magnificent mountain barrier separating France and Spain. The Vignemale in the centre of the chain (10,821 feet/3,298 metres) had been ascended in 1834 by the guide Cantouz of Argèles with an English gentlewoman, Miss Anne Lister, but the mountains remained largely unvisited by outsiders until the 1860s. Charles Packe (inventor of the sleeping bag) and the eccentric Count Henry Russell did most to popularize Pyrenean mountain-climbing, even if for Russell at least their main attraction remained the Vignemale. Over forty

years he climbed it 33 times, was so attached to it, indeed, that he leased it from the local *Syndicate* for 99 years – at the grand price of 1 franc a year. Then he built a series of grottoes up its flanks, in which he would spend weeks at a time, and throw dinner parties for his friends!

Cecil Slingsby was largely responsible for opening up the vast mountainlands of Norway to alpinists towards the end of the last century. In Greenland (which we treat as Europe for the purposes of this essay, but recognize to be geographically more closely allied to North America) exploration and epic journeys, particularly across the inland icecap, took initial precedence over mountaineering, although from the 1930s onwards, expeditions usually incorporated some peak-bagging. The highest point, Gunnbjorns Fjeld in the Watkins Mountains, was climbed in 1935 by members of L.R. Wager's expedition. Air travel has done most to bring Greenland's icy mountains within the reach of small expeditions. A bewildering number of peaks, many still virgin, make this a particularly attractive area, and university

LEFT: *Caucasus, Tatra, Pyrenees, the mountains of Scandinavia, Britain and the Mediterranean countries, to say nothing of the numerous sea cliffs and the tempting inland out-croppings: Europe has plenty to offer the serious mountaineer besides the Alps.*

RIGHT: *Twin-headed Ushba in the Caucasus (seen here from the northeast) is considered by many to be the World's loveliest mountain. Its lower North Summit was first climbed in 1888, the South Summit in 1903.*

in 1492. In the mid-fifteenth century, local men scaled Mount Sourlotis and some of the other spectacular conglomerate towers in order to graze sheep on their summit plateaux. The sheep were hauled up by their legs afterwards! These bizarre pinnacles, not unlike those of Montserrat in Spain, have attracted modern mountaineers since the mid-1970s.

German, Swiss and Austrian climbers plucked obvious prizes in Corsica. The Pindus mountains of Greece, the Spanish Picos de Europa, the Frankenjura, the Carpathians – all have attracted their advocates. In 1934 the King of the Belgians was killed in an abseiling accident while soloing a pinnacle beside the Meuse, in the Ardennes mountains. The history of climbing in the Tatra and on Saxony sandstone is covered in later chapters of this book.

In Britain, where the Alpine Club had been formed in 1857, native hills were at first considered very much second best,

LEFT: Charles Packe (1826-96), a dour Leicestershire squire and one of the pioneers of Pyrenean climbing.

BELOW: The eccentric Irishman, Count Henry Russell, built a series of grottoes up the slopes of the Vignemale (10,821 ft) and was first to sleep out on its summit.

groups have long been responsible for much of the activity here, as they have in Spitsbergen and other Arctic regions. The northernmost mountains in Greenland, the Roosevelt Range, were first climbed by a British Joint Services expedition in 1969 who grabbed no less than twenty-one relatively easy peaks.

Some people think the Meteora mountains of Thessaly in northern Greece, with their precariously-perched medieval monasteries, may have been the first difficult rockfaces ever scaled. Some ascents here must certainly predate that of Mont Ventoux in Provence in 1336 by the Petrarca brothers, or of Mont Aiguille in the Dauphiné by a band of King's mercenaries somewhere to train in winter when not in the Alps. But things soon changed. From initially being concerned merely with 'bagging' first ascents, usually by the easiest route to the summit, climbers later sought out hard rock for its own sake, opening up limitless possibilities on mountains large and small. British hills and cliffs then came into their own, different areas evolving individual characteristics and cultures. Climbing historians always enjoy trying to push back the boundaries of their sport. Who was the first rock-climber of all? The Romantic poet Coleridge, descending Broad Stand on Scafell in 1802 during a walking tour of the Lake counties? Or a youthful Wordsworth, earlier still, birdnesting on naked crags ere he had seen nine summers? Or was it one of the botanists who clambered after specimens on the East terrace of 'Cloggy' (Clogwyn du'r Arddu) in 1798? The Pillar pinnacle, in Lakeland's Ennerdale, received its first ascent in 1826, and thereafter scaling it became a popular feat for young bloods – and the not so young. The Reverend James 'Steeple' Jackson first clambered to its top at the age of eighty, dubbing himself the 'Patriach of the Pillarites', but while making another attempt three years later he lost his way and fell to his death.

The true Father of British rock-climbing is generally reckoned to be Walter Parry Haskett Smith, a gentleman lawyer who began swarming up Cumbrian crags while on a reading holiday in 1881 as a Cambridge undergraduate. During that first summer and those immediately following, he and his friends tackled many of the obvious lines on the major crags (the cracks and gullies), including putting up a number of atmospheric routes on England's highest mountain, Scafell. In 1886 he soloed the eye-catching Napes Needle. Systematically, Haskett Smith searched out, climbed and catalogued routes in the different mountain centres, ultimately producing the first British rock-climbing guidebook in 1894.

Gradually, as climbers gained in confidence, they moved out from the perceived security of the gullies onto the rock faces themselves, and in the years running up to the First World War, British climbers – particularly in the Lake District – were paralleling the bold athletic climbs of their Eastern European counterparts. Siegfried Herford and George Sansom, with H.B. Gibson and C.F. Holland, climbed the Great Flake on the Central Buttress of Scafell in 1914, employing a rope cradle around the chockstone and combined tactics: impressive nonetheless.

The late twenties saw some very bold efforts on big British crags. Piggott's climb on Clogwyn d'ur Arddu also used slings, as well as rope tensioning and artifical chockstones, which raised the hackles of traditionalists. On the other hand, Longland's route, led in gym shoes and without rope runners on Whit Sunday 1928, the first to breach that black cliff's western buttress, marked the real opening up of climbing on Cloggy. This brooding crag has remained a focus of developing technique for more

ABOVE: Early rock climbers clung to the security of gullies rather than venturing out on to open faces. Here, a party tackles Kern Knotts Crack on Great Gable, in Britain's Lake District.

British folk heroes: Hard man and purveyor of cryptic wisdom, Don Whillans (above) is seen in action on Heptonstall Moor. His 1950s partnership with Joe Brown (left, on the left) is perhaps the most famous in British mountaineering history and changed the face of rock climbing just after the War. Tom Patey, seen with Brown on St Kilda (left, on the right) and with Johnny Cunningham at work on the Left Fork of Y Gully on Cairn Lochan (above right), was a leading figure in Scotland, pioneering the exploration of islands and seacliffs and giving impetus to modern Scottish winter climbing. He was killed in 1970, abseiling from a Sutherland sea-stack.

than half a century. In the early thirties, Colin Kirkus dominated the scene, as did Menlove Edwards in the latter part of the decade. Edward's routes stand as a fine memorial: Chimney route and Great Slab, among others, are still highly rated.

After the War came what is popularly called the working class invasion, when city-dwellers took to the hills in great numbers. This is an over-simplification, of course: not all climbers had come from universities or the leisured minority heretofore, but it was an unstoppable tide made possible by full employment and a five-day week. Standards rocketed in much the same way as they had in the Alps (for opposite reasons) during the depression years of the thirties. Joe Brown and Don Whillans, two plumbers from Manchester, spearheaded the new initiative, and their ferocious lines on gritstone and in north Wales have remained classics and brought hand-jamming to a high art.

The sixties saw the introduction of man-made chocks and a short explosion of artificial aid-climbing on steep limestone, but over the following decade came a relaxation in dependence on equipment to assist ascent, allied to improved protection techniques and – above all – the advent of sports training. Climbing walls began to appear and to have their impact. At first they simply offered the opportunity to climb in urban centres away from the crags, but ultimately provided weatherproof gymnasia even in rock-climbing areas. The superbly fit climber whose interest is purely in rock now travels widely for greater challenge – and clement conditions. The sun-washed limestone crags of southern France, Germany, Italy and Spain, which had produced native rock athletes with the public profile of filmstars – Patrick Edlinger, Catherine Destivelle, Wolfgang Gullich, Stefan Glowacz – became international meccas.

Then, there was the escalation of competition climbing, very much a feature of recent years, but that is another story. . . .

Robin Hodgkin

Caucasian Prelude

Throughout the whole climb this was its chief fascination: tower after tower, a snow saddle between each, and all the time we were on the edge of immense sweeps of ice and rock of the most impressive angle.

Sitting in a field in the Cotswolds the Caucasus seemed infinitely remote as we made our plans for that summer. There were four of us – Bob Beaumont, John Jenkins, Michael Taylor and I – and we came from Birmingham and Oxford University Mountaineering Clubs. We elected ourselves to important executive posts, but had no leader; we did have impressive note-paper which was sometimes useful for scrounging supplies – chocolate for example; all of us read up what we could about the mountains; and with the assistance of Intourist we made our plans and eventually found ourselves with some bulky sacks of equipment and bulkier boxes of food crossing the plains of Germany and Poland. During much of this trip we were going to be hungry. Very little real food or currency was likely to be available once we were off the Intourist tramlines. Some fifty-five years later, the cold taste of hunger or the delicious flavour of herring roes and chocolate is still strong in my memory.

On the crowded wooden seats of Russian trains we rumbled eastwards across the Ukraine, along the edge of the sea of Azof, until after five days travelling we reached the sunny health resort of Naltchik. Another 80 miles in an ancient bus brought us up into the Caucasus by the great limestone gorges of the Baksan, and then to Tegenekli near the foot of Elbruz, where we were dumped at a small Intourist hotel.

It took us three days to get our first base camp pitched, up in the Jailik group, one of the finest of the several spurs which

BIOGRAPHY

In 1937, Robin Hodgkin (above, far left) took off on a shoestring budget for the Caucasus with three young friends. He was twenty-one, with a heartache, as he says, for high Asiatic mountains, and drawn by the prospect of untried climbs. It proved no disappointment. Besides the northeast ridge of Adyrsu Bashi, which he describes for us here, the party traversed Gulba by a fresh route and put up formidable new lines on Ushba South and the north face of Tetnuld – all with the very minimum of equipment. 'Our unprotected runouts, with that delicious, wayward hempen rope, were sometimes very long indeed' Hodgkin says.

In the Karakoram, on Masherbrum, the following year, he was at 24,600 feet with a companion when their tent was avalanched. Both were badly frostbitten during a stormy descent and a night spent sheltering as best they could in a crevasse, resulting in the serious loss of fingers and toes.

During and after the War, Hodgkin, a committed Quaker, worked as a teacher in the Sudan for sixteen years, and for ten years afterwards was headmaster of Abbotsholme, where he placed great emphasis on outdoor education. Writer and broadcaster, one of his books is titled Playing and Exploring.

RIGHT: The frosty Caucasus are the highest mountains in Europe. Kazbek, seen here, is the peak in legend to which the god Prometheus was banished. It was first climbed by in 1868.

LEFT: Hodgkin, Beaumont, Jenkins and Taylor in 1937.

buttress the Caucasus on their northern side. Those three days gave us an idea of the real difficulties and pleasures of Caucasian travel: the barren valleys of the north; their fine wild-eyed inhabitants – Balkaris – who, despite their dash, seemed never in a hurry; villages where smiling children stared from mud and wattle houses; the numerous young Russians coming to the mountains, not so much for the climbing as for air and friendship; and the trials of transport – the intransigent donkeys and the exquisite misery of heavy loads.

*

Beaumont and I returned to camp across the moraines in the hot afternoon sun, having spent a day climbing Yunomkara-Tau (4,365 metres), whose steep and shattered final pyramid had offered a fine route and a finer view. A bathe in a blue pool and some cocoa at the camp put us in an ideal frame of mind for sunny relaxation. We had had eight days of continuous climbing, each of which provided a fine new route or a virgin aiguille. The

best of these had been a route straight up the south face of Jailik (4,533 metres). I felt that a day's rest in our sunny hollow was justified.

But this was not to be. There was one great peak, Adyrsu-Bashi (4,370 metres), which remained to be climbed. On our side it presented nothing but steep, intimidating ice-slopes, and an extremely long ridge consisting of a screen of ice and rock crowned by a row of jagged teeth and buttressed by three great towers which fell away to the Golubev pass. John Jenkins kept eyeing it; sketching it in his diary.

'That spiky ridge! It would take at least two days,' I objected, having a picture in mind of the Peuteret climb on Mont Blanc. Wrong again. Jenkins, who had spent much time mentally minimising its difficulties, and visualising its possibilities, was convinced that the whole ridge could be climbed in a day by a fast-moving party of two. With a lot of encouragement and persuasion I agreed to make the attempt with him on the following day. After the usual preparations for an early

ABOVE: Adyrsu-Bashi. Looking back down the multitowered northeast ridge during the first ascent.

start and a possible forced bivouac, we went to bed as the sun set with that vaguely tense, slightly depressed feeling which comes before a big climb.

At 3.30 after a hot breakfast we started off over the moraines and out on to the open glacier. We were accompanied by Beaumont, who was going to make a solitary and exceedingly rapid ascent of Oru-Bashi (4,310 metres). The full moon which had made pleasant our plod up the glacier was dipping as we approached the Golubev pass. Beaumont left us and started up the steep névé towards his summit. The red light of the sun was creeping across the great upper snow slopes as we arrived at the foot of the ridge.

A short halt and we were off along the first of the many snow arêtes of that day. Then we came to the first tower where, on loose scree ledges, we climbed up into the sunshine of its summit. After a quick sardine, we were off again. We knew the next item would be one of the many little snow sickles between the towers. We came on it suddenly: only six metres away, below a little overhang. A jump was necessary on to the narrow crest of hard snow. It wasn't difficult, but frightening because of the extreme steepness of the slopes on each side. Throughout the whole climb this was its chief fascination: tower after tower, a snow saddle between each, and all the time we were on the edge of immense sweeps of ice and rock of the most impressive angle.

The second tower we climbed by a slippery slaty groove which brought us up to another little snow sickle, steep and corniced. The rhythm of the route was beginning to establish itself; gendarme and snow arête regularly followed each other and seemed to slip away beneath our feet; we were well ahead of schedule, but knew that the chief obstacles lay ahead. The third tower was the most formidable feature of the ridge. It was over 300 metres high, very steep, and cut from top to bottom by an unpleasant couloir of black ice. The rocks on the far side tempted us across. Jenkins went ahead and for half an hour hacked a line of buckets across the tough and extremely steep ice. Once across, on the fine-grained granite of the other side, the climbing became superb. It was hard, but always there were just sufficient holds to provide steady and rapid upward progress. It seemed like an everlasting Tryfan buttress, but instead of the dark and friendly gullies on either hand there were those incredible sweeps of blue-black ice forcing us to keep to the jagged crest.

From the top of the third tower we saw ahead the horizontal section with its line of notches and gendarmes. Our progress became less regular: sometimes we climbed over the gendarmes, more often we sidled along their icy skirtings and

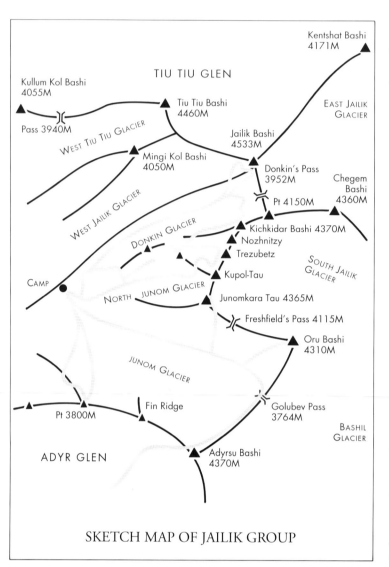

SKETCH MAP OF JAILIK GROUP

LEFT: Sketch map of the Jailik Group, the blue lines showing routes followed by the 1937 party.

RIGHT: Looking across the precipitous north face of Adyrsu-Bashi to the summit of Elbrus, 20 miles away.

BELOW: The Twin Peaks of Ushba.

crest which led easily to the rocky summit 100 metres away. We were in good time and were surprised to find that so far we had taken under nine hours. We made a long halt on the summit and lounged among the boulders admiring the view and brewing some tea in our emergency cooker. To the east clouds were piling up behind the great Bezingi Horsehoe (all the peaks around 5,000 metres high); south-wards Ushba (4,710 metres) stood out blunt, black and vertical above its neigh-bours; while to the west was Elbruz (5,633 metres), whose gentle bulky cone formed a striking contrast, detached from the gen-eral scene. But Ushba's twin summits were our magnet. Within ten days we would be on that red southern and higher tower, pushing our luck, pushing our limits.

In the hope of finding somewhere to sleep in the main Adyrsu Valley we started down the original route towards the southwest, leaving the summit at 1.30. A steep slope of soft snow led to a ridge running westwards. Here we met a slow-moving party of Russian climbers who were making heavy weather of what seemed to us easy rocks. They were perplexed by the absence of any tracks – how was it we were already above them? They indicated all the local places where rash climbers were liable to fall off. They only had a short rope and curious leather head gear. Friendly exchanges; then we continued, finding that the rocks below justified what they'd been telling us – steep smooth slabs for about fifty metres.

Slopes of hard ice followed, leading down to a long névé which took us to the upper glacier. A long glissade was followed by two little ice falls which we descended

shattered bases; once we were involved in a difficult pitch in search of running water; once dislodged a mass of black, wobbly blocks which echoed and re-echoed as they crashed to the glaci-ers far below. A moment of apprehension – but soon forgotten. Tooth after tooth was left behind till at last, after a short and foolish excursion off the ridge, we reached the final rocks where they merged upwards into the snow and ice of the face above. Our first acquaintance with the snow was unpleasant: a woolly mass of slush which I had passed slithered away from under my feet and separated me by six metres of bare ice from Jenkins. Conditions improved slightly above, but the snow remained soft and wearisome to body and mind. We were feeling the effects of the pace at which we had been going, and there was still a large obstacle to be overcome, a gaping bergschrund which cut across the whole face. We took it direct by a wall of crumbling crusty snow and ice. Then followed a final steep section guarded by what looked like a cornice, but wasn't. It was a pleasant snow

in crampons to reach the first moraines. Patches of grass and clumps of gentians began to lull us into the satisfaction of a nearly finished day but we soon found that we were deceived, for we reached one of the most desolate valleys where the recently retreated glaciers had left behind huge dumps of dust and boul-ders. Here we plodded, slithered and swore for two or three hours, before eventually reaching the greener and more open valley beyond. Just as the long-threatened and habitual evening thunderstorm was breaking, we presented ourselves at a camp of Russian students and begged the hospitality so rarely refused in the Caucasus. We were entertained to large bowls of prunes and rice by future Soviet engineers and architects.

Next morning, after being made to do physical jerks and wash with distressing thoroughness, we found a route back to the old Junomkara camp and rejoined the others in the valley. We would soon all be on our way, over the Betsho Pass, down to the meadows and tall, fortified towers of Svanetia.

Dietrich Hasse

Saxony Sandstone

First and foremost, in the spirit of classical mountaineering, it is a self-evident requirement that the first ascent of a summit or of a climbing route . . . must always start from below.

Where the river Elbe flows through the 'Dresden Gate' on the German-Czech border, a surrealistic array of eroded mountains and pinnacles rises from a landscape of dark forest and grey plain. This is the Elbsandsteingebirge, popularly known as Saxon Switzerland (or Saxon-Bohemian Switzerland). Its deep-cut gorges, sheer rock walls, remarkable clusters of sandstone towers and the occasional rounded volcanic top, present a fairytale country which has long attracted visitors and climbers.

The rocks were laid down under a Cretaceous sea which extended over what is now southern Saxony and northern Bohemia over a hundred million years ago. Massive layers of sandstone, more than 600 feet thick, were consolidated, uplifted and then, under pressure from neighbouring land masses, riven with a network of vertical fissures. Weathering deepened and sculpted these clefts even further to give here a tight valley, there palisades of cliffs or freestanding cuboid blocks. The unique needles which so characterize the region are the last eroded fragments of this primeval sea-bed.

The main Elbsandsteingebirge covers some 15 by 25 miles and ranges in height from 360 feet in the Elbe valley at Pirna to an ample 2,360 feet atop the Hoher Schneeberg in Czechoslovakia. It divides naturally into several regions, each with its own characteristics. In places the rock, containing elements of clay, offers little resistance to weathering; elsewhere you find a tougher calcareous cement, or a silicified sandstone which is the most durable

RIGHT: View of the Gansfelse, near Rhaten, from the north. In the background, left, is the Monchstein, where climbing vertical Elbe sandstone first took off in 1874.

BIOGRAPHY

Dietrich Hasse is a Bavarian climber who has a long association with sandstone climbing, in the Greek Meteora and Sahara as well as in Saxon Switzerland, where he has made a number of important new routes. He has also climbed in the Hindu Kush and Andes and has published widely. Here, he gives us a brief history of walking and climbing in the Elbsandsteingebirge.

BELOW: Steel engraving 1829 (from a drawing by Captain Batty), showing the Rathen area of the Elbsandsteingebirge with the Neurathener rock-tower and the Steinschlender.

of all. Where you get the most striking formations, with walls and pinnacles up to 330 feet high, it is safe to assume a relative firmness of rock. Slender, angular columns denote harder rock, whereas rounded, rather plump forms predominate on the more easily-weathered stone. Walls, too, vary enormously, presenting cracks of all widths.

When the Swiss draughtsman and copper engraver Adrian Zingg took up an appointment at the Dresden Academy of Art in 1766, most people in Germany (with the exception of such leading spirits as Goethe) still had a medieval perception of natural beauty. Influenced by his contemporaries in Switzerland – Von Haller, Rousseau and de Saussure – who had already set the essential style for a new way of portraying nature, Zingg brought a fresh appreciation of landscape. He settled happily into his new home and regularly wandered in the nearby Elbsandsteingebirge. Soon, he was leading his art students through 'Saxon Switzerland' (as the countryside became known, after him and his circle). Long before the opening up of other German districts to tourism, this immigrant 'promoter' – by virtue of countless romantic landscape pictures, engravings and etchings – had established a fashionable excursion trade, centred on Dresden, which from the second half of the eighteenth century onwards made this the most famous mountain-walking range in Germany.

After the appearance of practical descriptions of the country-side during the 1780s and 1790s, the first real walking guide to the Elbe sandstone region was published in 1801 – well ahead of the first Bavarian handbook for travellers. By the nineteenth century Saxon Switzerland was widely known, not just inside Germany. Streams of enthusiastic nature lovers poured in from all over Europe and further afield, so that besides numerous German-language publications there also emerged illustrated walking books in English, Danish, Swedish and, above all, French. In my possession I have an Elbsandstein wood engraving made by Edward Whymper, the first man to ascend the Matterhorn and inspiration to generations of climbers.

The area's great popularity lasted for over a century. Then, with the coming of the First World War, foreign interest in Germany declined markedly. After the Second World War, central and eastern Germany vanished completely behind the Iron Curtain, to be almost forgotten by the West. Even in the Federal Republic of Germany people remembered increasingly little about 'over there', so that in 1979, when we tried to launch a West German book about the Elbsandsteingebirge at the Frankfurt Book Fair, astonished dealers asked: Where on earth is that? Saxon Switzerland? Never heard of it! Such was the result of the region's virtual inaccessibility to ordinary westerners over just a few decades. Now, with the ending of the Cold War and attendant political change, the Elbsandsteingebirge can again be visited freely by everybody from the West, not just those from West Germany or Great Britain.

On a wave of enthusiasm, similar to the walking craze, the sport of climbing arrived in the Elbe sandstone region

LEFT: The Teufelsturm (Devil's Tower), where one of the first Grade VI climbs was achieved in 1906. It was four years before the same degree of difficulty was achieved in the Alps. Climbers here are repeating a 1936 Grade VII route, once considered the last great mountaineering problem of the area.

during the second half of the nineteenth century. Sporting climbing – that is to say, climbing for its own sake, the how-you-do-it being more important than what-you-climb – really took off here in 1874 with the first aidless ascent of the Mönchstein high above the Elbe Valley. There had been earlier artificial ascents, but this was quite deliberately a climb 'without any instruments of assistance'.

Until the turn of the century, climbing performance in the area ran parallel to overall climbing development, as evidenced in the standard of routes achieved. Leading routes in 1899, for instance, included the Campanile Basso in the Brenta Dolomites of the Alps and, in Saxony, the Blossstock, both rating UIAA

IV+ [Union Internationale des Associations Alpines, grade IV+] (which corresponds to V on the Saxon scale). Later on, the standards regularly climbed free (without aid) in the Elbe region outstripped those in the Alps. What we today call UIAA Grade VI (Saxon VIIb) was achieved for the first time on Saxon sandstone in 1906, and not once but in three instances, of which the Alter Weg (Old Route) on the Teufelsturm represents the best example. The earliest Alpine Grade VI route was not put up until 1910 – the same year that VI+ (Saxon VIIc) was reached on Elbe sandstone with the South Crack on the Kreuzturm. Grade VII- arrived with a variant to the Alter Weg on the Schrammtorwachter in 1911, and the West Arête on the Wilder Kopf in 1918 (both Saxon VIIIa). Grade VII was first put up on the Kunis Arête of the Rauschentorwachter (Saxon VIIIb) in 1921; VII+ on the Schwager-Talweg (VIIIc) in 1952; VIII- on the Frienstein-Konigshangel (IXa) in 1965; VIII on the North Face of the Schwager (IXb) in 1970; and VIII+ on the Grosser Wehlturm-Superlative (IXc) in 1977. UIAA Grade IX- was first achieved in the Elbsandsteingebirge in 1982 with the ascent of the Amselspitze Schallmauer (Saxon Xa); IX a year later with the Schwedenturm at the sixth attempt (Xb); and IX+ in 1986 with Heringstein-Barometer fur Stimmungen (Xc). In 1989 the UIAA tenth grade came to the Elbsandstein in Perestroika on the Schrammsteinkegel (UIAA X-, Saxon XIa), to be followed immediately by its Red Point ascent, rated at X (XIb). This is the limit of present day standards on Elbe sandstone. Meanwhile, Elbe sandstone climbing has lost the leading position it held in world climbing until the late 1960s.

With very few exceptions, the freestanding towers have alway been the most popular climbing goals in Saxon Switzerland, and still are, rather than the flights of cliffs with an easy way off at the back. On the 1,100 climbed outcrops in Saxony's Elbsandsteingebirge there exist today well over 14,000 routes. Around a dozen guidebooks and supplements have been published this century.

Rudolf Fehrmann, past master and pioneer of remarkable Saxon routes (as well as those Dolomite ascents on the Campanile Basso, Stabelerturm and Kleine Zinne named after him), launched the Elbsandstein guidebook in 1908. It set the course for the whole development of Saxon climbing. 'Non-sporting' routes, those on which artificial aids had been used for the first ascent, were simply omitted: such undertakings belonged to a past era. In 1910, for the first time, Fehrmann clearly defined what was meant by 'sporting' and what 'artificial'. *Fehrmann*, as his guidebook was universally known, was the first outcrop climbing guide in mainland Europe: only in Great Britain did something similar already exist.

LEFT: A 1970s route on the Wenzelwand in the Schmilkaer area, graded at UIAA VI.

ABOVE: East Face of the Teufelsturm (UIAA VII), first climbed in 1965 by K. Richter, W. Bohm and G. Kalkbrenner.

ABOVE: Rudolf Fehrmann (1886-1947), principle pioneer of Saxon climbing. He produced the first guidebook and set in train the high standard of sporting ethics for which the area is known.

59

Between its 1984/5 and 1991 editions, over 4,200 new routes were added to the guidebook, illustrating the surge of recent activity. The latest revision runs to six volumes and includes numerous extreme routes up to UIAA Grade X. That is impressive – although superficially it might appear less so if you allow yourself to be impressed by climbs in other areas where standards of difficulty have now surpassed those of the Elbsandsteingebirge. Surpassed, despite our having Bernd Arnold, the most successful climber of all time, whose performance is unlikely to be improved upon in the future. For more than twenty years Arnold has been the leading figure in this highly-developed climbing district, with over 600 first ascents of super-routes to his credit, plus the creation of five new grades of difficulty on Saxon sandstone (UIAA VIII, VIII+, IX-, IX and IX+).

Why, then, have we fallen behind in standards of difficulty? This perennial question faces us on Elbe sandstone: is it more desirable to keep up with the latest standards, which can involve top-roping, the use of chalk and perhaps even preparation of the face; or to maintain the tradition of pure, bold Saxon-style climbing? Two quite different interpretations.

In Saxony, we still see greater value in the latter, which absolutely prohibits any top-roping. Reconnaissances from above and the insertion of belay rings are equally ruled out, as is protracted rehearsal on projected holds and of combinations of moves on a more or less tight rope, as well as the employment of artificial holds. All these would mean an abandonment of some of our most inalienable and fundamental rules. Without them, our Elbe climbing culture would sustain real damage. First and foremost, in the spirit of classical mountaineering, it is a self-evident requirement that the first ascent of a summit or of a climbing route, or the 'conquest' of an obviously natural face, must always start from below. First ascents, even of contemporary trendsetting routes, should preserve local values as milestones for the reliable recording of developments in performance. Until now, that was universally accepted in outcrop climbing, as in alpinism and expedition climbing.

If such practices as top-roping had been adopted in the Elbe area, climbs like the West Arête of the Wilder Kopf, the Kunis Arête on the Rauschentorwachter, the Schwager Talweg or its north face, the Superlative on the Grosser Wehlturm, the Schallmauer on the Amselspitze, and all the other highlights and models of their time, could have been done a dozen years earlier – perhaps almost from the beginning. But these climbs would never have achieved the status and validity which they have won through their uniquely 'sporting' methods of problem solving. They are symbols of that epoch of inspired development, of intensely adventurous and bold rock climbing. What, by contrast, is lastingly remarkable about a climb done with psychological and physical help from above? It is as acrobatic as traditional climbs, of course – it would be laughable if it were not – but what else? Where is the profound mountain adventure? And

what of risk, of true standards of climbing, or mountain sportsmanship? We do not believe that such methods would provide stimulus and vision for our Saxon climbing youth.

So, all right, elsewhere people can adopt what we see as cheap practices, and in consequence do 'harder' climbs than exist on Elbe sandstone. But this new-fangled manner of forcing up climbing standards has had no appreciable effect on Saxon mountaineering to date. By far the majority of climbers stand by tradition, a majority prevailing also amongst the top-performers. That is not to say all of the special rules of Elbe sandstone climbing must remain for all time. For now, no artificial chockstones may be used, no ring pitons for a first ascent, no aids like sky-hooks or other temporary aid devices (wooden wedges, aid pitons or bolts, camming devices). But there are many concerned people who see a case for some change.

After a visit to the Elbe sandstone in 1976 by the top American climbers Henry Barber, Rick Hatch and Steve Wunsch (who

RIGHT: The Sonnwend-kegel in the Schramm-stein area. This route, the Sonnwendfeier, is graded VIII+ and was first climbed in 1985 by Berndt Arnold and companions.

made the first ascents of such inspired American climbs as Supercrack in the Shawangunks in 1973 and Psycho in Colorado in 1975), Wunsch wrote:

'If the unaccustomed mode of Saxon climbing makes a comparison with other climbing practices difficult, I can certainly say – and in this my friends unreservedly agree with me – that on our trips through America, Great Britain, Europe and Australia, nowhere have we come up against such matchless standards as in the Elbsandsteingebirge.

'. . . I mean that the isolation of the Elbsandsteingebirge, together with the uncompromising application of its traditional ethic, has produced a basis of challenging climbing routes, which put a climbing aspirant arriving there in his place

BELOW: Exposed climbing in the Schrammstein area.

ABOVE: Berndt Arnold, 'most successful climber of all time'. For more than 20 years he has been the leading figure on Elbe sandstone. He is pictured here in 1978 with his wife Christine.

more than the difficulties of any other climbing district known to me. I have never found a harder single climbing area . . . We all agreed that, if 'top-roped', the hardest routes in the Elbsandsteingebirge would not appear harder than extreme routes of many other districts. The attempt to lead these routes from below seems to us, nevertheless – especially following Fehrmann's rules – as something completely different. The most aggravating difference, which first gives Elbe sandstone climbing spice, is the problem of the poverty of protection. . . . There are plenty of climbing districts in the world which offer purely gymnastic problems . . . To my mind the aesthetically ideal exposition of the vicious circle of fear and safety has been positively resolved only in the Elbsandsteingebirge, a history that spans almost a century. The great tradition of ethical steadfastness was an advantage to the Saxon climbing community, in that it strengthened confidence in inner reserves, in strength and courage, so as to take on sporting challenges to such a high extent. To this bear witness those numerous monumental climbing routes, which during all the phases of mountain sporting development have their equal nowhere in the world. In addition, think of the era in which the rock climbs were first begun . . . Alone the fact that the ethical standards (the sporting rules) adopted by all Saxon climbers over so long a period give to Elbe sandstone climbing its purity, which vis-à-vis technological development has been preserved here far longer than in the rest of the world. . . . The younger generation should, before it resorts to material aid, remember the courage and ability that the old Saxon tradition has developed and taught.

'. . . In this context it seems to me worthwhile to question the mountaineering mentality which demands common standards and climbing practices. . . . Such levelling is typical of the western world. Actually the loss of individuality of climbing style in one region or another seems to me rather deplorable.'

RIGHT: Concentrated over 375 sq miles (970 sq m) on the German–Czech border, easily accessible from Dresden, are collections of surrealistic pinnacles. This is the unique Elbe sandstone region of Saxony, celebrated for its challenging climbs and uncompromising ground rules. No artificial aids are allowed.

SAXON SWITZERLAND

GERMANY

N

Dresden
Hohnstein
Elbe   Wehlen   ▲2   Rathen   ▲   Ulbersdorf   ▲3   Sebnitz   ▲16
Pirna   15▲   Hertigswalde
▲4   Waltersdorf   Lichtenhain
▲6   Porschdorf   17▲   Ottendorf   Saupsdorf   18▲
Ostrau
5▲   Bad Schandau   Zeughaus   Hinterhermsdorf
Konigstein   Pfaffendorf   ▲   9▲   11   Zeughaus   ▲
Neundorf   7▲   8▲   Krippen   ▲   14▲
1▲   Reinhardtsdorf   11
Schöna   12   Schmilka
Cunnersdorf   10▲
Berggiesshübel   Kleingiesshübel   C Z E C H   R E P U B L I C
Bielatal
▲13
Bad Gottleuba   Rosenthal

▲ Hoher Schneeberg 721M

1 Cottaer Spitzberg
2 Bastelwände
3 Waltzdorfer Berg
4 Bärensteine and Rauenstein
5 Königstein
6 Lilienstein
7 Pfaffenstein
8 Gohrischstein
9 Kleinhennersdorfer Stein and Papststein
10 Spitzer Stein, Müllerstein and Katzstein
11 Kaiserkrone
12 Zirkelstein
13 Kl. and Gr. Zschirnstein
14 Gr. Winterberg
15 Hochbusch
16 Buchberg
17 Ottendorfer Höhe
18 Steinberg

Paul Nunn

Skye Wars

These pleasures are unsanitized, adventurous, for adults only,

transcending the grading trivia invented to bamboozle the gullible.

The Misty Isle offers two alternatives to rock-climbers: heaven in drought in early summer; or a frustration of endless drenching rain.

Not that rains and mists lack charm. With relaxed mind, time, patience, food, a roof, a good book and an occasional dram, they would matter hardly at all. But gentlemanly leisure, sadly, has passed me by; my forays past Kylekin have been vulgar, short, incongruent with mood of place or people. Still, icons of gentle memory remain, amidst dazzling recurrent visions and nightmares from far bigger mountains, unalloyed happy images punctuating twenty years without serious scar.

The Cuillin require an adjustment in consciousness, the steep unknown rock demanding extra self-denying ordinance. Most climbers delight in the magnificent existing climbs, even in busy Glen Brittle holiday weeks, when the seashore is colonized by escaped Londoners. Yet there is a powerful pull to other corries, for despite a good number of modern (E grade) ascents since Robin Smith's Thunder Rib on Sgurr a' Mhadaidh in 1960, Skye remains relatively untouched. More 'Stairways to Heaven' await discovery, and dozens to equal the best on Scafell.

Sceptics are right to retort that despite gabbro's classic roughness, the rock is unreliable, cliffs inconveniently remote and long to prepare by abseil. There is no 'pocket pulling' and weepy streaks persist in fine weather; natural protection is sparse, and leading on sight makes 'high standard' climbing impossible. 'Old believers', however, slope off into their

BIOGRAPHY

Paul Nunn is a lecturer in Economic History. He began climbing in 1956 and in 17 years missed only one Alpine season. He has climbed in the Caucasus, Pamirs and Baffin Island, and taken part in 13 expeditions to the Himalaya and Karakoram. For more than three decades Nunn has been an astringent and widely-respected commentator on the climbing scene. He is President of the British Mountaineering Council.

fastnesses, rucksacks stuffed with wires, chocks and friends, wire brushes, trowels, and old ice hammers for cleaning earth-filled cracks. Heads buzz with would-be lines and vectorish links through wall and roof, corner and slab – many remained

filed for years, from Tom Patey's wall-map Hit List in an Ullapool garden shed in 1968 to our own times – stache without end, its key, imagination, the prize, a recurrent oasis of new excitements. There is little scope for parched narcissism. These pleasures are unsanitized, adventurous, for adults only, transcending the grading trivia invented to bamboozle the gullible. Rain-blasted craggy heights in remote coires can never become Klettergarten, or Ecoles des escalades.

Obsession with the sacred shows, an illusion of wholeness in a natural theatre – indefensible philosophically in a shattered world. So be it. The soul of rock climbing is being contested, threatened, by organized recreation's unquiet minds and gombeen men collecting dues. Harsh words – passionate, elitist maybe: doubly incorrect! Therein lies the rub. For climbing is, too, uncleansed of its essentials, without the castration of hazard and redefinition for competitive convenience. Uncustomized rock in high corries is a temple greater than any built by man, essential to more than climbers, a Calling for those who know.

*

The early seventies was a time of endings and beginnings. Within two weeks in the summer of 1970, Ian Clough had died on Annapurna and Tom Patey on the Maiden Stack in Sutherland. By coincidence, as if fulfilling a mythic ritual cycle of generations, their close friend Hamish MacInnes had agreed to join us in the Central Caucasus. An epic drive across Europe, a cold three days and two freezing bivouacs

ABOVE: *Clach Glas from near the Summit of Blaven.*

RIGHT: *The northeast face of Sgurr a' Mhadaidh, still presents many new route possibilities.*

on a new route on Pik Shirovski forged strong friendship. Like Tom before, Hamish pointed us at possibilities in the northwest of Scotland, reinforcing an already terminal addiction, acquired from climbs in Torridon, Loch Maree and Foinaven over the previous few years. Bob Toogood, Chris Boulton and I drove to Glencoe, making stately progress in the secondhand Renault 16 which temporarily boosted my ego and drained my pocket before a subsequent seven year exile to a Ford van. At his cottage above the meeting of the waters, Hamish sang the praises of Blaven, echoing the sentiments of Martin Boysen, who had done first ascents of Jib and Bargain Offer there with Dave Alcock in May 1969. Hamish had also climbed Jib, and enthused over photographs on his table.

To Skye in drought is 'glory road', heady intoxication for anyone with an ounce of affinity for the sharp bright light of Western Britain. To be 'on form' justified a new route or two, without the risk of exaggerating modest difficulties in imagination's distorting mirror.

The final scree-fan below Blaven awakened other realities, a Purgatorial flog on a warm day. After passing steep shorter walls, the crack and lower bulge of Jib loomed through evaporating morning mist, but we were drawn further, to the wall above, reminiscent of Scafell East Buttress and split by Clough's Cleft, but otherwise scarcely touched.

A classic feature sliced into its eastern face, a long thin slab of modest angle cutting through overhanging walls, the evident 'Moss Ghyll Groove' of the cliff. Entry required a widish bridge and high step onto a chest-level hold. The slab provided delicious delicate climbing, with only pause to lift occasional loose flakes or gabbro particles obstructing key holds. There were few runners until a larger foothold and a few cracks made a small stance and belay.

Excitement and pleasure brimmed. It seemed a pity to have to wait for Chris and Bob to climb up. Out of the north face shadow it had grown to a baking day, without another person sighted, like early morning on Cloggy at the end of the late 1950s. In the shadows sweat dripped from my nose end.

The continuation slab was much the same, padding on small holds with little protection, sixty or seventy feet to a substantial ledge under a soaring crack. What a life being a gritstoner, seeing fierce cracks as allies rather than uncompromising enemies!

The others roosted comfortably, and I swarmed my outsize body up the crack to a steep little sting in the tail, out into hot sun. It was shirt off before rescue of the others from below. Pasty from my non-Alpine summer, this was worthy recompense, if shortlived, as one midge, then another, smelt the blood of an Englishman. *Ecstasis* we called it, not for difficulty, but beauty, exhilaration and associations, all carried off on a hunch from afar.

We slept in the Glen Brittle Hut, finding old friends on the beach there and in the Sligachan pub. One, Nikki Clough, Ian's widow, had a broken half-shaft on her Daf car. As the garage in Portree had promised another in a week, we motored over on the next damp day – fruitlessly. Giving up on machinery, we visited Glendale, hoping to see seacliffs or stacks. Instead, amid sea mist were relaxed-looking retired bank managers disguised as crofters, at the site of one of the last real resistances to Clearance in the 1880s. The half-shaft never came. Nikki went south to care for her daughter, trekking back a month later, when the miracle happened and the car was repaired. In Gaeldom still, time has a different meaning.

Better weather and Chris' knowledge took us to Sgurr a' Mhadaidh, and a few pitches of what later became Megaton, then he took a day off and Bob and I did Atropos, Hamish's route (with Ian Clough) in 1958. An old piton turned to dust like a staked vampire when I tried to clip it on the second main pitch. At last more 'weather' sent us south.

The eventual ascent of Megaton in April 1974 was manna from heaven, the fifth route in five days. Tut Braithwaite and I had travelled up together and grabbed a route near Loch Carron before Martin Boysen joined us for three more, at Carnmore, Mainreachan Buttress and another on Loch Carron (this last had probably been done not long before by Les Brown). Mo Anthoine, Ian Campbell, Al Harris and a few others put in occasional appearances until Cam collapsed near Sligachan – wimped out, so Mo maintained, though a doctor pronounced pneumonia

and incarcerated him in Fort William Hospital. We kicked steps in hard névé up the slope to the Sgurr in a temperature and atmosphere akin to the eastern Alps rather than Scotland. At our previous stalling point, combined tactics suggested the only solution. Echoing past times, Martin sat on my shoulders and I levered myself upright to enable him to reach a jug hold above. As he heaved up, I sank back, victim of belayer's droop. The ramp led up and out like a dream. When it faded into the wall, a few leary moves over nothing led to a groove. Martin, belayed above, bridged across a groove of uncertain outcome. I followed, pulling on a sling he had left behind; Tut, waiting below, froze in the April shadow. The ramp was hard, the situation astounding. I continued up the groove and across an exposed wall, which yielded holds where required, to easier ground. There was a lot of climbing before we all escaped, to whoop down to Hamish, drink his birch wine and compete in jumping McLeod's Leap.

After Megaton, it was presumptuous to expect another way through the belt of overhangs on the Sgurr a' Mhaidaidh. Nor did Chris Boulton, author of *Thor* and companion on the ascent of Megaton's lower pitches, seem convinced when I mooted the scheme. In 1976, after returning from the Ressau Felix Trombe, a monster cave in the Pyrenees, Bob Toogood and I had done a few climbs in the Vercors. A second hot summer made the Chamonix Aiguilles disintegrate, which seems to have continued ever since. Our ropes were chopped to pieces by stonefall on the Plan west face, and we headed home. With a few days of freedom left, good weather was reported and Chris, Tony Riley and myself headed north, leaving England in a lurid 'Gone with the Wind' backdrop of forest fires.

Next morning the overhangs of Tairneilear loomed again.

Not far right of Thor a fine direct groove led to the slabs below its steep crux pitch. Since Chris' ascent with Ginger Cain in 1967, his memory seemed to need refreshment, and I sensed him pondering its difficulties again. Probably the rock itself appealed to his sculptor's eye. As Tony joined us on the shelf I craned my neck to view a groove a hundred feet up, sweeping down through even steeper rock. Apprenticeship had conditioned me to expect holds in unlikely places; on this one I was not so sure. Tony produced his Hasselblad, an ominous signal for action.

ABOVE: Blaven (3,044 ft) with Clach Glas (2,590 ft, left) and Garbh Bheinn (2,655 ft, right). Seen from the east across Loch Slapin.

RIGHT: Classic Cuillin-scrambling on the Blaven-Clach Glas ridge.

A first corner was wet, black and basaltic, protection a wobbly large hexentric the wrong way round after slippery bridging. Fear forced me to place a poor piton as protection or means of retreat, a blade tied off which inspired little confidence. Then the bottomless wall, right, had to be crossed, thankfully dry, into the hanging groove. There followed a haze of tricky climbing, aiming towards a small bottomless person-sized slot. The rope came around two corners, insufficiently slinged, and threatened to pull me off. Once in the slot, scarcely able to budge another inch of rope, I placed the only available dubious anchors and belayed.

This took less time to describe than to do, and a cold Tony was beginning to abseil before Chris set off to follow me. My suspicion was that they hoped I would get fed up, and I was. However, I would hardly have dared lower down on those anchors. For Chris to get into the slot I had to move out onto a small hold above.

There was insufficient security until I fixed a sound but small wire in a wall. Chris fitted better into the slot than I had, but still hung from the belays as there was little to stand on. A steep wall above was discouraging, running up to a steeper roof, with little sign of holds. Chris had difficulty paying out the ropes, so constricted was his hole. In a tense half-hour I slowly moved upwards and avoided plunging down the groove.

At last, with trepidation, I touched the underside of the roof, standing up on small holds. The roof was flat and smooth, and tired fingers gravitated towards its junction with the black wall. Three fingers of my right hand locked into a damp undercling, too high above my face to feel secure. The other hand excavated small loose rock chips next to the attached hand, gradually working towards the entry of a fourth finger. Then a small sliver of rock flirted out under the leverage, and I saw light through a thread leading to the fingerlock. There was a breathless, timeless little struggle as a sling slid through and emerged near my attached hand five inches to the right. Clip, it was in the bag!

I shouted to Chris to relax, although not so much as to pull out the wonky belays, then made newly-friendly moves around the roof to the right into less steep ground. It just did not seem possible that we had done it again.

Other times, other friends, other acres of gabbro. In May 1980, after a winter trip to Everest West Ridge, Clive Rowland took us to two crags he had found. On one, above the Broadford-Sligachan road, he'd one climb done, another attempt unfinished. While Clive, John Smith and Mike Richardson did a steep crack, Alec Livesey and I repeated Clive's former route, then effected another, similar in concept, rock and sparse protection to Golden Slipper on Pavey Ark.

Next day we were directed to a good rock face on the left of Waterpipe Gully. Our companions attacked a parallel line to the left, and the day was punctuated by Mike Richardson's oaths and crashing as detritus left the crag.

Alec and Clive sent me off first, up a rib of compact rough gabbro right of the cliff centre with interjections of slippery splintery gabbro, most of a rope length to a grassy small ledge in a beautiful curving groove. Alec bridged the next immaculate section, pointed features peeking from a white Arran hat, slipping occasionally on wet patches. After a good runner he speeded up, because it was harder, to a perfect shelf. Clive finished an uncracked wall with little protection. Revelation was a classic, equivalent to finding one of the great Hard VS standards of Llanberis. Not far away soared an overhanging Crack for thin fingers.

ABOVE: The moon over Sgurr a' Fheadain and Sgurr a' Mhadaidh, Coire na Creiche.

Like everywhere on earth, Skye is vulnerable. Roadstone interests seek to pulverize whole landscapes in the northwest as they have the Peak and Yorkshire Dales for decades, 'National Parks' or no! The scale of planned despoliations is astronomical, a response to overcommitment to roads and automobile transport inherent in anarchic 'free market' government policies. They beaver away, buying gutless lairds, promising handfuls of jobs to the Highlands and Islands Development Board and strapped communities. Should they continue, they will create abominations in the eyes of the whole of Europe.

All of us sometime betray what we love. One sunny afternoon in 1985 I soloed up the long rough slabs right of Revelation, not too far left of Waterpipe Gully. About to go to Gasherbrum 3 with Clive Rowland, the day did not weigh heavy. One thought did, as I lazed on top of the buttress and put the climbing shoes away. Some years earlier in the Indian Himalaya I had arrived in Kishtwar after a long wet walk, homeward bound, footsore and alone in darkness at the dak bungalow. The Chowkidar was very kind, organized food, and sent a boy for my Delhi bus ticket. Then he sat by, and chatted in the bungalow, preventing me from remaining unnaturally alone. After rice and dahl, he gently asked if I would like to see photographs of his English Memsahib

65

the deadweight film boxes grated down onto the gabbro. Unleashed, the net spread, as on water. Then the contents began sliding out in my direction. Several large boxes of equipment poised momentarily in disequilibrium – someone had blundered!

Unlinked in customary way by rope, they emerged like a slow-motion cluster bomb, each pursuing a potentially lethal trajectory. Although belayed, I half expected to be knocked backwards over the edge, while instinctively clawing for the closest boxes. Two were seized, another two stopped, but inevitably one trundled off into oblivion as I balanced full-handed. Depressingly thunderous, it boomed and banged hundreds of feet down steep slabs and grooves to perdition. Naturally it was the camera, worth around £29,000, although at the time my shouts were directed at innocent wretches possibly hidden below in its path.

Of course the sunset fight scene in *Highlander*, Sean Connery's cinematic pastiche of modern and medieval, survives. Two swordsmen, an older ex-Olympic specialist and young stuntman who had made his debut in a milk advertisement on top of Cheddar Gorge, were fitted with pianostring stunt wires to hidden harnesses, one up his kilt. A slip would have seen them suspended upside-down on vertical Cioch side walls, perhaps minus their privates. Another camera came and Tony filmed, from a slot in the rockwall behind, as the sun did a clichéd 'sickening goldie' over Glen Brittle.

friend. Unfolding the plastic, out came two or three photographs, barely discernable in the candlelight. Nikki Clough stood on the tidy grass outside the dak bungalow. There was another picture with her daughter. She had been there twice, once with Audrey Whillans in 1970, during the time of the Annapurna expedition when Ian was killed by a falling sérac, and again some years later.

Sitting on the gabbro slab I again pieced together the jigsaw, so many parts, some did not fit. Now she was dead.

In the summer haze a helicopter clattered and echoed in Corrie Lagan. A filmic human cluster pretended to be busy by the Lochan, hustling nets of equipment around, ready to be hoisted on to the Cioch, when not hustling one another. On the Cioch top, Tony Riley waited for the heavy 35 mm camera to come up. It was my job to guide the net from below as it dangled beneath the chopper, landing it on the sloping slab of the Cioch summit. One load lay safely stowed at the Cioch neck, fastened together by a loop of rope. Hamish MacInnes was close. Others kept well out of the way.

The chopper rattled high over the Cioch and gradually descended, the weighty net, around 180 kilogrammes (400 pounds) at least, swinging in my direction. Still supported from the aircraft, it slumped onto the slab above me, and rested in uneasy balance. At a signal the pilot released his safety hook, and

Those shots complete, our trials were not over. With an hour of light, Tony and I were flown to the ridge above by helicopter, where we reassembled the 35 mm movie camera in great haste. With almost no time to spare he was ready, aiming the Arriflex into the void above Corrie Lagan. On cue the chopper came buzzing up, hovering in space out of his shot, another camera mounted. From a high rock I picked up the first of three enormous two-handed swords, and at a signal threw it up and out into space, where it spun and flashed two or three times in the sunset before disappearing below. Just to be sure, the performance was repeated twice more, before an accelerated dismantling and helicopter dive into the darkness of the Glen.

Next day a promising film scene amidst the tottering spires of the Quiraing was prevented by lashing rain and howling gales. Skye took revenge and location shooting finished. Driving past the Seven Sisters of Kintail towards Clive's house near Cawdor next day, I was light-hearted yet pensive, a Gallowglass released and uncommitted to another master.

RIGHT: The Cioche, an outcropping pinnacle on the Sron na Ciche cliffs, where Paul Nunn waited to receive a net of film boxes from a helicopter hovering overhead. The French actor, Christopher Lambert (far right) is 'the Highlander'.

BELOW: Ruadh Stac and Marsco (on right), with Sgurr nan Gillean in the distance.

Mick Fowler

A Weekend Away

The wind whips the spindrift into a frenzy as our stinging faces peer up to where Chris is, somewhere above us in the clouds.

Ian is an old school friend, one I cannot disappoint. Still, it was inconvenient of him to arrange his wedding to Margaret for a Friday afternoon. It meant that, despite the Scottish forecast being excellent this weekend, we are later than usual weaving in and out of the tired commuters grinding tediously up the M1. So many trips in the past have coloured this road North with memories. . . .

Scratchwood, 5 miles from the North Circular Road, that's where Victor Saunders started the 630 mile drive to Torridon by taking the wrong exit and driving South, back to Staples Corner. And Junction 19, the M6 interchange, where Bob Gookey missed the exit and reversed along the hard shoulder until his 850cc minivan could make a slow start in the fast lane of the M6. Passengers remember it well – almost as well as those ejected onto the hard shoulder on a later occasion when Bob lost control and thumped into a bridge support with such force that the back doors popped open.

Near Junction 25 Henry Todd demonstrated how challenging it can be overtaking on a single lane section of motorway – even for Al Baker's trusty company Citroën. The base of a concrete bollard imprinted itself interestingly in the wheel, forcing a serious limp through the rest of that section and an altercation with the driver of another car. He seemed to think Henry was to blame, and needed some persuading that the damage to his car was insignificant.

Then, there's Ma Shepherd's on the A74, the only stop we allow ourselves, where

BIOGRAPHY

When leading British mountaineers were asked by a Sunday magazine who they felt was at the pinnacle of their sport, the name Mick Fowler emerged as 'the mountaineers' mountaineer'. A full-time tax officer, Fowler for many years has successfully divided his life between traditional respectability and the precariousness of high-performance mountaineer. Weekends find him making climbing raids across the Scottish border; summer holidays take him to the Himalaya. Victor Saunders, who regularly partners him and was with him on the first ascent of the awe-inspiring Golden Pillar of Spantik in the Karakoram, says it is his stability and incredible organizational skills which allow him to cut loose when he is climbing. 'He can't stand indecision. If I say to him I don't like the look of something, he'll say get on with it or go down.'

Fowler here takes us through a typical Scottish weekend in the winter of 1986, when the climbing included two new ice routes. Since then he and Saunders have both moved out of London to position themselves nearer the mountains.

the trusty Anne serves weather forecast updates along with the pie, beans and gravy, before tying up our breakfasts in separate Mother's Pride bags, cheese rolls for Saturday, ham for Sunday. (There's a science to this: cheese rolls dry out faster than ham.) Even the slip road here has a story to tell. It's where a rather over-enthusiastic Sonja Vietoris managed to leave the road and end up in distressingly close contact with the Little Chef cesspit. It wasn't even her car. . . .

On to Loch Lomond, scene of one particularly heroic manoeuvre by Chris Watts: a 360° rotation, including a reverse movement, across a narrow bridge. No damage except to the nerves. And Ballachulish, where Bert Simmonds – snoozing contentedly behind the wheel – took a hired Sierra over a roundabout and into a field. John English tested the famous Volkswagen durability north of Fort

William when his Scirocco negotiated a forty foot bank and partially immersed itself in the loch. Even then, the tow back onto the road by a drunken JCB driver was perhaps the most severe test. But the car passed and the weekend continued.

But this trip: it's 4.30 a.m. and the car has stopped. The occupants need several moments to register the fact. All the memory-jogging landmarks are behind us now, and in front the road dips into a calm sea – the Kyle of Lochalsh. The Skye ferry. Bedtime. Vic Saunders – 'Slippery Vic' for the difficulty of pinning him down on any subject, 'Slipper' for short – and I collapse haphazardly outside the car, leaving Chris and Sonja in situ. The first ferry is not till 5.30 a.m. One hour to wait.

I wake to the startling realization that a huge articulated lorry is edging past my head in its bid to be first aboard. Its exhaust pipe brushes uncomfortably close to my nose, ensuring that pollution intake levels far exceed my weekday London norm. The team struggles into action, marvelling at both the ferry crew and lorry driver, who are apparently oblivious to the fact that a car parked on the slipway and surrounded by dozing bodies might conceivably want to catch the first boat.

By 7 a.m. we are there. Glen Brittle. I suppose I should admit here to a degree of insider dealing affecting the 'on sight' situation.

George, my father, is still enthusiastically ticking off the Munros in his retirement and is often in a position to provide us with on-the-spot weather reports. Last night he phoned London at 7 p.m. to give us the all clear: a fine, crisp night with sea level snow and a glittering Cuillin. Twelve hours later, here we are. Every climbing team should have one!

Waterpipe Gully is top of the list for the weekend. George checked it out yesterday, when the signs were good. Unfortunately, though, the poor old boy must be a bit short-sighted as he failed to notice Doug Scott's team engrossed in a first ascent. (Such talented competition in these far flung spots!) To be fair, their ascent only becomes really obvious as we follow their footsteps and pick placements up the ice-choked pitches of what we believed to be our unclimbed line.

Somewhat to our surprise, Slipper and I are more competent than usual – either that or (more probable) the gully is easier than expected. Whatever the reason, we arrive on top with time to spare. South Gully, away to our right, had stopped me at

ABOVE: The glittering winter Cuillin, seen across Loch Hourn from the Scottish mainland, a distance of some 21 miles away. Blaven is the prominent peak (right of centre), with Garbh Bheinn on the far left and Sgurr an Gillean to the right.

Christmas, but today we leave most of our gear at the bottom and manage a quick solo.

Inspiring possibilities open up above. At the head of the amphitheatre containing Doug Scott's earlier line, The Smear, a continuous narrow ice streak, culminates in an icicle-ridden overhang. The urge which overcomes us is irresistible. In such situations, it is necessary to ignore inconveniences – like the lateness of the hour, or having left most of our gear more than a thousand feet below – and just concentrate on the task in hand. Soloing a few short Grade IV sections saves some time, and means that the lack of gear is not really noticeable until we have gained the line proper and effectively committed ourselves.

Slipper leads off on our single 9 millimetre rope. His time is not wasted placing gear: having so little, our progress is still fast. After a gradually steepening ice ramp, a short but expletive-packed struggle with a brittle icicle leads past a small overhang to a stance from where the rest of the line is clearly visible. It consists of a steep and narrow, but continuous ice runnel, leading directly to the capping icicle-draped overhang. Such sights make leaving the tax office desk (where I work) and rushing to Scotland for the weekend particularly worthwhile.

A couple more steep and spectacular pitches on perfect ice lead us to the obvious crux of the route, where water seeping through the overhang has frozen to form two huge icicles, one dropping from a point midway across the roof, and the other adorning its lip. From a constricted belay in a shallow ice cave, it looks just possible to climb up beneath the roof and cross it by transferring from one icicle to the other before moving round on to the front face and pulling up to gain the easier ground above. As luck would have it, the ice here is better than that of the icicles with which Slipper has been struggling lower down. Happily, a couple of ice screws survived our gear rationalization, and with these safely screwed in (as easily as the Russian salesman on the Ushba glacier had promised!), a series of lurches and much scrabbling of crampon-clad feet take me out onto the outer face of the outermost icicle.

At times like these my poor arms have sometimes let me down, and I've been known to end up dangling inelegantly from my rucksack straps, which I have judiciously attached to my ice axe wrist loops for this very purpose. Today, though, it's a good day without the excitement of such embarrassments. Basically, it is easier than it looks. A quick pull on bomb-proof placements and the sun is glinting on my face as the upper slopes come within reach. Only 150 more feet and Icicle Factory is over, and we stand on the deserted Skye ridge, surveying the scene. Despite it being a perfect day, we have seen no-one since leaving the car.

We linger, admiring the view, before heading down in gathering gloom towards the spot where we so foolishly abandoned much of our gear below South Gully. And at this point it dawns on us that our head-torches are among those items we considered suitable for load-lightening. Fortunately, there are no witnesses to the resulting grope-in-the-dark fiasco before we are eventually reunited with our gear.

The homely atmosphere of the Sligachan Hotel with its log fire, cosy armchairs and resident golden retriever induces lyrical reminiscences of the day's adventures. And the derelict garages just outside provide superb accommodation for the discerning weekender. Only the Ladies' toilet in Glen Torridon (with hot shower and working lights) can really be said to offer a superior bivouac.

Sunday, 4.30 a.m. Cold. Dark. For me, the crux of a winter weekend is getting started on a Sunday. The last ferry to the mainland on Sunday evenings is 5 p.m., so an early start is essential, if distressingly unwelcome. The long cold spell looks at last to be coming to a close. The wind is rising and streamers of cloud can just be seen racing across a darkening sky.

A quick reconnaissance down Glen Brittle yesterday showed an impressive streak of ice adorning the back wall of Coire a Ghreadaidh. We cannot see any mention of this line in the guidebook. Despite the worsening weather, this clearly deserves attention before we head back to London.

Having parked at the Youth Hostel, an hour's hopeful groping in the general direction puts us right for locating a path of sorts at first light. With the wind now gusting heartily and the first snowflakes falling, air conditions promise to be better for the complexion than the day before. Four of us started out, but only three retain sufficient enthusiasm to make it to the foot of the route. Not a good sign.

RIGHT: Mick Fowler on Waterpipe Gully, Sgurr an Fheadain.

ABOVE: On the ridge after making the first ascent of Icicle Factory.

LEFT: The Icicle Factory; an irresistible line on Sgurr an Mhadaidh.

Thrashing around, lost, on steep snow slopes, I ruefully recall last year when Slipper and I had been even more incompetent than usual in descending on the Ullapool side of the Fannichs, when our car was parked at Fannich Lodge. The penalty on that occasion had been a 20-mile walk. Here, though, the gods are on our side – or maybe it's gravity. We slither and stumble down to emerge from the mist with our approach route spread before us.

Back at the car a couple of inches of snow have fallen, but the thaw is setting in and the best cold spell of the winter is drawing to a close. A challengingly slippery exit up the hill from Glenbrittle leads us out onto the main road and back to Kyleakin in time for the last ferry.

Fourteen hours later I am back in the Tax Office, listening to colleagues' accounts of how they 'went shopping', 'caught up on a few odd jobs', or simply, 'had a nice rest' at the weekend.

'And you?' they say. 'Had a good time? Been away?'

I launch into an enthusiastic account, but winter climbing is a difficult one to explain. I can see from the blank expressions that your average Civil Servant just doesn't understand the attraction.

Chris, Slipper and I fumble blindly in the worsening blizzard, theoretically revelling in the contrast between workaday desk-bound dreariness and character-building weekend excitement.

A stimulating smear of ice disappearing into the clouds provides the necessary impetus, and after a spot of soloing it is time to fish out the ropes and get going properly. The wind whips the spindrift into a frenzy as our stinging faces peer up to where Chris is, somewhere above us in the clouds. Two long pitches and we are back to soloing again, dodging in and out of steep sections until the ground eases. White Wedding is complete and a characteristically hesitant descent is possible somewhere in the mist to one side.

Victor Saunders

Sheep Story

I looked down. Ten feet to a big ledge. Worst that could happen would

be a broken ankle, I reasoned. I was right.

Big boots, sacks, and hydroscopic Gore-Tex V Diffs in the rain. What else should one do on a blustery rain-soaked day? Jim Fotheringham had brought cling-filmed sandwiches, two each for himself, Chris Bonington and me. We sipped from flasks of coffee. Watched the downpour fade to a drizzle. High in the air, a pair of falcons were quartering the sky.

Jim turned to me with his uniquely mischievous grin. 'Which way now Victor?' I stared blankly at the guide book, it wasn't at all obvious. We were sitting in the back of a small cave, yet the route description didn't suggest leaving. Chris, who had done the climb before, couldn't remember either. Jim, who believes that Climbing Is Not Competitive, waited just that fraction of a second longer, to confirm to himself that we were indeed totally confused, before setting off.

'Come on, it's easy,' he said, disappearing like the Mad Hatter. A few minutes later he popped out of the cliff fifty feet above us. Chris and I followed the cave pitch, and resurfaced into the drizzle to find the Hatter had disappeared up the next pitch. The finish came suddenly and presented us with a walk off to the left, or a boulder problem up a slabby groove. The Hatter ignored the groove. Chris retreated from it half-way, saying it was too wet and greasy. This I could not resist, even though Climbing Is Not Competitive.

I reached Chris's high point and began to have uneasy thoughts. Some swine had definitely covered the holds in Vaseline. I looked down. Ten feet to a big ledge. Worst that could happen would be a

BIOGRAPHY

Victor Saunders came relatively late to mountaineering, at the age of 27, and since then has climbed all over the world: the Alps, the Caucasus, India, Pakistan, Nepal and Bhutan. He is an architect by profession, although these days his time is mostly divided between climbing and writing. His self-deprecatory, quirkily observed Elusive Summits, *describing four lightweight alpine-style expeditions in the Karakoram (including the Golden Pillar of Spantik), won him the Boardman-Tasker prize for mountain literature in 1990. He has recently returned to live in Scotland, where he was born.*

broken ankle, I reasoned. I was right. Not long after, there was a slithering, and a loud snapping crack. Like glove puppets, the two faces popped over the top.

'Be a'right in a min.' I gestured at my boot which was now pointing sideways, 'just twisted it a bit.' Jim, a dentist, by profession and therefore a great expert on feet, said he thought it looked worse than that, but didn't offer to carry my sack.

'It'll be okay,' I insisted. 'I've got to be. The Guides' test starts tomorrow morning.' I don't know what Chris thought, but I like to think he was genuinely concerned and sincere when he said it was something that could happen to anybody, and that risk was an essential part of climbing anyway. Nice man. I hopped uphill to clear the top of the crag. an unpleasant grinding noise, such as my car often makes, accompanied me. Near the top of the cliff Chris and the Hatter were deeply engrossed on a small ledge. As I hobbled closer, I could see a sheep's tail sticking out from the huddle.

'How disgusting,' I thought.

'Needs rescuing,' they said.

Of course it does, I thought . . . it needs rescuing from you. The animal had jumped down to a ledge the size of a small bed. The grass had by now been eaten up, and it could not make the jump back up. Down was 150 feet.

'Pass me your harness,' Jim said to Chris. 'I'll try to creep around its back, slip the harness over, and we can haul it up.'

'I don't think this is a good idea,' said Chris, getting the rope out. I had to agree with him. I remember the famous sheep

LEFT: Jim Fotheringham in Urchin's Groove, Scafell Pike.

They could barely bring themselves to remain aground long enough to poke their sharp beaks into the rabbit hole. But the pigeon had disappeared in the warren. The falcons would soon get bored. Chris and Jim got bored too, and joined me at the stream. The Hatter was clearly disgruntled.

'What about the sheep?' I asked.

'We had to leave it. Chris's harness isn't big enough.'

'Oh,' I said 'lucky sheep, eh?' The falcons flew off. I have often wondered about that pigeon. Did it find another exit from the rabbit hole or perhaps the warren was home to a fox? As for the sheep . . . I wonder if it realized how lucky it was.

LEFT: 'I'll try to creep around its back, slip the harness over, and we can haul it up.' (Cartoon by Victor Saunders)

rescue at Cummingston, when the tide had cut off a sheep and the rescuers hauled it up by waist line, which somehow slipped. The farmer's face was an awful sight when he saw the line had become a noose, swinging his once magnificent prize-winning animal by its neck.

I continued downhill. Soon I had to sit every five or six hops. Voices drifted on the breeze. 'I can't get round it's back, it keeps turning to face me.' Sensible animal, I thought. '. . . I don't think the farmer would like this. . . . what if the sheep decides to jump?' So it might, so it might, I thought to myself. I certainly would. '. . .It's okay, I'll try getting round this way, I'll surprise it with the harness. . . . can you belay us both?'

Spring had arrived that weekend. I hopped onto a small yellow flower, and ground it out of existence. A squeal tore the air as the two falcons began to harry a passing pigeon. In the background the breeze-wafted voices continued. '. . . damned beast keeps turning to face me . . . perhaps it doesn't trust you Jim . . . Chris can you *please* attract its attention so I can get behind. . . .'

Exhausted by the hopping descent, I collapsed on a mossy stream bank. The falcons had struck their quarry, which spun to earth, leaving a trail of feathers. The pigeon landed by a large boulder. The falcons spiralled down for the kill, describing an elegant double helix. Their intentions were not lost on the pigeon, which immediately popped down a rabbit hole conveniently located under the boulder. By now I was too far away to hear more than the odd phrase from the others: '. . . Won't let me . . . Farmer won't like this.'

Perhaps if I dunked the foot in the stream it might get the swelling down for the morning. Unrolling my socks revealed a monstrously swollen joint, about the size of a melon. The falcons had landed and were stalking round the boulder. They were clearly nervous. Strange to see these soaring birds of prey look so frightened. They kept looking over their shoulders.

BELOW: Here we see Jim Fotheringham trying to rescue a sheep.

Ed Douglas

Modern Times

Climbers were running up against a ceiling in this continual rise of standards and it would take a transformation in attitudes to overcome it.

RIGHT: Ben Moon climbs Hubble, his 1990 limestone testpiece at Raven's Tor in Derbyshire. Although short – barely half a dozen moves – at 8c+, this was nonetheless immediately hailed as 'probably the hardest route in the world'.

You could argue that the last embers of optimism and exuberance born of the 1960s were finally extinguished on the day in 1980 when John Lennon was gunned down outside his apartment block in New York. Russian tanks were rolling through the Afghan countryside and Mrs Thatcher's government had begun deconstructing all the systems and beliefs that had propped up postwar Britain. That world seems a long time ago. The café in Stoney Middleton still opened midweek. Climbers wore Whillans harnesses, thought Joe Brown's routes were hard, and ate large cooked breakfasts. The term 'PA' still meant something other than public address.

There are two routes in North Wales both climbed in 1980, and by men who would dominate the first part of the subsequent decade. The first caused an ethical storm over the tactics used by its first ascensionist, and the second terrified cognoscenti to such a degree that nobody dared repeat the climb until 1986. Both routes gave an indication of where climbing would go through the 1980s – if anyone had been wise enough to see it – and both retain a reputation for difficulty.

Ron Fawcett's Strawberries on Craig Bwlch y Moch above the village of Tremadog is a breathtaking line, spearing up a blank wall above the 1960 Joe Brown classic, Vector. Routes had been climbed on the Vector headwall's periphery, but Fawcett's ascent of the thin crack-line straight up the middle remains one of the most important achievements in British rock climbing. The climb encapsulated all the changes that had been steadily acceler-

BIOGRAPHY

Ed Douglas is well placed to comment on the British rock scene of the last decade. In 1987 he burst upon mountaineering consciousness with a snappy new domestic rock climbing magazine, On the Edge. *He was nineteen and had been climbing for six years. There was a degree of arrogance in his precocity perhaps – that he admits – but he feels it is the role of the young to question tradition. They must always do that. The magazine still flourishes, but Douglas has moved on. In 1993 he launched his second new publication,* Mountain Review. *Influential and international, it is a magazine reflecting all aspects of mountaineering, not just rock climbing, and includes films and literature.*

ating throughout the late seventies – increasing technical standards, greater fitness and a scientific approach – and illustrated just how far Fawcett had outstripped the achievements of his older mentor Pete Livesey.

Ron, a quiet but hugely determined man, graded Strawberries E5 7a – unheard of in those days and guaranteed to grab climbers' attention. Its second ascent went to a brash newcomer called Jerry Moffatt who would pursue and then finally overtake Fawcett throughout the early 1980s. Still E6, Strawberries wasn't climbed without a fall until the middle of the decade when Stefan Glowacz from Germany finally obliged. By the standards of the 1970s, Glowacz's should have been acknowledged as the first ascent, but by that stage Fawcett's controversial tactics had long been submerged in an entirely new approach.

John Redhead's The Bells, The Bells, (E7) on Anglesey's North Stack – the other great route from 1980 – did not allow the luxury of repeated falls. Its grade has remained undented by the progress of time, and a further indication of Redhead's achievement came when Andy Pollitt's on-sight repeat six years later gained universal acclaim. Redhead epitomized that other strain in British rock climbing – that of bold commitment. An artist, and something of a mystic, Redhead climbed intuitively without bothering to train – a real contrast to Fawcett's professional approach. The Bells showed just how dangerous that style of climbing could be; climbers could push their technical limits to unimaginable lengths if they were safely protected, but Redhead's heart-stopping achievements would not prove popular.

It is also worth remembering that in 1980 climbers still wore EBs. These seemed perfectly adequate at the time, as illustrated by the above two routes, but the changes in equipment over the next ten years made climbing appear more of a different sport than anything else. The boots (although the word itself is too heavy) now used make EBs feel like Wellingtons. The habit of using climbing walls, of climbing abroad in winter, of taking a more athletic approach, have improved the overall level of fitness of climbers. While the method of protecting routes is not dissimilar, those climbs with

fixed protection have become very popular. Climbers are now less inclined to walk long distances; opportunities for climbing in the rain are no longer as readily welcomed.

While it might appear that there has been a wholesale move towards the cult of the grade at the expense of exploration, it's worth observing that far more new routes were climbed in the 1980s than all the previous decades put together.

Areas like Pembroke and Pen Trwyn in Wales, the southern sea cliffs of Devon and Cornwall and many crags in Scotland were transformed by this attention. Whether it was Mick Fowler climbing some obscure Scottish sea stack – often driving up from his London home for the weekend – or Pat Littlejohn adding another outstanding line in the southwest, the rise in standards offered new and exhilarating challenges in the old idiom. But climbers were running up against a

ceiling in this continual rise of standards and it would take a transformation in attitudes to overcome it.

Strawberries illustrated the problem. There had to be a limit to what could be climbed – first try – without technical error or a failure of strength, and Fawcett had more or less reached it on Lord of the Flies (E6) in 1979. In the early 1980s more and more climbers yo-yoed routes of increasing difficulty, working out sequences before falling, returning to the ground and starting again. Fawcett is now uncomfortable about the tactics he used and hardly sees the route as his. Yet the tactics he used can be seen as a precursor to those of the mid-1980s.

But in the beginning the word was Fawcett. His free ascents of the Cave Routes in Gordale, both E6, offered climbers a new challenge. 'It became obvious,' wrote Martin Atkinson, 'that natural talent and weekend climbing were

LEFT: German climber Stefan Glowacz was first to make a fall-free ascent of Strawberries, Fawcett's 1980 line on the Vector Buttress at Tremadog. The route is now graded E6, 7a.

approach, and the 1980s – in every sphere and sector of life – demanded style and outspokenness.

Moffatt the prophet, who had dispensed with Colorado's famous testpiece Genesis, necessarily provided us with Revelations (E7). The 30 feet of severely overhanging limestone at Ravens Tor was ahead of its time, certainly, and arguably the hardest route in the country, but its greatest significance was the passing of Fawcett's heavy mantle to the muscular shoulders of the new school. Fawcett's ascent of the arête right of Green Death at Millstone at E7 in the same year was an achievement to match that of Moffatt's, but Fawcett must have been aware of the irony when he called it Master's Edge.

If it sometimes appeared that all rock climbing took place in the Peak District and occasionally Yorkshire, Moffatt corrected that with his ascent in 1983 of the Master's Wall (E7) on Clogwyn d'ur Arddu, finishing a line begun by John Redhead. It was a bold ascent that dispensed with Redhead's controversial bolt. Redhead maintained that Moffatt had avoided the real challenge remaining on the Great Wall, but the latter's achievement should not be underestimated. It was left to Johnny Dawes to solve the problem in 1986 with Indian Face. There can be few ascents that have troubled the imagination of climbers more than this palm-wetting adventure and it remains Dawes' finest achievement. Still unrepeated in 1993, few top climbers have even bothered to consider climbing it, such is the threat it poses of serious injury or death.

no longer sufficient to climb the hardest routes of the day.' This resulted in a hard core of unemployed men (women are only now making an impact on British climbing), most notably those centred on the Stoney Middleton café, climbing full-time. The favoured rock was limestone, which could be protected more readily and where training could make a real difference.

There were others who chose alternatives to the steep and powerful limestone routes waiting to be climbed. Johnny Woodward's Beau Geste at Froggatt Edge is a blank and overhanging gritstone arête which is still rarely climbed. Woodward soon departed to Colorado but he had showed the way, most notably to Johnny Dawes.

A short stocky figure with an unerring sense of balance and a soul that was born to climb, Dawes practised his skills on the back of the fives courts at his public school before unleashing his talent on the crags. Fearless, intuitive and determined, he climbed a string of gritstone lines of a new order of difficulty, which have received much attention but few repetitions. Dawes, like Redhead, took an artistic approach to his climbing; it was a mode of expression for him and he once described gritstone – his preferred medium – as 'like water and like wind'.

On limestone, Jerry Moffatt had drawn level or even overtaken Ron Fawcett by 1983. His unerring self-confidence and complete dedication earned him the reputation of a superbrat, but with hindsight such a personal assessment can be seen in a broader context. Moffatt was simply leading the next generation in, and they weren't going to bother with the tight-lipped understatement of its predecessors. Brash times require a brash

In 1984 Malham Cove in Yorkshire rose to the fore. A number of former aid lines, with their bolts still usefully in place, provided two major players of the time, Fawcett and the dreadlocked Ben Moon, with two E6s, New Dawn and Superdirectissima. Malham's wings had long been appreciated by climbers, but the central section offered climbers in the eighties apparently limitless scope. The only problem was protecting them. Gary Gibson's Clarion Call and Fawcett's Tequila Mockingbird, both in Cheedale, had made use of bolts, to the distress of traditionalists, but the tide of change was sweeping in from across the Channel. Climbers travelling to southern France watched the French streak ahead in terms of technical difficulty, and visiting superstars like the Le Menestrel brothers showed how far the British were falling behind.

By the mid-1980s the growing obsession with limestone and the irresistible demands for new lines allowed the floodgates to open and the bolts poured in. At Malham that meant a huge number of short but powerful lines for lesser mortals and a string of longer and hugely demanding routes for the more talented. John Dunne was Malham's finest contributor with a large number of E7s and E8s to his credit and an E9, the Superdirect. Mark Leach's Cry Freedom, also graded E9 by the first ascensionist, showed how practising a sequence of moves again and again allowed climbers to contemplate routes that had been considered impossible by previous generations.

Dunne's involvement with Malham prompted the first attempt to organize a climbing competition. They were proving popular on the Continent and those who were riding on the sport's new-found commercialism saw an opportunity to further enhance climbing's wider appeal. For the first time in its history there were enough recreational climbers to support a small band of professionals, working at the extreme end of what was possible. The resulting event was quickly forgotten, but by the end of the decade indoor competitions, previously viewed as the work of the devil, were accepted, if not established in Britain.

All this variance from tradition caused ageing pundits to view the scene with some displeasure, but in retrospect the decade was characterized as much by its bold and inspirational climbs as by the more gymnastic testpieces. Johnny Dawes led the way for many in this respect, solving a large number of long-standing gritstone problems in the Peak like Gaia (E8) at Black Rocks and End of the Affair (E8) at Curbar. But there were many other gifted contributors, including John Dunne, whose New Statesman (E8) at Ilkley and Partheon Shot (E9) at Burbage rank with Dawes' best. Dunne, a massively strong man whose training regime would eventually force him to have surgery, straddled the two branches of the sport, taking part in the Malham competition one month, to the fury of the traditionalists, and then adding a new and fearsome line the next.

The golden period of this adventurous period came in North Wales between 1986 and 1988. Gogarth returned to fashion with Pollitt's mind-chilling repeat of Redhead's The Bells. Dawes climbed the Indian Face on Cloggy and Paul Pritchard added Super Calabrese (E8) at Red Wall. Furthermore, the discovery, if examining your backyard can be termed thus, of the slate quarries created a new-routing boom to equal that at Pembroke in the first part of the decade, and the nearer goldrush at Pen Trwyn, which offered another gymnastic venue to the superfit.

Dawes found another medium – slate – to suit his fluid style, climbing The Quarryman up the sobering wall of Twll Mawr above Llanberis in 1988, and Big Things, Little Things on the Rainbow Slab in 1991 (E9). Scores of new routes were added in this period from the likes of Redhead, Pollitt, Haston, Williams and many others, and the rock is now seen to offer a quick-drying alternative to the Llanberis Pass.

The one aspect of this rapidly changing era that remained consistent with previous periods of exploration was the obsession with specific areas. Yorkshire, the Peak District and North Wales seemed to be the only places good climbers went to, an impression reinforced with the parochialism of mountaineering magazines. In recent years that has changed, with climbs of E7 and E8 appearing in the southwest and Scotland, and there are a number of activists operating in such areas who would be recognized as amongst the best by their peers if they lived in Sheffield or Leeds. Martin Crocker, for instance, or Dave Cuthbertson contributed steadily to British climbing, and at the hardest standards, throughout the eighties.

More acknowledgement could have been given to climbers like Pat Littlejohn, whose enthusiasm, eye for a line and spirit of adventure provided routes that have proved as popular as anybody else's. There were climbers who made a point of visiting remote and demanding places, Mick Fowler for instance, whose low-key and businesslike approach produced some of the most sobering lines in the country. These extend from Stairway To Heaven on the Isle of Skye to Caveman at Berry Head in Devon.

Inevitably, though, it was those areas closest to the traditional postwar home of climbing that would provide the climax to the decade and perhaps show the way for the nineties. Ben Moon has proved to be the most technically gifted of the current crop of limestone devotees, and following his first major routes in 1984 like Statement of Youth (E7) at Pen Trwyn he has steadily worked at pushing the grades even further. He has climbed extensively on the limestone of southern France and this experience came together in 1990 on Hubble at Ravens Tor, the crag that epitomized the climbing of the late 1980s. Some have tried to dismiss the line as an extended boulder problem, but at French 8c+ it is undoubtedly one of the hardest in the world.

Moffatt too has continued to improve, despite a long period in the middle of the decade when the continual training necessary took its toll. He required surgery and a long break to recover. When he did, he returned to a climbing scene that had changed. French style and competitions had been accepted and he threw himself into the latter with his usual gusto and to some effect. More recently he has followed the fashion for projects, his finest being Liquid Amber at Pen Trwyn, climbed in 1991 and given the grade of 8c.

Climbing has always been about testing the limits in the purest form possible, and whatever the critics might say of recent

RIGHT: Pat Littlejohn grew up in Devon where he began climbing at the age of 14. His haul of new routes over a long career runs into hundreds, and he has been the leading exponent of exploratory seacliff climbing.

achievements, British climbers continued that tradition throughout the 1980s. The sport changed but then so did the rest of society, and the reasons for both lay in the past and not in the hands of a few individuals desperate to impress. Inevitably the wheel will turn again and there are already interesting possibilities. Many talented rock climbers, like Paul Pritchard, are returning to the mountains to add hard new routes to the world's high places. A new batch of bold young climbers are covering the ground of Dawes, Dunne, Redhead and Pollitt and the boulder problems appearing on the Plantation boulders at Stanage and elsewhere will lead to harder full-length routes. Climbing has always been, and always will be, a game without frontiers.

NORTH AMERICA

Audrey Salkeld

The 'history' of mountain-climbing in North America begins with the white man, which is not to deny that Amerindians roamed through and over the rugged ranges long before European settlers saw the continent as their New World. Some tribes, like the Sheepeater and the Ute, lived their whole lives among high crags, having of necessity to be nimble climbers, but they left few traces. And even if today archaeologists can be certain that some rock shelters and other structures on prominent mountains like Middle Teton predate accepted 'first ascents', this cannot alter the written record. Thus, the earliest verifiable climb of significance remains that of Mount Washington in 1642. This giant of the Presidential Range – at 6,288 feet the highest peak east of the Mississippi and north of the Carolinas – is known for catching some of the worst weather in the world: its windswept summit was attained by Darby Field of New Hampshire in company with two native Americans.

Pike's Peak, Colorado, was the first 14,000-footer to receive an accredited ascent. In 1820 Edwin James, a young botanist with a military survey detachment, led the small party which scrambled to its summit late in the afternoon of the second day's climbing, so late in fact that there was no option but face an unplanned bivouac on the way down.

Seven years later another young botanist, David Douglas of Glasgow, crossing the Athabasca Pass on his way home from two years' plant collecting in the Canadian Rockies, on impulse scaled one of the great snow mountains that rose to the west of the trail. Five hours' hard trudging in snowshoes brought him to the top of a peak, which looked to be the highest, and which he called Mount Brown. He estimated it, mistakenly, at 17,000 feet, and for some years it was regarded as one of the highest in North America. Now we know it to be a mere 9,156 feet (2,791 metres), and posterity remembers Douglas, if at all, for the fir tree that bears his name. But he was perhaps the first person to have climbed a North American peak for no better reason than an irresistible desire to do so.

ABOVE: Scottish botanist David Douglas (1798-1834) climbed Mount Brown in the Canadian Rockies but over-estimated its height. His niece made this sketch two years after his return from America, when he was 30 years old.

In the second half of the nineteenth century, high peaks throughout the continent were climbed, or walked up, the majority in the course of exploration and survey, but always the odd one or two out of sheer curiosity or fun. Mount Saint Helens, in the Cascade Range (9,677 feet), was topped in 1853 by Thomas Dryer, editor of *The Oregonian*, as a publicity stunt for his Portland newspaper. This great snowy dome, near-perfect in its symmetry, was popularly known as America's Little Fujiyama, although to the Indians it had always been Lawelatla, the smoking one. Rounding the summit crater, Dryer noticed a steady blast of steam issuing from its volcanic depths – unmistakable evidence, so he told his readers, that the fire was not yet extinguished. As if to underline his words, the mountain re-erupted a few years later and for a decade spewed out ash and fiery lava. Even this, we know now, was only the trailer for a far

more spectacular blow-out towards the end of the twentieth century.

Dryer's subsequent claim to have scaled nearby Mount Hood (11,235 feet) in 1854 was considered to be stretching the truth, and the climb was more convincingly completed some time later by another party. Doubt, too, hangs over the first ascent of Mount Rainier, which at 14,410 feet is the pride of the range: parties in 1852 and 1855 gained the crater rim, but neither left any account of going on to the summit proper. August Kautz in 1857 we know turned back just short of the prize, but the fourth contesters, in 1870, certainly completed the climb. Hazard Stevens and Philemon Van Trump bivouacked in a cavern near the crater before continuing to the summit the following morning.

Long's Peak in Colorado (14,255 feet) has been described as 'the boldest and biggest of the promontories that rest the prairie-tired eye of the traveller'. It might be thought curious that it should also have been likened to the Matterhorn, since there is little beyond steepness to suggest any similarity. But no landscape, it seems, is complete without one: Matterhorns are metaphors, springing up wherever there are mountains. Oral tradition tells how one Indian, Old Man Gun, regularly climbed Long's Peak around the middle of the last century to visit an eagle trap he had built on the summit; but it was Major John Wesley Powell with William Byers, founder and editor of the *Rocky Mountain News*, who led the mountain's official first ascent in 1868. They came by way of the south wall, its easiest aspect, which soon became a popular climb, to be accomplished within five years by women, too. The adventurous Scotswoman Isabella Bishop, who was touring Colorado on horseback, has left a particularly vigorous account of the perils of her ascent in 1873. The granite precipices of the east face had to wait until 1919 to be climbed.

An ascent of Wyoming's Grand Teton (originally called Mount Hayden) was claimed in 1872 by N.P. Langford and his companion James Stevenson, and written up in *Scribner's Magazine*. But the account failed to satisfy sceptics, as did that of the next claimants in 1893. It was 1898 before William Owen, Franklin Spalding, Fred Petersen and John Shive made a positive ascent. Devil's Tower, a volcanic plug of columnar basalt, also in Wyoming, was climbed – after a fashion – as a Fourth of July stunt in 1893. Two ranchers, Willard Ripley and Will Rogers, advertised the feat as chief attraction of a local fair and picnic. Having previously driven long wooden pegs into a crack between two of the columns, and bracing them with an outer,

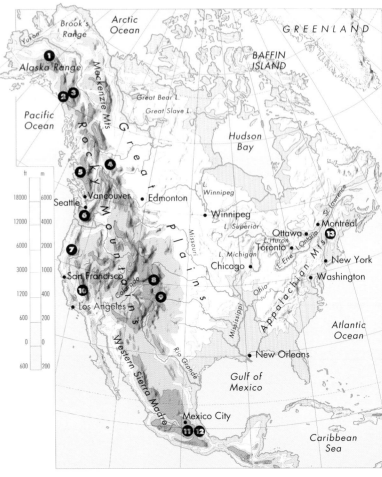

RIGHT: The great ranges of North America.

KEY TO MOUNTAINS
1 McKinley; 2 St Elias; 3 Logan; 4 Robson; 5 Waddington; 6 Rainier; 7 Shasta; 8 Elbert; 9 Blanca; 10 Whitney; 11 Popocatepetl; 12 Citlaltépetl; 13 Washington

BELOW: John Frémont jubilantly planting the Stars and Stripes on the 'summit of the Rocky Mountains' during a reconnaissance of the Oregon Trail in 1842. Today, it is not clear exactly which was his 'highest peak'.

RIGHT: One of Dr Collie's exploratory climbs in the Canadian Rockies towards the end of the last century, when the area was being opened up following the construction of the transcontinental railroad.

support-cum-handrail, on the great day they moved up their prepared 'ladder', by now roughly 350 feet long, clambering to the summit where they unfurled the Stars and Stripes to the delight of the gathered crowd. The first 'legitimate' ascent had to wait another forty-four years.

While the most accessible North American mountains were being picked off more or less piecemeal by enthusiastic opportunists, in Europe Alpine climbing had become a popular and formalized activity. Americans were among those to clamber the Alps with delight, seemingly oblivious that back home vast tracts of alpine country just north of the 49th Parallel remained unvisited and unknown, even to geographers. It was not until the forging of the Dominion of Canada in 1871 that a viable transcontinental crossing was deemed necessary through the rugged Selkirks and Canadian Rocky Mountains and serious exploration began. This led to the construction of the Canadian Pacific railroad and, in turn, to the springing up of settlements along the route with accommodation for tourists. A concerted effort to 'sell Canada' as an alpine resort was made by the railway company, which built chalets and imported Swiss guides into the area. Edward Whymper, as the most famous mountaineer of the day, enjoyed an all-expenses-paid peak-bagging holiday with four guides in the newly-accessible upper Yoho valley on the promise of writing and lecturing about its vacational opportunities. The Canadian Alpine Club was formed in 1906, holding annual well-attended camps in the lone pinewoods around the great peaks. Within a few years most of the major summits had been climbed, although the highest, Mount Robson, at 12,972 feet, had to wait until 1913 for its first ascent by Albert MacCarthy, William Foster and the great Austrian-born guide, Conrad Kain.

For many years Mount St Elias, visible from the sea, was considered the highest peak in Alaska. Only from 1875, when white men began penetrating inland, travelling up the Tanana and Yukon rivers, did they become aware of Mount McKinley, albeit without at first appreciating its superlative height (20,320 feet). It was sketched and named by W.A. Dickey, who in 1897 saw it from a distance of a hundred miles while prospecting at the head of Cook Inlet. The first climbing attempt was in 1903 when Judge James Wickersham reached 10,000 feet. In the same year Dr Frederick Cook led his preliminary expedition to the mountain, and returned three years later with a larger party. After a siege of several months failed to yield success, Cook declared all attempts over for the season and his men dispersed to conclude their various investigations. When they reunited, however, Cook surprised his fellows by announcing that he and Edward Barrille had successfully made it to the 'Top of the Continent' in a last bid via the north arête. The claim was openly doubted at the time and has since been convincingly disproved, as has Cook's subsequent assertion to have been first at the North Pole. The McKinley evidence hinged on being able to demonstrate that Cook's 'summit' photograph was a fake. The first undisputed ascent was made two years later by the Reverend Hudson Stuck and Alaska pioneer Harry Karstens with two companions. Mount St Elias had already been climbed at the end of the previous century by the Italian Duke of the Abruzzi.

Canada's highest peak, Mount Logan (19,850 feet), lying in a particularly remote and rugged area of the Yukon inland from Mount St Elias, demanded a 140-mile approach march largely over icefields, and was accomplished in 1925 by a team led by the veteran mountaineer Albert MacCarthy. He tackled the problem much as a polar enterprise, employing sledge-hauling and pre-cached supplies; it was to prove an epic of endurance,

moving the British *Alpine Journal* to comment: 'Greater hardships have probably never been experienced in any mountaineering expedition.' The climb was not repeated for another twenty-five years, and the area – noted for its intense cold, gales and frequent blanketing fogs – remained a virtually unmapped wilderness until the National Geographic Society sponsored land and aerial surveys in the mid-1930s, under the leadership of Bradford Washburn.

Washburn was one of the pivotal figures of the closeknit Harvard Mountaineering Club which had reached the forefront of American mountaineering. As his contemporaries turned to objectives in China and the Indian Himalaya, he – following an Alpine apprenticeship – concentrated on exploration and ascents in Alaska and the

ABOVE: A sledging party of the Duke of Abruzzi's expedition of 1897, when the Italian flag was hoisted on top of Mount St Elias.

RIGHT: 'The Top of the Continent' photograph published by Dr Frederick Cook after his claimed ascent of Mount McKinley in 1906. It subsequently proved to be a fake.

LEFT: Fred Beckey in Monument Valley in the 1960s with Eric Bjornstad (right). For five decades, Beckey (who was born in Germany in 1923) has been climbing's most famous hobo and master of the first ascent.

Yukon. In 1930 (aged 20) he led a six-man expedition to the unclimbed Mount Fairweather in the Alaska Coast Range, and in the winter of 1932-3 explored and mapped Mount Crillon (12,726 feet) in the same area. He also led the 1935 National Geographic Society Yukon Expedition which made the first crossing of the Great St Elias Range from Canada to Alaska in the dead of winter. This was followed by photographic survey flights over McKinley and in 1937 the Lucania expedition described in the following essay. For more than fifty years Bradford Washburn has been the leading authority on the topography and history of North America's far north.

The 1930s saw the emergence of a new band of climbers in the western states of America, prepared to use the pitons and running belay techniques developed in the Alps. Higher Cathedral Spire in Yosemite Valley was one early and impressive technical rock climb. Later the same year, 1934, the same party of Bestor Robinson, Dick Leonard and Jules Eichorn also bagged nearby Lower Cathedral Spire. As a teenager, Fred Beckey was laying the foundations for a career which has spanned some seven decades, climbing increasingly challenging routes in the

RIGHT: Yosemite Valley in California, postwar climbing mecca. This view, looking east, shows El Capitan on the left, Half Dome in the far distance and (right) Cathedral Rocks and the Bridalveil Falls.

LEFT: Climbers on Lost Arrow Spire – see how a Tyrolean traverse has been used to link the tip of the spire with Yosemite valley rim. The spire was first climbed in this manner in 1946, but it was the full-length Chimney Route, forged by Swiss emigré John Salathé the following year with Anton Nelson, that launched the era of Yosemite multi-day big wall climbs.

Cascades and Olympic mountains. In 1942, he and his brother thrashed through the wilderness of British Columbia to grab a second ascent of the elusive and notorious Mount Waddington – the last 500 feet by a new route. On their feet they wore tennis shoes with felt 'pullovers'. But the Beckey brothers apart, little was done anywhere in North America during the war years beyond training mountain troops and advancing material technology. However, the period immediately following signalled a new belle époque as climbers moved out onto the great rock walls of Yosemite and the southwestern deserts. Swiss-born John Salathé, a blacksmith, hand-forged a new range of rugged carbon-steel hardware – pitons, angles, skyhooks – with which, in 1947, he then forged the Chimney route on Lost Arrow Spire with Anton Nelson. The climb took five days and nights. With Allen Steck, Salathé (then aged 51) claimed Sentinel Rock two summers later, another five-day climb in temperatures at times reaching 105° F (40° C). During the 1950s, spoils were divided largely between the camps of Royal Robbins and Warren Harding. The same names featured in the following decade, too (and still do), reinforced by Teton climber Yvon Chouinard, Tom Frost, and a strong Coloradan contingent, epitomized by Layton Kor.

Robbins' routes include the northwest face of Half Dome (with Jerry Galwas and Mike Sherrick), Salathé Wall and North America Wall on El Capitan, as well as Tis-sa-ack on Half Dome. Harding was responsible, in 1958, for the formidable

Nose route on El Capitan with Wayne Merry and George Whitmore, the culmination of an eighteen-month siege involving a number of protagonists and thirty-seven hard climbing days. Two years later Robbins, with Chuck Pratt, Tom Frost and Joe Fitschen, repeated the route in a continuous seven-day push. Robbins was consistently refining his big wall technique in an endeavour to keep reliance on 'artificial aid' to a minimum. After Harding forced Dawn Wall with Dean Caldwell in the autumn of 1970, in a climb lasting twenty-seven days and employing what many considered excessive aid, Robbins endeavoured to 'erase' the route by chopping the bolts on a repeat ascent with Don Lauria. After removing 40 of the 330 drilled anchors, he gave up on the task, explaining afterwards that the climbing was of a much higher calibre than he expected, inspired even, one good lead after another.

Dawn Wall proved the ultimate in artificial climbing. These days, the emphasis is on free climbing, and we publish here Paul Piana's account of the freeing of the vast Salathé Wall, what he and many consider to be the greatest rock climb in the world. Canadian Peter Croft has soloed his favourite climb, The Nose on El Capitan, in a remarkable four hours and twenty-two minutes, but the Great Roof at around mid-height was always seen as a stumbling block to a true free ascent. However, in September 1993 Lynn Hill and Brooke Sandahl finally freed the whole route, after familiarizing themselves with individual hard pitches. Hill gives the route an overall 5.13b rating. For the future, Croft foresees routes like this and Half Dome, and perhaps more, eventually being 'enchained' into more demanding challenges, as is the mode with major Alpine routes.

For all this activity on rock, there has been no slackening of interest in hard snow and ice, or mixed climbing. One family to have particularly influenced the development of the North American ice experience has been the Lowes from Utah. George Lowe III and Jeff Lowe are cousins, each coming from large, close-knit families. Jeff's father, Ralph, had been an early Teton climber and with his brother, George's father, introduced the clan to camping and climbing at extremely tender years – Jeff himself was only seven when he first climbed The Grand. They started ice-climbing in the mid-sixties when the discipline was evolving fast. Various permutations of brothers and cousins put up hard winter ascents in the Tetons, and took an active part in designing specialized ice equipment. Introduced to climbing frozen waterfalls by his older brother Greg, Jeff with Mike Weis climbed the exquisite chandelier-like Bridalveil Falls in Telluride early in 1974.

Throughout the 1970s George was establishing some of the most difficult routes in the Canadian Rockies – the north face of Alberta with Jock Glidden, north face of North Twin with Chris Jones (unrepeated in twenty years), Aurora Borealis on the north face of Geikie with Dean Hannibal; and in Alaska, he climbed the hardest route of the day, Infinite Spur on Mount Foraker. The Lowes are still making news, climbing hard, at home and abroad. Their active contemporaries have included Rob Wood, George Homer, and Bugs McKeith, who were responsible for Weeping Wall. McKeith, with fellow expatriate Britons, the Burgess twins, and Charlie Porter, climbed Polar Circus, an awesomely long Canadian waterfall; John Laughlan and Jim Elzinga pioneered Slipstream, another frozen cascade of 2,800 feet on Snowdome in the Columbia Icefields. In the same way that rock classics were gradually 'freed', so various methods of aid, like a form stirrup-sling or étriers, were dispensed with on ice routes. John Roskelley and Jim States thus 'cleansed' Bourgeau Left Hand waterfall in midwinter 1975.

Jim Bridwell and Mugs Stump climbed the committing east face of Moose's Tooth in Alaska in 1981, and later that year Stump established Moonflower Buttress on Mount Hunter with Paul Aubrey, a route he considered his best climb ever. Throughout the decade Barry Blanchard, Kevin Doyle, Karl Tobin and Dave Cheesmond were responsible for a string of extremely hard and dangerous winter routes in the Canadian Rockies, unimaginable twenty years ago. Blanchard here describes one such on the north face of Howse peak, completed over four days in 1988 with Ward Robinson.

BELOW: Half Dome from Ahwahnee Meadows. Its 2,000-ft high northwest face was first climbed over five tense days in 1957 by Royal Robbins, Jerry Gallwas and Mike Sherrick.

Bradford Washburn

Close Call

For the first time in our lives we knew what it was like to be really up against it: we were not trying to make a first ascent of the west face of Steele – we had to.

BIOGRAPHY

Born in 1910 and educated at Harvard, Bradford Washburn gained his early mountaineering experience in the Alps. In the early 1930s he made a remarkable crossing of the St Elias Range and in 1938 carried out an aerial photographic survey of Mount McKinley. A noted cartographer and photographer, he has been responsible for definitive maps not only of McKinley but the Grand Canyon, Mount Everest and New Hampshire's Presidential Range, the last being the haunt of his childhood and inspiration for his lifelong love of adventure. For 40 years he was Director of Boston's Museum of Science until in September 1985 he was elected Honorary Director for Life. His many books include the handsome Mount McKinley, the Conquest of Denali.

LEFT: *Honeymoon picture of Brad and Barbara Washburn on the summit of Mount Bertha, Fairweather Range, Alaska in 1940. Barbara later became the first woman to climb Mount McKinley. She has been an active partner in most of Washburn's field projects.*

RIGHT: *The South Face of Lucania (17,150 ft) in Yukon Territory. Lucania's still-virgin summit was the big challenge to North American mountaineers in the 1930s. Washburn and Bates were flown by light aeroplane on to the glacier in the foreground from where then made their bold climb.*

With the ascent of Mount Logan in 1925, Mount Lucania became the big challenge for North American mountaineers. Rising to an altitude of 17,150 feet in the extreme southwest corner of the Yukon Territory, a few miles east of the Alaskan border, it was the highest unclimbed peak as well as one of the most remote mountain summits on the whole continent, clearly a difficult and involved mountaineering problem. The mountain had been first seen by the Duke of the Abruzzi – from the summit of Mount Saint Elias on 31 July 1897 – and was named by him after the liner which had carried him across the Atlantic. Nearly forty years passed before it was approached closely. Then, in April 1935, Bradford Washburn, with Robert Randall as pilot, flew over the southern and eastern approaches of the Lucania massif on a photographic survey for the National Geographic Society. Later in the same year, Walter Wood's Yukon Expedition succeeded in climbing Mount Steele (16,600 feet), a peak rising less than 10 miles to the east of Lucania's summit. And in March 1936, Russell Dow (working with Washburn's camera) took a beautiful series of detailed aerial pictures of the valley system at the head of Walsh Glacier. With the facts gleaned from all these reconnaissances, Washburn, together with Robert Bates, who had been with him on Mount Crillon a few years before as well as on the Yukon expedition in 1935, planned a serious attempt on Lucania for the summer of 1937. The peak's isolation made it financially impossible for the pair to contemplate coming

in by pack-train from either McCarthy to the west or the little outpost of Burwash Landing on Kluane Lake (Canada) to the east. A major part of the difficulty of climbing Mount Logan had been the long and gruelling approach up the Chitina Valley and Logan Glacier: to tackle Lucania from the west would not only have duplicated this but added another 30 miles of ascent up the Walsh Glacier for good measure. Yet the only alternative –

to reach the mountain from the east – had to be directly over the summit of Steele, when that mountain itself was already an arduous march from Burwash Landing.

Here, Washburn tells how he resolved the dilemma – how he and Bates audaciously snatched their peak during an epic fight for survival when all their plans went wrong. At 27, this was Washburn's seventh campaign to the American sub-Arctic.

*

Experience in the Yukon had already taught us the value of the airplane in solving problems of difficult access, and our pictures showed an excellent landing-place near the head of the Walsh Glacier. We decided to land our party there, along with supplies for the climb, hoping it would also be possible to pick us up again in August after the climb was over. Still, 'just in case', we took the precaution of making up a little waterproof album of

aerial pictures showing the route out to Burwash Landing. And though well aware of the problems of retreat down the Chitina River, we also armed ourselves with maps of the Logan area and the Chitina Valley.

We were to be a party of four: Russell Dow and Norman Bright would join Bob and me. With our pilot Bob Reeve, Dow made three flights into the Walsh Glacier in early May, safely caching all our

LEFT: *Thunderclouds over the Yukon. A view eastwards from the summit of Mount Steele.*

BELOW: *After their plane stuck in the wet snows of the Walsh Glacier in 1937, Brad Washburn and Bob Bates (seen here, digging) were obliged to hike 125 miles over the mountains back to civilization. Lucania was grabbed en route.*

supplies there at an altitude well over 8,000 feet. On 18 June, Bates, Reeve and I took off at low tide from the Valdez mud-flats in Alaska, 185 miles from Lucania. Reeve's Fairchild 51 brought us in three hours to Walsh Glacier, where we landed, halfway up our wing-struts in slush late in the afternoon, in the face of a heavy southeaster.

Unseasonal rainstorms in the preceding month had riddled the glacier with crevasses, and the storm burst upon us before we could get unloaded and our camp established a mile away beside the bedraggled cache of stores. It took many hours to dig out the plane and taxi it closer to our campsite. Without snowshoes we would have sunk to our waists in the morass. There wasn't the remotest hope of the plane taking off again without a significant drop in temperature. Instead, that evening it rose to nearly 60° F (16° C). The clouds dropped, and a wild thunderstorm was followed by torrential warm rain all night. For two days it poured and snowed intermittently, and a thick impenetrable fog covered the glacier: the plane was hopelessly bogged in.

In next to no time the surface of the glacier aged months. The short landing strip we had trampled was sliced nearly in half by a myriad crevasses. On the 20th Bob tried to take off, but the slush was too deep and loose, and as he was taxiing back towards camp, his left ski plunged into a deep hole in the treacherous slough. The left wing-tip disappeared beneath the surface. We dug for hours – pushed, pulled, and dragged frantically. Finally, we got her out safely, back to the top of the steeply inclined runway once more.

Two days later, after a light freeze and having altered the pitch of the propeller, Bob Reeve at last took off on his fourth attempt. It was the closest shave that I've ever seen, or ever hope to see; and he left with absolutely no intention of returning with the other two men. We couldn't hope to be so lucky again. Thus, Bob and I found ourselves abandoned on the glacier, with 100-odd miles of desolation between us and all civilization.

Our predicament was made doubly serious by the terribly broken nature of the lower Walsh Glacier. This offered our shortest way out to safety, but we rejected it as too dangerous for two men alone. There was a pass near Mount Walsh, 10 miles south of Steele, but neither of us cared to risk our all trying to get down to the valley that way. To fail and then have to climb back over the crest of the range to replenish our food supply before taking another try elsewhere would have been devastating, if not impossible.

We finally decided that the safest and surest way out would be over the top of Mount Steele. It would be a grim business. For the first time in our lives we knew what it was like to be really up against it: we were not trying to make a first ascent of the west face of Steele – we had to.

It meant climbing to a great altitude with heavy loads, but at least once atop Steele, we would be where others had safely reached from Burwash Landing, 60 miles to the east. The conviction that anything Walter Wood could get up we could get down buoyed our spirits.

Reluctantly abandoning practically all our valuable photographic and survey apparatus, we set out for Steele on 25 June with 50 days' food, a Logan tent and the minimum of climbing equipment. Using a small ski-sledge, we dragged two loads of supplies to a second camp five miles up-glacier at about 9,000 feet and thence, working on foot, relayed our supplies ahead as rapidly as possible, reaching our Camp 5 at the very head of the Walsh Glacier on the morning of 1 July. Up to that point we'd had but few clear hours. The incessant snow and fog forced us to keep camps tight together because of the labour of breaking trail: by having them only 2 miles apart, instead of 5 or 6, and by relaying loads over the trail in two or three shifts a day, we constantly kept our tracks well beaten down, and despite the weather managed to make fairly speedy progress. Willow wands were used as markers, and without them we would scarcely have been able to move at all.

Camp 5 was located in a superb basin at the foot of the great 4,000-foot wall that drops south from the 14,000-foot plateau between Lucania and Steele. A small ridge buttresses this wall, and was by the way we felt sure we could reach the pass easily and from thence the summit of Steele.

An evening clear-off on 1 July permitted us to reconnoitre and

ABOVE AND RIGHT: On the Walsh Glacier. Drying out (above) on the first good day, and (right) excavating pre-cached supplies on their arrival. The bundles of black-tipped willow wands were for trail-marking in the recurrent fogs. Most of the climbers stores and equipment had ultimately to be dumped in a lightweight race for life.

mark a route up the lower part of the wall, advancing through a barrier of séracs to the site for Camp 6 on the ridge at a height of 12,500 feet.

At Camp 5 we jettisoned one of our sleeping bags, an air mattress and half our gasolene, along with a good many incidentals that we reckoned we could do without. Climbing on the ridge was abominable. The snow ranged from knee- to waist-deep and we were completely fagged out when Camp 6 was finally established late on the night of 3 July in a niche hewn out of snow and ice on the crest of the ridge. A 2-foot snowstorm further complicated matters and made the steep upper part of the ridge particularly hard going in several places, especially as it was nowhere gently-inclined enough to let us use our very effective 'bearpaw' snowshoes.

After three relays to 13,800 feet through heavy snow and dense fog, we dug ourselves in at Camp 7 at midnight on the 5th. The following day, working with our aerial photographs and in dense clouds, we succeeded in worming our way around a very high serac barrier at the head of the buttress, and by noon had willow-wanded a route to the Steele-Lucania pass. We could only tell we'd arrived on the pass because the ground dropped away very gently on the opposite side. One load that night and three the next day over the short, steep route between Camps 7 and 8 and we were finally etablished on the great divide later on 7 July.

Our only plan till that moment had been to save our skins by a speedy retreat to civilization over the top of Mount Steele. We knew it would be hopeless to try to relay down the east ridge of the mountain: when we left our camp on this pass we needed everything on our backs necessary to get us out to Burwash Landing with no relaying whatsoever. But finding ourselves with about ten days' more food than we needed or could carry for our dash into Canada tempted us to think again about Lucania. Rather than simply abandoning our climbing plans, why not make one desperate bid to 'bag' it? We had worked unceasingly to this point, without a single day off, hoping that by using the bad weather low down, we could profit from clear skies higher up where our every move depended on them.

Unfortunately, we were not allowed a very long rest. After a good sleep on the 8th, the weather suddenly cleared. Lucania towered invitingly on the other side of the pass, and a glorious sea of silver clouds rolled gently along the valleys below us, its surface lightly ruffled by a fresh clear-weather breeze.

We loaded our camp rapidly onto our backs, leaving a cache of food and gasoline

ABOVE: First to stand on Lucania's summit, Washburn (right) and Bates photograph themselves with Brad's camera perched on his ice axe. The summit was a narrow ridge of snow-covered ice, barely 12 ft in length.

at the pass, and at ten that night established a ninth camp on the wide snow plateau at the very foot of the final mass of Lucania. We'd been forced to descend about 1,000 feet on the north side of the mountain in order to traverse and make camp at the bottom of a good route up the last steep slope.

The next day, climbing unloaded at last, we wallowed our way upward through interminable powder snow towards the summit of Lucania. One thing was clear: if we could not use snowshoes most of the time, we were licked. I took mine off for a second to test the snow and went in halfway up my chest. There wasn't a sign of crust anywhere, no matter how deep down. We took turns climbing the 40° slope in big zigzags, each breaking the trail for fifty steps, then climbing aside for the other to lead; and after nearly eight hours of continuous climbing, we finally stood on top at 4.45 in the afternoon.

The view was magnificent and it was perfectly still, not a breath of wind. With the temperature nudging zero, you could hardly see a cloud in any direction except to the east over the great lowlands of Canada. Every peak in the St Elias Range from Bona, 50 miles to the northwest, to Fairweather, 100 miles to the south, stood out crystal clear. Hubbard, Alverstone, Jette, Seattle, and Vancouver, all our old Yukon Expedition friends, rose 60 miles to the south. And how could Mount Logan possibly be over 30 miles away, with its immense summit ridge and cliffs standing out in such colossal scale?

Late that night, stiff, weary but triumphant, we straggled into camp and had a royal banquet as the sun set in a glorious blaze of colour behind the lofty crest of faraway Bona. Our long shot had paid off: Lucania was ours!

Thrilled as we were with our success, we were by no means out of trouble. Sixty miles of mountain, glacier and muskeg, as well as the summit of Steele, still lay between us and our next sound sleep in a bed! On the morning after the climb we threw away nearly all our food, our largest cooking pot, most of our clothes, and cut half the floor out of the tent to save weight. By noon we had again reached Camp 8, on another cool, clear, windless day. That night we reconnoitred and broke trail to a point 200 yards below the summit of Steele, leaving two 50-pound loads where our willow-wand supply ran out at 15,500 feet.

Almost every night above Camp 5 the temperature had hovered about zero, with the minimum of -14° F (-26° C) the night before we climbed Lucania. On the night of July 10, an icy northerly wind bore down on our little camp. The thermometer dropped to only -9° F (-23° C), but blowing snow and the raw cold prevented us from getting started till nearly nine on the morning of the 11th. That noon, with two 75-pound loads, we made it back to the 16,400-foot shoulder which we'd climbed the previous evening, and leaving our loads there, climbed the final cone of Steele under ideal weather

LEFT: *The ninth camp on a snowy plateau below Lucania's summit, from where Washburn and Bates launched their attempt, and to which they returned, stiff and weary, after a long day's continuous climbing in snowshoes.*

RIGHT: *The upper slopes of Lucania were loaded with tremendous drifts of dry snow. Bates is snapped by Washburn shortly after noon with the summit still nearly five hours away.*

FAR RIGHT: *Pilot Bob Reeve (right) is seen here with Washburn in Valdez before the expedition. He flew them in but was unable to get them out.*

conditions. The St Elias Range was again cloudless from end to end, except for a reddish haze over the peaks to the south-west – a sign that is the certain forerunner of bad weather.

One of the grandest thrills of the whole expedition was the discovery now, on the very tip-top of Steele, of a large bundle of willow-wands jammed into the highest snowdrift two years before by Walter Wood. The fact that these had not been buried in their long cold vigil on that exposed outpost is mute evidence to the terrific wind that must scream and lash across that desolate drift when the weather is not so pleasant as we found it on that balmy July afternoon.

Half an hour's exultant rest on top of Steele, and we returned to our loads at 3 o'clock. In a further desperate effort to cut weight, we now threw away food, our last spare clothing, the shovel, tent pegs, our only air mattress, and all but three pints of gasolene. We cut the entire bottom out of the tent and sliced off all the guys.

At 3.20 we started down the long East Ridge and, after an endless tussle with deep snow, ice and breakable crust, finally pitched camp 9,000 feet below on a moraine at the head of Wolf Creek glacier at 8.35 that night. Continuing in general along the route followed by the Wood party two years before, we descended the glacier next day to a point 2 miles below Wood's Advanced Base Camp. We'd been told that the Wood party had left a huge cache of food behind, easily identifiable, but we found when we got there that bears had destroyed everything, even the cans. All they'd missed was one small tin of Peter Rabbit peanut butter. Instead of being able to rest and build ourselves up here, things now began to look desperate. The night of the 13th saw us camped on the shores of the Donjek River, 20 miles nearer Kluane Lake and Burwash Landing.

Crossing the Donjek proved one of the most formidable and harrowing obstacles of the trip. Its treacherous icy waters – impossible at times to pass even when on horseback – forced a detour of nearly 20 miles upstream before we could find a safe ford. We spent a night in the rain on the Donjak glacier with our poleless tent wrapped around us. Descending the east shore of the river, we bolstered our nearly empty larder with a red squirrel (just like eating piano wire) and a rabbit killed with our ancient six-shooters, along with quantities of tempting mushrooms picked from the mossy floor of the forest.

A week of navigating 'by Gosh and by God', and we finally met a friendly pack-train on the afternoon of 19 July, just as we were bogging our weary way through a swamp on the last pass before our goal. They took us to a nearby cabin, where we feasted with them for twenty-four hours before riding into Burwash in state, each astride an unpadded pack-saddle on one of the most docile pack-horses in the whole of the Yukon.

That 35 mile ride will always linger in my memory as the most excruciating torture I have ever endured. The proudest of mountaineers, unfortunately, may find themselves the very humblest of horse-men! The superb reception given us by Gene Jacquot at his Burwash Trading Post, however, remains one of the happiest of a long store of memories. Never have I eaten so much sheep steak nor lemon meringue pie in all my life!

Ed Webster

The Desert Song

For those climbers who welcome the adversity of loose rock, frost-wedged blocks, and long, parallel-sided cracks, their loyalty to desert climbing borders on religious fanaticism.

To the tourist, hiker, or climber, the Canyonlands of east central Utah present many wondrous and unexpected surprises – sublime pastel coloured sandstones, and unusually shaped landforms. It is the stark unreality of this barren landscape, however, with its dramatically eroded spires and towers and sheer canyon walls that makes the region so appealing to rock climbers. It is an area I have visited frequently and will forever return to.

Truthfully, desert rock climbing attracts a relatively small group of devotees because the quality of the sandstone varies greatly, from extremely soft to near-granitic firmness. But for those climbers who welcome the adversity of loose rock, frost-wedged blocks, and long, parallel-sided cracks, their loyalty to desert climbing borders on religious fanaticism. A sane climber, if there were such a thing, might well wonder why. To sit atop one of the desert's pointed, isolated summits, to hand-jam up an unbelievably smooth Wingate sandstone crack, to smell the pungent aroma of sage, and to hear the silent song of empty, untouched spaces are all reasons climbers visit the Canyonlands of Utah. While the largest spires were climbed by the early 1960s, in the late 1970s other new routes beckoned.

*

BIOGRAPHY

Talented rock climber, all-round mountaineer, photographer, Ed Webster made his name on big North American desert walls. In the Himalaya, he has soloed Changtse and taken part in several Everest expeditions, climbing the east face to the South Summit with Stephen Venables and Robert Anderson in 1988. Severe frostbite sustained on that climb resulted in the loss of fingertips and toes following seven gruelling operations. Now he is climbing and writing again with all his usual vigour, and in 1992 made a number of first ascents in the newly-opened mountains of Mongolia.

America's most famous desert climbs – Super Crack (5.10), to be found in Indian Creek Canyon, and The Primrose Dihedrals (5.11+) on Moses Tower, located in Taylor Canyon.

My first Canyonlands climbing trip was in November 1976. For months, Jim Dunn had fed me stories about a crack he claimed was the best jam crack in the world. So Jim, Earl Wiggins, Bryan Becker, a few other friends and I headed west to the then unknown and unclimbed walls of Indian Creek Canyon. We were not disappointed; if anything, we were awed into speechlessness. The fabled crack, slicing 300 feet up the middle of a smooth, burnished sandstone wall, was an arrestingly pure line – but could it be climbed? In 1976, rock climbing protection had not evolved particularly far. Our rack consisted of Chouinard hexentrics, which had limited holding power in parallel cracks, plus two new, double-pronged Lowe camming nuts, which looked better designed for entry into a science fair than for use on an actual climb. Then there was the Wingate sandstone, soft enough that if the leader fell, there was a high probability that all the hexentrics would shear out of the crack, and the leader would hit the ground.

The atmosphere, I recall, was tense yet circus-like on that crisp November day. Earl was the highwire walker attempting the never before completed stunt. When he began jamming, he climbed with steady, practiced movements. Twenty foot runouts marked his progress up the crack. Every eye was rivetted on Earl while we held our collective breaths, watching him climb the hand to forearm-width crack with machine-like precision. When he threw himself into a belay niche, our

Even in my wildest dreams, I'd never imagined such a crack, a fissure so parallel-walled, so eye-catchingly straight, so perfect! Here was a crack so flawless God must have sliced it on a lucky day in Heaven. Also located in the Canyonlands, and equally improbable in architecture and beauty, is a slender 500 foot tower hidden in a remote canyon, an immense exclamation point mocking the forces of erosion which created it. They are two of

RIGHT: *Moses Tower at sunset, with Webster's Primrose Dihedrals centre. He later free-climbed the route with Steve Hong. Moses is the grandest of the desert spires in Utah's Canyonlands but remains well hidden in Taylor Canyon.*

cheers echoed around the narrow canyon followed by sighs of relief. He had not fallen. I followed Earl's lead, removing the protection while marvelling at the crack's dramatic beauty. We had managed the first pitch, the section we were least sure of climbing, but the climb wouldn't be completed until we arrived at the canyon rim, old-style thinking compared to today's 60-foot sport climbs, where reaching the cliff top is inconsequential – but for us it was important.

I began jamming the second pitch above Earl's hanging belay. The crack was insecure, fist-sized to off-width, but here the Lowe camming nuts came into their own and I surprised myself by getting good protection. I continued jamming to another

route would infrequently, if ever, be repeated because of the doubtful protection. Our ascent of Super Crack also broke the long, summit-oriented tradition of desert climbing which dated back to Layton Kor and Huntley Ingall's first ascent of Castleton Tower in 1961.

How times change! We could never have foreseen Ray Jardine's invention of Friends, the spring-loaded camming device which revolutionized rock climbing protection from 1979 onwards. With Friends, smooth, parallel-sided cracks are easy to protect, and many of Indian Creek's other ultimate cracks have now been done. In fact, Canyonlands has become an international destination for rock climbers. While today you might have to wait in line to climb Super Crack, at least the protection is superb, and the beauty and magic of this remarkable climb lives on.

By 1979 I had climbed many desert spires, but not the grandest of them all, the well hidden Moses Tower, which boasts an uncanny resemblence with the desert Prophet. When I finally saw a photo of Moses the majesty of the then unclimbed east face dihedral was fixed in my memory. In April that year, Buck Norden and I approached Moses carrying food and water for several days. First, we repeated Fred Beckey's North Face route. Cold temperatures, no sunshine, a stiff breeze, and uncomfortable hanging belays made for a miserable, if spectacular climb. Ice climbing seemed blissful by comparison. When a dangerous shave with loose rock quenched Buck's appetite for unpredictable sandstone, I decided to attempt the east face corners alone.

The next day, I followed signs of a previous ascent to the top of the third pitch, where I found a rappel sling. The climbing was entirely artificial, leap-frogging hexentrics and stoppers up the parallel-sided cracks. Friends were not yet in common use, but a month later I purchased my first two Friends directly from Ray Jardine, from the trunk of his car, in Yosemite.

My preconceived notions of the spirituality of a desert solo quickly vanished on my second day. On pitch five my rope jammed, tangling 90 feet higher as I tried to pull some slack back down. Rather than jumaring up my haul rope to fix the snag, I decided to save my strength and jumar the jammed rope instead – a stupid decision, but I was too drained by the heat and strenuous climbing to grasp my potentially fatal blunder. After clipping into my protection with a sling, I jumped up and down

ABOVE: Bryan Becker (bottom) and Ed Webster in action during the first ascent of flawless Super Crack of the Desert (5.10) in Indian Creek Canyon, 1976.

exposed belay at which Earl joined me. We now decided to pendulum right into an easier crack which Earl followed to the top, then Bryan came third, combining the first and second pitches, and soon we were all on the rim celebrating.

We were thrilled to have free climbed The Super Crack of the Desert, or Luxury Liner, Earl's name, but we assumed the on my jumars to check that the rope was still jammed. It was – until I had cleaned 70 feet of protection, removed one of the last nuts, and without thinking, swung out on the rope. Dramatically, instantaneously, the rope untangled and sent me flying for a 50 foot free-fall down the dihedral. A foot or two away from my nose, the overhanging sandstone walls sped by with increasing velocity as I contemplated my error. Luckily, my jumars caught me, with a tremendous upward jerk.

Far below, Buck was sun-tanning on a rock. 'Did you see *THAT*?' I shouted.

'Weren't you a bit higher a few seconds ago?' he answered.

Above me, the Ear, an overhanging, leaning flake, held a vile off-width crack. Dazed by my fall, I painstakingly drilled a bolt ladder up the Ear. Another pitch with more bolts gained the summit. Exhaustion and dehydration cancelled any exhilaration

RIGHT: *Moses Tower, with Steve Hong belaying at the top of the second pitch during the first free ascent of Primrose Dihedrals.*

BELOW: *Another shot of Super Crack.*

ABOVE: *Webster, back on Super Crack in 1992. By now, the advent of Friends has made it possible to protect such smooth, parallel-sided grooves, so that you often have to wait your turn to climb them.*

I felt at completing my solo new route. No smile came to my lips, no hand clasp signalled a triumphant finale. I fell asleep, waking only when my fingers and arms began cramping uncontrollably. Could I descend? Five adrenalin-filled rappels later, I returned to earth.

At home in Colorado, I pondered free-climbing The Primrose Dihedrals, as I'd named the route after the primroses growing near the climb's base. That October I ran into Steve Hong, a good friend from college. I had barely told him about the possibility of free-climbing Moses before another impromptu desert trip was born.

Since leaving Moab on the last leg of our drive, the normal dimensions of time and space no longer seemed to apply. Vast expanses of sky and earth seemed to swallow us whole as we headed across the Island in the Sky toward Taylor Canyon. When the regular road ended, an unexpected and rather surprising encounter

LEFT: Moses Tower with climbers on Pitch 2 of the Primrose Dihedrals.

ABOVE: Ed Webster climbs the fourth pitch during the first free ascent of Primrose Dihedrals. (He named the climb for the flowers at its base.)

with a nude jeep enthusiast – who fortunately put his clothes on – gave us a lift to the canyon rim. Before dawn, stars dropped from the clear desert sky as we rappelled into the silent depths. Steve climbed ten feet into a shallow, inverted slot, which looked almost climbable using chimneying and palming techniques. Baffled, he lowered off several times, finally handing me the rope. Boosted by my extra height, I latched onto an elusive hold, muscled up and reached the belay.

Steve led off in the still bearable early morning heat, wedging fingers and toes into perfectly tailored jams. When the going got tough, he plugged in a Friend and continued without losing momentum. The Primrose Dihedrals was the first major desert climb I know of where Friends played such a key role. All previous desert climbs had been protected by stoppers, hexentrics, and/or pitons. We were astonished by how well Friends worked in the parallel-sided cracks, and it honestly felt like we were cheating. After downclimbing slightly, we traversed to several exciting, stacked flakes, and arrived at a comfortable ledge below the upper corner system, well satisfied with our progress. At every perplexing move a positive edge or bucket appeared, rare holds for these generally smooth Wingate walls.

Our luck stayed strong on pitch four, although our pace slowed as the rock became hot to the touch. Bridging up the beautiful corner system following a crack that widened from finger to fist, and finally snaked around a five foot roof, I lost my mind to the dance. It was one of the most heavenly free pitches ever, like climbing up the inside of a cathedral, the soaring walls arching overhead and behind you. Steve followed quickly, joking that he didn't have my oversized hands to fit the crack.

At a semi-hanging belay we sorted gear while surveying the Ear's leering, overhanging offwidth crack. Given Steve's enormous strength, I felt he could pull the rabbit out of the hat again. Wedging himself into the offwidth, he struggled slowly higher, panting. Then, appearing to defy gravity, he extricated himself, swung free, and clawed and laybacked up the Ear's outside edge, finally reaching up for a ledge big enough to collapse on. Every move was at my limit as I struggled to repeat his performance, frantically unclipping from the bolts, laybacking wildly up the exposed, overhanging flake. Sand blew into my eyes, then the flake's brittle edge snapped, but I hung on and heaved up onto Steve's belay, my mouth so dry I could barely croak my congratulations to him.

After regaining my senses, I climbed up the final ridge to the summit of Moses. It was Steve's and my best climb together. Savouring our success we surveyed the magnificent isolation of our perch, admired the canyon's earthen colours, and listened to the desert song of peace and solitude. We had free-climbed Moses, the desert prophet – and the prophecy we now knew with conviction, was that Friends would forever change desert free climbing. A storm was brewing to the west and, if we hurried, we could still get to Moab in time for dinner.

LEFT: Swiss climbers on the summit of Moses Tower.

Barry Blanchard

Striving for the Moon

Above me the cornice bulged in the moonlight, the luminous belly of the great white whale. If Ward's efforts disturbed it, it would wipe me out like a D-10 hitting a strawberry.

The moon. It spread silver on the road and the trees, on everything in front of my windshield. Made me feel I was sitting in a drive-in, not doing a hundred and ten clicks, watching this highway charge at me from the silver screen. Would I still spook at elk eyes nailed in my highbeams? My mother once told me how she hates barmaiding during the full moon because of the craziness, 'People get strange during a full moon, son.'

Ward's car was idling in the Lake Louise parking lot when I pulled in. He had the seat reclined and his arms crossed over his chest. 'What's up, Ward? How long you been here?' 'Since two,' he said. 'Couldn't sleep, so I drove on up.' Ward lives an hour away, close to Golden, on the west slope of the Rockies. He hadn't done much Alpine climbing over the last couple of years because of full-time logging and a new family. I figured he was either really keen, or that Sam – his newborn, and second child – was up and accentuating the household tension: Ward's wife, Jan, doesn't dig risky climbing.

Funny to me how Ward and I seem to have switched lives over four years. In the winter of 1988 we established new lines on the north faces of Edith Cavell and Howse Peak; later that spring, with Kevin Doyle and Marc Twight, we got our alpine-style asses kicked on the Rupal Face of Nanga Parbat. At that time Ward was a complete climbing bum, living in an eight-by-ten Banff basement and cooking on his camping stove. I had a wife – no kids – and we ate out a lot. These days Ward heats his wooden house with an

BIOGRAPHY

For more than a decade, Barry Blanchard has been one of Canada's leading alpinists. In the early 1980s he made a name for himself with the first one-day ascent of Polar Circus and a winter climb of the Grand Central Couloir on Mount Kitchener – both in the company of Kevin Doyle. His North Pillar of North Twin, climbed in 1985 with the late Dave Cheesmond, was long considered the hardest alpine route in North America. Blanchard has climbed in the Alps and the Himalaya: he took part in a bold alpine-style ascent of the north face of Rakaposhi. Born and raised in Calgary, Blanchard is seventh-generation Metis – French Canadian and American Indian – a cultural legacy which has emphasized his love of wildernesses and his spiritual awareness. He lives now in Canmore, near Banff.

airtight stove, has a modern gas cooker, and maintains his chainsaws in his own workshop elsewhere on the property. I'm divorced and living at No. 6, Shady Lawn Motel, Dead Man's Flats, Alberta: fifteen-by-seventeen, with a two-burner hot plate. My cell, I call it.

RIGHT: The Northeast Face of Mount Temple, often likened to the Eigerwand in the Alps. The route, Striving for the Moon, follows the central water-ice system, then traverses into the lefthand gully at three-quarters height.

The North Face of Mount Temple has been called the Eigerwand of Canada, but I prefer to think of the Eiger's North Face as the Templewand of the Alps. Either way, all similarities end there. Temple is a huge pyramidal massif, isolated from everything else, yet dominating the rest of the Louise group – Victoria, Hungabee, Deltaform included. This year a water-ice system had etched a 2,500-foot line from Temple's east shoulder to a small lake below the northeast flank. The ice was unclimbed and – avalanche hazard permitting – could connect with the classic east ridge route and the summit 2,000 feet higher. I liked the idea of standing on top of Temple in December, beating the sun-starved seven-and-a-half hour winter days.

The cold predawn air held my breath in clouds in front of my face. I skied through them and saw white feathers grow on Ward's hair, an encrusted halo reach down his chest and across his shoulders. We cached our skis off the road, under a large spruce, and I thought about how the

ABOVE: Robinson negotiates avalanche debris at the start of the climb, providing the first real test for a new titanium rod in his leg, put there six months earlier after a bad break.

forest was midway here, neither the dry pine of the east slope where the walking was easy, nor the impossible jungle of the west where walking was . . . well, walking was more like climbing, climbing through nets of snakes. Ward usually worked in that big timber: his last six months had been spent convalescing after a root he was cutting sprung and drove a piece of his tibia through his shin. (At the hospital they'd had to turn him and his bush splint – a treebranch – sideways to get in the door.) This route would be the first real trial of Ward's leg and the titanium rod that is now in there to stay.

'How's the leg?' I hoped for a positive answer, yet Ward was someone I value beyond my own convenience, and would truly not begrudge if his pain turned us around . . . I knew, too, that if he admitted to any pain, it would be simply – honestly – debilitating. 'Fine, so far.' 'No pain?' 'Not so far, and I'm happy about that.' (My friend Ward is not a man of many words.)

We tacked uphill, sticking to the trees. I'm always suspicious of wide open white. Calf-deep snow parted effortlessly before my feet, like a matrix of crystal shards suspended in air. It was the shallowest snowpack in living memory. Looking east I saw the sky heating up, the last stars sputtering out in a deep blue that faded to pale and was cut ragged by the Rockies' horizon. There was no wind.

At dawn we stood on a small moraine, gearing up and studying the cinder blocks of snow at our feet. A metre-thick slab had kicked out of the cone at the base of our route. It ran on the ice and I guessed that the heavy winds of several days before had loaded it too fast. We were in the absolute lee of Temple. Ward bowed to my theory – I being the trained mountain guide and avalanche-forecaster and all. The bare ice was obviously safe and I cramponned up it, dragging the rope behind me. At the fracture I waited for Ward: it would be stupid to kick off what was left and have it bulldoze your friend into a trough where the snow would back up and bury him deep. Ward agreed and eased up over the fracture, close on my heels.

The gully made me feel safer. The snow was supported here, and there were smaller areas of it. It felt firm underfoot and I visualized the spindrift avalanches pouring down here during the windloading, tried to see the individual snow particles driving into each other and, hopefully, bonding. I thought about the ice cone below: why hadn't that bonded? Everything comes to rest there. Too much too fast – easy to say, but what was the equation?

Thunk. Ahead Ward had planted his axe into the first of the ice. I focused on the present and the task of catching up. Everything *felt* okay.

'Do you want the rope above your head or below your feet?' I asked. We were standing on a small stomped-out platform beside the first hard pitch. Ward smiled and said, 'Ya. I'd like to lead this.'

The 10-mil [millimetre] rope shuffled through my belay. Occasionally I'd let go and snap a picture on my new, handy, drape-around-the-neck, weatherproof, point-and-push 28mm camera. Then Ward was out of sight and I settled back and studied the goat track. The goat had cut across a shale ridge to the west. The ridge was in the sun now and I bet that he was lolling in it somewhere too. Perhaps the next ridge over. I'd seen him up there in mid-October when a client and I had been stormed off the Anderson couloir (a classic route west of where we were now). Like most of the lone billies I've seen he seemed more curious than afraid, in an aloof sort of way. Probably wondering what drives us above the treeline in winter when all the other critters go to sleep, or head down lower. I'd once had an *Oreamnos americanus* (Rocky Mountain goat) trench his way peacefully through the snow twenty feet above me as I stood tied to a tree belaying my partner up a waterfall. The surface slide that goat started was large enough to thump snow into every opening in my partner's system, including his mouth.

I have a large soft spot for mountain goats. I respect their incredible scrambling ability and the way they can sprint straight uphill for a hundred metres. We can't. And I find them beautiful, often a pure white, always jet black in nose, hooves, horns and eyes; and so powerful. Their muscles bulge, even under their thick winter coats. Once, roped-climbing up a 50° snow couloir in north central British Columbia, I was scared by a fall-line series of craters. I thought a large boulder must have bounded down the gully; and where there was one . . . Topping the gully, though, I saw the goat tracks leading in, and the first crater 10 foot down, the next 15, and the rest 20, until they disappeared a thousand feet down. I'd have given my front seat in hell to have seen him shred that chute.

'Off belay!' Ward's strained shout shattered the calm over the valley and got me to tying his pack onto the 5-mil, ready to

us hung a drape of huge ice daggers topped by a pillar spilling out of a gunsight in the gully, obviously the hardest passage on the route so far, probably a full 60 metres. If we didn't get over it now we'd be descending the Anderson couloir tomorrow because Ward had told Jan that we'd be down by tomorrow night. There wouldn't be time enough to go to the summit.

I gained 15 metres by bridging between dead vertical daggers, sporting, and *très* physical. I was dredging up the bottom of my lungs when I finally pulled into balance and twisted in a screw. I started again, sooner that I would normally have done, believing that aggression and risk would be the key to getting us both up before dark. The next 25 metres spiralled me to the right edge of the ice and all the way back left. It was a type of climbing that I am good at: insecure ground, moderately anaerobic, monstrously huge falls and snippets of time to listen to my internal chatter: '*Go* man *go* . . . Forget the screw *GO!* . . . that came out too easy, Barry, make sure . . . Oh, man , should've taken that screw . . .'

The long screw bit solidly in the flank of the pillar. I torqued it home and pulled up onto the edge. Five metres higher I planted my right tool blindly on the frontside of the pillar. Following it out there was like stepping out of an airborne Hercules to handrail the fuselage. I thought I had it, too. Five metres of 90° ice went by and, like a moth clinging to a light bulb, I was holding it together. Then it bulged out and I could taste my lungs

BELOW: *Another shot from Day 1 on Mount Temple. Canadian ice climbing has been pushed to new limits in recent years, with Robinson and Blanchard as consistent high performers. One week in 1988 they made first winter ascents of two major north faces.*

LEFT AND ABOVE: *Robinson leads during Day 1 of the first ascent of Striving for the Moon. Although the two* climbers take turns to be at the sharp end, all the photographs here are by Blanchard and thus feature his partner.

haul. To save time I climbed the grade four ice with my pack on and we fell into a rhythm of soloing the easier ground and having the leader haul his pack on the steeper stuff. And so we toiled and sweated through our afternoon, and despite the toll I was reaping on my muscles, inside I felt as calm and clear as the day.

'So that's what we've got to do today if we want to go over the top tomorrow.' Ward had summed up the situation. It was 4 p.m., and the sky was already gaining grey. It would be dark in an hour. Above

and smell my heart. My left arm trembled when I locked off on it . . . then it failed and extended and I felt that sick feeling that a bullrider must feel when his hand hangs up. I'd been in this situation before, sometimes I reslot the other tool, regain some composure, and go again (you can add some support by biting the sleeve of your locked-off hand). Several times I've cheated with a fifi hook that I carry for just that purpose. Over my left shoulder I glimpsed the rope: it cut a clean arc into the cave, way, way down there. I groped for the fifi hook that I couldn't see, my right tool thrashing about like a marlin's tail, an enemy then . . . and then a cantankerous friend who wouldn't get into my hand so I could weight the hooked fifi. I hung and twisted in a good screw. Three metres higher I pulled over the top, totally pumped and trembling again.

The thin Spectra-cord cut hard into my hands. I was hauling both packs. Ward hung on the rope to get out the last screw and pulled over the top exhausted. The sky was blue-black.

'Nice lead, Barry.' 'Thanks, Ward.' I grinned with closed lips, happier with the climb now, the hard pitch had enriched the route, even in the dying light everything was now a notch brighter, glowing. Sacred ground.

Half a rope's length up I walked onto a catwalk of snow and laughed. It was perfectly flat, spacious and protected by an overhang that supplied us with ledges for our crampons, helmets, boots etc. The moon rose and I was no longer watching the drive-in screen. I was in it, and the night wasn't charging me, it embodied me.

Some time later we rolled onto our sides and watched the northern lights. I knew I would never see that again and for a while I didn't think about my troubles . . . I grinned my ass off.

*

The hammer snapped clean off from the head of the tool and I swore. My other tool was an adze. I wouldn't be getting the pin out with that. Ward gave me one of his two hammers and took my adzed tool.

'D'you want this one?' he asked, nodding at a pitch which looked hard, another silk-thin katana falling from the sky. 'It's yours.' 'What do you mean?' 'I did my work last night, so this pitch is yours, dude.' Ward laughed. We both knew that I may be faster on it because I was now the 'lifestyle climber', but speed is only god in the Alps, or for the ego, or youth or something; in this country, if a guy wants to go for it, I say *bravo*, give me the belay line – and I hope you get something for yourself up there!

He did. I could see it in his eyes when he told me how well my tool worked compared to his. His picks had been sharpened to the point that a pair of tennis racquets would have been an improvement, and I suggested he quit being such a cheap redneck and spring for some new ones. I got the full Ward Robinson laugh, something never used as a social grace but which comes booming out when Ward's fancy is tickled. I appreciated it.

I led up and onto the transfer ledge that I'd scoped with binoculars. We had to get into the parallel gully to the east, where the ice was. The solid quartzite took good protection and I was glad to see metamorphic rock so high in the Rockies. Ninety-five per cent of the time we are on sedimentary limestone, which is often poor, and so complicated, if not terrifying.

Midday we arrived at a windowsheet of ice tacked to an overhang. 'Kinda looks like a shower curtain, hey, Ward?' He chuckled. 'Ya, funny how these things always look bigger from the road. Guess it's your pitch, I did my work this morning.' My attempts to set my feet broke the ice for the first three moves, creating an overhang. I did my pull-ups. (The Gore-Tex suit sleeve had a surprisingly fresh taste.)

We entered the upper basin and wallowed to the ridge. Wind, harsh and out of the west; it was 4 p.m. We cowered

behind a block the size of a storage shed, the size of my place. Going down the Anderson couloir would have been the conservative and thoughtful thing to do, but we came up with rationale against it. Principally we were betting on hearing a dial tone at a payphone three and a half thousand feet below us at the summer lodge on Moraine Lake; and we both knew we'd have the moon. Really, in the course of this life, how often do we get to strive for anything by the light of a full moon?

I sprinted into the logic of 'seeing how it goes'. We had to traverse a massive basin and find a gully through the Black Towers. It was dark and under all my layers I was soaked. The protection had run out an hour ago and I'd charged on, assuring myself that there wasn't a continuous snowpack. I was on top for five steps, then shin-deep for two, then pulling on rock to get onto the next bench. I had my headlamp on backwards so that any of the friends that Jan might call up would see us. Now I stood wedged behind some snow, bringing Ward in on a body belay, my headlamp pointed directly at the highway.

Ward took over and I heard his unspoken protest in every piece I took out: 'Hey, jerk, I've got kids.' Anchored to his

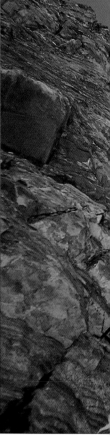

LEFT: Robinson leaves the bivouac on Day 2. The two climbers took turns to be at the sharp end during the climb; the photographs featured on these pages show Blanchard's view.

last pieces, he belayed me up. I led into the gully, placing bomber pieces as I went.

The steeper passages were still summer névé, bright yellow, but taking even Ward's blunt picks with a solid drywall *thunk*. Ward got the cornice, and for one hour I stood alone in the narrows of the gully. Cold walls of limestone crowded my shoulders and I bowed my head before sporadic waves of spindrift sent down by Ward. Like liquid, the cold seeped through my clothing and spread over my skin in a growing stain. I tried to focus on the sling lopping off a pillar of ice in front of me. It was material – real; I strived to anchor my psyche to it in the same way that I was anchored to it. But the shivers came, and so did the fear. Above me the cornice bulged in the moonlight, the luminous belly of the great white whale. If Ward's efforts disturbed it, it would wipe me out like a D-10 hitting a strawberry.

I stood and waited . . . the rope came tight. I understood some of Ward's fear as I levered sideways to pull over the cornice. His last pin had been thirty feet lower in rotten limestone that he'd dug through a foot of snow to reach. I stepped onto the ridge, and the cornice and the fear disappeared below my feet. The wind stole my words and I had to thank Ward twice for a good lead. We started moving, the summit was 250 metres higher across almost a kilometre of ice ridge.

Towards midnight Ward and I traversed the last of the glacial arête. The west wind was steady and bitter and I had everything on, including my neoprene facemask. Behind me the apex of the ridge sliced the world into a dead black that fell away to the north and a soft silver glowing on the south.

I pulled in the rope for Ward and together we stepped onto the summit. His leg was strong. Physically I hurt, but spiritually I was feeling no pain.

Six and a half thousand feet lower I could see the lights of Lake Louise, and all its bars. I thought about people down there now, staggering out. There'd be more at closing time. I hoped they'd all escaped their crosses for a while. Ward and I stumbled off into the wind. At five in the morning we crunched up to a payphone. I lifted it and put it to my ear: *Uhhhhhhhhhh*, a dialtone. We bedded down on picnic tables on the porch of the deserted lodge. I'd been out of my bag for twenty three hours.

'So what did Jan say?'

'She's happy that we're down; she really wasn't worried yet.'

'That all?'

'Pretty much . . . She did say she thinks we're crazy.'

I rolled onto my side. The full moon shone down on us all.

RIGHT: First pitch on the second day.

ABOVE: Ward 'getting a little something for himself'. The two climbers top out towards midnight on the second day in a bitter west wind. Another five hours' descent still lie ahead.

Paul Piana

The Free Salathé

This headwall must be the grandest climb in the universe, an exquisite, inspiring crack system splitting the 100° sweep of golden wall at the top of El Capitan. The essence of the Salathé is distilled in this one incredible fissure.

In 1961, a great expanse of unclimbed granite lay on the southwest face of Yosemite's El Capitan, the wall named for John Salathé, Yosemite pioneer. That year, using Salathé's hard-steel pitons, the young and supremely talented team of Tom Frost, Chuck Pratt and Royal Robbins established a route up the centre of the face which even today is called 'the Greatest Rock Climb in the World.' At the time, the climb crossed all known frontiers and was state-of-the-art in technical difficulty. Pitches were created, both free and aided, as hard as anything that had previously been done. Had they blown it, the three could only have relied on themselves for rescue – and in 1961, being 2,000 feet up on a Yosemite wall was a good deal further off the deck than it is today!

More than a generation later, the sport's focus has changed. Even though more difficult modern aid climbs are being established, the goal is no longer merely to reach the top but to climb to the summit. Todd Skinner and I aren't aid-climbers – we are free-climbers, using rope and hardware only for safety, not to pull ourselves up. Unlike all previous ascents of the Salathé Wall, we climbed upward only by the strength in our hands and the will to hang on. Todd and I consider the Salathé the greatest free-climbing goal in the world. There are pitches that may be tougher, but nothing even remotely as grand or sustained in difficulty. From some of the toughest climbs in the United States and Europe, we have compiled an extremely valuable library of techniques

BIOGRAPHY

With his longstanding climbing partner, Todd Skinner, Paul Piana has 'freed' a number of North American aid-routes. Their style is controversial in that, rather than climbing 'on sight', the harder gymnastic sequences of moves are first rehearsed and memorized with a safety rope in the manner of modern sport climbing. Holds may be brushed clean of detritus, necessary fixed pitons placed, and stores cached before the full free climb is made from the bottom of the wall. Such preliminary 'recons' can last weeks, if not months. After the Salathé climb described here, the pair, climbing with Galen Rowell, freed the north face of Mount Hooker in Wyoming and created a new high grade route, The Great Canadian Knife, on Mount Proboscis in the Logan Mountains, taking a line which, Piana says, runs 'laser-straight for 1,500 vertical and overhanging feet.'

which proved to be invaluable on problems facing us more than 2,000 feet off the ground. We knew that we would never be able to climb the Salathé free with a full daypack of gear. An unheard-of amount of continuously-difficult climbing would be involved, and it was obvious that the Salathé Wall couldn't be touched without a lot of preparation.

RIGHT: El Capitan soaring above Yosemite Valley with the Nose towards camera. The Salathé takes a devious line up the lefthand side of the face and was first climbed (with some aid) in 1961 by Chuck Pratt, Tom Frost and Royal Robbins.

We decided that a series of 'camping trips' would allow us to gain the necessary knowledge and become accustomed to life so far off the ground. Our strategy was to spend six or seven days at a time working on different sections of the wall. These trips were used also to cache water and the occasional can of beans at critical sites. After working low on the route – that is, up to Pitch 24 – it became difficult to haul enough water and food to points higher. So, changing our tactics, we carried an enormous amount of gear up the twelve miles of trail to the top of El Capitan, then from a reconnaissance camp on the rim, began making outrageous rappels to put us in position to work the upper section of the climb. What had seemed like hideous exposure on Pitch 24 suddenly became no worse than the void experienced on short free climbs. Leaving fixed ropes anchored to a big block just over the rim, we began work on the crack

When, after a month of recons, the time came for the final push from the ground up, we knew we had a good chance of pulling it off if we could stay together physically and mentally, and if the weather held cool and dry.

The Salathé Wall begins with ten rope lengths of climbing called The Free Blast. This section posed no difficulty and we soon found ourselves on Heart Ledges. From here, the climbing becomes steeper and increasingly spectacular. About 700 feet above Heart Ledges we encountered the first of the really difficult pitches. At 5.13b, it turned out to be a beauty, the first crux requiring a wide variety of crack techniques. We found power flares, 5.12+ moves from them into pin scars and back out again, thuggish laybacking, and then we found the hard part!

Many leads above, pitches became harder and harder. The amazing Headwall loomed over us like a dark cloud. Especially memorable was the pitch below the Great Roof: powerful, open-handed laybacking and technically desperate stemming, protected by horribly frayed bashies and an unwillingness to fall. This flaring 5.12b dihedral ended at a dangling stance below the Great Roof. This bold feature stairsteps over and out for twenty-five feet and, with the walls of the corner below, cocooned us from the wind. We hauled our bags and set up our portaledge camp.

The first night of several was spent here, lives and gear tangled across the hanging corner like some giant cobweb. Our little world was quite secure, but we could never truly relax. The position was too spectacular. Gear dropped a long, long way before we lost sight of it.

From the top floor of our camp, the route moved out right with lots of cool morning beneath our heels, an easy but spectacular traverse leading to an attention-getting series of dead-point surges to sloping buckets. From here it is possible to brachiate wildly to the right, feet swinging a hundred miles off the deck, and then to throw your leg up and over. What a place! The first 5.12+ flare moves, just above the belay, were harder than any I had ever experienced and were unprotected as well. The jams were so bad that Todd had to visually monitor his hand through each move. So flaring were they that it was impossible to down-climb and the slightest error, even a change in the blood pressure in his hand, would see the Salathé flick him off and send him screaming far below the roof, until the force of the fall crashed onto my belay anchors with Todd wild-eyed and spinning thousands of feet off the ground. We were both glad he didn't fall. Power, grace, tremendous skill and the essence of boldness were some of the practices Todd pulled from our cheat's

repertoire. We were ecstatic to see the second 5.13 pitch done, but sobered because two more waited just above.

These two pitches, spanning the beautifully overhanging orange wall, were a joy to look at but could well have ended our free attempt. This headwall must be the grandest climb in the

ABOVE: Paul Piana leading the Roof pitch (No 29) on Day 6 of the Free Salathé.

LEFT: Free Salathé – Piana jumaring on the wall.

universe, an exquisite, inspiring crack system splitting the 100° sweep of golden wall at the top of El Capitan. The essence of the Salathé is distilled in this one incredible fissure.

'The most beautiful pitch I've ever seen', Todd said of the first, but we feared its unrelenting pump. More than mere technique would be needed to free it: beyond the ability to make difficult moves, it called for a marathon endurance effort. This was an 110-foot physical nightmare, demanding power and technique to the bitter end. Any mistake at the beginning of this long, overhanging pitch had a cumulative effect. The error might be fixed or powered through but only with a great deal of additional energy, robbing the arms of the control needed at the most difficult section of the crack, the last eight feet. In addition, the pitch was so strenuous that if success was to be had, one had to run it out rather than waste energy placing protection. I thought Todd had it in the bag twice, but he failed just a move away from the anchor. A thirty-footer later, Todd hung a few moments, toes brushing the wall. Then I belayed him to his highest piece so he could unclip and down-jump far enough to be lowered to the belay. Against all hope, Todd went up again, but even ten feet off the belay, it was obvious he was too tired to succeed. Still, he gave more than his best. He fought upward with violent karate-chop jamming, frantic foot changes and missed clips. Then ninety feet up, a dejected murmur in the gloom and I was yanked upward and into the wall as Todd hit the end of the rope.

The morning brought one of the longest breakfasts I have ever known. After having put things off long enough we started up the fixed lines to do battle with the Headwall. Todd felt a bit hesitant so early in the morning and needed to clear his mind. He climbed fifteen, then twenty feet above the piece he hung from, and then dramatically hurled himself into the void. He repeated this six or seven times until it became fun and the reluctance to go for it was completely gone. Back at the belay, we looked down at the still dark valley floor. The sun hadn't hit the face and the winds on the Headwall were still. Todd flowed through the stillness and all the difficulties, slowing at the last few moves, taking care

LEFT: Life on the wall; Piana reading in a portaledge.

BELOW: Still jumaring. There are some 35 pitches on Yosemite's Salathé Wall.

to make no mistakes. Then, all was laughter as he clipped the belay and I started up to join him.

We spent at least an hour cleaning my hands with alcohol, superglueing the rents in my fingers and then carefully applying a wrap of tape over the glue. The morning's lethargy became adrenalin as the thin jams were suddenly below and I found myself wedged into a pod-like slot. Exiting the slot seemed particularly rude to my tattered hands, its flared jams as painful as backhanding a wire brush. The pitch flowed together until I found myself staring at the dyno target. Todd was screaming, 'Hit it! Hit it!' Long seconds passed as I pondered failure, either from missing the dynamic move or from lack of trying. A deliberate lunge and I pinched the knob so hard that Arnold Schwarzenegger would have been proud. I cranked to the belay, laughing and waving my arms like a lunatic. We had it in the bag now. We rappelled down the headwall and under the roof, packed our gear and

slowly hauled it to Long Ledge. After this chore we had a little daylight left and were hungry for the top. The face-climbing pitch off Long Ledge is a gem, a continuation of the headwall. After Todd had danced up this wonder, I enjoyed a superb 5.11- thin hand crack which put us only one pitch from the top. Todd made light work of this last bit of 5.11 and the Free Salathé was done!

The next morning was perfect. We breakfasted and started hauling freight to the rim. We joked about being extra careful, remembering that most car accidents occur within two miles of home. I was first over the rim and selected the best anchor I could find, the huge block we had used before, as had years of Salathé climbers. Off to one side were a couple of fixed pins to which I anchored Todd's fixed line. I plugged in a Number 1 Friend to make sure. While Todd jumared the pitch, I used the block as a hauling anchor and also as my tie-in. When the bags reached the lip, I was unable to pull them over myself and waited for Todd to arrive.

While waiting, I felt I might as well be embarrassingly paranoid and clipped the fixed pins as well. Todd reached the rim and as he pulled up the extra ropes I began taking out the anchor. I removed the Friend and turned to lift the haulbags

ABOVE: Paul Piana leads the last pitch on the steep headwall.

small, gouged and bent piece of metal had saved Todd's rope from being cut. I had been held by the loop I'd clipped to the fixed pin. The 11mm rope which I'd tied into the block had sliced through as easily as a shoe lace. Two other 9mm ropes were in eight or nine pieces and the haul bags were talus food. We coiled the remnants of rope and started down the east ledges. A descent usually taking under two hours required almost nine. We arrived at the base of the Manure Pile Buttress looking much worse than the average wall climber who staggers down the trail.

We had dreamed, we had trained and we had struggled. Even though the climb ended in a nightmare, we had triumphed. The ecstasy we feel at achieving our dream will live inside us forever.

Sometimes at night, as I am drifting off to sleep, I suddenly hear that big block move and see Todd tumble over the rim. I think how difficult it would have been for our families if we had been killed, shudder at the remembrance of being dragged off the summit of El Capitan, in certain knowledge that we were going to die. For me, the definition of 'horror' is now an emotion. Now that several years have passed and Todd and I have healed, I am even more pleased with our climb. We worked harder than anyone else was willing to work, harder than we thought we could. We were prepared to risk our most shining goal becoming a tormenting failure. Yet we were prepared to fail and fail and fail until we could succeed.

Live your life like a thrown knife. Begin it!

when there came a horrible grating sound. Spinning round, we saw to our terror that the block had come loose.

I am not clear exactly what happened next. Todd tells me I put out my hands to the block, yelling 'No!' I do recall the two of us being battered together and the horror of seeing my best friend knocked wildly off the edge. Then I felt a tremendous weight on my left leg as I was squeegied off the rim. There was a loud crack like a rifle shot, more pummelling and suddenly everything stopped spinning and I could just peek back over the edge.

All was in tatters, ropes pinched off and fused – it seemed as if they had all been cut. I was afraid to touch anything and sick with the knowledge that Todd had probably just hit the talus. All of a sudden, a startling bass squeak sounded below me, followed by a desperate 'Grab the rope!' I hauled myself over the top and soon a bloody hand on a crushed ascender slid over the rim. I helped Todd up and we lay there for a long time, terrified because Todd was having trouble breathing and his pelvic area hurt badly. My leg was in a really weird position and reaching a crescendo of pain.

I don't know how long we were there, frightened to move lest we unravelled the braid of cut ropes that held us. When we did get up, we discovered that Todd's line appeared to be okay. He'd been held by one of his ascenders. Apparently, the rock had scraped over it and miraculously that

RIGHT: The west face of El Capitan with the Salathé Wall. For a long time after their free climb, Piana and Skinner were still awed at its difficulty and doubted that it would be climbed again in a hurry.

Audrey Salkeld

SOUTHERN HEMISPHERE

South America The Andean Cordillera form an elongated spine along the western edge of South America, from the Caribbean coast to the isolated fjords and lakes of the Magellan Straits. Their 4,500 miles make them the longest continuous range of mountains in the world. In a final thrust, they erupt from the sea again in Tierra del Fuego, to bristle on towards Cape Horn. Geologically young, with many still-active volcanoes, they rise in places to more than 22,000 feet, and encompass wide climatic variations, from the dripping jungles of their Amazonian slopes to the bleak deserts of Peru, Bolivia and Chile. Patagonia, at the remote southern tip of the chain, has been called the uttermost part of the earth, with its perpetual icecaps and cataclysmic winds.

To the native South Americans the Andes were sacred; to the Conquistadors who so brutally blazed through Peru and into Ecuador in the first half of the sixteenth century they presented a formidable obstacle, and the lurking threat of ambush. They were the last refuge of the Incas. The impregnable fortress of Machu Picchu, high in the rainforest, was never discovered by the Spanish invaders. Archaeological evidence shows that a number of Andean summits were ascended, possibly even occupied, by local Indians three centuries before the first ascent of Mont Blanc: the Chilean volcano Llullaillaco 22,057 feet (6,723 metres) was climbed, we know, by Atacama Indians, making it probably the highest mountain ascended anywhere in the world, until the Schlagintweit brothers reached the slightly higher summit of Abi Gamin in the Himalaya in 1855. Documentary evidence of Andean ascents – possibly of any mountains outside Europe – starts with a climb of the Ecuadorean volcano Pichincha ('Boiling Mountain', 15,423 feet) by Spaniards anxious to observe its crater after an eruption in 1582. In the eighteenth century a Franco-Spanish expedition, led by Charles Marie de La Condamine and Pierre Bouguer, carried out the first scientific explorations at high altitudes. Over eight years, in their attempts to determine the degree of the meridian near the Equator, they set up many high signal stations and scaled a

RIGHT: South America: the Andean mountain chain, longest continuous range in the world, runs 4,500 miles along the western edge of the continent. Geologically young, it contains a number of active volcanoes. In 1970, a devastating earthquake in Peru claimed thousands of lives, including all 16 members of a Czechoslovakian climbing expedition to Huascaran.

KEY TO MOUNTAINS
1 Pico Bolivar; 2 Roraima; 3 Cotopaxi; 4 Chimborazo; 5 Huascaran; 6 Ancohuma; 7 Pico da Bandeira; 8 Ojos del Salado; 9 Aconcagua; 10 San Valentin

number of peak, including Pichincha (again) and Corazon (15,718 feet). On Chimborazo, 'Watchtower of the Universe', which for a long time was believed to be the highest mountain in the world (and indeed is, if you measure it radially from the earth's geocentre!), a height of 15,565 feet (4,745 metres) was reached. They also observed Cotopaxi during an eruption.

Ecuadorean volcanoes featured again in 1802–3, when the German scientist and geographer, Alexander von Humboldt, arrived to investigate and climb Cotopaxi (19,344 feet) and Chimborazo (20,702 feet). Though he failed to reach either

ABOVE: *Edward FitzGerald, an early visitor to New Zealand's mountains and to the Andes, seen here in a portrait by Sir Edward Burne-Jones.*

ABOVE: *Mount Cotopaxi erupting in 1743, when flames reputedly licked 2,000 ft above the cone.*

LEFT: *Baron Alexander von Humboldt (seen here in his study), an important scientist-explorer of the early 19th century. He went almost to the top of Chimborazo.*

LEFT: *'We were then 20,000 feet high' – a sketch by Edward Whymper illustrating his 1880 ascent of Chimborazo.*

summit, he did attain a height of over 19,000 feet on Chimborazo. Wilhelm Reiss, another German scientist, and a companion eventually climbed Cotopaxi to its crater rim in 1872.

The first ascent of Chimborazo, which marks the real start of 'mountaineering' in the Andes, was made in 1880 by Edward Whymper of Matterhorn fame, climbing with his old rival Jean Antoine Carrel, the 'cock of Val Tournanche', and a kinsman of Carrel's. They also scaled Corazon and Cotopaxi, besides bagging an array of lesser virgins: Sincholagua, Antisana, Cayambe, Sara Urco and Cotocachi. The two Carrels also climbed Illiniza.

Aconcagua, at 22,840 feet (6,962 metres) – by the latest measurement – is the highest peak of Argentina, of the Andes, of the Western hemisphere, of anywhere outside Asia. It has attracted plenty of attention over the years – as it continues to do with the current craze among globe-trotting mountaineers for ticking off all 'Seven Summits', the highpoints of each of the world's continents. Aconcagua is a complex, twin-headed mountain and was first ascended in 1897 by the celebrated Swiss guide Mattias Zurbriggen, climbing solo. He was the strongest in an expedition led by the swashbuckling alpinist Edward FitzGerald, a young man who'd already made a name for himself with exploratory climbs in New Zealand. Other members of the team later repeated the climb, although not FitzGerald himself, for whom Aconcagua represented 'an intolerably monotonous slagpile.' Sir Martin Conway, next to near the summit almost two years later, felt much the same: 'The whole mountain is falling to pieces and all the stones dividing'. He forebore treading the ultimate snows in deference to FitzGerald, but it was a courtesy he afterwards regretted. Conway also

ABOVE: *Annie Peck, a teacher from Providence, dreamt of being first to reach what she called the 'Apex of America'. With two Swiss guides she climbed Huascaran Norte in 1908.*

climbed Illimani (21,200 feet) in Bolivia.

The Peruvian Andes comprise some twenty or more separately identifiable ranges, and offer some of the finest mountaineering in the world outside the Greater Himalaya. The highest and most popular group is the Cordillera Blanca, easily accessible from Lima. Perhaps the first European to penetrate this area was C.R. Enock, who crossed the high Abra Villon pass in 1903, and two years later attempted to climb Huascaran, its highest summit at 22,205 feet (6,768 metres).

Another early traveller was Annie Peck, a middle-aged Classics teacher from Providence, Rhode Island. She had been enamoured of mountains since a visit to Europe some years before, when she vowed to return and scale the 'grand old Matterhorn'. This she did in 1895, and 'the unmerited notoriety attained thereby' (as she put it) spurred her 'to the accomplishment of some deed which should render me worthy of the fame already acquired'. She certainly had a flair for self-publicity, which she quickly learned to exploit to find sponsors for her schemes. Above everything else, she desired to be the first to stand on the 'Apex of America', stubbornly refusing to acknowledge Aconcagua as this apex, and Zurbriggen therefore its first-footer. Instead, she launched into a series of expeditions to Bolivia and Peru to satisfy in her own mind which was the highest peak, at length settling upon Huascaran. Success attended her fifth attempt to climb the mountain, in 1908, although it is now known that the north summit which her party reached is the lower of Huascaran's twin peaks.

Harper's Monthly Magazine carried an exclusive account of Miss Peck's triumph (as it had of her earlier attempts). On this occasion Annie was accompanied by two Swiss guides, Gabriel Zumtaugwald and Rudolf Taugwalder from Zermatt. It irked her that the guides attached little importance to her earlier efforts (complaining to her readers that one of the chief difficulties in a woman undertaking an expedition of this nature was that 'whatever her experience, every man believes that he knows better what should be done than she'), and even more that in the final, windy stages of the climb, while she and Gabriel were nobly taking altitude measurements with her hypsometer, Rudolf should nip ahead to the summit instead of staying to help. She was free to acknowledge her guides' 'instrumentality' in the expedition's success, but nonetheless devastated not to have been first to imprint the tipmost snows. That much was her right, she felt, as leader; what she had paid for. So, poor Annie: robbed not only of her ultimate kudos, but in time proved to have gone for the lesser summit. . . . Huascaran itself fell short of her estimate and clearly was not the Apex of the Americas as she had hoped. It was not even high enough for her to snatch the women's altitude

record from her compatriot and arch rival Fanny Bullock Workman, who had climbed Pinnacle Peak in Kashmir (22,808 feet) two years before. Some sceptics have doubted whether schoolmarm Annie got up her mountain at all. Nonetheless, her fame rang round the world and she received a gold medal from the President of Peru for her 'meritorious ascent'.

The true summit, Huascaran Sur, was climbed from the west in 1932 by a German expedition led by P. Borchers. The same party made first ascents of Nevados Chopicalqui (20,998 feet), Huandoy Norte, Artesonraju and Copa, among others.

The last thousand or so miles of mainland South America, those parts of Chile and Argentina which lie beyond 45° South, comprise what is known as Patagonia. Here the Andes are lower, rarely exceeding 10,000 feet (3,000 metres), and are mostly broken into small groups by deep fjords and west-flowing rivers (the continental watershed lying well to the east of the main Andean crest). In these southern latitudes, so close to the Pole, the Ice Ages were particularly severe and remnants of what was once a gigantic ice sheet linger in the form of two extensive ice caps: the Hielo Patagonica del Norte, stretching for some 125 miles (200 kilometres) between latitudes 46 and 48° South and containing Patagonia's highest peak, Monte san Valentin (13,204 feet, first climbed by an Argentinian expedition in 1952); and the more southerly Hielo Patagonica del Sur, between the Baker Channel and Union Sound. Between them they encompass some 9,000 square miles of crevassed ice, pushing glaciers out into the surrounding forest.

The southern ice cap was visited three times by the Argentine explorer Dr Frederick Reichert, in 1914, 1916 and 1933. On the last occasion, he reported having glimpsed – during a lull in the storms – a live volcano in the middle of the ice-sheet. No-one took much notice. But in the southern summer of 1959-60, Eric Shipton, leading an exploring party up the O'Higgins Glacier on to the ice-cap, also spotted a peak with vapour pouring from its black vents. Bad weather prevented his group mounting an attempt upon Reichert's elusive volcano, Cerro Lautaro, but it was eventually ascended four years later by two Argentines, P. Skvarca and L. Pera. Shipton returned to the ice-cap in 1961-62 to make a very ambitious 150 miles (240 kilometres) journey along its entire length from Baker Fjord to the northwestern arm of Lago Argentino, a sledging trek of 52 days. He was accompanied by Jack Ewer, C. Maranghunic and E. Garcia. On the way, the party climbed Cerro Don Bosco, but was turned back by bad weather from the summit ridge of El Murallon. Eleven years later, after more Patagonian travels, Shipton, with Garcia, Maranghunic and M. Gomez, made a six-week traverse of the northern ice cap from the San Rafael Glacier to the Rio Cochrane, taking in ascents of Cerros Arco and Arenales (the latter a second ascent).

The Patagonian massifs of most interest to climbers are the Paine and the FitzRoy mountain groups, each a collection of steep granite spires, about a hundred miles apart. Mount FitzRoy (nowadays, officially, Chalten) at 11,170 feet (3,405 metres) the highest in the area, had been attempted several times before it was successfully surmounted in 1952 by Lionel Terray and Guido Magnone of France. Terray, whose career included many fine Alpine and Andean climbs, notably the first ascent of Makalu in the Himalaya, used to confess that FitzRoy was the

ABOVE: *Patagonia – the Paine Group, from the west. On the right, the Central Tower, which was climbed in 1962-3 by a British team, their route going easily to the col, then following close to the lefthand skyline.*

RIGHT: *The Cuernos del Paine at sunrise (from the south). Highest in the group, Cuernos Principal, went to Chilean climbers in 1968.*

climb which brought him most nearly to his physical and moral limits. Though less extreme than some of his Alpine routes, FitzRoy's remoteness from all possibility of help, its almost incessant bad weather, its plastering of verglas, and above all its terrible winds, made the whole climb more complex, exhausting and mortally dangerous than anything in the Alps.

Nearby Cerro Torre, 10,280 feet (3,102 metres) has been described as 'a scream in stone'. And 'a nightmare aiguille emerging from a bubbling devil's cauldron of cloud, like a glittering lighthouse'. In 1958 it was attempted unsuccessfully by two Italian expeditions, before a spectacular first ascent was claimed

the following year by Cesare Maestri (also Italian). Six days after setting out with the Austrian ice expert Toni Egger to make an alpine-style assault of the North Face, Maestri was discovered, confused and half-buried in the snow of the glacier.

The pair had reached the summit, Maestri said, but Egger was swept away by an avalanche during the descent. Years later, as more climbers attempted the dramatic peak and failed, people began to question whether Maestri and Egger could really have climbed Cerro Torre. In defiance of the sceptics, Maestri returned in 1970 and bolted his way up the Southeast Ridge and East Face using a compressed-air drill! Outraged, climbers

111

RIGHT: *The controversial Italian climber, Cesare Maestri. Doubt still hangs over his claimed ascent of Cerro Torre in 1959. His partner, Austrian ice expert Toni Egger (far right), was swept away by an avalanche and killed.*

BELOW: *Aerial view showing Cerro Torre (right), with Torre Egger and Cerro Stanhardt. Beyond them rises FitzRoy (left), now known as Chalten, and Aiguille Poincenot.*

around the world denounced such tactics; and since, by his own admission, Maestri had not this time surmounted the overhanging mushroom of snow which tops the mountain, they still denied him the honour of first ascent. During the winter of 1973-4, another Italian team, led by Casimiro Ferrari, climbed the West Face *and* the crowning mushroom. But whether they were first or not on Cerro Torre's lonely summit has to remain a mystery. Maestri has never wavered from his story despite many probing interviews. Egger's body was discoverd in 1975, a mile and a half down the glacier, but his camera which could have contained vital summit evidence was never found. Maestri's 'bolt ladder' was 'freed' in 1978 in a remarkable day-and-a-half alpine-style climb by Americans Jim Bridwell and Steve Brewer.

The sky blue Towers of Paine are less extensive geographically than the FitzRoy-Cerro Torre group, but can probably boast a greater number of severe peaks. Bavarians Stefan Zuck and Hans Teufel made the first ascent in the range in 1937 with their climb of Paine Orientale, one of the lesser peaks, but it was not until the 1950s that the area's full potential began to be realized. Paine Grande, the highest peak, yielded in 1958 to Italian climbers following a route pioneered a month earlier by Argentines. The Central Tower was climbed by Don Whillans and Chris Bonington in 1963, and the Fortress five years later by another British group – John Gregory, Gordon Hibberd and Dave Nicol. The same year the Shield and Cuerno Principal went to Italians and Chileans repectively, and in 1971 the fine Catedral peak was climbed by all members of Dave Nicol's northwest ridge expedition. South Africans, led by Paul Fatti, claimed first ascents of the Sword and Cuerno Norte. Other peaks followed and attention turned, as elsewhere, to the harder faces. Over the years there has been no let-up in popularity: despite the unremitting and ferocious weather, which can seal off peaks for weeks on end, climbers continue to be drawn to the fine Patagonian granite.

New Zealand and Australasia Samuel Butler (author of *Erewhon*) wrote of New Zealand's Mount Cook in 1860 that although it was hazardous to say so of any mountain, he did not think any human would ever reach its top. And he upbraided himself for admiring a mountain which was of no use to sheep. Two volcanoes of New Zealand's North Island had been climbed earlier in the century, but mountaineering interest in the Southern Alps really dates from 1882 when the Reverend W.S. Green visited the area and was almost successful in climbing Mount Cook, the highest summit (12,350 feet). It was a remarkable effort; while the mountain was ascended in 1894 by three young New Zealanders – G. Graham, T. Fyfe and the 17-year old J. Clark – nearly thirty years were to pass before Reverend Green's route was successfully completed. E.A. Fitzgerald and M. Zurbriggen, robbed of Cook, their desired prize, pulled off several other firsts, including ascents of Mounts Tasman and Sefton. The 'father' of New Zealand mountaineering is held to be A.P. Harper, one of the co-founders of the New Zealand Alpine Club in 1891 and author of much exploratory survey work, particularly among the glaciers of Westland. By the turn of the century there was a small, flourishing corps of professional guides, among them the brothers Peter and Alec Graham who dominated the country's mountaineering for a quarter of a century, climbing most of the remaining giants and opening up many new routes and traverses. Their most famous client was Miss Freda du Faur, a pioneer of women's climbing in New Zealand, who made a number of notable climbs just before World War I, including the first traverse, in a single expedition, of all three summits of Mount Cook. The most celebrated New Zealand alpinist remains, of course, the erstwhile beekeeper, Sir Edmund Hillary, who scaled Everest with Sherpa Tenzing in 1953. He had learned his craft from Harry Ayres, an outstanding guide with a tremendous reputation for brilliant ice-work. The New Zealand Alps continue to produce top rank mountaineers, known for their exploits at home and in the greater ranges.

Australia can boast no mountains of similar scale. The Great Dividing Range, which extends for over 2,000 miles, consists largely of eroded plateaux no more than a few thousand feet high. Mount Koscisuko (7,328 feet) is the highest point. Other lesser ranges are scattered across the continent and in the island of Tasmania. In the absence of Alps, Australian climbers have turned to their crags and gorges, sea cliffs and sea stacks, making Australian rock climbing a dynamic and individual force.

The first man to claim ascents of all Seven Summits, Dick Bass, included Kosciusku for his highest peak in the Australian continent – which of course it is. But these days Seven Summit-baggers head for New Guinea and the highest mountain of Australasia. The Carstenz Pyramid (16,023 feet) is a grey rocky peak rising from the dense, steamy jungles of Irian Jaya. Its remoteness, unique scenery and, above all, the fascinating Dani people who live in its shadow – until quite recently a fierce warrior tribe with a reputation for cannibalism – all combine to make a climbing trip here a magical experience, a visit back in time. Heinrich Harrer, the Austrian Eigerwanderer, with New Zealander Phil Temple, made the first ascent of the Carstenz Pyramid's three highest summits and recorded his adventures in *I Come from the Stone Age*.

BELOW: Carstenz Pyramid is the highest peak in New Guinea, and in all Australasia – one of the collectable Seven Summits.

Antarctica The vast continent of Antarctica extends over almost five and a half million square miles (14 million square kilometres) and carries an ice-cap with an average thickness of over 6,500 feet (2,000 metres): remarkable statistics.

It contains extensive mountain ranges, the highest peaks being found in the Sentinel Range of the Ellsworth Mountains, first seen and named by Lincoln Ellsworth during his Trans-Antarctic flight of November 1935.

Mountaineering began on the continent in 1908 with the ascent of Mount Erebus (13,250 feet), a still-active volcano on Ross Island, by a polar party led by Professor Edgeworth David and including the famous explorer Douglas Mawson. Members of Scott's last expedition, making a memorable second ascent, were driven off the mountain by a minor eruption. The highest peak in the Sentinel Range, Mount Vinson (16,067 feet), received its first ascent by an American party under Nick Clinch in 1966, who also climbed Mounts Tyree, Shinn, Gardner, Ostenso and Long Gables. Vinson these days is a tourist attraction, climbed frequently as another of the Seven Summits. The late Mugs Stump soloed the west face of Tyree, wryly claiming it as 'probably the hardest climb done by man'.

The Antarctic Peninsula, the crooked finger of land stabbing towards Cape Horn across the stormy seas of the Drake Passage, carries the second longest mountain chain. Its highest peaks, Mount Francais (9,456 feet) and Mount Andrew Jackson (11,316 feet), have both been climbed, as has Mount Gaudry (8,049 feet) on the offshore Adelaide Island.

General mountaineering on the 'Last Continent' will remain difficult, however, not only because of the shortness of the Antarctic summer and the atrocious weather, but because of a bureaucratic reluctance to sanction high risk ventures, as well as the high cost of support. Having said that, overland journeys to the Pole, alongside full Trans-Antarctic crossings, are becoming more frequent, and the people who take up these challenges have very often proved themselves first as mountaineers: one thinks particularly of Sir Edmund Hillary, who reached the Pole in 1958 as part of the first crossing of all, of Naomi Uemura, Reinhold Messner, Roger Mear, Sue Giller . . . This close association is mutually beneficial.

BELOW: Antarctica is home to some splendid landscapes and summits. The highest mountains, the Sentinel Range, were first seen and named by Lincoln Ellsworth during his Trans-Antarctic flight of November 1935. All the main peaks on the continent continue to attract exploration.

KEY TO MOUNTAINS
1 Vinson; 2 P3657;
3 P3630; 4 P3355;
5 Minto; 6 Murchison;
7 Erebus; 8 Markham;
9 Kirkpatrick; 10 Sidley

Many of the bleak sub-Antarctic islands offer promise to private parties. The explorer H.W. Tilman made several voyages to southern waters, climbing peaks on Possession Island and Kerguelen in the Crozet Islands, and taking part in the expedition to make the first ascent of Big Ben on Heard Island. He was lost at sea in his eightieth year, on his way to the South Shetlands. Weatherbeaten Brabant Island in the Palmer Archipelago boasts a number of mountains up to 8,200 feet (2,500 metres] and was the destination of a Joint Services Expedition in 1984. South Georgia has seen various mountaineering forays with ascents of its major peaks Paget (the highest at 9,565 feet (2,915 metres), Brooker and Sugartop. The 'Southern Ocean Mountaineering Expedition' of 1989-90, which included Stephen Venables, Julian Freeman-Atkins, Kees 't Hooft, Brian Davison and Linday Griffin, claimed first ascents of the island's Vogel Peak and Mounts Kling and Carse.

Africa Inland was a high mountain, 'Kilimansharo', crowned with a white substance resembling silver, an early East African missionary was told in 1847, and the whole place so full of djinn (a spirit in Muslim mythology) and evil spirits that legs stiffened and people died from the bad effects of their presence. The only man brave enough to have attempted to climb this mountain crept home with his hands and feet destroyed. Snow was a baffling commodity to the dwellers of the African lowlands, and

Ice cap

Permanent ice shelf

Permanent bases

the existence of snow on the Equator was for a long time disbelieved by Europeans. The explorer Henry Stanley was told by a boy on the shores of Lake Albert of a mountain covered in salt, and looked up to discover the snowclad Ruwenzori.

Kilimanjaro, as we know now, is, at 19,340 feet, the highest point in Africa. A dormant volcano, Kibo, its major peak, was first climbed in 1889 by Hans Meyer and Ludwig Purtscheller. Kilimanjaro is another of the collectable Seven Summits; and there is a popular tourist trail, not technically difficult, although the effects of altitude frequently catch people unawares. Ice routes, such as The Icicle on Breach Wall (first climbed in 1978 by Reinhold Messner and Konrad Renzler), are among the most formidable in the world. The development of climbing on Kilimanjaro and Mount Kenya owes a lot to the partnership and the vital inspiration of Iain Allen and Ian Howell, particularly during the 1970s.

Batian, 17,058 feet (5,199 metres) and the highest of Mount Kenya's two summits, had been climbed in 1899 by a large expedition led by Sir Halford Mackinder and Campbell Hausburg. Eric Shipton and Percy Wyn Harris made the second ascent in 1929, taking in the lower summit of Nelion as well. The following year, Shipton with Bill Tilman climbed the long, classic northwest ridge. A famous attempt was made in 1943 by three prisoners of war – who had escaped from a camp at Nanyuki – with stolen rations and improvised equipment. After a plethora of attempts, the fine ice-bound Diamond Couloir on Kenya's south face fell at last, in 1973, to Phil Snyder and Kenya National Park Warden P. Thumbi, who became the first black African to have been known to climb a Grade VI route.

The Ruwenzori mountains lie along the western border of Uganda and are popularly known as the Mountains of the Moon. This mysterious area, with its bizarre bog plants, was thoroughly explored in 1906 by the far-ranging Duke of the Abruzzi, whose party – which included four Courmayeur guides and the famous photographer Vittorio Sella – accounted for most of the major summits. Activity here has been sporadic over the years and was all but impossible during Idi Amin's rule.

In Southern Africa, there is a strong climbing tradition, the famous Table Mountain and the fold mountains of the Western Cape, and the basaltic Drakensberg, providing the bulk of the climbs. Elsewhere in Africa – although not in the southern hemisphere – the High Atlas of the north present a complex of jagged ridges and a dozen summits over 13,000 feet, with rock climbs and longer expeditions. In the Sahara, the Hoggar and other outcropping desert ranges have become highly popular with today's international sun-loving rock climbers. Catherine Destivelle's vertiginous climbs in the remarkable rocky regions of Mali have been immortalized in the film *Seo!*

BELOW: Ellsworth Mountains, Antarctica, showing the Heritage Range at 80° South (from Wilson Nunatak).

John Earle

Patagonia with Shipton

*This storm-lashed wilderness gave him all he looked for, with its
unexplored mountain ranges and glaciers. It suited his philosophy of
lightweight exploration and travel with a few friends.*

On New Year's Day 1963 we set off at last
for South America. Eric Shipton wore his
heavy climbing boots to save weight,
although his luggage, to my eyes, already
appeared fairly frugal. As we settled down
in the plane he turned to me and said, 'By
the way, have we got any tents? I think I
may have left one down in Punta Arenas.'
This marvellous vagueness that I came to
understand was not an act. To him, there
were more important things to think
about in planning an expedition than
whether or not he had a tent.

To many, Eric Shipton may have
seemed an enigma. He often appeared
diffident and was ill at ease in large
groups. But this belied his enormous
strength of will and determination that
sometimes could almost be taken as stub-
bornness. Huge reserves of physical
strength and courage were not readily
obvious in this slight, apparently frail,
retiring man. Yet, when he talked in that
quiet voice of his, there was an almost
hypnotic presence.

In the days of huge expeditions with
hundreds of porters and luxurious tinned
foods he was often known scathingly as
the 'bag-of-rice-a-day explorer', living off
the land where possible, on meagre
rations, striking into unexplored and
unknown mountain areas with just one or
two friends, for months on end. He was
way ahead of his time, of course.

It wasn't that he sought out hardship for
its own sake, but he certainly enjoyed
travelling in strange lands, with all their
problems of access, route finding and
mountaineering difficulties. He gained a

BIOGRAPHY

*John Earle runs the Dartmoor Expedition Centre for
Outdoor Pursuits. He has climbed in the Alps,
Himalaya, South America and Baffin Island, and has
also made a number of freelance television documen-
taries. He first met his childhood hero, the explorer
Eric Shipton, in the early 1950s when he went to
work at the Outward Bound School in Eskdale, where
Shipton was briefly Warden. In 1963 he joined
Shipton for the two-part Patagonian expedition that
he describes for us here.*

great spiritual release from living this way.
In many senses he rejected what most
would call a normal way of life. He had
few personal belongings or clothes, most
of which he kept, latterly, in the flat in
London's Tite Street of his dear friend and
companion Phyllis Wint. He could pack
and be ready to travel in a few hours and
literally plan an expedition 'on the back of
a postcard'.

A lot of his time was spent at the Royal
Geographical Society, poring over maps,
talking to friends, lecturing, and often
surrounded by the admiring 'ladies of
Kensington Gore', as he called them. He
loved friendly argument, frequently
calling black white and white black to
stimulate conversation.

By 1957, a few years after I first met
him, Shipton was moving into a second
phase of travel and exploration. After his
rejection as the leader of the 1953 Everest
Expedition he had more or less turned his
back on the Himalaya and now began
looking towards the 'uttermost part of the
earth', Tierra del Fuego and Patagonia.
This storm-lashed wilderness gave him all
he looked for, with its unexplored mountain ranges and glaciers. It suited his
philosophy of lightweight exploration and
travel with a few friends. There was a
saying going around that if you followed
in the footsteps of a Shipton expedition,
you could pick up enough gear and clothing to equip your own trip from all that
he had thrown away.

Our first objective this time was to try
to reach and climb the small volcanic peak
of Mount Burney on the Munoz Gamero
Peninsula in the very remote southwest
corner of Patagonia – just the sort of trip
Eric revelled in, although it infuriated Jack
Ewer, a British lecturer working at Chile's
Santiago University, who had joined us.
He felt it was a complete waste of time
and resources.

We set off in a Chilean Army truck that
took us to the edge of the fjords and lakes
system beyond Estancia Skyring. From

ABOVE AND RIGHT: Eric Shipton in Patagonia. The picture to the right shows the tough, pyramidal Antarctic tent he favoured, pitched below the icefall of the Frances Glacier.

We found what was probably the Passo del Indio and set about relaying our gear over to a further lake system. Even with its wooden floorboards removed, the dinghy still weighed 150 pounds (67.5 kilogrammes) and was an appallingly awkward and bulky load. We carried it for ten-minute spells. Getting to one's feet with it lashed to a pack-frame was a terrible struggle and, once up, it nearly drove us into the ground. One television critic, after watching this part of my film, referred to Eric as 'this ageing masochist'. It took six hours to carry everything across, going backwards and forwards many times.

The gruelling relaying was repeated three times into new lake systems, bringing us closer and closer, we hoped, to Mount Burney. With the almost gale-force prevailing westerly winds, the waves on the lakes were huge and we plunged up and down into the spray. Within minutes of launching, we'd be soaked to the skin, and constantly had to bail the boat out as the water swirled around our feet. The weather most of the time was driving mist and rain.

At the head of what proved the last lake, where we left the dinghy, we were able to see, beyond a long, marshy plain, the

there, we travelled in a large RFD inflatable dinghy powered by an outboard engine. Leaving caches of food and petrol at suitable places, we pushed into this completely unknown and unexplored country of forest and mountain. There were legends that the Alacaluf Indians had carried their bark canoes from one lake system to another and this was exactly what Eric proposed to do with our inflatable dingy, food and equipment, not to mention the film and cameras that I had with me for the BBC television documentary I was making.

LEFT: *Shipton's love affair with Patagonia began in middle life, after he had turned his back on the Himalaya. The storm-lashed wilderness gave him all he looked for, with its unexplored ranges and glaciers, and drew him back time and again.*

BELOW: *Eric Shipton on ice.*

winds. Not once did we ever see the little volcanic peak as we struggled across its glaciers and moraines, radiating like the spokes of a wheel.

When we arrived back at our lakeside dump and came to inflate the RFD, we found both pumps had perished and we had to blow it up by mouth. Our lives depended on getting the boat afloat. We each took three- or four-minute stints, at the end of which we reeled away, giddy and sick. Eric with his 'high altitude' lungs seemed able to manage longer spells, and after an hour the boat appeared hard enough to launch. It was no wonder that Eric felt, in some ways, that this was the most dangerous expedition he had ever been on. We were more out on a limb, with no hope of rescue or reaching help and civilization through the dense forests of Patagonia, than on many of his previous trips, including Everest.

glaciers pushing down from what must have been Mount Burney, hidden in thick cloud.

We now had a decision to make. Were we going to look for a chance to climb the mountain by establishing a camp as high as we could on a ridge below the clouds and sit it out, waiting for the weather to clear; or should we keep moving and explore a larger area of this unknown mountain?

Eric, not one for peak-bagging, had no difficulty in making the decision. He suggested that we should try to make a journey right round Mount Burney. It took us eighteen days of double-loading to complete the circuit in mist, rain, snow and shrieking

After a brief rest of a week in Punta Arenas, we were off again, this time with the Chilean Navy in the little ocean-going tug, the *Cabrales*, down the Magellan Strait, escorted by dolphins rolling over and over in the bow waves, out into the Pacific and then back east into the Beagle Channel. Eric's objectives were the largely-unexplored mountains at the eastern end of the Darwin Range of Tierra del Fuego, an area almost as large as the European Alps with only three or four peaks that had been climbed, most of them by Eric himself on an earlier trip.

With his fine sense of history, Eric was clearly thrilled to be sailing the Beagle Channel, past the deep, forested fjords cutting back both to the north and south into the tall peaks and cascading glaciers that reached the water's edge. This dramatic stretch of water, linking the Pacific to the Atlantic, was the way that FitzRoy and Darwin had sailed in 1831.

Eric had invited Argentinian Peter Bruchhausen and Claudio Cortez from Chile to join the expedition, and the four of us were rowed ashore by longboat into a little bay called Puerto Olla on the northern shore of the Beagle Channel. A great wall of dripping Nothofagus forest rose up from the beach, barely visible through the heavy rain and drizzle that fell as snow only slightly higher up the mountains. We saw at once why other expeditions, hearing about Darwin's supposedly impenetrable 'temperate jungle', had not attempted to climb these mountains.

As we moved all the equipment and food into a delightful dell, we came across the remains of a wooden wigwam, probably left there years before by the Yahgan Indians who used to collect mussels and hunt in these waters. At the same time the weather cleared and the whole scene was transformed. We could see the bay of Puerto Olla fully now, a half mile crescent of sand backed by forest almost encircling the turquoise waters of the lagoon. Brown fronds of kelp waved languidly in the gentle swell and a pair of kelp geese swam along the shores. A sea lion poked its inquisitive head out of the water, watching us with huge, limpid eyes and twitching whiskers. The sun shone brightly now from a blue sky. An hour ago it had been grey and cold with steady rain, sleet and snow. It brought home very forcibly how unpredictable and changeable the weather was in these mountains of Tierra del Fuego. The man who had climbed and explored in the great ranges of the world sucked on his pipe, enjoying this strange and haunting land, and we gorged ourselves on mussels cooked over a wood fire.

The next few weeks were again typical of a Shipton expedition. We double-loaded huge kitbags of over 70 pounds (31.5 kilogrammes) through the thick, clawing forest and up on the glaciers of the mountains, often with sudden onslaughts of wind grabbing and pushing at us, whirling the powder snow up in stinging clouds that peppered our bare

BELOW: Roncagli, Tierra del Fuego, from the east.

faces like shot. We carried a four-man Antarctic Pyramid tent made of ventile and cotton. It weighed over 50 pounds (22.5 kilogrammes) when dry and certainly proved to be one man's load when wet. Eric reckoned it was the only tent on the market at that time that would stand up to the hurricanes of Tierra del Fuego. At least four times this wisdom was proved right.

The storms that hit the tent as we lay at some 5,000 feet on the ice-cap-like glaciers of the Darwin Range were ferocious. Sudden blasts, violent and demented, hurled themselves at us. We could hear them coming above the general continuous roar of wind and rattle of powder snow on the tent, a higher screaming rapidly approaching over the glacier. Laying, waiting for them to arrive, wondering if the tent could survive another onslaught, the sound was like an express train arriving in a sudden explosion of noise, a blast that tears at your eardrums and swallows you completely. At one stage of our enforced rest Eric decided to halve our rations in case this fearful weather continued for weeks, as apparently it might. We lay and read. It was hard to talk above the cracking of the tent, but when we did Eric kept us enthralled with stories of his earlier trips. For him,

conversation was one of the delights of life. He had an incredible calming contentment and, with his ability to discuss a wide range of subjects, the time passed very quickly. Still, as he reminded us, in that classic remark of his: 'Bedsores are the most likely injury on an expedition.'

On days of fine weather during the next few weeks we crawled out of our tent like children let out early from school. We explored the glaciers and pushed out towards the heart of the Darwin Range, finding an extraordinary land-locked glacier lake, very like the one beside the Grand Aletsch glacier in Switzerland. We climbed two virgin peaks, Monte Bove and Monte Francés, both only just over 7,000 feet but festooned with huge glaciers that plunged down to the Beagle Channel. The summit of Monte Francés consisted of three enormous cauliflower-mounds of ice crystals formed by the damp winds from the Pacific freezing into amazing feathers of ice.

We had a final fight for survival on leaving our glacier-camp to return to the Beagle Channel when we were caught in a terrible storm that grabbed and buffeted us like a thing possessed. The air seemed to be almost solid and visible, and it was as if we were straining into an endless barrage of rushing waves. Several times we were plucked and hurled twenty or thirty feet on the steep ice.

Eric was carrying the tent, which had been encased in ice and frozen snow when we dismantled it and must have weighed 80 pounds or more. He tried to jump a crevasse and failed. With horror, we watched as almost in slow motion he disappeared through the hole he had made. The rope tightened and the wind yelped in triumphal fury.

I had never heard Eric raise his voice, nor did he now. I shall always remember his faint, 'Er, I say . . . ' barely audible over the roaring wind. 'Are you going to be able to get me out?'

BELOW: Monte Frances, first climbed by Eric Shipton and John Earle.

BELOW: Southern Patagonia, Land of Tempest, where ice caps still linger from the last Ice Age. (Co stands for cerro, meaning a peak not rising above the permanent snowline.)

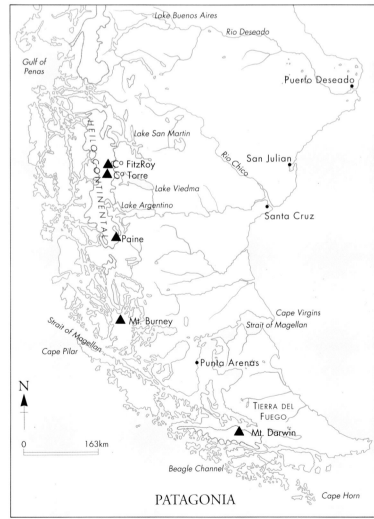

PATAGONIA

We did, but both he and I suffered mild frostbite that day in our toes and fingers. Reaching the calm of the Beagle Channel, we lit huge fires to warm and dry ourselves and to cook more *moules à la Beagle*. Again that great contentment flowed over us, engendered mainly by Eric's love of this desolate, wild but beautiful primeval land.

*

Eric Shipton never returned to Tierra del Fuego, but a few years later he climbed Mount Burney with an approach from the Chilean Channel to the west of the peak. We remained close friends until his death from cancer left me with a great gulf of grief and sadness. He had been, and still is, an inspiration for me. His sense of wonder and, as he put it, 'enchantment' never left him. The last paragraph of his autobiography sums up the unique quality of the man:

'The springs of enchantment lie within ourselves; they arise from our sense of wonder, that most precious of gifts, the birthright of every child. Lose it and life becomes flat and colourless; keep it and

*All experience is an arch wherethro'
Gleams that untravell'd World,
   whose margin fades
For ever and for ever when I move.'*

Alfred, Lord Tennyson, *Ulysses*

RIGHT: Earle and Shipton (seated) with Claudio Cortez on Frances ice cap, working towards Monte Bove, another first ascent.

BELOW: Eric Shipton was a dreamer of dreams, and at heart a poet. He died in 1977, but he has left us many books of his wide-ranging explorations, to be enjoyed for generations.

Adrian Burgess

Starving on Huascaran

We took a too-short look at the small photograph of the face, packed our gear and five day's food, and hitched a ride up the Llanganuco valley to begin the climb.

I arrived in Huaraz with a sprained thumb. Not the sort of thing to bother me normally, but I could barely hold an ice-axe and we were there to climb. I was annoyed with myself because it needn't have happened. We shouldn't have set up those two black market con-men, even if they were about to fleece us. And certainly, I didn't need to get into a skirmish with one of them once they knew the game was up – especially as the other had already escaped. The noise had drawn crowds from nearby offices and we'd had to pretend we were special police to effect our own escape. My only consolation in all this was that my brother's hand was as swollen as my own. Brian Hall simply looked at us and shook his head.

It was 1977 and we had just travelled overland from Buenos Aires. Brian had climbed Cerro Stanhardt with John Whittle, while my brother Al and I had picked off FitzRoy. John returned to the United Kingdom, satisfied; our friends Al Rouse and Rab Carrington were over in the Huayhuash, and we three settled on the Blanca. Maybe we were a little too laid back in those days: all I knew about the area was that Huascaran was the highest peak in Peru. That pretty Lima girls spent their summers in Huaraz we only discovered on arrival. . . .

We needed an objective. Something powerful. Something compelling. There wasn't a guidebook and so we began to ask around for ideas. An old copy of the French magazine *La Montagne* materialized, which carried a story about the first ascent of the North Face of Huascaran

BIOGRAPHY

'Twin terrors of the Himalaya', 'living legends on four continents', 'oddball luminaries of the brightest magnitude' – an American outdoors magazine wrestled to categorize the roistering Yorkshire-born Burgess twins. Adrian, 'Aid', is the half of the legend who now lives in the United States. In a career spanning several decades he has climbed around the world from Alaska to Patagonia, has summited Everest, been many times to the Himalaya in winter, and is an outspoken champion of the environment. In 1977, he took part in an extended 'Super Trip' to South America with Al Rouse and friends, of which the climb he describes here was one of the highlights.

Norte. As I'd once had a French girl-friend, it fell to me to make the translation.It didn't seem to matter that I had failed my O-level French. I managed a few words, but nothing that told me of the climb's real length and difficulty.

RIGHT: Huascaran (on the left, 22,205 ft) is the highest mountain of Peru. The author's ascent of the North Face of Huascaran Norte (right) took nine days, following the prominent ridge seen in the photograph.

The original idea had been Lionel Terray's. He was with a French national expedition which, failing to get a permit in the Himalaya, sought an objective elsewhere. They finally went to the North Face in 1966 as a team of over ten climbers, including such names as Paragot and Seigneur. After almost a month of fixing rope in Himalayan siege-style, they reached the summit, although sadly one member was killed during the descent. Since then, the mountain had not been climbed again.

We took a too-short look at the small photograph of the face, packed our gear and five day's food, and hitched a ride up the Llanganuco valley to begin the climb. The following day the three of us hiked up towards the foot of the face and camped beneath a rock-band, well out of the way of a nasty-looking glacier. From there we could observe the face at close quarters. It looked big – maybe five thousand vertical feet – especially when considering the altitude (over 21,800 feet at the summit). Not wanting to admit that we might have underestimated the

RIGHT: The Burgess brothers sheltering from the sun on a small ledge 1 x 2 m, the first bivvy on the Paragot route. Climbing was impossible after midday because the heat was too great.

RIGHT: Steep snow climbing had to be done early or late, when the surface was frozen solid.

BELOW: Day three: no protection on flutes of unconsolidated snow.

climb, we compromised by allowing we needed more time to acclimatize. This would leave us short on food, and so I returned to the valley to re-supply: we could then afford to wait a few days before setting off up the mountain. It was a cold, clear night when we strap-ped on crampons and climbed out onto the tottery icefall. At one point we reached an impasse which could only be solved by a tricky climb over a short ice-cliff. We certainly had no wish to descend that par-ticular section and felt all the more committed to our task.

The climbing was at once steep and technical. We followed steep flutings broken by crumbling rock bands until we emerged onto a pinnacled ridge. We had brought only one snow picket and so were faced with the frustrating decision: should the leader take it, or the second belay to it? That day seemed too short for the climbing we needed to perform. As dusk settled over the mountain we fumbled to set up our bivi on tiny ledges. 'Don't drop the boots, don't drop the boots', I re-minded myself, as fatigue weighted flick-ering eyelids.

The day had been a hard one and next morning we found ourselves so dehy-drated we decided to take a rest day. Thinking back, I can't believe we did that.

Of the hundred or more alpine climbs that I've done, before and since, I have never taken a day to rest, just got on with the climb, no matter what. So my conclu-sion has to be that we were really, really done in.

On the third day we climbed some steep ice around to the right of a buttress of friable rock. The climbing was both insecure and tiring, made worse by our sizeable packs. Then a couple of steep and unprotected ice pitches took us up towards a left-sloping ramp. When we began looking around for somewhere to sleep I thought we might have to spend the night on our feet. Then I spotted – off route to the right – a tiny patch of snow. Al and I burrowed into that while Brian lashed himself to the 45° slope.

LEFT: Morning on the final bivvy: from left, Huandoy, Santa Cruz, Quitaraju, Alpamayo, Artesonraju, Piramide, and, on the right, the twin peaks Chacraraju Oeste and Este.

BELOW: Day seven, and difficult mixed snow, ice and rock climbing. The impressive ice flutings, common to the Andes, are seen in the background. Similar flutes provided very difficult climbing on the route.

How we wished for a better stove. One that would turn out pints of hot soup and gallons of tea. That was a pipe dream: our one-pint Primus coughed out only enough heat to melt water for a cup of tea each. Our food was eaten cold.

Day five arrived and we were still only halfway up the climb. We followed old traces of a rotting white rope over rock bulges and into some open chimneys. When we spotted tiny rocky ledges, we decided to call it a day. Brian took one, Al another, and I stood, like a lemon, wondering what to do. Finally, I built my own ledge from slabs of rock perched one atop the other. It was two feet wide – luxury!

By Day six we were getting hungry. . . . As we belayed each other up some snowy corners, we'd urge each other on with calls of, 'We'll have a whole roast chicken when we get to Huaraz.' I didn't know how many days that would take, but I knew that chicken was important. It snowed that particular afternoon and we cut a good snow ledge while cloud swirled around us. Three tiny people, lost on a huge face.

Visibility was poor the next morning and Brian led out 300 feet of rope before he placed the picket. Another, steeper pitch of ice and the granite cliffs were blocking our way. This was the start of the famous traverse. Well, hardly famous exactly, but I remembered it was mentioned in the magazine. I commenced a series of rappels-cum-tension-traverses across to my left. Then it was more traversing obliquely left and up some rocky corners.

'Think of the chicken!' rang out across the wall. 'A whole one, and roasted, too!' As we climbed towards a steep rock corner the sky cleared and the horizon showed a sea of cloud with shark-tooth peaks floating among the billows. The ledges were small that night. I half-stood, sank, collapsed into my rucksack.

The hours dragged by – and cold they were, too. I dozed and dreamt of chicken, Peruvian girls and water. Maybe they were all on the same plate – I don't recall. . . . But the eighth day I remember clearly. Al led a hard rock pitch which eased into an easier gully. We all thought we had finally escaped – only to be disappointed. There was another hard rock section – including three pegs for aid – and then the ice wall. Looking suspiciously at Al's belay, I began to cut steps up hard ice. I should have been able to front-point it, but my legs were too wobbly and our nerves too strained. Gradually the angle eased and I sank into soft snow to belay the others. The climb was ours and we bivouacked immediately.

Day nine I awoke and vomited, in one and the same moment. Al's stern voice reminded me to survive: 'Get a grip lad.'

And we did.

Sean Smith

El Regallo de Mwoma

The wind howled past the Towers with the speed of an express train.
Whenever it gusted there was a crashing, ripping sound, as though the
very substance of the air was being rent by the gale.

Paul Pritchard, the 'Mr Bold' of Welsh rock climbing, had changed his spots. After an epic and disastrous first expedition to the Himalaya, he decided mountaineering was what he wanted to do. A winter in Scotland and a season in the Alps prepared him for another trip, and the granite walls of Patagonia seemed a worthy objective. He invited Noel Craine, Simon Yates and myself to accompany him. We made a well-balanced team, two mountaineers and two rock climbers. Simon and I (the mountaineers) would show the others how to dig snowholes, zip up cagoules and perform sundry mountaineering-type tasks. They (hopefully) would teach us how to inch our way up acres of vertical granite. It seemed to work. We dug a snowhole at the foot of the wall and after four weeks had fixed nearly eight hundred metres of rope on the East Face of the Central Tower of Paine.

Only Noel had climbed a Big Wall before, and all he would say was that El Cap was 'a picnic compared to this'. The rest of us were newcomers to jumaring, sac-hauling and the like, and were finding it hard, both mentally and physically. Still, we'd made good progress and our confidence was high. Operating as two pairs, and climbing in shifts, helped us maximize the brief periods of good weather in a Patagonian summer. Now, in the first week of January, the four of us had teamed up and were bivouacked on a tiny ledge some 250 metres below the summit. We hoped to top out the following day.

Watching the evening clouds gather I thought back over the past weeks, of all

BIOGRAPHY

By the early 1990s, Sean Smith had been climbing for over a decade. He was one of the first 'Alpine Binmen', a group of mainly Sheffield climbers who took on a cleaning contract in Chamonix, and the apartment that went with it, to give them the freedom to climb and ski in the Alps the year round. Now most of his time is taken up on expeditions further afield – Nanga Parbat's fearsome Mazeno ridge, Patagonia, the Tien Shan mountains. Based in London, Sean works as a freelance photographer. A portfolio of his Tibet photographs have been used to illustrate a book of poems by Kathleen Jamie.

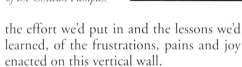

RIGHT: On a rare sunlit morning, the Towers of Paine, at the head of the Ascencio Valley, rise dramatically from the surrounding grasslands of the Chilean Pampas.

the effort we'd put in and the lessons we'd learned, of the frustrations, pains and joy enacted on this vertical wall.

*

During that period, although our progress had been relatively rapid, the climbing itself was slow and nerve-racking. Originally we had hoped to free climb much of the route, but cold, wind and rain precluded any chance of that. We'd had to resort to sustained aid climbing techniques, and were pleased if we led two pitches a day.

Hanging on tied-off pegs and leap-frogging RP's up icy cracks and dodgy flakes was a new game for me. There was a lot of fear and a lot of adrenalin. We were all pushing ourselves hard and our absorption in the climb was total. We all took big falls.

Noel led the crux pitch, and led it carefully. This was one place he couldn't afford to fall. Working slowly, he engineered RPs, knifeblades and rurps up a thin crumbling seam, then around a ten metre Damoclean flake. He graded the pitch A4.

While this was the only pitch of that grade, the climb as a whole was still very sustained. It followed a thin crack system in the vertical pillar separating the German and South African routes, and most of the 38 pitches were A2 or harder.

Although this was the steepest, blankest section of the East Face, the crack line was just about continuous and we never needed to place any bolts. Bolts – other people's, that is – became a bit of a sticky issue on this climb. We had brought two of our own from England in case we needed to establish a portaledge camp. However, as it transpired, where we had our ledge camp was already equipped with about a dozen bolts and a mass of other gear. The presence of all this paraphernalia (transistor radio, Himalayan overboots, etc) seemed to underline a profound difference in attitude between ourselves and our predecessors.

Our ideal was to try a major, difficult new line and climb it as cleanly as possible. Although we decided to fix ropes on this climb – realizing the impossibility of trying such a thing 'Alpine style', and acknowledging the commitment involved in a 'capsule' ascent on a wall of this steepness, especially with the Patagonian weather – inherent in that decision was the need to descend the line of ascent and clean the ropes after the climbing was finished. This was a feeling we all shared. To be on a technical and serious new climb didn't give us carte blanche to leave what is essentially litter scattered over a mountain. To do so seemed to us illustrative of a basic lack of respect and sensitivity for an increasingly beleaguered and fragile environment.

The line we were on had already suffered in this way. It had been attempted on two separate expeditions by a Spanish team who had climbed the bottom (easiest) third of the wall before retreating. This section was peppered with unnecessary bolts and pegs and hung with tattered

LEFT: The East Face of the Central Tower is one of the most impressive rock walls in the world. Its 1,200-m high sweep of granite offers a variety of lines for 'big wall' climbers. El Regallo de Mwoma follows a thin crack line splitting the slender pillar that directly faces the camera.

127

remnants of fixed rope. The mess incensed us, and to make matters worse, we later heard a rumour that these climbers had broadcast a television film in Spain showing that they had finished the climb and reached the top of the Central Tower, when in fact they had dumped all this gear at their high point, intending to come back and try again.

Mind you, failure is not uncommon in Patagonia. Since its first ascent in 1963, the Central Tower has only been climbed a handful of times. Most expeditions have been thwarted by the typically atrocious weather.

The same thing was to happen to us on our first attempt.

＊

While I'd been day-dreaming, the clouds had crept closer. During the night they enveloped the Tower.

Next morning, leaving the top bivouac, the four of us were jumaring through waterfalls. Everything was soaked, the rock was streaming with water and freezing rain beat hard against our faces. The wind howled past the Towers with the speed of an express train. Whenever it gusted there was a crashing, ripping sound, as though the very substance of the air was being rent by the gale. Leading difficult aid climbing in these conditions was an impossible task. Wet through and without food and gas, descent was our only option. We embraced it with a vengeance: that night we were at the estancia and the next in Puerto Natales. Our friends in town said it was the worst storm in years.

Four days later Paul and I were back on the wall. We'd left camp quickly and in relative silence, battling with our individual doubts. If nothing else, we would at least bring down the equipment from our climb. The memory of our retreat was still fresh in our minds. Jumaring back up to the ledges we looked for damage to the ropes caused by the storm. They seemed okay.

Night was falling as we reached the portaledges. We drank tea and cat-napped standing up. Quietly we packed food and bivvy gear. An unspoken resolve had formed: we would climb until we were turned back.

At 1 a.m. we began to jumar. Climbing through the night was almost hallucinatory. The stars glinted with a cold brightness and

ABOVE: Paul Pritchard jumaring fixed ropes to the bivvy ledge on the upper section of the wall during the climbers' first attempt on the summit. Below him the face drops away to the glacier, some 900 m below.

RIGHT: Paul Pritchard again, leading one of the harder aid pitches on friable grey granite in the central, steepest section of the climb. Sustained and overhanging, the thin cracks ascended in this part of the climb formed the crux of the route.

FAR RIGHT: Simon Yates leading into a feature the team named 'the coffin'. This pitch was about half-way up the climb, just past the overhanging crux section, and was climbed on one of their rare sunny days. In the distance is one of the peaks of the Cuernos group of mountains.

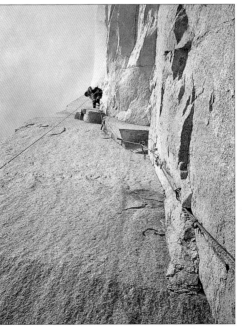

the Tower's presence was only betrayed by an inky shadow. Minute on the surface of this darker darkness, Paul and I progressed upwards like two clockwork spiders.

The ground retreated invisibly, and shortly after daybreak we had reached the upper bivouac ledge. After a brief rest we continued to our high point, where we untangled ropes and sorted the rack. Paul led a long aid pitch which brought us to easier-angled mixed ground. Several pitches of rock and ice decorated with German fixed rope now led to the foot of the seven-metre summit block.

Without realizing it, we had been climbing all day. The weather had become increasingly unsettled and the wind was blowing with hurricane force. Coming from the ice-cap to the west, it was bitingly cold.

Tired, and unprepared for this gale, we had no choice. We decided to begin our descent on the relatively sheltered east side, stripping the ropes as we went. There just wasn't time to wrestle with this final ice-encrusted obelisk.

Working quickly, we arrived at the top bivouac by nightfall and settled down to a much needed sleep. Continuing the descent the next day was a nightmare. The howling gale was still in force, and cleaning the route became increasingly frustrating. The air was malevolence itself. Updrafts and eddies would blow the ropes in all directions until they invariably stuck. On several occasions we had to resort to the knife.

Surprisingly, though, I was getting used to this vertical world. I had simply adjusted to being a point on a line, capable only of one-dimensional movement. But it was still infuriating, watching a snarl-up ten metres away, and being unable to intervene.

The abseiling became exhausting, swinging around with bivvy gear, several hundred metres of rope and a massive rack. It took eight hours to clean down to the portaledges which, if we'd just abbed the ropes, would have been a quick and simple rappel of an hour or two at most. But it had to be done.

Darkness was approaching as we reached the ledges. Swiftly, we scuttled back to base camp. Paul and I would return and collect the gear in a few days time. First we needed a rest. . . .

*

For several days after the climb I felt subdued, humbled, as though I'd been allowed entry to a special place where I didn't really belong. Paul described a similar feeling. It was as if we had been granted some strange momentary identification with the element of chance, and we acknowledged this in our route name. Translated from the Spanish, it means 'The Gift of Mwoma', the Tehuelche (Indian) god of the mountains who, in their extinct mythology, lived among the mountain towers of Paine.

Roger Mear

After Dark

'Out of Chaos, the void from which all things arose, there issued Erebus,

the darkness, and his sister Nyx, black night. From their incestuous

union were born Aether, the pure air, and the brightness of Day.'

BELOW: Mount Erebus and pressure ice, Ross Island, photographed during the Footsteps of Scott expedition.

Theoretically, on the 23rd April, the sun at its zenith should have been about half a degree above the horizon. At a little before noon the northern sky reddened and slowly, imperceptibly sunrise turned to sunset without the sun's warm red disk ever becoming visible above the black silhouette of the ice cliffs. There followed days of failing twilight until there was only a faint reminder of the sun's existence, a band of red-grey sky on the northern horizon, so unremarkable that it did not even provide an incentive to gaze out of the ice-framed windows of the hut.

By the beginning of June, Cape Evans had been enveloped in darkness for nearly a month. Against the black volcanic sand of the beach lapped a frozen tide; angular plates of ice were heaped in disarray on the shore. Antarctica had turned its face from the sun towards the black emptiness of space, and was held by a cold so profound that it seemed that beyond the perimeter of the hut's yellow light, time and all existence must cease. The hut had become a besieged oasis of warmth on the edge of a continent that in winter is again, as it always was, incognito, unknown and unexperienced.

By the standards of modern mountaineering, an ascent of Mount Erebus is little more than a walk, but in the darkness of winter it would be a walk into an alien world, where the only warmth would be that of my body and the only movement the wind and the slow rotation of the stars and moon. A world where the steel air is too cold for snow to fall or for clouds to form. The temperature that

BIOGRAPHY

Born in 1950, Roger Mear has a degree in Fine Art. In his climbing he has shown a predisposition for cold ascents. He scaled the Eigerwand in winter, and made the first winter ascent of McKinley's Cassin Ridge in temperatures that fell to 60° C below zero (-76° F).

He has worked with the British Antarctic Survey in Grahamland, and in 1985 walked to the South Pole in the footsteps of Scott. (His book of that adventure, In the Footsteps of Scott, *written with Robert Swan, won the Boardman-Tasker Award for 1987.)*

In 1991, with Dave Walsh, he made the first British ascent of Nanga Parbat; this was a summer, lightweight climb of the Kinshofer route on the Diamir Face, with its direct finish, taking eight days up and down. More recently Mear has been guiding in Antarctica with Doug Scott and Sharu Prabhu.

morning had been -30° C (-22° F). The summit of Erebus 12,448 feet above us would be as much as 30° C colder (-76° F).

The volcano was first sighted by Sir James Clark Ross in 1841 and named by him for his ship, Mount Erebus. In 1908 men from Ernest Shackleton's expedition clambered up and down the mountain during six March days; the ascent was repeated by a party from Captain Scott's expedition in December 1912.

As with those of the heroic age, ours was an expedition with grander ambitions than the summit of Erebus, but I wanted something for myself, an experience that I did not have to share, to dilute with anyone. I wanted a jewel to carry away uncut, for me, miserly to turn and polish. I wanted a communion with the landscape that was uninterrupted by other perceptions. I wanted to experience the hard cold infinity of Antarctica.

In the darkness the desire germinated, but I found it hard to leave the warmth and security of the hut, afraid of the forces that I had seen playing on the Cape. I waited for the feeling that said it was right to go, until there was no reason for hesitation. Then

one fine day turned into three and then a fourth, cold always cold, but colder and clear. The air streaming unusually from the north, a steady current flowing across the polished back of the glacier. A wind, that seemed dependable, not suspiciously still, tempting, playing the trick, the calm before the tempest that would come, roaring, thick with drift to obscure the sky, rattling the hut, blasting its walls with black grit torn from the Cape. It was time to make the decision and go.

Mike cooked a breakfast for the two of us, using my departure for Erebus as an excuse for indulgence. Gammon steaks, tinned tomatoes, slices of home-baked bread, toasted with fork and fire and spread thickly with butter, and eggs, fried eggs. These were amongst the last of several hundred brought from New Zealand almost four months since, and we took the precaution of immersing them in water, to test if they were good or bad, before cracking the shells.

We left the hut together at 4.30 p.m., Mike accompanying me to the glacier's edge. I had informed him of my plans without

offering him the option of joining the adventure, and he was disappointed. We could see only blackness as we emerged from the shell of light that surrounded the base. Then, as our eyes became accustomed, the Cape revealed itself enchanted under the light of a full moon. From the beach we made our way over and around the humps and bumps of the lava beds, in and out of the contorted rocks, our boots crunching on the pea-like gravel, or squeaking as the rubber made its imprint on the chalk-hard and faintly luminous snow that hid in every lee.

We descended slightly to the flat alluvial bed of Skua Lake. In February, when we had first landed at Cape Evans, it had been a shallow ice-covered pan edged with bright green algae. Now the lake was a solid transparent lens 50 yards across, shrunken from the edges of its hollow. To follow this route in summer meant running the gauntlet of angry skuas, a bedlam of screeches, gaping beaks and aerial attacks. Now there was only silence.

Mike scurried on ahead as we began to climb the steep embankment of loose moraine that divides Cape Evans from the Barne Glacier. I felt clumsy and unfit after weeks of inactivity, and would soon have begun to sweat if I had attempted to keep the pace he was setting – and the sweat would freeze in my clothing, allowing cold to creep jealously into the warmth that was an aberration in this land.

He was waiting for me on the level ground beyond the rise, where the boulders gave way to burnished ice. It was as if he stood on the shore's edge, unable to go any further without trespassing upon my private adventure. He wished me well and returned to the hut.

I began to walk, in awe of the wondrous moonlit landscape and the uniqueness of the experience that lay before me. No one had ever climbed an Antarctic mountain in the dark of winter.

From the rocks of Cape Evans the glacier rose gently toward the shallow re-entrant at the head of which stood William's Cliff. For several hours I made my way towards this shadowed crag, surveying the ground ahead with manic intensity, left and right, perceiving in the half-light all sorts of phantom signs that said 'Crevasse!' We had all of us crossed this glacier on more than one occasion, and always unroped. Yet now, despite what reason said, my fears loomed large.

I arrive at William's Cliff feeling very tired at 11.30 p.m. In a shallow scoop that curved around the base of a small buttress of broken rocks, I hacked at the ice with my axe to cut a bed that would not cause me to toboggan in my sleeping bag, back down the slope to the crevasses on the glacier.

Spread out below was a luminous achromatic world, leached of the hard reality of dazzling snows and ink-black shadows that the sun would bring. Across the frozen waters of McMurdo Sound rose the incorporeal summits of the Royal Society Range, for in the silver half-light the air seemed as substantial as the mountains. The floating ice tongue of the Erebus Glacier stretching into the sound was visible only by the bright band of ice cliffs that weave in a florid wave along its seven-mile length. In each bay the cliffs shrink in height to insignificance, punctuating the edge into a line of silver hyphens. Beyond this, Hut Point Peninsula, limiting my southern horizon, shone like bone in the light of a full moon that now circled high to the north.

I slept warm and comfortable, without interruption, until just before 8 a.m. The only token of a new day was the moon's

changed position, now a little lower in the sky and to the south of Mount Discovery. After a breakfast of hot chocolate, Alpen and soup, prepared and eaten with little more than a hand escaping from the sleeping bag, I dressed, still inside the bag, and then grudgingly left its warmth to pack. The thermometer read -32° C (-26° F), and the cold was no small incentive to begin moving. Teetering upon crampon points I crossed to the base of an icy ramp and began to climb. Emerging through broken rocks I found myself on a level summit scattered with isolated tors. From here the glacier forms a broad saddle, descending slightly to a point midway between William's Cliff and the sudden steep rise of Erebus. It was 12.30 p.m. by the time I had trudged the three miles to the base of the mountain and drawn level with the Three Sisters, volcanic cones that protrude mysteriously from the ice like Neolithic barrows. It was -39° C (-38° F) with a light wind blowing from the south, blowing from the interior of a lifeless continent.

It was easier to relax now that I had gained the snowfields of Mount Erebus, with the glacier and the constant worry of hidden crevasses behind me. I continued climbing until 5.30 in the evening when I arrived at the rocky niche we called the

LEFT AND ABOVE: Mike Stroud on the slopes of Erebus on Ross Island with the Erebus glacier in the background. Erebus was first climbed in 1908 by members of Shackleton's Antarctic expedition.

Pulpit. As the moon slid behind the mountain I unrolled my sleeping bag and contentedly prepared myself for another comfortable night.

My complacency evaporated as I was sharply reminded of the vulnerability of my position. The mattress was punctured. Examination revealed a small angular tear, perhaps caused by a crampon point. I attempted a repair with an adhesive patch, but despite warming it on the flame of a cigarette lighter the glue would not stick. I tried to restore the necessary insulation by spreading my rucksack, jacket and down salopette under the deflated mat, but it was not enough to keep out the incipient cold. I curled, shivering, with my knees pulled to my chest. Yet it was not the prospect of a few nights' discomfort that alarmed me, but the knowledge that it would now be difficult to survive a bivouac of any duration if a blizzard should pin me down.

The stove spluttered and its blue light died, leaving the fragments of chipped ice unmelted in the pot. Without a functioning stove I would have no option but to retreat. Dismantled, cleaned and reassembled, it purred once more as I warmed my fingers in its flame. After a cup of hot chocolate the world seemed less threatening. I lay on my back gazing up at the 5,000 feet of Erebus that had eclipsed the moon. It was unbelievably cold, much colder than the -39° C displayed on the thermometer, and the higher I climbed the colder it would become. I wavered, undecided – up or down?

Was it coincidence that the moon's disappearance had brought so many doubts? The weather was as fine as could be wished, not a trace of cloud in any direction. Mount Discovery and the mountains of the Scott Coast all seemed without substance. To the south, the Great Ice Barrier, a plain of unimaginable size, stretched in interminable flatness, unbroken and devoid of any feature that could give sense to the scale of its barrenness. To the north the sea was frozen beyond the horizon, for 200 miles, and this more than anything expressed the utter isolation of the land. Deprived of sleep I watched the moon's glow progress from south to north behind the dark silhouette of the volcano, and reasoned that by midnight it would begin again to cast its light upon the face. What point was there, I reasoned, in staying here until convention said it was morning? At midnight I began to drink and eat, before packing and making ready to go.

I took a line up snowfields left of a rib of volcanic lava, sidestepping upwards in a succession of tacks, first left, then right, then left again. For 5,000 feet I climbed, avoiding where possible outcrops of rock and bare ice and keeping to the chalk-hard snows that predominated. In places, great plaques of snow, a remnant of a newer, softer layer that had been eroded by the wind, stood proud of the underlying surface. These had to be negotiated with care. Often they would fracture underfoot, and lumps of the slab would slide back down the slope into the gloom beyond.

Soon I reached the final steepening below the rim of the old crater. Here, at the line between moonshine and moonshadow, I had a square of chocolate and a rest before embarking upon the slope. In the darkness this short climb was intimidating. The ice was marble hard and the points of my crampons skittered ineffectually on its surface. After so many months living at sea level my breathing at this altitude was heavy and laboured, and despite the cold I was soon sweating, unable to pause with such precarious footing. At last the slope relented and I emerged from the shadow on to the great flat expanse inside the ring of the outer crater. The ground was littered with large felspar crystals and blocks of pumice into which the points of the crampons sank. The pointed summit cone was still a mile distant, and between me and it loomed several ghostly towers, scattered indiscriminately across the plateau. These polymorphous growths, some of which were 20 feet in height, were the ice-encrusted vents of fumaroles. Clouds of vapour billowed from their bulbous tops.

It took another hour to reach the summit and I did not stay there long. Although there was only the slightest breeze my hands quickly began to freeze. I stood on the lip of the crater and gazed down into its black depths. Foetid, sulphurous fumes grabbed the breath. Enormous silvery boils of cloud filled the chasm and drifted in majestically slow rises out above my head. Thinner tears of yellow-tainted vapour were pulled by swift currents up the vertical inner walls and over the rim. Nine hundred feet below in that mist-obscured cauldron glowed an iron-red heart, and when for a moment the air cleared, I saw rents of soft orange heat. It seemed strange that the temperature at the summit was the same as it had been at the bottom of the mountain, -39° C.

I raced back along the narrow ridge that divides the active and dormant craters of the summit cone, and with plunging steps leapt down loose scree into the breach in its northern face and out of the wind. Somewhere directly below me was the wooden cabin once used by parties from McMurdo as a base for studies of the crater, but now abandoned due to increased volcanic activity. It was with relief that I realized the vague shadowy block to which I walked was indeed the hut. I had never been confident of finding it in the dark. As I dug my way into the drift I uncovered a notice on the door which said, 'This is definitely a hard hat area'. I pondered what I would do if Erebus erupted now.

The temperature inside the hut was also -39° C. (Later I discovered that mercury freezes at this temperature.) I lit a candle and soon had the stove purring. After about an hour the temperature rose to -28° C (-18° F). Water vapour rising from the pot of melting ice froze before it reached the ceiling, falling as minute particles that covered every surface as if dusted with icing sugar. On a shelf in one corner was a bottle of Glenlivet buttressed by its own little snowdrifts. Imprisoned behind the

green glass was a frozen block of Scotch that rattled but would not pour. I was affected by the altitude to a far greater extent than I had expected. The simple task of unlacing a boot left me breathless. I had no desire to eat and watched the noodles I had cooked freeze in the pan. I forced myself to drink, feeling weak and queasy. It is well known that the relatively low barometric pressure near to the Poles markedly increases the effect of altitude. Though I was no more than 12,000 feet above the sea, it felt as if I had rushed to a far greater height.

I decided to descend without delay. In all probability my recovery would be swift as I lost height, and I knew that the period of peace in which I had snatched the ascent would not last. When the winds returned there would be nowhere to hide on the 13 miles of polished ice and blasted rocks that lay between the summit of Erebus and our hut at Cape Evans.

As I strode out across the mile of gentle slope towards the rim of the old crater, the moon cast before me a deep shadow of my rucksack-laden form. The air was absolutely still. It was as if the cold had frozen time. Nothing moved, nothing changed, nothing lived. I felt like a phantom, my passage as insubstantial as my shadow, viewing the world as in a dream. I reached the rim and plunged into the shadow of the mountain. The ground fell away, to slide out of the shade 8,000 feet below, as a moonlit glacier. Zig-zag, zig-zag, down, down, down, over ribs of rock

ABOVE: Erebus sporting a volcanic plume. In 1912, a climbing party from Scott's last expedition were driven from the summit by a minor eruption.

RIGHT: Erebus and Scott's Hut at Cape Evans.

and sheets of ice, seeking out the soft layer of snow I had avoided on the ascent, because it cushioned my plunging steps. I kept pace with fractured slabs that my heels dislodged. Down, past the Pulpit, where twenty-four hours before I had bivouacked. Down, the last steep slope of snow, the Three Sisters coming up to meet me, and then I was below the tops of their pointed cones and walking out across the level ice into the moonlight with the dark face of Erebus behind.

Five hours after leaving the summit hut I reached the top of William's Cliff and traversed around its northern side. On the crest the scalloped ice was scattered with fist-sized rocks, blasted from the crag by the wind. What was it like here when the tranquillity was shattered by a roaring stream of air? An icy whaleback laced with chalky ribbons of snow-capped crevasses led steeply down to the Barne Glacier. Stretched out below me were the six miles I hated most, the spread of ice cut by crevasses that had to be crossed. I knew that no matter how carefully I probed each crevasse bridge the step from ice to hollow lid always filled me with fear. In the milli-second when the first footfall found only empty air you would know and, faster than the body could react, you would be gone. There were perhaps a hundred crevasses between here and Cape Evans, some only a foot or two in width, others 15 feet across. Sometimes, where the ice was bare of snow, they were as proud as scars on suntanned skin, but in the gentle hollows of the glacier, where a sastrugied crust of snow had formed, they were hidden.

I was tired now. Cape Evans was close, and although it was a rule I did not like to break, I pushed on into fatigue. Running on empty is a game I have often played, but not here, where inactivity all too quickly brings frostbite and exhaustion, hypothermia and death.

Ahead, the summit of Inaccessible Island rose and fell beyond my horizon as I walked the rolling undulations of the glacier. During those last hours, I saw in the silver light some vivid illusions. Perhaps it was the fatigue, but more probably the eye's need to make sense out of its deprivation. I saw, even though I knew it could not be, a scattering of black rocks on the bare ice, and then as I gazed more intently, they rose and flew, turning this way and that, like a flock of autumn starlings. Twice I saw in the separated red and green of a 3-D movie, people at a distance of 400 yards. Two figures suddenly multiplied into a group of fifteen or more, shuffling in line and each carrying a pike or perhaps a placard which made them reminiscent of delegates at an American political convention. But there was no one. Once I came upon something so beautiful I had to stop, and sank to the snow to watch it play. From the shadow, beneath the cornice of a low sastrugi, emanated a small mandala of pointillist light, viridian and orange. It hovered like a timid pet, and even when I broke the concentration and looked away it reappeared.

In the last painful mile of jarring ice the black moraines of Cape Evans came into view. I tried not to want their arrival too much and make the last moments interminable. Then, crossing the last crevasse, reaching the first rocks and knowing the journey was safely done, I was flooded with the friendliness of the Cape. Though it is a barren piece of ground, it is claimed by men, it is known, it has a history and all its parts are named.

Relieved of care, my energy fled and the pain of feet flayed by 13 miles and 12,000 feet of cramponed descent surged forth. I stumbled through the rocks and crusted snow to the flat gravel bed of Skua Lake. The hut did not appear until I rounded the last hillock above the beach. A warm yellow light fell from the windows. I dropped my sack in the pitch-black porch and, still wearing crampons, stepped into our warm and pleasantly grubby home. Mike had risen especially and made tea. I sat down as I was, stripping off ice-encrusted layers as I became warm.

A little over eight hours ago I had been on the top of Erebus; in another eight hours, when I woke from sleep, the experience would be a memory. Gareth, Robert and John were still at the American research station at McMurdo. If Mike had been with them and not at Cape Evans, no one would have known that my climb was not a dream, least of all me. Other people assure us, as we assure them, that because the experiences we share are not contradictory they are real. On Erebus how could I tell?

Greg Mortimer

Jousting at Icebergs

I felt more joy on this summit than on any other, and that joy came from a luxurious sense of isolation. What a treasure. What happens when these opportunities for isolation are gone I wonder. Whither will we wander?

The best I could do was to hang on to the cold metal wheel and hold it straight while the fluorescent flashes went whizzing past the sides of the boat. The harder I looked into the black of the night, the denser it seemed to be. The battle was constant but the conditions changed every few minutes when there was an overwhelming sense of speed as we dropped like an arrow through the night, surfing down the front of the 20-metre swell. At the bottom of each trough of water the nose of the boat pitched up into the air, but I could only gauge a change of speed by the slowing of the phosphorescent squid. Below decks the others slept soundly, oblivious of my struggle to stave off the feeling of vertigo in the blackness.

Even after three weeks at sea my stomach still churned like a viscous bubbling pot. But poor Lyle – from the minute we had turned right out of the haven of Sydney Harbour and headed into this daunting mass of water he had been violently ill. Somehow he was surviving, on a diet of intravenous maxilon and sleep.

I had learnt from the outset that it doesn't do to have a sense of urgency when travelling in a 20-metre yacht. There is only a narrow window of five or six weeks each summer when a little boat like ours might safely travel through the pack-ice and return before the sea freezes over. We didn't really know if a yacht could get safely through the pack-ice at the mouth of the Ross Sea, but, then again, the lure of Antarctica and entire mountain ranges where the highest peaks are unclimbed, is pretty strong. We had

BIOGRAPHY

Greg Mortimer, from Sydney, is a geologist whose work has taken him to many of the world's remote places. He has made difficult climbs in Australia, New Zealand, Africa, Britain and Europe, the Himalaya and North and South America. Particularly impressive have been ascents of Yerupaja and Piramide in Peru, Mount Kenya's Diamond Couloir, and the South Spur of Annapurna.

In 1984 he was one of the five-man team attempting a hard new route on the avalanche-swept north face of Everest and, climbing alpine style, reached the summit with Tim Macartney-Snape. He added the world's second-highest summit in 1991, when with Greg Child and Steve Swenson he reached the top of K2 by its north ridge. The ascent of Antarctica's Mount Minto, described here, took place in February 1988, in the Antarctic summer.

left Sydney two weeks late, because of gear-box trouble, so from the outset we were racing against the clock.

After two and a half slow weeks we entered the latitudes nick-named the 'Furious Fifties', but even the fire in the engine room did not blow away the last of our impatience. It was on a calm, overcast Southern Ocean evening. Jonathan was on watch while the other ten of us crammed into the tiny galley. Flames, flames on a grey sky over a grey sea, leapt from the engine room. Then a grizzled flash as Colin Putt – engineer, member of Mensa, mate of Bill Tilman – darted his 57-year-old frame into the red heat. More than any of us, he knew the danger. Two minutes later, flushed with success and fear, he emerged on to the steel deck. We stood in the damp air, mouths gaping as he described how close the fire had come to the fuel lines. Staring blankly into the fog, or quietly looking into each other eyes, we realized, in unison, how very vulnerable we were. From that point our intricate plans fumbled along on a slow

BELOW: Mount Minto from the Man o' War Glacier.

wave of hope until we reached the mouth of the Ross Sea, where a thin belt of pack-ice, some 5 kilometres wide, barred our way. Skipper Don gently danced the boat through the tight, white maze until, at the southern side, with open water in view only a few hundred metres away, the ice closed behind us and we were stuck. Lyle thought being held tight in the ice was great. For the first time in a month he could stay out on deck without vomit-ing. But for me it was a nameless dread. Directing Don from the crows-nest I had pushed the boat too hard, had been too ambi-tious, in too much of a hurry. Now we waited, expecting to be squashed like a pip.

Thirty-six sleepless hours later we had a stroke of luck with a change in the wind. We are set free to sail on to the Antarctic coastline. From Cape Adare, that lonely finger of rock warning of Antarctica's harshness, we glide down the side of the Trans-Antarctic mountains to the inviting mouth of Mowbray Bay. We turn towards the tonsils through a line of huge white teeth and are welcomed into the back of the bay by golden puffs of spray

from a dozen whales who are cruising for dinner in the rich evening light. The backdrop is the white walls of the mountains dominated by the immense East Face of Mount Herschel which roars out of the sea to 3,500 metres.

At the back of the bay the 15 kilometre-long Edisto Inlet is locked with sea-ice. Eighteen hours later we are leaving the relative safety of the yacht, laden with 1,000 kilogrammes of food, film and fantasy, towed by a puffing motor toboggan. For three days we shuffle and grunt to the top of Football Saddle, overlooking the mighty Tucker Glacier; 120 kilometres long and 15 kilometres wide. It is our highway up to Mount Minto.

At the saddle, Jonathan and Chris head back towards the ship to pick up more fuel for our overladen mechanical monster. The plan is for them to travel quickly, unladen and to return the following day. But out on the sea-ice they stumble into a catastrophic display of natural power as ice breaks out of the inlet and in 24 hours, 150 square kilometres of ice moves out to sea like a gigantic floating jigsaw puzzle. A small piece of ice has them on board and they are plucked from it as they float towards oblivion by Pete and Ken in the ship's inflatable. Our skidoo then sinks in 200 fathoms of cold blue.

What follows is best described as a frank and open discussion of our altered circumstances. To walk or not to walk? Fifteen kilometres per day, 100 kilogrammes per person. It didn't sound too much, but it meant a race against the clock. Lose the race and we would be locked in for one year by winter's mandatory

sentence with the freezing of the sea. We hadn't wanted to man-haul; after all, we had been weaned on the grim stories of Shackleton, Mawson and Scott. Once we made the decision to walk and took those very first steps up the Tucker, it seemed like we were carrying the burden of their legacy. What a vile form of human endeavour. Our bodies craved calories so that five or six thousand a day barely seemed enough.

Our daily bite at the distance was a different matter, seeming puny against the volume of the Tucker Glacier. Morning after morning I would step into the shackles of the man-hauling harness hoping that it would be an easier day, only to be disappointed after a few hundred metres. I would set my sights on a prominent ridge thinking we could reach it by lunchtime, but inevitably it would take a full day.

But, great God, it is a beautiful place! Such a massive, lonely land with little variation in colour, no smells, no sound and once you get about 20 kilometres inland, it is devoid of life. You would think that your senses of smell, hearing and colour might be deadened by this deprivation, but they are vigorously enlivened. You feel Antarctica's raw and cutting edge which leaves one thinking that any minor mistake would be treated with disgust by the forces that drive the land.

The further we plugged up the Tucker, the lighter our loads became because we left a cache of food and fuel every two days for the return trip, but the elastic band that connected us to the relative safety of the shore became tighter.

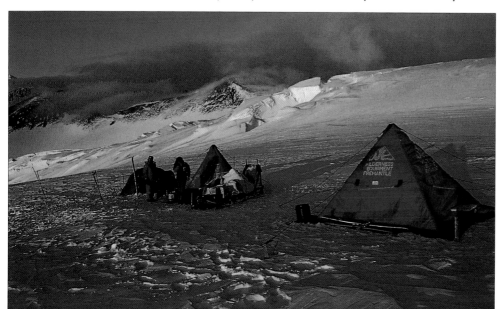

Eighty kilometres inland, we turned right into the Man o' War. I felt like we were reliving the emotions that the first expedition into Everest's Western Cwm must have felt, because the end of the glacier is a cirque of unclimbed rock spires and ridges and beyond them are the curving ridges of Mount Minto. Who had set foot on this glacier before? Probably no one.

We crossed a pass and set up a camp at the foot of the southeast ridge on the névé of the Ironside Glacier. We were down to bare bones with two tents, a packful of gear each, five days' food and a couple of pairs of skis. Five days was all we could allow for this push if we wanted to get home this year: summertime was ticking away. Lincoln would miss the birth of his first child, it could cost us a small fortune to get a boat back the following year to pick us up. I didn't mind so much and the thought surprised me. I felt quite at peace in the ice desert and there was a budding romance with Margaret, the expedition cook.

Two days later we left our cramped nylon havens and beat a way to the bottom of the southeast ridge. The previous morning was thwarted by a vicious ground storm that left us dispirited, but today felt like a summit day. It was clear and cold with a nasty wind off the polar plateau; so cold and clean that the air seemed to crackle.

ABOVE: Sledging down Tucker Glacier.

LEFT: Chris Hilton leaping from floe to floe, trying to find a way back to the ship.

BELOW: Moubray Bay.

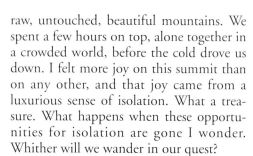

ABOVE RIGHT: On the summit of Mount Minto, where it is -60° C (-76° F), with wind chill.

ABOVE: The constant freezing conditions of the region have created a beautiful, dramatic landscape.

LEFT: Tracks in the soft snow of Man o' War Glacier.

raw, untouched, beautiful mountains. We spent a few hours on top, alone together in a crowded world, before the cold drove us down. I felt more joy on this summit than on any other, and that joy came from a luxurious sense of isolation. What a treasure. What happens when these opportunities for isolation are gone I wonder. Whither will we wander in our quest?

When our feet touched the cold steel of the ship's deck five days later the anchor was lifted immediately and we turned for home. In the previous few days the first fragile panes of ice on the sea had hinted at the start of the winter freeze. This had sent a wave of distress through our beleaguered captain and he called on a Greenpeace ship that was luckily passing by at the time. Greenpeace sent their helicopter into the lower reaches of the Tucker Glacier to collect us.

Back on board the six of us went below and slept. Glenn, the expedition doctor and cameraman, had come down from the mountain with a frostbitten big toe but had somehow managed to ski 120 kilometres back to the lower Tucker Glacier. When we woke two days later we were in the midst of a Force 11 gale. For five days we sat at the mouth of the Ross Sea, dodging bergs, unable to put up any sail or to motor out of the storm. We were totally at the mercy of the storm. In the middle of the third night, while everyone was asleep except for the one person on watch, the insides of the boat exploded.

Each person was spat from their bunk, the timber floors blew out, and flying tin cans filled the air. The tip of the mast dipped 15° below the waterline. We know it was 15° because that was the trajectory of the batteries as they broke loose from their mounts and smashed into the electrical instruments on the far side of the engine room. The galley was a vile mess. No sooner had we recovered and cleaned up the chaos then it happened again. Twice we had been knocked down in the one night, presumably by rolling off the top of big waves, but we had survived and the hull had stood the strain.

In the middle of the following day as the storm was abating, our attempts to sleep were broken by a cry from Pete warning that a huge tabular Ross Sea berg was appearing out of the fog on our lee side. Out on decks we all worked in a frenzy trying to free the ice-encrusted halyards. The sails were brittle from days of storm seas and we stood in chest-deep freezing water as waves

The climbing was technically easy but it was wickedly cold. At -60° C (-76° F) it felt as if our eyeballs would freeze. Jonathan developed two horns of ice on his bushy eyebrows from constantly taking his goggles off and on in an effort to balance the sticky-eye feeling of freezing eyes with the problem of foggy vision. Lyle solved the problem by cutting the eyebrows back to the skin. And then suddenly, there was the summit.

The day had passed, the steep 200-metre gully system was behind us, and we were there, right there, nowhere else, with no thoughts of other places. This flat area, half the size of a football field, had never been trodden by humans before. One hundred kilometres to the north lay Cape Adare, then beyond that the Southern Ocean, peppered with bergs. To the south and west are the Trans-Antarctic Mountains: hundreds of kilometres of clean, washed across the open decks. In the meantime the skipper was trying to start the motor. Each time I looked up from the work at hand the berg was closer. They were minutes of sickening horror and I felt paralysed by the power of the forces that were playing with us.

The berg was less than a kilometre away and we could see enormous waves breaking onto its 50-metre high flanks. Finally the motor started to turn over. At the same time someone noticed that a large halyard was hanging over the stern, and as the motor started to crank over, the halyard – which must have been wrapped around the propeller – tightened like an enormous rubber band. Then suddenly there was a frightful pop and the strain on the halyard released. With the pop a large white object was flung out into the foaming sea like a ball. It was the radar dome which had been mounted on the mizzenmast and ripped from its steel mounts by the halyard. But, miraculously, the tailshaft and propeller held together and we slowly pulled away from the berg.

It seemed like Antarctica would not let us go. It was shaking its cruel fist at the young upstarts. The next few weeks were a series of horrible Southern Ocean gales from the west. We made little progress, the sails were falling apart, we were running out of water and, as a last straw, the tailshaft broke. But somehow, and it amazes me to this day, the crew held it together. There was no way that we could get to Australia to sail triumphantly through Sydney Heads as we had imag-

ined. Instead New Zealand was to be our final destination.

For the last five days we had champagne sailing with a stiff southerly wind up our tails. We had been released and we cruised up the eastern side of the South Island of New Zealand with the rich smell of tepid earth wafting from the land. On our last night at sea, in the relative warmth of a southern autumn and with land on our left shoulder, I remember thinking clearly that (now that I was safe and warm) I liked it out there. What form of madness is this?

LEFT: Man-hauling to Minto.

BELOW: Mount Ajax.

Geoff Tabin

Antarctic Solitude

'Probably the hardest climb done by man,' Mugs replies with a wry grin. He is serious. Mugs Stump knows about hard, scary routes.

The highest mountain in Antarctica is the 16,863-foot Mount Vinson in the Sentinel Range. It was first climbed in 1967 when Nick Clinch's ten-man American Antarctic Mountaineering Expedition, supported by U.S. military planes, succeeded in making first ascents of the three highest peaks on the continent. In 1983 Dick Bass and Frank Wells hired Giles Kershaw, the world's most experienced polar pilot, and a modified Tri-Turbo airplane to make the second ascent. Kershaw returned a year later to climb the mountain with Pat Morrow, and the pair set up a company, Adventure Network International, to service adventurers in Antarctica. Now they have hired me to guide an ascent of Mount Vinson.

My five clients include two other professional climbers, and two who will find the mountain a struggle. Ken Kammler, a 46-year-old New York surgeon, has the quiet confidence of a man who has succeeded in many endeavours, but, unfortunately, climbing mountains isn't one of them. Peter Kinchen is a 59-year-old Dutch businessman who has paid full fare for his personal mountain guide, Klaus Wagner, from Germany, to join us. My final group-member is Rob Mitchell, a guide for a Canadian adventure travel company which wants to be able to offer Vinson in its programme next year.

In Punta Arenas, Chile, we make optimistic plans. After Vinson, we will attempt the virgin, fourth highest mountain in Antarctica, Mount Epperly (15,100 feet). First, though, we have to get there. We wait 10 days for the weather to clear before climbing the aluminium painter's ladder into the unheated, non-pressurized cargo plane, and settle into canvas seats. After a five-hour flight over glimmering white wilderness the plane lands on the blue ice runway of Patriot Hills. It is eleven at night. We step into bright sunshine and a sharp, cold wind. We build full igloos around our tents, anticipating a long, cold wait before getting to the mountain.

However, a few hours later a tiny orange aircraft lands on skis near our tent. Giles Kershaw and Max Wenden have just

BIOGRAPHY

Geoff Tabin has climbed all over the world and is well known as a writer as well as a climber. He contributes an adventure travel column to Penthouse *magazine. His ascent of Everest in 1988 was, he believes, the first by a Jewish person. He was the fourth man to climb all 'Seven Summits', the highest mountains in each of the world's continents, and he has told his adventures in his book* Blind Corners. *A graduate from Harvard Medical School, he is a physician currently practising in Rhode Island.*

completed the first single-engine crossing of the Drake Passage. Giles, hatless and gloveless, strolls over, saying, 'I'll grab a quick nap, then take you to Vinson. Can you be packed in three hours?'

We fly over the spectacular Sentinel Range, rising 8,000 feet from the Antarctic plateau, with no foothills. Behind them extends a seemingly infinite sea of whiteness. We set down in a snowy valley under the massive, vertical West Buttress of Mount Tyree.

The first task is to secure our base camp against Antarctic winds and create an area in which to cook. After one sleep, which is how we delineate time in this perpetual sunshine, we make an acclimatization ascent of a small peak west of base camp and are shocked to find two planes and a cluster of tents on the other side, when we had expected nothing.

Thirty minutes later, Colonel Campos of the Chilean Airforce welcomes us with hot coffee and fresh apples, telling us that one of their planes had a hard landing here a month ago. He flew in

ABOVE: Mount Vinson (from the south), highest peak in Antarctica.

RIGHT: Summit day. Looking southwest from near the top of Vinson towards Mounts Shinn and Tyree. The South Pole is far to the south on the ice cap.

142

with a repair team. 'We have plenty of food and fuel. Come back anytime,' he says.

One sleep later we carry heavy packs to our first camp site on the mountain, at the base of a steep ice face, finally alone with our climb. Or so we think. Just as I finish stripping off four layers of clothing and wiggle into my tight, overstuffed sleeping bag, I hear a roar outside.

'Howdy, mate!' Astride three snowmobiles sit Paul Fitzgerald, a New Zealand geologist, and two mountain guides – another Kiwi, Rob Hall, and an American friend of mine, Mugs Stump. 'We're camped twenty kilometers away,' Paul says. 'When you get off your climb, give us a radio call and we'll party.' He smiles 'We've got lobster tails, steaks, and Mexican food.'

Above Camp One we climb a 1,500 foot ice wall and enter a fairytale valley leading to the massive bulk of Mount Vinson, towering 4,000 vertical feet above us. To gain the peak we must climb 3,000 feet up a steep snow ridge to the plateau between Vinson and Mount Shinn, then cross a long flat crevassed section to reach the summit cone.

One sleep later we begin the summit push. Short-roped together, Ken and I reach the col between Vinson and Shinn after five hours. A strong wind gusts along the plateau. The mercury in Peter's thermometer shrinks past forty below the bottom of the bulb. The sun moves behind the peak. I am wearing two sets of heavyweight polypropylene underwear, bib overalls, thick pile jacket, a one-piece insulated windproof suit,

ABOVE: *Giles Kershaw with the three-engined DC-3, which flew the first independent mountaineering expedition into Antarctica.*

RIGHT: *Camp I on Mount Vinson, Ellsworth Mountains.*

Peter sleeps in his tent. I shake him awake, yelling, 'How's your foot?' 'Good,' he mumbles, sliding down in his bag and snoring once more. There is nothing I can do. Ken and I drink a few cups of water and join Peter in slumber. Our summit 'day' took 27 hours of continuous climbing.

Eighteen hours later I am awake, priming stoves. Peter groans. I find him staring at his right foot peeking from the side of his unzipped sleeping bag. The first three toes are black, and the entire foot swollen to twice normal size. Huge blisters have already formed. It is serious. He won't be able to put on his boot, let alone weight the foot. If the blisters break and become infected, he might die. We must get him down.

'Didn't hurt yesterday,' Peter mutters flatly, looking in wonder at the deformity at the end of his leg.

We discuss the options. It seems possible to bring a snowmobile around from the next valley, which would be the least traumatic way of transporting Peter. I head for the Chilean camp to radio the geologists for help.

The Chilean radio operator cannot reach the geological party. Our message is intercepted by the American station at the South Pole, which monitors the field team's frequency. 'Why do you want them?' the operator demands.

'Is for rescue of climber,' the Chilean radio operator answers; I take the microphone to add, 'Nothing serious. Only a little frostbite that will be safer to move by snowmobile.' But it is too late. The chain of protocol has started. Increasingly exaggerated reports of the 'dying' climber are the talk of Antarctica. South Pole calls Siple. Siple calls Rothera base. In a giant game of telephone-whispers, word of Peter's near-fatal condition spreads. Everyone is contacted except the people we want. Adventure Network at Patriot Hills call the Chilean camp offering to send a plane with a snowmobile for us as soon as the weather improves. Meanwhile, there is nothing I can do but drink Chilean coffee and eat cookies.

Three hours later, Mugs, Rob and Paul roar into camp. 'What's up?' Mugs wants to know.

I explain the situation.

'No problem! We'll be with your boys in a few hours!' The rescue squad fire up their engines and disappear into the mist.

But no! The snowmobiles cannot reach our camp. 'The ridge is too steep,' Mugs reports.

Rob Hall, Mugs and I climb back up the ice face, dragging a sled. We carefully place Peter in the sled, then Rob Hall, Klaus and Mugs lower him down. I belay Ken. Rob Mitchell heads back to Camp Two to carry out all the garbage left by previous expeditions. At the bottom of the face Paul and the snowmobiles take us to camp.

The rescue is successful, but an Antarctic storm blows in and it is five days before the weather improves. Peter remains optimistic and cheerful in the hospitable warmth of the Chilean camp. We shuttle between camps by snowmobile and dine like kings. Looking at the impressive rock walls of the Sentinel Range, I

goggles, neoprene face mask, three layers on head and hands, vapour-barrier socks, plastic boots with alveolite inners and neoprene overboots. And I still feel cold.

'How're ya doing Ken?' He gives a thumbs-up. Rob, climbing solo, vanishes from sight above us; Klaus and Peter slowly drop behind. Ken and I take one step per four raw breaths. Reaching the base of the final impressive pyramid we pause and look around. The sky is still blue with a few high cumulus clouds. Below, two figures slowly descend into a swirling mist of wind-blown snow. Another climbs steadily upward.

Five hundred vertical feet beneath the top Klaus joins us, screaming into the wind, 'Peter is so tired, he must go down. Rob is helping him down. I make tracks for you and wait on the summit.' Unroped, he moves confidently up the 45° ice. Ken and I slow down. Ten breaths per step. Ten steps, then a sitting rest. We have been climbing for 16 hours. Ken shows no signs of altitude sickness and assures me he is warm. So we continue, inching towards the continental climax.

Above there is only a short, easy final ridge to the top. Klaus passes us on the way down, joyous. 'It is the greatest summit I have made!' With incredible inner fortitude Ken continues, onward and upward. An hour later we embrace at the pinnacle of Mount Vinson. Klaus was right: the views across the jagged summits of the Sentinel Mountains and out over the vast white wilderness are stupendous. But, boy, is it cold!

The descent takes nine hours. Back in camp, Rob is worried about Peter's right foot, 'It was frozen solid when we got down.'

forecast the technical routes which await the next generation when Mugs lets it slip that he has climbed the West Face of Mount Tyree.

'You did!' I stare in amazement at the 8,200-foot sweep of vertical quartzite. 'How was it?'

'Probably the hardest climb done by man,' Mugs replies with a wry grin. He is serious. Mugs Stump knows about hard, scary routes. His Moonflower Buttress on Mount Hunter with Paul Aubrey was a quantum leap in technical difficulty in the Alaska Range. The epic he had with Jim Bridwell on the East Face of Moose's Tooth has achieved legendary status for its boldness and difficulty in frigid conditions. Mugs has soloed El Capitan in winter, the north face of the Eiger, and the Cassin Ridge on McKinley in 15 hours.

In an even voice, Mugs tells me how he worked his way up a series of snow and ice ramps leading to a near-vertical runnel of brittle ice that was the key to getting through an overlap at one-third height. 'No way could I have down-climbed that ice,' he tells me calmly. With the temperature at 30 below, Mugs still had a vertical mile of difficult mixed climbing and uncertain route findings above him. The

ABOVE: Mugs Stump, who died in 1992. One of the boldest and most experienced of mountaineers, he solo-climbed the West Face of Mount Tyree.

BELOW: On Mount Vinson.

crux was a rock move three-quarters of the way up, where an overhang required a pull-up on a two inch edge of rock frozen into the face while balancing his crampon points on a sliver of rime ice. From the south summit he traversed to the higher north peak before descending.

I marvel at Mugs' confidence in attempting the wall in such temperatures. 'Oh, I warmed up with Mount Gardner's Southwest Face,' he explains. This 7,200-foot route is nearly as impressive as the one on Tyree, and took Mugs a mere 12 hours. Mugs extols other route possibilities in Antarctica, particularly the clean granite of the Gothic Mountains. His enthusiasm is infectious. However, with Peter's frostbite there is no chance even of attempting Epperly on this trip.

The weather finally clears enough to evacuate us to Patriot Hills. But, the onward fight situation sounds bad. 'We've sent to Miami for a new DC-6 engine,' is the message from Punta Arenas, 'and a mechanic who knows how to install it.' Finally, the radio announces that the plane is fixed. Then, that the pilot has quit. Another ten hours and the cavalry arrives in the form of a big DC-6 filling the sky above camp. Giles Kershaw has 'nipped back from Hong Kong' to rescue us from the ice.

*

A few months after our trip, Giles Kershaw died in a crash in Antarctica. Mugs Stump perished in a crevasse in Alaska in 1992. Giles was the main force in opening Antarctica to mountaineering; Mugs pushed it to a new level of boldness and difficulty. Thanks to these two, the doors are now open, with an expanded concept of what is possib!e. First ascent and great exploration opportunities in Antarctica will remain for generations to come.

Stephen Venables

HIGH ASIA

Long ago a Hindu sage wrote that a hundred ages of the Gods would be insufficient to tell all the glories of the Himalaya. Today the Himalaya still evoke a picture of infinite vastness. For mountaineers, obsessively seeking ever more tightly defined superlatives, they remain the ultimate sporting arena for the gratification of our vanities. But much more than that: even the most single-minded seeker of records cannot fail to be moved by their abundance, the complexity of their glaciers, the variety of their cultures and landscapes, and the continuing history of their exploration. There is still endless potential for going where no-one has gone before. Because of this element of exploration, this blurring of distinctions between travel and sport, my overview of Himalayan mountaineering starts way back in the last century when travellers with no mountaineering experience whatsoever began to investigate the world's greatest mountain range.

The Greater Himalaya sweep in an arc over 1,500 miles, from the Afghan Hindu Kush to the jungles of Burma, separating the Indian subcontinent from the desert highlands of Sinkiang and Tibet. Even along the Nepal-Tibet border, where the mountain chain is comparatively narrow, the landscape is infinitely vaster and more complex than the European Alps. In the northwest, where the Indus river cuts its tortuous gorge between the Karakoram and the Himalaya proper, the barrier is nearly 500 miles wide; and travelling up the miraculous new Karakoram Highway by bus still takes three gruelling days to cross the range.

RIGHT: Geologically young, the mountains of High Asia are still rising. This aerial shot shows Everest and Lhotse from the southwest; the giant wall of Nuptse can be seen extending to the left, concealing the Western Cwm. In the foreground, the peak with the dog-leg ridge is Chamlang.

BELOW: The Greater Himalaya.

KEY TO MOUNTAINS
1 Tirich Mir; 2 Nanga Parbat; 3 K2; 4 Nanda Devi; 5 Dhaulagiri; 6 Manaslu; 7 Everest; 8 Makalu; 9 Kangchenjunga

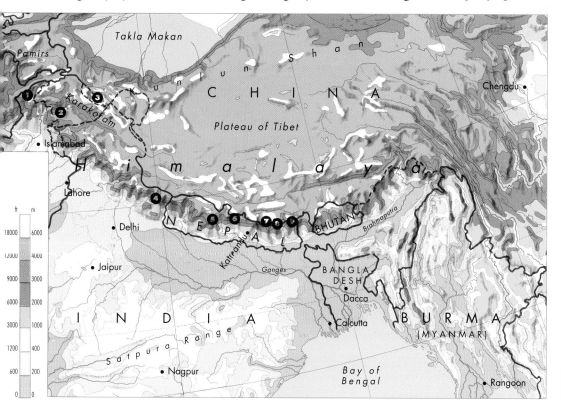

ABOVE: Captain John Noel in the Tibetan dress he wore in an attempt to reach Mount Everest illicitly from Sikkim in 1913.

RIGHT: Towards Mount Kailas. Dr William Moorcroft and Captain Hearsey (the figures on yaks, left) cross the Niti Pass into Tibet in June 1812, disguised as Hindu pilgrims.

People have lived in the high valleys for thousands of years and the most important passes were known long before Europeans arrived. Our Eurocentric history of Himalayan exploration is therefore, in its initial stages, one of re-exploration and mainly the story of a single colonial power – Great Britain. Alexander the Great had reached the western Himalaya in Classical times; Marco Polo had written a geographically vague account of his journey through Badakshan and the Pamirs, skirting the northwest fringes of the Himalaya; Ippolito Desideri, an Italian Jesuit missionary, made an extraordinary journey from 1716 to 1721, travelling up through Kashmir to Ladakh, continuing along the Indus and Tsangpo valleys to Tibet's capital, Lhasa, then returning south across one of the high passes into Nepal. But to all intents and purposes, when British settlers began consolidating their control of India in the nineteenth century, they knew virtually nothing of the wild mountain country on their northern frontier.

The first probe north was made by a Lancashire vet, William Moorcroft, after years of badgering the East India Company for permission to visit the famed horse-markets of Turkestan (or Sinkiang, as it is now usually known). In 1819 he set off through the powerful Sikh empire and continued north to Ladakh. In a journey lasting five years, he twice attempted to reach the fabled Karakoram Pass, only to be rebuffed by the Chinese authorities in Turkestan. Forced westwards into Afghanistan, he disappeared there, almost certainly killed by a local chieftain. In his prolific journals, Moorcroft advocated Britain extending her influence into Kashmir and Ladakh, for military and commercial advantage against the expanding Russian Empire. Twenty years passed before such a policy was officially adopted.

Godfrey Vigne was the next private British explorer to brave the vast unknown of the western Himalaya. Between 1836 and 1838 he explored extensively around the Vale of Kashmir and into Baltistan and Ladakh, attempting to reach the Hispar, Mustagh and Karakoram passes. On his return he published the first map of the Karakoram range, wildly inaccurate but hinting for the first time at the immensity and complexity of the mountain ridges and vast glaciers of the region.

The British Raj finally pushed north in the 1840s, defeating the Sikh empire and effectively taking over Kashmir and Ladakh. In 1847, Dr Thompson, a border commissioner appointed to explore the boundaries of Ladakh, finally succeeded in following the trail of bleached mule bones over the series of gorges, glaciers and passes that lead to the Karakoram Pass, 5,570 metres above

sea level, at the gateway to Central Asia. A hundred years later Eric Shipton was to follow the same route to Kashgar, where he served as British Consul. Even he, probably the most widely-travelled Himalayan mountaineer of the day, was awed by the immensity of the Central Asian Trade Route.

Karakoram exploration after Vigne reads like a *Who's Who* of famous mountain explorers: the Schlagintweit brothers' discoveries of the 1850s, Godwin-Austen's survey of the Baltoro Glacier in 1861, Francis Younghusband's perilous crossing of the East Mustagh Pass in 1897, Conway's expedition of 1892, the legendary exploits of William and Fanny Workman,

LEFT: Watercolour of the Panmah Glacier, from Skeenmurg, Karakoram, painted in 1872 by H.H. Godwin-Austen.

RIGHT: HRH Prince Luigi di Savoia, Duke of the Abruzzi, first to attempt K2 in 1909.

LEFT: The Lower Rimo Glacier, Kashmir, photographed by Filippo de Filippi on an expedition to investigate K2 in 1915.

BELOW: George Mallory and Andrew Irvine, setting out from the North Col for their fatal attempt on Mount Everest on 6 June 1924.

Tom Longstaff's discovery of the Siachen in 1909, largest of the Karakoram glaciers. The Duke of the Abruzzi made the first attempt on K2, and in 1914 his colleague, Filippo de Filippi, explored the Rimo Glacier. Then a Dutch couple, the Vissers, filled in huge gaps in the map during the 1930s and Kenneth Mason discovered the Zug Shaksgam to the north of the range. Finally, in 1937 and 1939, Eric Shipton masterminded a wide-ranging survey of the remote glacier systems around Snow Lake.

Exploration was now linked inextricably with mountaineering, and, as elsewhere, many of the European explorers brought with them Alpine guides. Conway set his sights deliberately on summits, claiming the Silver Throne and attempting the larger Baltoro Kangri. The Duke of the Abruzzi, despite protestations of scientific endeavour, came to this remotest corner of Kashmir to find, amongst other things, a climbing route up K2 – a route later followed by Charles Houston's American team and called the Abruzzi Spur.

The Duke made little progress on K2, but nearly succeeded on Chogolisa, attaining a new altitude record of over 7,400 metres. Three years earlier Longstaff had climbed Trisul, 7,120 metres, in Garhwal, and as early as 1895 Alfred Mummery, the British alpinist often referred to as the 'father of modern mountaineering', made an audacious attempt on Nanga Parbat, the gigantic western bastion of the Himalaya, towering above the great bend of the Indus river.

That was a remarkable expedition. Not only did Mummery and his companions carry out a major reconnaissance of the mountain, furthering the explorations of the Schlagintweits, they also attempted a technical climb way ahead of its time – the central rocky rib up the Diamir Face. Mummery and Raghobir Thapa, a Gurkha, reached the top of the main rib and would have continued up easier slopes had Raghobir not been taken ill. Their highpoint is usually quoted as about 6,000 metres, but was probably nearer 7,000 metres. Mummery had no support team, no fixed ropes, no prepared camps. He was climbing 'alpine-style' on the most direct route up Nanga Parbat. Another 83 years would pass before Reinhold Messner, climbing solo, achieved success in the same manner on the same face.

A few days after his attempt, Mummery and two Gurkhas disappeared trying to cross a high pass. When attempts on Nanga Parbat resumed in the 1930s, they were massive sieges, supported by Sherpas and headed by large teams of German climbers. The British, meanwhile, had become obsessed with a peak 700 miles to the southeast.

In 1852 the Survey of India's computations had disclosed that its distant 'Peak XV', on the Nepal-Tibet border, was the highest mountain in the world. It was named after Sir George Everest, a distinguished former Surveyor General. In 1913 a young army officer, John Noel, attempted illegally to reach Everest from Sikkim, coming within 40 miles of his objective before being turned back by soldiers. The British had been trying to organize an official attempt on Everest ever since Lord Curzon became Indian Viceroy in 1898. Although the Nepalese approach was to remain firmly closed to foreigners until 1950, through a mixture of bullying and diplomacy, links were established with the Dalai Lama of Tibet, who in 1921 at last gave permission for a reconnaissance party to pass through his territory.

The expedition was organized jointly by the Alpine Club and the Royal Geographical Society and was led by Charles

ABOVE: Sherpas on the East Rongbuk Glacier, approaching the North Col slopes. In 1922 seven died in an avalanche.

RIGHT: *The Sherpa 'Tigers' of 1933, who established a high Camp 6 on Everest.*

LEFT: *Party ascending the North Col of Mount Everest, one of the most dangerous sections of the climb.*

Howard-Bury. It comprised mainly seasoned explorers, the most experienced mountaineer being Dr Alexander Kellas, who had already climbed several peaks in Sikkim and whose theories on man's physiological capabilities at extreme altitude were much later to be borne out by the first oxygenless ascent of Everest in 1978. By cruel irony Kellas died on the approach march, and thereafter the driving force behind finding a route onto Everest was George Mallory. He spearheaded the protracted search up the Rongbuk Glaciers on the north side, round to the Kangshung Glacier on the east, and eventually reached the head of the East Rongbuk Glacier to discover a route onto the North Col and North Ridge.

Mallory was one of Britain's better alpinists, though probably not as competent as the Australian-born George Finch, who joined the first full-scale attempt in 1922. Finch was a scientist: his invention of down-filled clothing and commitment to oxygen equipment foreshadowed postwar developments, but in his day he was a lone voice in the wilderness, suppressed by the overbearing weight of British amateurism and snobbery.

Yet despite feeling their way in the dark, the British achieved astonishing things on Everest. Most remarkable was Colonel Norton's attempt in 1924, when he pushed to nearly 8,600 metres on the North Face without bottled oxygen. Nine years later Frank Smythe gained the same highpoint. Both had thrust on alone, leaving weaker companions to turn back – the sort of action which years later would earn others the accusation of selfishness or egotism. Smythe and Norton each felt that, despite the crippling effects of hypoxia, given more time they could have

carried on to the summit. When Messner and Habeler finally climbed Everest without oxygen in 1978, they had the huge advantage of improved technical experience and light equipment, enabling them to move much faster. Their insulated clothing could probably have saved them in the event of an unplanned bivouac. Now, it has become commonplace for people to survive bivouacs at extreme altitude, and to climb at night, but the pioneers were restricted by the limits of daylight.

There were seven unsuccessful prewar expeditions to Everest. Like the Germans on Nanga Parbat, the British never quite achieved the coincidence of lucky timing and correct logistical planning. The size of team seemed to make little difference, although Eric Shipton was convinced that too large a party was actually a hindrance. He said the leader should always be an active mountaineer able to lead from, or close to, the front.

Shipton, like Mummery, like Finch, was an innovator. His first Himalayan experience was the successful Kamet expedition of 1932, led by Frank Smythe. Within two weeks of reaching base camp it had climbed the 7,756 metre summit, the highest so far achieved. Almost an anticlimax, Shipton said. What left a deeper impression was the subsequent discovery of the Bhyundar valley, immortalized by Smythe as 'the Valley of Flowers'. Everest, Kangchenjunga and Nanga Parbat are 'duties', Smythe wrote, but 'mountaineering in Garhwal is a pleasure, thank God.'

Garhwal, the most immediately beautiful, verdant corner of the Himalaya, and also the most accessible in the 1930s, was where Shipton chose to organize the first of his streamlined expeditions. In 1934, at the suggestion of Longstaff, another, earlier prophet of lightweight exploration, he penetrated the Rishi Ganga Gorge to reach the elusive sanctuary of India's highest peak, Nanda Devi.

Shipton's method was simple and economical. He took just one European companion – his old climbing partner from Kenya, Bill Tilman – and three proven Darjeeling Sherpas, including the incomparable Angtharkay. Clothing and equipment were kept to an absolute minimum and, apart from a few tins, all food was bought locally in bulk. Add to those minimalist logistics the human factor – two very tough, enterprising individuals, hardened by pioneer farming in Africa – and you have an extremely effective, mobile way of exploring difficult mountain country.

The following year Shipton built on the method for a small experimental expedition to Everest during the monsoon. Besides accomplishing important survey work, over twenty peaks were climbed. But as far as the Himalayan Committee in London was concerned, this was just a filler before the next full-scale attempt in 1936, when Shipton handed leadership back to Hugh Ruttledge. Tilman had not acclimatized well in 1935, so was omitted from the 1936 Everest 'show', leaving him free to return to the pleasures of the Garhwal. He retraced his steps up the Rishi Ganga to make a successful attempt on Nanda Devi – establishing a summit altitude record that would stand until the French climbed Annapurna in 1950. Charles Houston describes this memorable expedition in the following essay.

Three years after the ascent a Polish team climbed Nanda Devi's lower but equally spectacular east summit, the first in what was to be a long line of phenomenal Polish successes in the Himalaya. It was also the last great climb before the Second World War. Several expeditions that summer came abruptly to a halt. Heinrich Harrer and Peter Aufschnaiter were interned by the British after their attempt on Nanga Parbat; in Lahul, another Austrian, Fritz Kolb, was detained after climbing Mulkila.

Further west, at the heart of the Karakoram, Eric Shipton was camped on Snow Lake when a young botanist on his expedition, Scott Russell, came up from the Hispar with news that Britain had just declared war on Germany. Shortly before abandoning the expedition to report to the authorities, Russell reached the crest of the Khurdopin Pass and gazed across an unknown glacier winding its way down towards the remote valley of Shimshal. Many months later, incarcerated in a Japanese prison camp, he wrote of his disappointment: 'Clear before us lay . . . the route for which we had hoped but could not now follow . . . it seems that a gate was then closed – the gate that led to free planning of our lives, and the key to reopen it is still in an uncertain future.'

The War brought Himalayan mountaineering almost to a standstill. Soon afterwards the whole political map of Central Asia changed. Kolb's 1947 exploration of the Kishtwar was one of the last foreign expeditions to Kashmir before Partition wreaked havoc in that province, whose vague status and ambiguous boundaries were a direct legacy of the first British probes northward a century earlier. In Tibet, Aufschnaiter's detailed mapping of the area round Shisha Pangma was the final foreign venture for many years.

The Chinese invasion of Tibet coincided with a change of government in Nepal, allowing foreigners for the first time to visit Langtang, Annapurna, the west side of Kangchenjunga and Sola Kumbu – the Sherpas' homeland immediately south of Everest.

Suddenly the great giants – the 8,000 metre peaks – began to fall, as though mountaineers had finally broken some intangible barrier. It is hard to pinpoint precise reasons for this. Technology has been cited and there is no doubt that the French team which climbed Annapurna in 1950 was better equipped than prewar expeditions, though they used no oxygen. For Everest, the British took advantage of wartime advances in military equipment, including effective oxygen apparatus. The 1953 expedition was meticulously organized along the lines of a military campaign, and there was a strong spirit of patriotism: what the French could achieve on Annapurna, the British could do on Everest . . . and the Germans, a few weeks later, on Nanga Parbat . . . the Italians, in 1954, on K2.

This kind of generalizing can be misleading. Ed Hillary certainly achieved success on the back of an elaborate full-scale siege. But in the two previous seasons he gained his experience as a roving explorer, travelling light with Shipton, Lowe, Evans and others, climbing peaks, exploring untrodden glaciers and linking unknown passes across the newly-opened mountain paradise of the Nepal Himalaya. On Everest itself, despite the careful preparation, illness reduced manpower at a critical stage, forcing Hillary to carry a 28.5-kilogramme load (63 pounds) to the final assault camp at 8,500 metres, an astonishing feat, even allowing for supplementary oxygen.

John Hunt's masterly leadership on Everest became almost a blueprint for climbing great Himalayan peaks. The Italian veteran Ardito Desio employed a similar approach on the much harder peak of K2. Yet this was not the only way of attempting big mountains. Just before the War, Charles Houston had made the first serious attempt on K2 with a small team, backed only by a handful of high altitude porters. He also describes that expedition for us in his essay, graphically reconstructing the physical nature of the Abruzzi Spur: long, steep, insecure and very hard to follow in bad visibility. The crux pitch, led by Bill House, is still regarded with great respect. But Houston's main interest is with the moral issues of high altitude climbing – specifically risk and

ABOVE: *Professor Giotto Dainelli with one companion and 57 'coolies' explored the Siachen Glacier, Karakoram, in 1930.*

responsibility. He takes pride in the fact that his team did not push on for glory at any cost: far better in his view to return alive. He is also adamant that the climber's top priority must be the well-being of his companions, not the summit.

This emphasis on the moral dilemma is coloured retrospectively by subsequent events, specifically the disastrous summer of 1986 when thirteen climbers of several nationalities died on K2 in a series of grisly accidents. At the time Houston was publicly critical of what he felt was unacceptable ambition leading to callous disregard for companions' safety. He may have been overreacting, but his criticisms had some validity. He was a world authority on the physiological risks of high altitude, and by then had also experienced tragedy on a later attempt on K2.

In 1953 he very nearly reached the summit. Even after sitting out a seven-day storm at nearly 8,000 metres, he was still considering a summit bid, until one of his six companions became paralysed by thrombosis. Ambition was forgotten in the urgency of getting Art Gilkey off the mountain. What followed was one of the great Himalayan epics. Houston realized that to get the paralysed man down could kill the whole team. Yet he never considered abandoning Gilkey. A slip at one point resulted in everyone but Pete Shoening falling in a tangle of ropes. With extraordinary skill, Schoening held the entire team on an ice axe belay. But later the same day, while the others were preparing a camp, the helpless Gilkey was swept away in an avalanche. His final calamity undoubtedly saved the rest, for even without the encumbrance of their invalid companion, they had a desperate struggle to escape alive from the Abruzzi Spur.

The late fifties and early sixties was a golden age of Himalayan mountaineering, as expeditions helped themselves to the most tempting fruits. The Karakoram offered the ripest pickings –

Rakaposhi, Trivor and the Mustagh Tower to British teams; Distaghil Sar, Gashergrum II and Broad Peak to the Austrians; Hidden Peak and Masherbrum to Nick Clinch's American expeditions; Gasherbrum IV to an Italian expedition led by the alpine legend of the thirties, Riccardo Cassin, and spearheaded by the young virtuoso, Walter Bonatti.

These were all giant peaks, over 7,000 metres, and though they were usually climbed by their easiest routes, we should be wary of the myth that Himalayan climbing at this time consisted purely of 'boring snow plods' by universally large teams, relaying loads between a tedious succession of fixed camps. Gasherbrum IV in 1958, even by its easiest route, involved hard technical climbing at nearly 8,000 metres, taxing the greatest alpinist of his day. On Distaghil Sar in 1960, Wolfgang Stefan had a team of just four climbers. Three years earlier, his old friend Kurt Diemberger was party to a similarly small-scale venture on Broad Peak, a climb indeed that had been a pointer at things to come, both for Diemberger himself and for Himalayan climbing.

The dominant figure in the Broad Peak quartet was Hermann Buhl, who in 1953 had made an extraordinary impromptu solo push to the summit of Nanga Parbat, arriving on the final snowy cone on his hands and knees after 16 gruelling hours. He spent the night on a tiny ledge above 8,000 metres, only staggering back into camp the following afternoon, unable to speak and looking ten years older. Buhl was lucky on Nanga Parbat, escaping with just frostbite to a few toes. Four years later on Broad Peak, he and his companions proved that, without any help from high altitude porters, a small team could climb an 8,000 metre peak. But it was Buhl's last summit. Some days later, attempting Chogolisa, he fell through a cornice to his death.

Political difficulties closed most of the great mountains for much of the 1960s, but in 1970 the Nepal Himalaya were again opened to foreign mountaineers. By now all but one of the 8,000 metre peaks had been climbed, as well as many seven-thousanders. People were eyeing the huge untouched steep walls on previously climbed summits. A young British team, led by Chris Bonington, used siege tactics and thousands of metres of fixed rope to force a brilliant and difficult line straight up the South Face of Annapurna. The same year on Nanga Parbat, Dr Herrligkoffer organized an attempt on the Rupal Face, said to be the biggest mountain wall in the world. Reinhold Messner reached the summit first, soloing the difficult exit gullies, his brother Günther in hot pursuit. But Günther was so weakened by the effort that the brothers decided to descend by a marginally easier, unknown route on the far, Diamir side of the mountain – the face attempted by Mummery back in 1895. They almost made it: Günther was killed by an avalanche in the closing stages of their unplanned traverse. Reinhold went on to climb Manaslu by another new 'big wall' route, and ultimately to surmount all fourteen of the eight-thousanders, soloing both Nanga Parbat and Everest, and never using oxygen.

Messner revolutionized Himalayan climbing; but there are perhaps limitations to his ruthlessly lightweight approach, occasions when 'alpine style' purism is less appropriate than good old-fashioned teamwork. Diemberger discusses here his dream of a route up the forgotten east side of Everest, a face relegated by Mallory in 1921 to 'other men, less wise'. The dream was brought to reality by American team-effort and Diemberger was invited to film the first full attempt on the face in 1981. Even with double fixed ropes, the ascent of the initial buttress was a masterpiece of difficult dangerous climbing, calling for all the skill and determination of one of America's best technicians, George Lowe. The Americans succeeded on their second attempt on this Kangshung Face in 1983, when six climbers reached the summit, using oxygen on the final stage.

However, when it comes to disciplined teamwork the nation that excels most repeatedly is Japan. From the first ascent of Manaslu in 1957, Japan has swept up unclimbed peaks with assiduous regularity. In recent years particularly, with new possibilities opened up by China on the north side of the range, the Japanese have picked the plums – the first ascent of K2 from the north, first ascent of Everest's north face, of Kula Kangri on the northern frontier of Bhutan and, far to the east, by the great bend of the Tsangpo River, first ascents of Gyala Peri and the great eastern bulwark of the Himalaya, Namche Barwa. No other country seems to have the energy, resourcefulness and sheer cash demanded by the Chinese to compete in this extraordinarily expensive game.

In less expensive areas one nation that has reaped the benefit of big team effort is Poland. Voytek Kurtyka's essay stresses the individualism and sheer toughness of Polish mountaineers, perhaps underplaying their capacity for team spirit, as evidenced in the first ascent of Kunyang Kish, for example. He personally favours the very hardest walls, attempted in uncompromising alpine style with just one or at most three companions.

Pierre Béghin of France was one of several climbers pushing back the boundaries of possibility during the eighties. Others included his Swiss friends Erhard Loretan and Jean Troillet, who in 1986 climbed Everest's north face, up and down in just 40 hours. Tomo Cesen's astonishing claims are still being disputed by mountaineers, but his fellow Slovenians Andrej Stremfelj and Marko Prezelzj quite definitely made a committing ropeless ascent of Kangchenjunga's South Ridge in 1991 and the elusive first ascent of Menlungtse in the following year.

BELOW: Nanga Parbat seen from the air from the southwest over Babusar Pass.

Wanda Rutkiewicz, who died on Kangchenjunga in 1992, was one of few outstanding women in an activity that is still dominated almost exclusively by men. Of all the major first ascents of Himalayan peaks only two – Nun in 1953 and Gasherbrum III in 1984 – were made by women. But in recent years women have shared in difficult new routes: Alison Hargreaves on Kantega, Cathy Freer on Cholatse – both famous 6,000 metre peaks in the Everest region. Catherine Destivelle has attempted the much-tried North Ridge of Latok II in the Karakoram, having already free-climbed the fiendishly difficult Jugoslav route on the Trango Tower. Perhaps the most outstanding female climb to date has been Kitty Calhoun Grissom's ascent of Makalu's West pillar, which she modestly describes here.

Some of the best routes in the Himalaya are now festooned with slowly decomposing fixed ropes, which certainly spoil the aesthetics of mountaineering whether or not they represent any environmental threat. If we are to protect mountains for future generations, the answer probably lies in keeping expeditions as small as possible, paring down logistics, tackling more with less, as Mike Thompson suggests in his piece, so that it is the capabilities of the climbers themselves that are being explored.

For those who remain explorers at heart, there are still huge tracts of mountain country, particularly in southeast Tibet, that remain virtually untouched. Even in better-known areas of the Himalaya we have only scratched at the surface of climbing possibilities. There is much still to be done.

Charles Houston

Heyday Climbs

Like imagined castles, cathedrals and towers, separated by valleys of ice,

the beautiful granite stood many thousand feet above our heads. We were

in the Land of Giants.

Were the Nanda Devi and K2 expeditions of the 1930s really as magical as we remember, or has time magnified them beyond reality? It's hard to believe how naive and presumptuous we were – Ad Carter, Art Emmons, Farnie Loomis and I – American college kids inviting the best British climbers to join us! True, we had paid our dues (dues were lower then), cutting our teeth in the Alps and on expeditions to lesser but wilder Alaskan peaks.

We were fascinated by Paul Bauer's fabulous assault on the ice-towered Kangchenjunga and Elizabeth Knowlton's account of Nanga Parbat. The British Everest efforts were the stuff of legend. And in 1932 three Americans had penetrated eastern China and climbed unknown Minya Konka. One of that little band, Emmons, spent painful months in Tatsienlu having his frozen toes amputated. He talked with Loomis and Carter who were contemplating an Alaskan climb and urged them toward the Himalaya; they came to me, and late in 1935 we began planning in earnest. We would aim high – Kangchenjunga, no less.

I was struggling in the first year of medical school, Carter was finishing an Alaskan survey with Washburn and neither of us had time to spare. Emmons and Loomis became the spear-carriers! And how did we attract the British? Peter Lloyd reminds me that the link was Graham Brown, who'd been with me on the first ascent of Foraker in Alaska in 1934. Giving him carte blanche to approach other Britons, his starting point was to look at those climbers who'd been

BIOGRAPHY

Charles Houston enjoyed walking holidays in the Alps with his family, making his first climb in 1924. Here he describes two expeditions of the 1930s, to Nanda Devi and K2. He returned to K2 in 1953, and was booked for a third attempt in 1955. When an Italian team succeeded in 1954, there was regret but also the satisfaction of knowing that they had followed the route he and his teams had reconnoitred. In 1950, he took part in the first trek to the south side of Everest.

As a doctor, Charles Houston became interested in the effects of high altitude, and used his experience as a flight surgeon during World War II. During 1962-1965 he directed the American Peace Corps in India, and afterwards taught environmental health and medicine at the University of Vermont.

considered but turned down for Everest that year. All three of those he recruited fell into that category. Bill Tilman had not acclimatized well in 1935, Noel Odell was thought to be too old at 46, and Lloyd had not scored well in the required RAF medical (one of the great strokes of luck in his life, he later concluded, since Nanda Devi in the event proved incomparably more worthwhile). We became a wonderfully happy group!

Most American equipment was unsuitable, so Loomis went shopping in Britain, where he was warmly welcomed but gently advised that Kangchenjunga might be a bit much for us. Soon he cabled that our Brits would be happier if we went to Nanda Devi. This was generous of Shipton and Tilman, who had been first to penetrate the Nanda Devi Sanctuary in 1934, since it was 'their' mountain. We knew nothing about Nanda Devi, but were excited, if intimidated, by the great names now in our team. Noel Odell was familiar for his extraordinary accomplishments on Everest in 1924 and his climbs in America while a professor at Harvard, Bill Tilman was already a legend, and Peter Lloyd seemed promising. Both Emmons and I knew Graham Brown to be good company and a strong climber – although 53! Altogether, they were a powerful bunch, and we quickly changed our name from Harvard Kangchenjunga Expedition to British-American Himalayan Expedition.

I was interested in how the altitude might affect us, and Dr Ross McFarland, airline altitude expert, gave me articles to

RIGHT: Nanda Devi. At 25,645 ft, this was the highest peak in the British Empire, and is here seen from the northeast, with Nanda Devi East to the left.

ABOVE: K2, second highest mountain in the world. It is pictured looking north, up the Godwin-Austen Glacier, from the glacier junction known as Concordia.

read and 'took me up' to a simulated height of 28,000 feet in a low oxygen room, thus starting a lifelong interest.

Loomis arranged shipment to India of the best mountaineering equipment of the day. Each of us took his favourite sleeping bag. Mrs Duncan in Scalway, Shetland made us three light wool sweaters apiece. Grenfell cloth parkas with wolverine fur around the hoods were to wear over sweaters and a heavy shirt (down-clothing was still in the future). Leather boots – with tricouni and hobnails – were made by Robert Lawrie in London. Our food was varied and plentiful – we had agonized long over what to take, little suspecting Tilman's reaction: fruits and vegetables (sun dried by Mrs Kelly in Massachusetts), cereals, specialities and many meats; pemmican was added later.

My records are silent about money! Much of our food, but little equipment, was given to us. We each paid a share of the cost, but Loomis generously carried most; he and Emmons did most of the work. Food was shipped in March from Boston to Calcutta. We travelled separately: my family and I with Lloyd, Odell and Brown by P & O steamer. Tilman and Loomis had gone earlier and Carter started for China and would meet us at the mountain. A wise dean let me take my final exams six weeks early! We arrived in Bombay on July 2nd and took a train to Delhi. Visits to the Taj Mahal and Fatehpur Sikri gave us our first taste of the India we would come to love. All was over-whelming, straight out of Kipling's India.

It is amazing that before computers, before FAX, when inter-national telephone was dubious, we could put together such a party with such a goal in five months. There were no flights across oceans and only two per week from Europe to Asia. We were vaguely aware that a powerful man was stirring trouble in Germany, but not until we crossed Afghanistan and Persia two years later were we aware of his *Drang nach Osten* (eastward

expansion). British rule in India was peaceful, safe and efficient – but innocent!

Tilman reached Calcutta in mid-April and tried again for the Kangchenjunga permit. Silence indicated disapproval, so he sent our goods to Garhwal, where Loomis joined him and the two chaperoned porter food into the Rishi Gorge. They had a rough trip, moving fast with heavy loads, and Tilman broke two ribs. We all met for the first time on July 6th in the Forest Bungalow at Ranikhet. Only then did Tilman appreciate the extent of our supplies. With grunts and scowls he ruthlessly 'bagged and scrapped' half our treasured food, allowing us to leave there with six Sherpas and only 37 Dhotial porters.

The march-in was pure joy. For us everything was new and we showed our emotion. Leeches, rain, broken bridges, leaking tin roofs – nothing mattered when we were travelling the beautiful and romantic hills where our early heroes had climbed, and where Jim Corbett still hunted too plentiful man-eating leopards and tigers.

The view from the 11,000-foot Kuari Pass, veiled by clouds, was breathtaking; as were the wild flowers. Some visited the holy city of Badrinath, we bathed in a hot spring and in rushing waterfalls. Our Sherpas, who had been chosen in Darjeeling by Tilman, tended us in the tradition of the British Raj: greeted with bed-tea at dawn, we broke camp after a quick breakfast and were on the road an hour after waking. Pausing for lunch and for tea, we camped in mid-afternoon. We

Americans insisted on carrying packs; the Brits knew better!

The track disappeared as we climbed a steep ridge, slid into the Rishi Gorge and past the Inner Curtain – a great wall which guards the entrance. It rained hard for days; we were stopped by the roaring Rhamani river until Tilman somehow got a rope across. Here the Dhotial porters balked: this torrent was too much – how would they cross it on their return? They left and, with ten loyal Mana porters, we made three carries to camp under a great overhang. Drastic changes were needed. Tilman took charge, once again muttering 'nothing but chemicals!' as he culled our food. We were too much in awe of this strong silent man to protest. Two days later he was vindicated as we sweated loads through the gorge.

The Rishi has carved a canyon, in places 10,000 feet deep, through the rim of mountains which encircle Nanda Devi; the walls are steep and slippery rock and grass, interrupted by cliffs. We made several carries each day, exhausting but immensely exciting. Finally, we crested the rim and peered into the Sanctuary, a lovely rolling meadow with Nanda Devi towering from its centre. We relayed loads through grass and flowers to the glacier, up the moraine and finally on August 7th to base camp, where the Mana men were sent home. We celebrated with a bottle of apricot brandy, which Tilman has described with enthusiasm in his book of the expedition.

Above us, 8,000 feet of mountain was so foreshortened we could not guess at the route. For the next week we carried loads higher and higher, stocking camps, fixing a few ropes as handrails (jumars were unknown). Every few days heavy snow kept us in our tents, but usually we had a mix of sun, cloud and snow. The rock was steep and horribly rotten, interspersed with steep-sided snow ridges where we carved a track into one side. Much of the route was easier. A few cases of diarrhoea, touches of altitude sickness, some snow blindness and occasional 'sick' among the Sherpas did not slow us as much as did the weather. By August 14 we were camped at 21,000 feet. Our worst casualty had been the loss of all the tea – life's blood to the Brits, though less so to us. These were modified siege tactics – inching up the mountain, one camp after another. We were a small

LEFT: Stills taken from Charlie Houston's movie of the expedition, showing (from top): Bill Tilman; Ad Carter; Tilman again; Arthur Emmons (facing camera) with Peter Lloyd (left); Noel Odell; load carrying to Camp IV; Nanda Devi from Pisgah at the entrance to the Sanctuary.

RIGHT: Camp 4 on Nanda Devi, looking over 'Longstaff's Col' towards Nanda Kot (22,500 ft).

RIGHT: The southern flanks of K2 (28,253 ft/ 8,611 m) with Angel Peak (the Angelus) – seen from across a crevasse at Concordia.

vulnerable party, without radio, and a long and difficult way from help. Complete self–sufficiency brought a level of conservatism not present today. We spent much time moving loads. We were also concerned that the Sherpas should not travel unescorted: in those days they were seen as the responsibility of the climbing party, and not to be left to their own devices. This was unnecessary for Pasang Kikuli who had much Himalayan experience and had survived the dreadful Nanga Parbat disaster in 1934.

For six weeks we resolved everything by consensus, but it was becoming clear to all that we needed a leader to take some tough decisions. Tilman was the obvious choice. So, on August 21st, huddled storm-bound in a tent, we charged him to choose two teams for the summit. The smoothly concave slope would provide only a tiny platform for a final camp. Storm kept us in camp for two more days. Tilman quietly proposed that Odell and I should try first, with Lloyd and Loomis next. The 25th dawned crystal clear, and despite deep new snow – which fortunately had blown off the steep route – we all climbed to about 24,000 feet where Odell and I were left to make camp.

Next day we climbed steadily up the steepening face to a ridge. By early afternoon we were making slow progress, feeling the altitude in waist-deep snow. We continued to 25,000 feet where an easy snow slope led to a rock wall and the summit. The weather was perfect, the view magnificent and we were joyfully confident. Thinking it too late to continue – one did not climb at night in those days – we returned to our bivouac, planning to move camp higher and go for the summit. We celebrated with corned beef hash; I served Odell first, not noticing that the bottom of the tin had been punctured. Two hours later I was sick, very sick, with vomiting and diarrhoea, crawling apologetically over Odell onto the tiny platform, looking down forever. It was still and clear and cold, but for me anything but calm. The night passed. The next day Odell shouted down to the others,

who understood him to say 'Charlie is killed!' rather than that I was 'ill'. Consequently, they rushed up (if you can consider six hours a rush), led me down, and Tilman replaced me. Next day he and Odell moved camp 500 feet higher, and on August 29th reached the summit after a near fall. There, as Tilman inimitably put it: 'we so far forgot ourselves as to shake hands.'

We others had already started down. Once the poison from the spoiled meat had passed, I was weak but able to climb. Graham Brown was severely affected by the altitude, and only after much argument would agree to go with me; this was my first experience of the mental changes which today we call high altitude cerebral oedema. Safely at Base on August 31st, our rejoicing was tempered by the death from dysentery of the sick Sherpa, Kitar. We buried him there, with a suitable service and a carved slab, and turned toward home. A runner carried a cable to *The Times* of London: 'Two reached summit August 29th', for we were determined (ridiculously, as it turned out) to give no names.

Tilman and I with Pasang Kikuli had decided to try Longstaff's Col, to the east, while the others returned the way we had come. I will never forget that 100 miles after we crossed the pass – 'a little dicey in places,' said Tilman. There was the glorious sense of fitness, power, and a job well done. We travelled a major caravan route from Tibet with many travellers, intensely curious at our tattered appearance. On the 12th of September we reached Ranikhet, in time for me to catch the twice-weekly flight to Europe and the boat home, only a bit late for medical school.

Tilman's story ends with words which mountaineers would do well to remember: 'It was but a short three months that we had met, many of us as strangers, but inspired by a single hope and bound by a common purpose. The purpose was only achieved through teamwork, teamwork the more remarkable on account of the two different nationalities. . . . The Americans and ourselves do not always see eye to eye, but on those rare occasions when we come together to do a job of work, as, for example, in war or the more serious matter of climbing a mountain, we seem to pull together very well. Where each man has pulled his weight each must share the credit; for, though it is natural for each man to have his expectations, it is in mountaineering, more than in most things, that we try to believe "The game is more than the players of the game, and the ship is more than the crew." '

*

After Nanda Devi we each went our way in the real world, but having tasted the joy and excitement of the great mountains, longed for more. The chance came in 1937 when the American Alpine Club obtained permission to attempt K2, the most remote of the great mountains. Fritz Wiessner, chosen for the attempt, could not go, and I was asked to lead a reconnaissance. Heady stuff, K2 – second only to Everest, virtually untouched – 'beyond the passes', as Kipling wrote.

Success on Nanda Devi made planning easier. My close friend Bob Bates was first to join, but none from Nanda Devi was able to get away. We asked Dick Burdsall, summiter on Minya Konka, and Bill House of Waddington fame; Loomis sent Paul Petzoldt from the Tetons. The British government arranged a transport officer: Captain Norman Streatfeild, veteran from the harsh, romantic Northwest Frontier of India. As on Nanda Devi, we were advised that we were too small and weak a party for such a great challenge – but we paid no heed.

Charles Houston

Wiser from Tilman's stern teaching, we used Brad Washburn's Alaska system: each food bag was complete for two men for one day; three of these in a larger tougher bag would provide six-man days. Bates weighed and counted and packed. Burdsall researched maps and literature, both scanty, and became our treasurer. Some Nanda Devi equipment was serviceable; we added down sleeping bags, new tents and boots from Switzerland and Britain. We would be lean and spartan, travelling far and light. Generous donors provided the $9,000 budgeted. Supplies were sent in April to Marseilles and on to the same ship the team took to Bombay. My exams in medical school made me late and I flew from London, joining the others in Rawalpindi on May 9th. After three busy days in Srinagar we took trucks to road's end, where we and our six Sherpas, Shikara, cook and cook's helper, with 25 ponies, began the long walk.

The 350 miles took 31 days – long, hard marches in hot, dry, spectacular country. It was tremendously exciting, this wild and little-known region. First over the snow-covered Zoji La pass into Baltistan, past a white cliff carved with the initials 'H.H.G-A, 1861-2-3', where Godwin Austen had passed. On the ninth day we followed the mighty, muddy Indus, where the track ran sometimes five, sometimes a thousand feet above the torrent. Beautiful green oases in this vertical desert showed where generations had built irrigation ditches. We were welcomed as curiosities – but friends – everywhere. Here was polo where it had originated, dances, dinners, and always the tiring, satisfying long day's travel. . . . This march-in was a wonderful time to shakedown, get to know each other, to dream, to plan, to hope together. Here, where the Great Game was even then being played, we were already 'inspired by a single hope and bound by a single purpose.'

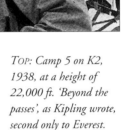

This journey was in sharp contrast with the shorter march to Nanda Devi. In Garwhal, the constant rain made for lush forests and hillsides, great trees and streams and acres of flowers. In Baltistan we strode across dry sand and rock and up gigantic red cliffs. Water was rare, and an even rarer rose bush bloomed unseen. This was a hard land, wild and wonderful; Garwhal was soft and seductive, inviting rather than threatening. For me the contrast was unforgettable and wonderful – even forty years later when I returned briefly.

Half-way to base camp, on May 25th, we reached Skardu, a busy trading centre where cast-offs from the French 1936 expedition were for sale. In great confusion, we selected 55 porters to carry gear to the final village, Askole, eight days of hard rough scrambling away. First we took a barge across the Indus – allegedly a relic from Alexander the Great – then a goatskin raft across the Braldu, and then many rope-bridges, steep cliffs, and sand. A porter strike threatened, but the Sherpas and intervention from Skardu saved the day. Finally we came to the huddle of poor stone houses that were Askole, where we were warmly greeted, given handfuls of apricot pits (eaten like almonds), and found men eager to help us on the next part of the journey. We caught rare glimpses of pale-faced Moslem women with Grecian noses, and Greek coin jewellery: truly we were deep into the past.

TOP: Camp 5 on K2, 1938, at a height of 22,000 ft. 'Beyond the passes', as Kipling wrote, second only to Everest.

ABOVE: Charlie Houston at Camp 5.

RIGHT: Houston seen climbing above Camp 4.

Then, disaster. Petzold, our biggest and toughest member, became delirious with high fever and pains in every part of his body. After two days, during which I had no idea what ailed him, we agreed that the party should move on without us. If Paul recovered, we would try to catch up; if he died – well, I would bury him and hurry after the others. After one last bathe in the Askole hot springs, with 75 porters carrying gear and food for all, they started for our mountain. Petzoldt slowly improved and, though very weak, we overtook our friends.

After rough days we reached the huge Baltoro glacier, unimpressive and ugly, retreating behind its terminal moraine. But once on that 80-mile ice-flow, we were in a magical land. Like imagined castles, cathedrals and towers, separated by valleys of ice, the beautiful granite stood many thousand feet above our heads. We were in the Land of Giants. Rounding the corner at Concordia, the vast amphitheatre where half a dozen glaciers meet, we saw our beautifully symmetrical pyramid, towering two miles above its base and awesome, even 20 miles away. We camped near a glacier river, paid off the porters who were anxious to get down, and gave the leader 45 stones. 'Throw one away each day and come back when they are all gone,' we told him.

We had only six weeks to examine this huge mountain and to find a route for the 1939 party. Above base camp, broken cliffs and jagged ice falls, showered with avalanches, were unthinkable to us then. Further to the east the face fell in a steep unbroken avalanche slope 10,000 feet to the glacier. Twice we went to the west, spending several days over a dangerously crevassed glacier, and climbed to 22,000 feet on Savoia pass, to be turned back by steep green ice. Two pairs laboured five miles eastwards, towards Windy Gap, shuddered at the cornices of the Northeast Ridge and, after a token climb to 22,000 feet, returned to base.

By June 27th we had examined those routes we thought feasible by the state of the art in 1938. Today every route we inspected and many others even more dangerous and difficult have been climbed – and too many climbers have paid a fearful price. Though eager for the summit, we were not willing to take such risks. What were we to do? The South Face offered many erratic little ridgelets of rotten rock, twisting into each other. These were our last hope and for the next 25 days we struggled up to the final summit pyramid. As each recce-party found a camp site, others packed loads to stock it with fuel and food. We leap-frogged in half siege-, half alpine-style. Although monsoons rarely have much impact here, we had severe blizzards alternating with beautiful clear sun and the black sky of altitude.

These were wondrous days with moments of incredible beauty, hours of fatigue, and seconds of panic when stones whirred like shells about us. The route was unceasingly steep and became more difficult and dangerous the higher we went. Jumars were unknown. We had little rope to fix and few pitons – all these were yet to come, a mixed blessing. Finally, with the party intact and still strong and keen, July 20th saw Petzoldt and I established in Camp 7 on the lower edge of the great snow shoulder. The weather looked clear; the others returned to lower camps to wait their turn. We climbed steeply, then across a gentle slope to the foot of the final barrier – 1,500 feet of rock and ice cliffs. I could go no further; Petzoldt was a bit stronger, but the summit was beyond us, then. Back in camp we were horrified to find only a few matches remaining; with the last one we lit a feeble stove, melted water, cooked supper and went to bed. Without matches we would have no more water and not enough food. A ring around

the sun and high cirrus next morning were ominous. We went down to bring up the others, but as we did, the weather thickened.

Very much aware of the steep, avalanche–smoothed Black Pyramid, and the difficult chimney which Bill House had conquered, and the 60-foot overhang below this, we were not ready to tempt fate further. On July 25th, without mishap, we were together in Base Camp and the weather, though threatening, still held when the porters returned next day.

The march home took us to intoxicating green grass, warmth, running water, fresh food, and the exhilaration of strength, health and relief, tinged with sadness. We made Skardu easily over the Skor La, and then climbed to the flower–strewn meadows of the great Deossaie plateau and finally, sadly, to the Burzil Pass. There we sat alone, looking far down at Kashmir, journeys end. We had done what we had been asked to do: we had thoroughly scouted this magnificent mountain, found a reasonably safe though difficult route (for its time), and had come amazingly close to summiting. Could we have gone further? In today's world, certainly. Should we have tried again? Bound by the standards and practice of that time, facing bad weather, and very tired from five hard weeks of exploration and load–carrying, we were right to turn back. Others, years later, pushed the envelope further; some did great and heroic deeds, others died, needlessly, victims to ambition and to the mind–numbing effects of great altitude. We lived to climb again, for many years. In true mountaineering, the summit is not everything. It is only part.

LEFT: The 'Dudley Wolfe Memorial' at the foot of K2, commemorating, besides Wolfe, the Sherpas who died with him in 1939, as well as Art Gilkey, another American lost on the mountain in 1953. Americans had a long and special relationship with K2, in much the same way as the British identified with Everest.

Edmund Hillary

Everest: the Last Lap

The view was amazing, like a giant relief map before us. To the east Makalu stood out prominently, and I found myself automatically looking to see if there was a route up it.

Sometime around four o'clock I looked out of the tent door and could see it was going to be a perfect day for the job. Even as early as this, the view was indescribably lovely, with the icy peaks below glowing in the first flush of dawn above their still dark and sleeping valleys. We brewed more tea, nibbled a few biscuits, and thawed out our frozen boots over the Primus stove. By the time Tenzing and I struggled outside – wearing all the clothes we possessed at the time – it was getting on for 6.30 a.m.

Our little ledge was still sunk in deep shadow, but the way ahead, bathed in sunlight, looked inviting. Tenzing gave a cry of delight at being able to pick out Thyangboche Monastery far below – way, way down, 16,000 feet from where we were standing, faint on its prominent spur.

'Come on,' I urged. 'Let's go!' I was worried that we might get frostbite if we stood around too long. Willing as always, Tenzing grinned and scrambled past me, kicking a long line of steps around the bluff on which we'd been camping. We regained the ridge.

At first the going was not too steep although, here, the ridge had narrowed to a knife edge and its friable snowcrust demanded care. I took over the lead and swung out to the right, on to the Kangshung Face, instead of following the line taken by the first assault party, more or less directly up the crest. The snow was soft and very unstable. Sometimes we'd take one step forward, then slide back a couple of feet; all the time I feared the whole thing would avalanche with us on

BIOGRAPHY

This is the story of 29 May 1953, when a young New Zealand beekeeper and his Sherpa companion climbed into immortality, by becoming the first to stand on the world's highest point. Hillary had taken part in Eric Shipton's southern reconnaissance of Everest in 1951; Tenzing had been on six earlier expeditions, to the north and south of the mountain, and had narrowly missed reaching the summit with the Swiss the year before. John Hunt's 1953 expedition reached the South Col on May 21, to establish its Camp VIII. From there, Charles Evans and Tom Bourdillon, using closed-circuit oxygen apparatus, made a tremendous push to the South Summit but were unable to continue further. Another tent was then placed higher up, on sloping ground at 27,900 feet and anchored to oxygen bottles, there being no convenient rocks. Hillary and Tenzing spent an uncomfortable night inside, dozing and brewing tea. The temperature plunged to -27° C (-17° F), and once they had exhausted all the oxygen they had allowed themselves for the night, the two were extremely cold and miserable. Fortunately the wind, which had been alarmingly gusty early on, eased before morning . . .

it. Carefully, I packed down the snow as I made each new step. About half way up one particularly steep section I turned to Tenzing to see what he felt about it.

'Is dangerous . . .' he acknowledged, clearly not at all happy.

'So what do you think? Shall we go on this way?'

He thought for a while before replying. 'Just as you like,' he said at length – which to be perfectly honest wasn't a whole lot of help. Still, on we went . . .

Conditions improved. The surface got harder and at last we emerged onto the South Summit. This was as far as Bourdillon and Evans had reached two days earlier, at about 28,700 feet. We sat down gratefully, had a snack and a little to drink, and I did some mental arithmetic to figure out how our oxygen was lasting. In fact, I was doing elaborate calculations all the way up the mountain – and all the way down it again.

Ahead, the summit ridge looked daunting, what at lower altitudes one might call 'a good alpine ridge'. The first part rose gradually, but there were enormous cornices overhanging the Kangshung Face. One careless step here would be enough to send the lot crashing 10,000 feet down to the glacier below, and us with it. To the left, the Southwest Face fell steeply into the Western Cwm. Pretty impressive! Some way ahead I could see the steep black rock step which all along we'd thought would be the crux of the climb. Well, we would have to see . . .

Moving down off the south summit – quite a little dip down, it was – in the old-fashioned methods of those days, I cut a line of steps along the lefthand side of the ridge, above the rockface. To my great relief, and some astonishment, the snow was firm and crystalline: two or three blows of the axe fashioned a perfectly satisfactory step. Soon I had chipped a line of steps the full length of the rope – forty feet – and, belayed to my ice-axe, I brought Tenzing along to join me. Then I repeated the whole process, rope length after rope length, all the while uneasily conscious of the great drops at our feet. A good line of steps here was going to be especially important on our way down, after the climb, when we could expect to be feeling very weak and tired.

Before long we reached the rock step. It was about 40 feet

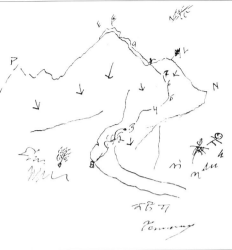

LEFT: A sketch by Sherpa Tenzing, illustrating the route by which Mount Everest was finally climbed.

ABOVE: Sherpa Tenzing crossing a deep crevasse in the Khumbu Ice Fall on an aluminium ladder. The 1953 expedition benefited from technological advances made during the Second World War.

LEFT: Hillary and Tenzing, roped together, make their way up to the final camp, from which they set out alone for the summit (photographed by George Lowe at 27,500 ft).

161

ABOVE: The crowning moment. Tenzing stands proud on the summit of the world, 29 May 1953. He raises aloft flags of Britain, Nepal, India and the United Nations.

high, and looked even steeper close to, formidably steep when one remembered the altitude, 29,000 feet. Then I noticed a narrow crack on the righthand side, where the ice was breaking away from the rock over the Kangshung Face. Crawling inside, I began to wriggle, forcing and jamming my way up it. It was tremendously hard work, and on reaching the top, I flopped, gasping, in the snow, like a beached whale. Yet even as I struggled for breath, I felt a surge of jubilation. For the first time it

struck me that we were really going to make it. Before that, all had been hope and surmise: now I was confident it would take a lot to stop us.

Tenzing joined me and we carried on. Still chipping steps, I hugged the lefthand slope. The ridge seemed to go on forever, its snake-like undulations bearing away to the right, each one concealing the next, raising hopes that at last we'd come to the end, only to have them dashed again.

I had no idea where the top was: for almost two hours I'd been cutting steps now, and my back and arms were exhausted. Tenzing, too, I could see was very tired.

A patch of shingle barred the way. This, too, I clambered over wearily, continuing on around the next bump. Only then, did I realize it was the last bump of all. Ahead the ridge dropped away steeply, revealing, as far as the eye could see, nothing but the barren highlands of Tibet.

Above us, to the right, was a rounded snow dome. Just a few more whacks of the ice-axe, a few more weary steps, and Tenzing and I were on top of Everest!

It was 11.30 a.m. on 29 May, 1953.

There came no feeling of extreme pleasure or excitement, more a sense of quiet satisfaction, and even a little bit of surprise. So many tough climbers had tried for the summit and failed. Now Tenzing and I were there: it seemed hard to believe. Behind his balaclava, goggles and oxygen mask, all encrusted with icicles, I could see Tenzing grinning beatifically. I reached out to shake his hand, but he would have none of it. Instead, he flung his arms around my shoulders. We hugged and thumped each other on the back until forced to stop for lack of breath.

Removing my oxygen equipment, I took photographs of my companion on top, waving a string of flags – Nepalese, British, United Nations and Indian. Then I sought to record all the leading ridges down from the summit, proof if we needed it that we'd really been up there. (I was mindful that it is a very disbelieving world.)

The view was amazing, like a giant relief map before us. To the east Makalu stood out prominently, and I found myself automatically looking to see if there was a route up it. Even Kang-chenjunga, 80 miles away, could be seen clearly. Over to the west was Cho Oyu, where I'd been the year before, and in the distance, Shisha Pangma. Peering down the north side, there were all the landmarks I'd heard about from the prewar attempts on Everest: the north col, Changtse or north peak, and the curving East Rongbuk Glacier. Tenzing, meanwhile, had scratched a little hole in the snow and was burying some sweets and biscuits as offerings to the gods for our success.

By now, I'd been without my oxygen for nearly eight minutes and was growing clumsy-fingered and slow in my movements, so I quickly plugged myself in again. At once, as it seemed to me, everything looked brighter. Maybe I was deluding myself, maybe it was a pyschological effect, but I could have sworn the world swung immediately into sharper focus.

After 15 minutes we turned to go, picking our way down the mountain slowly and carefully.

At our highest camp we stopped to brew up. By this time (2 p.m.) our oxygen had run out, but we continued steadily downwards, burdened now with our camping gear. A couloir on the Southeast Ridge had been swept clean by the wind and no longer

LEFT: Colonel John Hunt leads his triumphant team home. Left to right, at London Airport: Lowe, Band, Gregory, Hillary, Hunt, Tenzing, Wylie, Noyce, Stobart, Westmacott (Pugh and Morris, both concealed).

BELOW: News of the success (relayed to London in code by The Times *correspondent, James Morris), splashed into the world's press on 2 June, Coronation Day of Queen Elizabeth II.*

bore any trace of our tracks. I had to chip steps all the way down its hard surface and was relieved to see George Lowe coming up towards us bearing a flask of soup. Tomato, I seem to remember, and very welcome.

'How did it go?' he wanted to know.

My reply was in rough mountaineering form. 'Well George, we knocked the bastard off!' (Never, for a solitary moment, did I dream that the wretch would broadcast these great words to the world, over the BBC!)

*

Our success on Everest made a great difference to the lives of all of us. It certainly did to me. As a result, I became deeply involved in the welfare of the Sherpas and the other mountain peoples of the Himalaya.

Over the years the Himalayan Trust, which I set up with some friends in the early 1960s, has built some 26 small country schools in Nepal, as well as two hospitals and a dozen medical clinics. We have established a number of tree nurseries to replace the forests severely denuded by the increasing number of visitors, and have planted out a million seedlings. But growth has been exceptionally slow and only after five years did some of the trees start to sprout. It will be many years before much of the forest has been re-established.

In the 1980s the head lama of Thyangboche Monastery asked us to construct a school for the training of his 25 young monks. We agreed and it was a long and difficult progress. We were rather proud of the completed school and for a year it did an excellent job, but in January 1989 disaster struck. Thyangboche Monastery and our school caught fire and were completely destroyed. So it was back to fundraising again: we determined we would rebuild this focal point of Sherpa heritage. And we raised more than £150,000 – the Sherpas themselves, amongst their own people, found $50,000 – an absolutely colossal sum. Foundations for a new monastery were dug and 11,000 pieces of timber cut. Rocks were dressed and cemented together. Slowly, the building has risen again, in its old familiar shape . . .

Reaching the summit of a mountain gives great satisfaction, but nothing for me has been more rewarding in this life than the results of our climb on Everest, when we have devoted ourselves to the welfare of our Sherpa friends.

Tony Streather with Ralph Barker

Grim Days on Haramosh

Next morning I found I was suffering from snow-blindness. I had lost

my goggles and the two ice-axes, and I was also hallucinating.

'Come on up!' I called. 'You can't imagine what you'll see when you get here!'

For the four of us who made up the high-climbing party on Haramosh, this was a bittersweet moment. Forced to lower our sights by unseasonable weather, we had at last reached a point, between the mountain's twin peaks, from which its secrets were dramatically revealed.

After five weeks of frustration, it was some consolation to realize that even with favourable weather this 24,270-foot summit in the Karakoram would probably have been beyond us. A stronger party, not so restricted for time, might succeed, but for each of us other commitments intruded, and tomorrow we were going to have to start the descent.

Bernard Jillott, seeking an even more spectacular vantage point, urged John Emery, our doctor, to climb to a pinnacle a little further up the ridge, 'Then Tony can take a picture of us.' Roping up, the two had almost reached the pinnacle when there was a muffled, subterranean explosion, and simultaneously the snow on which they were standing started to move. With Rae Culbert, the fourth member of our group, I watched stupefied as our friends swept past with terrifying acceleration, down into the snow basin a thousand feet below. There seemed nothing to stop them being carried on with the avalanche straight over the North Face. When the snow flurries subsided, I moved across to the avalanche trail and, belayed by Culbert, peered down the slope into the basin. To my astonishment and joy, I could see two crumpled figures

BIOGRAPHY

Tony Streather served in the Indian Army during and just after the last War, in the north of that country and later in Pakistan, where his duties daily took him over high passes. In 1950, a Norwegian expedition drew on his expertise for an attempt on Tirich Mir, and he went with them to the summit. In 1953, as Transport Officer to the Americans on Charles Houston's K2 expedition, he was caught up in the epic attempt to save Art Gilkey (see page 152).

Two years later Streather took part in the expedition to successfully climb Kangchenjunga for the first time, making up the second summit pair with Norman Hardie. At the time he was the first person to have climbed two peaks over 25,000 feet. In 1976 Lt. Col. Streather, as he was by this time, was invited to lead an Army expedition to Everest, celebrating his fiftieth birthday the day base camp was set up. He was President of the Alpine Club from 1990-92.

emerging from the snow. Jillott and Emery had survived the fall, but they were trapped in an inaccessible place. I couldn't see how we were going to get them out.

Bernard Jillott, at 23 the prime mover of our expedition, was President of the Oxford University Mountaineering Club. The year was 1957. A few months earlier he had invited me to talk to the club about my experiences on K2 and Kangchenjunga, and this was when the subject of Haramosh was broached. Three other club members wanted to go, Jillott told me, but he felt they needed a 'veteran' – I was 31 – to lend credibility to the project. Would I be their leader? His single-mindedness impressed me, and I soon found myself drawn into the expedition by the enthusiasm of the group.

With the leadership settled, Jillott set about the planning and obtaining permissions and sponsorship with characteristic energy. His favourite climbing partner was a young medical student named Emery, and as one of my stipulations was that the party should include a 'doctor', Emery, keen to come, fitted the bill admirably. I found him less obsessive than Jillott, of wider interests and broader vision. Jillott's final choice for the high-altitude party was New Zealand forestry graduate Rae Culbert. At 25, Culbert owed his greater maturity not so much to his age as to three years surveying with the New Zealand Forest Service and a deep affinity with his work. Each of us, at various times, was to turn to Culbert for friendship. A fifth member of the expedition, though excluded from the high-altitude party by

inexperience, was the American, Scott D. Hamilton, Jr., 29 and a graduate of Cornell University. Devoted to Jillott and Emery, his puritanical upbringing left him wincing at Culbert's colourful language, but he recognized in him an ally from the New World.

From Heathrow to Karachi and forward to Gilgit, 40 miles west of Haramosh, we travelled by air, all except Emery, who voyaged by sea with the expedition stores. At Gilgit we engaged porters to help carry our stores to the high camps. A day's ride to the road-head at Sussi and two days on foot brought us to the high Kutwal Valley and the Mani Glacier, where we set up base camp.

Our initial aim was reconnaissance: to explore and survey the approaches to Haramosh. But I knew well enough that I had in my party skilful and ambitious climbers, capable, once a pyramid of camps was built, of a disciplined dash for the summit.

Starting our assault via the Northeast Ridge, we moved base camp up to the head of the valley, below the pass known as the Haramosh La. Soon we had established Camp I half-way up towards the La and found a site beyond it for Camp II.

Progress in the next few days was slow. The Northeast Ridge proved impossible for porters, and the detour forced upon us led through a grotesquely crevassed icefall, causing further delay. Then the weather broke, driving us back down. By extending our travel bookings I managed to devise a new 12-day assault

ABOVE: Haramosh (24,270 ft), photographed from above Camp 2. On this peak in 1957 an Oxford University expedition, led by professional soldier Tony Streather, was overtaken by one of the most epic tragedies in climbing history.

RIGHT: Bernard Jillott, who had organized the expedition, survived two falls into the snow basin, only to walk off the mountain in the dark, while trying to help his companions.

plan which still gave us an outside chance of reaching the summit. But when we finally left base camp on the 29th August, fresh snow combined with clashes of temperament to threaten cohesion. Yet gradually we were shedding something of our individualism, pooling our resources, becoming a team. Camp III was put in at 18,500 feet, Camp IV at 20,000. Hamilton retreated with orders to keep Camp III open, and on 15th September, in good snow conditions, we succeeded at last in breaking through to the Northeast Ridge.

same area wouldn't avalanche twice. As the slope steepened I was forced to turn and face into it, as though going backwards down a ladder. Sometimes I half-turned and shone my torch down the slope, shouting as I did so. Soon I heard answering shouts. When the rope pulled taut, Culbert joined me, and together we resumed the descent. It was tedious work, and we were astonished when it began to get light. The second day of our traumas had begun. Now we could see Jillott and Emery waving to us, and hear their warning shouts. A line of ice-cliffs lay directly below us, and there was no way down. We would have to traverse along the top of the ice-cliffs until they petered out. The effort taxed us both, and it was late afternoon before we approached the end of the traverse, by which time we had been climbing almost continuously since the morning of Day 1.

It was at this point that Culbert lost a crampon. I already knew that Jillott and Emery had lost their ice axes. Now, as I caught Culbert's eye, we both knew how significant this latest loss might be.

From the end of the traverse we started down a 400-foot slope, which ended in a bergschrund or large crevasse at the change of levels. Again we had to go down backwards, kicking steps. But at last we reached the bergschrund. Advancing to the upper lip, we lowered a rope, Jillott and Emery tied on in turn, and a moment was spared to celebrate our reunion. But there was no time to waste. Although the light was already failing, no one doubted that we must start the climb out that night. We had almost reached the traverse, on a single rope, Culbert leading, when something crashed into me and knocked me off the slope. It was Culbert, hampered by his lost crampon. Our combined weight dislodged Jillott and Emery and we fell together in a tangled mass straight over the bergschrund and back into the snow basin. No one was hurt, but I had lost my ice axe in the fall. Taking over the lead, using

I had watched continually for signs of avalanche conditions, and I felt perfectly safe on the ridge. But it was the first time we had stood on a slope facing northwest. A great weight of snow must have been driven against it to account for the avalanche.

Now, judging that Jillott and Emery would survive perfectly well in the snow basin for the night, I returned to Camp IV with Culbert, for sustenance, to fill thermos flasks of hot soup for Jillott and Emery, and to collect more rope. Then we set out again for the ridge, hoping to get down to the basin that night.

It was ten o'clock when we reached the ridge. The night was dark, but we had torches. Asking Culbert to keep me on a fairly tight rope, 300 feet of it, I started down the slope. Soon the snow hardened and I felt safer; I was in the track of the avalanche. The

Culbert's axe, I tried again. It was almost dark now, but later there would be a moon. Again we had nearly reached the traverse when I found myself falling: Jillott had gone to sleep in his tracks and dragged us off a second time. Exhausted, we spent the night jammed in the berg-schrund, huddled together to keep warm.

When it began to get light – it was now Day 3 – I climbed out of the crevasse. I felt fairly strong, but I knew the others had been less fortunate. We had a difficult day ahead of us. We had climbed about 300 feet, without roping up, when Emery spotted an axe sticking out of the slope; it was the axe I had been using during the night, Culbert's axe, and I could now cut much firmer steps. But on the traverse, first Emery and then Culbert felt themselves slipping. Digging in with his crampons, Emery arrested the slide. But Culbert, with his cramponless foot already frostbitten, called to me for help. I replied that I would give him a belay from the end of the traverse. Reaching it, I climbed a few feet up the slope to be sure of safe ground, then made way for Jillott and Emery and told them to go back to Camp IV. 'We'll follow you shortly,' I said. Almost immediately, Culbert came off the traverse. The jerk was too much for me to hold, and soon we were tumbling the lower half of the avalanche fall suffered by Jillott and Emery. But with no snow falling with us, to cushion us, we were shaken and concussed. Already it was getting dark, the end of Day 3. Jillott called down, 'We'll go on back to camp and get food and drink. We'll be back to help you as soon as we can.'

Culbert and I fell into an uneasy sleep. All our hopes now rested on Jillott and Emery. We would wake for Day 4, but it was plain to me that Culbert would not survive another night.

Next morning I found I was suffering from snow-blindness. I had lost my goggles and the two ice-axes, and I was also hallucinating. But we had to get going. Jillott and Emery would have reached Camp IV during the night, and I calculated that after food and rest they would be back at the point of the avalanche by about midday. I expected to meet them somewhere on the traverse. Twice more, as we climbed the steep slope to the traverse, Culbert slipped and fell off. The second time he sat where he landed, absolutely all in. I called to him to hang on where he was. 'The others will be down soon.' They would bring food and drink, a spare ice axe and a spare crampon. Between us we would get Culbert out. Yet as time passed there was still no sign of them. What could be delaying them? I began to fear that something had gone desperately wrong.

When I reached the point where I had belayed Culbert across the final stretch of the traverse, I saw something sticking out of the snow; it was the axe I had been using, Culbert's axe. It gave me renewed strength.

Picking up the track back to Camp IV I realized that Jillott and Emery had taken a different route from the original, and with much trepidation I followed it. It proved to be a dead short cut. After avoiding numerous hazards I joined up with the original track. Then, with darkness falling on the fourth day since leaving Camp IV, I picked out the two tents, dreading what I might find. Emery was lying on top of his sleeping bag, shaken and distressed.

There was no sign of Jillott. I asked the obvious question. 'Where's Bernard?'

'He's gone.'

'Gone? Gone where?'

'He's gone. He's dead. He walked straight off the mountain.'

I learned with mounting horror how Jillott, driven by his determination to return as quickly as possible to the snow basin, had forged ahead, and how Emery, trying to follow, had fallen into a crevasse, lost consciousness, and lain unprotected all night. When he came to that morning he had struggled out and followed Jillott's tracks until they reached a point where, in the darkness of the previous night, he had walked off the mountain.

Emery had called repeatedly but got no answer. Later I did the same. Meanwhile Emery asked his own question. 'Where's Rae?'

'I'm afraid he's still in the basin. He kept slipping off. We'll have to go back for him.' Even as I said it, I saw the utter hopelessness of it. With Jillott dead and Emery so badly frostbitten that he was almost totally incapacitated, the only practical task that remained was to try to get him off the mountain alive.

To leave a comrade to his fate on a mountain was an abandonment not to be contemplated. But I had known, when I left Culbert, that he could not survive another night. I could do nothing for him now. For hour after hour I kept melting snow in an effort to slake our thirst. Then we tried to sleep. For the first time on the expedition we took sleeping pills, but they brought no rest for me. I was too preoccupied with thoughts of Rae Culbert, the man who in our separate ways we had all loved, and of the tragic end to the highly promising life of Bernard Jillott.

Emery and I fashioned a halting means of progress that eventually got us down to Camp III, where an anguished Hamilton called to us as we approached: 'Are we safe?' Somehow I gasped out the truth. Hamilton, stunned by the news, broke down, as I did at that moment. I still believe that, but for the mischance of a lost crampon, we would all have got safely off the mountain.

Hamilton knew the route from Camp III to base camp better than anyone, and in the next two days and nights his help was crucial. When at last we spotted the Hunza porters coming up to meet us, Emery and I collapsed.

Haramosh was climbed in the following year by an Austrian expedition. The long ridge from the scene of the avalanche took them eight hours.

LEFT: Blessed sight! Hunza porters climbing up from the valley to help the stricken party. (By this time Streather and Emery were both in a bad way from their protracted exposure, barely able to move.)

Peter Habeler

From Space to Super-space

Our breath came raggedly and exhaustion overwhelmed us every forty to sixty feet, so that we had to rest our heads on our axes.

For me, the ascent of the 26,460-foot Hidden Peak in the Karakorum in 1975 was a very special experience. I feel very much that an adventure like this not only extends a climber's limits on rock and ice, but leads him or her into other very important fields. To any young climbers who may be ambitious to follow in my footsteps, I would say that what matters is not so much attempting the hardest routes on a Himalayan seven- or eight-thousander, as having enormous enthusiasm for mountaineering. It is vital that, heart and soul, you belong to mountains and to mountain-climbing.

This story really started with our ascent of the North Face of the Eiger, a climb still generally regarded as a big and dangerous wall. My perception of it at the time was of a vast space, aloof and unfriendly, not at all welcoming. I didn't fully understand the sensations then, but on the way to Hidden Peak they took on a more con-crete form and I was better able to describe what it was I felt, what it was really all about.

In considering the Eiger North Face as a great space, I had instinctively acknowledged how much we humans are part of a spatial world. For a number of hours this space became an ingredient of our short lives, to be hastened through, traversed, speedily surmounted, and as quickly deserted. The leap from Eiger to Hidden Peak was basically no more than a necessary and consequential leap from one space to another.

In the space of this eight-thousander, Reinhold Messner and I found ourselves

BIOGRAPHY

His one-time partner, Reinhold Messner, used to say of Peter Habeler, 'He's like a sky-rocket, really impressive once the fuse is lit!' Born in Mayrhofen in the Austrian Tyrol in 1942, he took up climbing at the age of six and by the time he was 21 had become a certified mountain guide and skiing instructor. Apart from the years between 1966 and 1971, when he climbed and taught in Jackson Hole in the United States, Peter Habeler has lived and worked in his native Zillertal, in 1972 becoming the Director of the Alpine School of Mayrhofen. He now runs his own alpine and ski school.

In the mid-1960s, Habeler began a fruitful climbing partnership with Reinhold Messner. The two gained their first high mountain experience in 1969 with an ascent of the east face of Yerupaja, and a first ascent on Yerupaja Chico in South America. In 1974 they climbed the Eiger north face in what was then a record time of ten hours. There had been 'West Alpine style' ascents in the Himalaya before – eschewing big parties, sherpa support and oxygen bottles – but the Hidden Peak climb (described here) turned the tide of high altitude climbing. The lightweight, 'fair means' ascent became the stylistic ideal. The oxygenless ascent of Everest in 1978 was the last climb of the partnership. Habeler remains At Home in the Mountains of the World, *the title of his autobiography.*

RIGHT: *Hidden Peak (Gasherbrum I, standing at 26,470 ft/8,068 m), seen here from the northwest. The Messner-Habeler route climbs out of the steep basin, left, to join the lefthand skyline at its shoulder.*

BELOW: *Reinhold Messner before the Hidden Peak climb, photographed in Camp I of the Polish Women's expedition which successfully climbed Gasherbrums II and III.*

ABOVE: The Baltoro Glacier. Looking northwest towards Concordia from below Golden Throne. Mitre peak is on the left, with Muztagh Tower beyond.

LEFT: Peter Habeler after his lonely 45-mile trek up the Baltoro – a hostile world, it seemed to him then, with death only a hair's breadth away at every turn.

even more isolated than before, completely cut off from normal life. The leap from Eiger-space to the grandiose space of this face forced us to the appreciation that we had laid ourselves open to a transformation: we had become 'spacemen'. I should explain what I mean.

Up until now, when I'd completed a climb, I would sit in front of a hut, chatting with friends, be content to watch the wind blowing through the long grass. I could gaze at the blue-green of an icy mountain lake. There was time enough for all that. Even the rain was a matter of course. Tomorrow, the sun would come out again and we could go climbing once more.

That was a different world. In the leap from space to super-space, everything became more urgent, more hurried. Time could not be so squandered. How would such careless waste affect the pleasure of it? How much now hung upon one or two wet or snowy weeks on the way to a summit!

For three days after leaving Paiju at the foot of the 45-mile Baltoro Glacier, I was completely on my own, climbing up the broken ice. I had forged ahead to find a suitable spot for base camp, from which we could ascend Hidden Peak. In those three days I felt as lonely as I've ever been in my life. The great peaks to right and left occupied enormous spaces in a hostile world. The higher I climbed, the more they began to oppress me, like passing silent companions.

Wading across one of the many broad rivers on the glacier, I stumbled to be snatched away by the flood. Death was only a hair's breadth away, but my luck held and I managed to clutch hold of a rock and save myself. That night was cold and icy, and laying in my wet sleeping bag in the silence I was plagued by a turmoil of conflicting thoughts, quite distinct arguments, all with something important to say about my life. But what was important now?

And what would become important?

To be sure, I wanted to reach the summit of Hidden Peak with Reinhold, who meanwhile had caught up with me. We wanted to do it as a two-man team. We had set ourselves a clear goal, a new idea. But it had been well thought through, systematically prepared for: it was a logical undertaking. Both of us had set our hearts on it – lost them to it, you might even say.

Only when your heart is really in something can you take on, or put up with, the quite enormous stresses involved in a project like this. But is it possible to lose your heart totally to such an idea? Certainly getting to the summit was an important factor. But I heard an inner voice telling me gently yet insistently that there was more to it than that. This voice won me over, persuaded me there was something more vital than the summit of Hidden Peak.

People I knew, people I felt close to, suddenly seemed to join me on the glacier, entering my thought-world; for a while they were more real than the mountains all around. And I understood that I was about to do something in my life which quite possibly was a mistake.

As a young man I'd devoted myself utterly to the mountains. I loved them, loved everything they offered me, which was a great deal, a very great deal. In this love, people only gradually came to play a significant role, but beautifully, for love comes in stages; it needs its own special gentle development. In the end there

the problem, I found myself able to live with it. I had been liberated.

When something becomes clear, like that, you transcend your present condition to be transported to a new level, higher and greater than where you were before. All at once I knew it was perfectly possible to live with absolute contrasts, individually and jointly!

With the dawn, my night qualms were banished. Everything shone in a new light. Even the dangers of the Baltoro Glacier became more bearable. Now all I had to do was simply put it to the test, this new-found ambiguity of mine. Meanwhile, there was nothing to do but apply my enormous restlessness to the continued march up the glacier, to find a spot for our camp and get it ready.

So how did we get on?

On 26 July we set up base at the foot of our mountain at a height of 16,700 feet. Our few porters trailed back to their villages, and we were alone.

should and must emerge a more rounded, complete person.

Here now, in the middle of the night, it suddenly became clear to me just how much I was in love with Regina, my girl back in the Zillertal. I loved her presence, her nearness, and I longed vehemently – even more vehemently than for our summit – that these joint loves of mine would find a place, a home.

But how could they be combined: my powerful drive to be off to the world's mountains and the just-as-clearly perceived and strong tie with life at home? Was such an apparent contradiction really irreconcilable? In the instant that I consciously faced up to

As soon as Reinhold and I had our tents up, we set off for our first reconnaissance. By way of two icefalls to the west of Hidden Peak, we reached the foot of the Northeast Spur. From here we got our first view of the face: it was steeper than we had pictured it. In fact the lower part looked horrific – an ice wall with a rock band at 20,000 feet.

We spent a night at 19,350 feet, then descended to base camp again, and for the next few days studied the weather. There

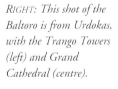

RIGHT: This shot of the Baltoro is from Urdokas, with the Trango Towers (left) and Grand Cathedral (centre).

seemed to be a definite pattern. Three or four fine days, then it would break up again.

At the start of a fine weather period we reascended to a height of 16,075 feet, bivouacked and next day set up a small cache of provisions and equipment, just above the start of the ice face. From here we got a marvellous view of what lay ahead. For the most part, it looked as if we had nothing to fear from falling stones and ice, and it was clear what we had to do. We would go down to base camp once more, rest up, then launch our assault at the start of the next fine spell.

We knew we'd have to climb the face entirely unroped, as we would the upper section to the summit. Quite simply a day wasn't long enough to get up the ice face using conventional rope protection, and a bivouac anywhere on it was bound to be risky. But that's what we were good at, that sort of climbing, moving unroped up steep mixed terrain. It was one of our strengths. We'd proved it long ago and were prepared for it.

In those few days that we rested, storms left a heavy precipitation on the mountain, but we set off at last on 8 August. The weather was still not good, but it was improving noticeably. We erected our little tent on the same spot as our reconnaissance camp. In our rucksacks we carried only the barest essentials. Every surplus gramme would exacerbate the strain of climbing at great height; every one too few could be deadly if the weather were to break suddenly. In the same way as we packed our rucksacks a year before for the North Face of the Eiger, we deliberated long over what to take and what to leave.

Very early on the morning of 9 August we were standing at the foot of the ice face. Almost 4,000 feet of the steepest ice separated us from our next planned bivouac site above the ice-glazed rock section. So this was it! No rope for this bit, no oxygen, no outside help. Everything we would need during the next three days was packed in our rucksacks.

Slowly we made height, thrusting in the tips of our 12-point crampons at each step. We climbed one behind the other, alternating the lead. After eight hours, and the ascent of an extremely hard and dangerous ice chimney, we came to easier ground and so to our bivouac site at about 23,300 feet. We were so exhausted we couldn't even stand up to level out a small platform for our tiny bivouac tent, and although we were plagued by thirst, could eat nothing. Five o'clock saw us already crawling into our sleeping bags.

At 6.30 next morning, when we got up, it was bitterly cold. Even the inside of the tent was thickly encrusted with ice. Carefully, we made our final preparations for the ascent to the summit. We couldn't put on gaiters without taking off our gloves, and within moments our fingers had lost all feeling. Clearly, we were going to have to work hard to avoid frostbite.

Apart from our cameras and some medication, we left everything else behind

in the tent. We wanted to be on top by 4 p.m. at the latest, but even if there were a delay, no way would we bivouac on or near the summit. We were coming back down to this camp, no matter what.

The terrain was easy to begin with and we made good progress, although the oxygen-starved air was already making life uncomfortable. After an hour the face steepened. Reinhold was filming, an almost superhuman exertion at this altitude. The snow was hard-packed by the wind and unpleasant to break trail in. Our breath came raggedly and exhaustion overwhelmed us every forty to sixty feet, so that we had to rest our heads on our axes, waiting for the strength to slowly seep back into our legs. Then another forty feet . . .

Around midday I crossed the summit headwall, out onto the ridge, and knew it couldn't be much further to the top now. Climbing the heavily-corniced ridge, we

BELOW: Peter Habeler on the steep ground of Hidden Peak's northwest face. The climbers had to descend the same way they went up, step by step, facing inwards.

ABOVE: Hidden Peak (Gasherbrum I), seen from Gasherbrum III. (This picture was taken by Alison Chadwick-Onyskiewicz, a British woman who was climbing with the Polish Women's team.)

ABOVE: Another shot of Hidden Peak, this time from the southwest, across the upper Abruzzi Glacier. The northwest flank (around to the left) is not visible from this viewpoint.

could only go about fifteen feet before needing a rest!

I reached the highest point half an hour after noon. The weather was glorious, the panorama out of this world. Reinhold joined me after a few minutes and we hugged each other with joy, as excited as small children. We'd done it! Attained our goal! Our plan had been successful!

Do successes like this gradually diminish the world? What if they keep happening, can everything go on just the same? How about in the long term: do they have a place in that, a value? Or will they evaporate with the next success?

Walter Bonatti sent us a cable that read 'Tremendous alpinism. You two are the only ones in recent years to have pushed out the boundaries of mountaineering.' And Fritz Wiessner wrote that it was an extraordinary performance: 'Probably the finest feat ever achieved in the great ranges. It surely heralds a new epoch in mountaineering. And it was only possible because these outstanding climbers are both incredibly fit, fast and extremely

able. They combine all the right technical, physical and phsychological elements.' To me, this was recognition indeed: more than that, the words gave fresh encouragement.

Even so, on the way home, I was careful not to forget the dangerous experience of my lonely march in to base camp. Now there was another voice to listen to – and possibly to welcome with still greater pleasure.

There is just one further brief observation I would like to make. To recognize that someone loves you for who you are at this moment, and, moreover, for that person to be the one above all to whom you can let yourself say, 'I love you!', then the world becomes a paradise. That was the joy I experienced as I travelled home to Mayrhofen.

Back in the Zillertal – in Mayrhofen particularly – so many people let us know that they had been with us in spirit on our way up Hidden Peak and were now very proud of us. Proud?

It made me really happy to be received in this way. I shall never forget the interest of my many, many friends in the valley and town. I really was able to forge a union between the two opposites, calm the tension which had tormented me on the Baltoro Glacier.

And where will be my home from now on?

The Himalaya, and the Zillertal – both!

Kurt Diemberger

Chomolungma's Last Secret

One morning, early, I take the picture which seven years later will bring me back with a large expedition into this mysterious Tibetan valley. The East Face, the fantastic East Face of Everest!

'Man, don't be crazy. Let me go!' My rope-mate rears above the abyss like a Lipizzaner horse on a string as he attempts to take another giant bound down the icy slope into Tibet where his beloved camera, an extremely expensive model, rolls just beyond his reach, away into the depths. Almost skittishly, the broken carry-strap flicks and dances at every turn in the snow. Close to tears, Hermann begs for more slack. 'I could still get it,' he insists, but a flood of irate Schwabian follows as his camera continues to elude him, making little jumps, for all the world like a mouse scampering down the slope. . . .

How it rolls and rolls, this Rollei! Teeth clenched, I hang on, hands locked, legs opposed in the deep snow, axe rammed in hard – I haven't moved a muscle since the moment the camera was lost and it was clear my friend was bent on hurling himself after it. To loosen my grip now would be disastrous – one stumble and we'd both fetch up sixteen-hundred feet down among the crevasses on the glacier, or somewhere between the pale moraine hills at the end of the valley on the Kangshung side of Mount Everest. Better far to be alive and the camera lost!

But Hermann is still annoyed. He wants us to climb down the face to retrieve it. Right away. There's no reasoning with him. I cannot believe the camera will have snagged anywhere, but Hermann Warth from Schwabia, my companion on this 1974 Shartse expedition, is as pig-headed as they come, and this was his most prized possession. So, we'll try. But it doesn't take us long to realize what a crazy quest this is.

BIOGRAPHY

Born in 1932, this legendary mountaineer has, in a career spanning more than thirty years, been on over twenty expeditions to the high peaks of Inner Asia. Kurt Diemberger is the only man alive to have succeeded in making first ascents of two eight-thousanders (peaks of over 8,000 metres). He has also won a number of film and literary awards connected with his mountaineering.

With Julie Tullis, he formed 'the highest film-team in the world', producing documentaries on Everest, Nanga Parbat and the Karakoram, as well as films about the life of those who live in the mountains. Julie died after an ascent of K2 in 1986, a tragedy Kurt tried to come to terms with in his book The Endless Knot. *Although he knows it can never be as it was before, he continues to return to the mountains. They have helped him in the past and will do so again.*

The face gets steeper all the time, and there's an edge below, beyond which who knows how many drops and overhangs lie concealed. The camera must surely have fallen to the very bottom, and even if it landed in soft snow, it's hard to see how it can be undamaged. 'I can always get it fixed!' Hermann pins his hopes obstinately on this one last chance.

Somehow we have to get to the foot of the face – but not this way. Once back at the top of the slope, I draw a deep breath: we were very lucky there! We head off for a distant saddle, from whose 19,000-foot snowslopes we hope to get down into the unknown Kangshung valley and around to the bottom of our face. It takes three days, and we don't find the camera, although all the gas cylinders and other stuff we chucked down as markers, to make the search easier, we retrieve without trouble. 'The yeti must have had it,' I joke, but Hermann is not amused. All the same, this is ideal yeti-country: great blocks, some grass, a hummocky basin with soft hills like whipped cream on the other side of the valley. And further out, glimpses of the hidden forests of Karma Chu. No man's land . . . plenty of cover . . . Snowman's land. We pass icy nights huddled together under a huge rock, frost crumbling off the waterproof skin of our bivvy bag every time we move. Our faces are rigid with cold. We count the hours until the dawn.

One morning, early, I take the picture which seven years later will bring me back with a large expedition into this mysterious Tibetan valley. The East Face, the fantastic East Face of Everest! A dream face. Shimmering ice-formations, gleaming facets, linked by thousands of ribs, like the pipes of an organ . . . and huge – maybe 13,000 feet high. An unknown face in a forgotten valley, unde-scribed since the British climber George Mallory led a reconnaissance here in 1921, promptly declaring it a far too risky way to climb Everest. (He went back to the north side of the great mountain, only to find his

BELOW: The Kangshung Face, Everest's last secret, seen here from the slopes of Makalu. Kurt Diemberger was haunted by this forbidden face for many years, as he gazed on it from various viewpoints.

ABOVE: Top of the great rampart guarding the approach to the upper Kangshung Face of Everest, which was later called Lowe Buttress. Fringed with massive icicles, this upper section resembles the jaws of a giant shark.

glacier-covered ribs, and reached by a pillar of really steep rock, over 3,000 feet high. Hermann and I had noticed this giant buttress from our icy bivouac when we were searching for the camera. In the two months we spend climbing Makalu, I keep looking across at my coveted face.

Five months later I am high on Everest, filming French mountaineers inching their way into a deep, dark sky. We are on the Southeast Ridge; it is 15 October, 1978, and we're bound for the top: Pierre Mazeaud, Jean Afanassieff, Nicholas Jaeger and me. Below us stretch the endless Tibetan highlands, the icy ridges of the Himalaya . . . Way down, beyond our feet, is the Kangshung Glacier . . . From its depths, the east face of the mountain reaches up to me. We are moving along its upper rim. It feels 'mine', somehow, or at this moment I feel I belong to it – it's hard to explain. Once again I see the route I picked out during my days on Makalu. It looks perfectly feasible, but of course, from here, I'm only seeing the upper part.

Suddenly, all that is unimportant – I am swimming, floating in the sky above Tibet, but with my feet rooted to the ground: we are on Everest's summit, on a never-to-be-forgotten day, above distance and proximity.

Another two years go by. It's autumn 1980. I am with my Sherpa friend Nawang Tenzing, who climbed Makalu with me and Shartse before that; he doesn't share my dream. 'You shouldn't disturb the Buddha of the summit more than once,' he admonishes. 'You've already been up there.' This time Everest isn't our only goal, but nearby Lhotse as well. Both elude us and misfortune clouds the expedition. A Sherpa dies in the icefall, and an avalanche pushes an Italian mountaineer into a crevasse on his way to the South Col. Terrible storms rage for days. Several of my companions suffer frostbite as we sit out one storm on the 25,936-foot col. The impact of the air-masses is so tremendous that an empty tent takes off like a balloon and disappears away down towards the Kangshung Glacier. Through whirling veils of ice crystals I gaze out over Tibet.

The Chinese have opened the border. Mountaineers are tripping over each other in Beijing to secure a permit for the north side of Everest. Soon the greedy clamour for honours will start there too. Can there still be gods on the summit of this mountain? Who now is bothered about its secrets? Yet there remains that one forgotten valley, one face about which nobody speaks, which nobody has ever tried. It seems unbelievable on this over-crowded mountain. The East Face. A picture in my drawer. The last secret of this big mountain. An image in my heart.

*

I am rattling along in a truck, enveloped in a cloud of yellow dust. Over my mouth I wear a gauze mask, as do my companions. The 1981 American Everest Expedition has the East Face in its sights. But as a kind of insurance, we also have a permit for the north side, the traditional ascent route from Tibet. For three days we have been travelling this dusty road over the Tibetan plateau, up and down, speeding between the mountains of the Trans-Himalaya, past lakes, through deserts and patches of green. Monsoon clouds rob us of our first expected sighting of Chomolungma, 'Goddess Mother of the World', from the top of a high pass. Only the summit of Cho Oyu peeps through the clouds.

We reach Kharta, a mountain village in the bottom of the valley of the same name, the birthplace of Sherpa Tenzing

death there on a later visit, while making a summit bid with Sandy Irvine.)

The face haunts me, becomes a treasured dream. But I don't speak of it. The Chinese don't let anyone into Tibet. No use building false hopes. I wonder about a secret expedition, slipping over the border like we did before? But that's unthinkable: you couldn't get gear in that way. No, this face is destined to remain a dream – and how many dreams come true?

A photograph in my drawer – for a long time, this is all that remains. Four years go by. Then, in spring 1978, I set out for my third eight-thousander, Makalu, with Hermann Warth again and a small international expedition. And once more, Everest's East Face rears up with her fluted ribs and icy slopes! Now I see clearly how to attack it if the chance ever comes my way. There's only one real possibility on a face so constantly scoured by avalanches: the wide rib of ice – more of a ridge really – one of the five 'fingers' of a hand-shaped feature draped across the face in such a way that its outspread fingers just touch the Kangshung Glacier. Again I think: 13,000 feet from glacier floor to the summit – that has to be one of the biggest ice faces in the world!

The finger to follow is the one on the left, the biggest of the

it back on his shoulders to his own valley, where hardly any trees grow. It takes several days – but here, time is no problem.

Even under heavy monsoon rain, which dogs almost all our approach, it seems like paradise to us. The fascination of the trees and flowers is overwhelming. We are travelling with almost 70 yaks and a dozen porters. The animals are not used to strangers: the only outsiders to have come into the Karma valley since Mallory's time are a French reconnaissance group, and Andy Harvard on a scouting mission for this expedition (both in 1980). Then on one exceptional day, the clouds open and there, shining white at the end of the valley, like a polished shield, rises the enormous wall of Chomolungma above the pale moraine hills of the Kangshung Glacier. It's almost the end of August: how long, we wonder, can the humid air from the southeast keep pressing monsoon clouds through the Arun and Karma valleys so that they strike Everest's East Face and the north side of Lhotse, blanketing them day after day with fresh-fallen snow?

Norgay who climbed Everest in 1953 with Ed Hillary. By pure chance the two met again a few days ago when we were in Lhasa. Tenzing was leading a trekking group and Ed is a member of our expedition. He and I are not the only ones in this team to have been to the top of Everest: Wang Fu-Chou, our liaison officer, climbed the mountain back in 1960. But apart from we three and a British cameraman, all the other 16 are American. Richard Blum and Lou Reichardt share the leadership. (It was Blum's wife, Dianne Feinstein, mayor of San Francisco, who secured our Chinese permit after that city was 'twinned' with Shanghai. Reichardt was the first man to climb K2 without oxygen.) We also have Gary Bocarde, an ice-specialist as strong as a bear; John Roskelley from Spokane, who has already stood on top of three eight-thousanders; and George Lowe, another 'big name'. There are several rock specialists, two doctors, two lawyers – and one woman, Sue Giller, whose first act is to see we draw up a roster for kitchen duties! It's a really impressive team. And how did I come to be invited as the expedition's film director? That I owe to a certain picture in my drawer, or, if I look further back, to a broken camera-strap. . . .

With its forests full of coloured birds and orchids, and tucked deep below the eternal ice of the summits, Karma Chu is one of the most beautiful valleys in the world. So the British described it in 1921 and so, too, we find it. Nothing has changed. It is practically uninhabited: only a couple of shepherds come over the high passes each summer to let their yaks graze the fine grasses, or now and then somebody in Kharta, in need of a log, will cross the 16,400-foot pass, descend into the jungle of the Karma valley, cut a tree, shape it roughly with his axe, and carry

ABOVE: The Kangshung Face, with the South Col of Everest forming the central dip in the skyline.

RIGHT: East Face, 1981 – looking down on the Kangshung Glacier from Lowe Buttress, with Dan Reid climbing.

I fancied I knew this face, having seen it so often over the years; I had already climbed it in my mind. But, here, with its thousands of tons of ice bearing down, enwrapped by it and the sounds of its cracking séracs and roaring avalanches – only now does this sinister, beautiful place of light and shadows really come alive, and I am forced to admit that what I knew was a dream. Yet there is still something dreamlike in its ominous beauty, something to link me with my earlier vision. Ice mushrooms, as big as houses, are stacked towards the skies, one atop the other, whole galleries of them, processions of white shrouded figures. And enormous balconies of blue-green ice, 300, maybe 500 feet high, high above our heads, poised, ready to break off. Icicles clatter almost continuously from that giant hand, whose fingers – the ridges – dip into the Kangshung Glacier. It is a place of voices, of cavities and corners – here an arena, there another – a palace of ghosts. There are wet-snow avalanches, like waterfalls, and others, originating higher, from 23- or 26,000 feet, which are silent fast-racing clouds, seeming to explode in boiling billows. The biggest sent its pressure wave as far as our base camp, three miles away, covering the tents with snowdust –

harmless, luckily, at that distance, but, by God, impressive! Some days and nights there are more than 100 avalanches, including the powder avalanches that sweep down 9,000 feet from Lhotse's vertical North Face – that face which seals in this wild spot on the opposite side.

So daunting and unpredictable is the avalanche danger that two of the best American mountaineers finally leave the expedition. Others, fascinated by the idea of being the first humans to hazard a route up Everest's most preposterous face, remain. Some have yet to make up their minds. It is a distinct disadvantage to have a second permit for the standard north-side route: there will always be mountaineers only interested in the summit. Which way you get there is immaterial to them, though a known route is usually faster. Success is what counts. To some people, speed itself is the dominant factor. But, even today, now and then, you can still find the frontline pioneer, who is body and soul an explorer. He has much less chance of getting to the summit, has to start from scratch, from the bottom, discover everything for himself. His main concern is not speed – and even the question whether or not to go with oxygen may be a secondary consideration, a matter of judgement. For him, the route and its problems are what count. Mastering the ascent as 'elegantly', or as 'sportingly' as possible can wait for those who follow. He will have found his satisfaction even if he doesn't step on the summit, will be content to have discovered the Where and the How.

At the end of August, after covering a distance of nearly five miles across the Kangshung Glacier, zig-zagging through its high moraines, John Roskelley, Jim Morrissey and I are the first to reach the enormous rock buttress. (This tiresome stumble would become our daily fare for the next one and a half months. We'd never get yaks across it, so base camp has to be quite a way from the mountain, among the last green meadows.)

The buttress is the lowest phalanx of the southernmost finger of that hand spread across the face. In my earlier observations I'd picked it out as offering the only hope of ascent, an ideal, straightforward route. But will it be possible? The spine of the buttress, where it is most difficult, may offer the only passage without avalanche danger up to the enormous ice ridge, which in continuous inclination gradually leads to the final face of Everest. Those upper slopes are criss-crossed with crevasses and nasty-looking séracs, but don't appear too difficult. Even so, bad snow conditions, the altitude, weather, snowfall, winds, avalanche danger – could yet conspire to rebuff us.

But first, the 'Ice Throat'! Three thousand feet above the foot of the wall is a menacing feature, like an open mouth with shimmering teeth – an enormous fish-maw. It is fringed with icicles, 50 feet long, with more tucked inside, growing towards each other from above and below. This weird formation, some 300

feet high, looms above the dark face of the buttress and was first given the name 'Jaws' for its resemblance to a Great White Shark. Now the Americans call it simply 'Helmet'. Despite the apprehension we all feel about climbing directly below such a monstrosity, it becomes increasingly clear: either we go this way or not at all!

This is where George Lowe becomes the 'spirit of ascent'. He's convinced the route should 'go'. I am, too, but to get up into

TOP: *Climbing towards the 'Helmet' at the top of Lowe Buttress.*

ABOVE: *Dan Reid and Sue Giller, frustrated at having to give up the hard-fought attempt on the Kangshung Face in 1981.*

RIGHT: *Shartse, Peak 38, Lhotse and Everest – seen at dawn from the Kangshung base camp.*

that gaping mouth will be one of the most technically difficult things I ever saw in the Himalaya, and without any doubt the most difficult climbing anywhere on Everest.

For a month and a half we climb under constant threat of falling icicles, on a double fixed rope . . . up and down and up again, over ground that is sometimes as sheer as the side of a house, hanging on jumars, puffing under heavy loads. Grass and edelweiss surprise us after the first 300 feet, but then the rock becomes increasingly difficult with 300-foot slabs, and snow-crests so narrow that it's a problem to pass one another. The 'Bowling Alley', above, is a dangerous couloir tilted between 50 and 60°, down which whistle chunks of rock and ice. It leads to 'Pinsetter Camp' (the bowling pins being set up for bombardment are us!), an eagle's nest of a camp, relatively 'safe' below an overhang, but one morning Kim Momb arrives to find a hole in the tent, and a stone lying exactly where he is to sleep. The concluding face of the pillar gives George a hard time; more than once a full day only yields one or two ropelengths! Difficulty 5.7, A3 . . . rotten rock with nowhere to put a piton . . . standing in slings with 2,500 feet of space below your feet. It's true that a climber gets used to almost everything, but never to the thought that the rope might be severed by a falling icicle: that's why we use the double line.

From advanced base at the foot of the wall (about 17,400 feet) three camps are established along a line of fixed ropes – the last at about 21,300 feet on the highest point of the Helmet, the Fish's Mouth. That solves the problem of getting onto the upper face of Everest, and is a sort of first ascent in itself. But now, our meagre luck deserts us. A storm with heavy snowfall creates wind-pressed slabs all over the face, bringing bad avalanche danger. We wait and wait, discuss and wait. . . . Three men and a woman are still for pushing on, but the pressure of reality becomes too great: how can we logistically transport stores along the pillar if there are not enough mountaineers? Heavy storms, borne in on the jet-winds, will be here in about two weeks. Time has run out on us. Heavy-hearted, we abandon our attempt. The last moment is almost a disaster. Dan Reid, one of the most insistent in pushing out the route, has his leg badly cut by a big block in the Bowling Alley. He sews it up himself (he's a doctor) and sits on the moraine for three days. There arc tears in his eyes when he starts limping for home.

*

Two years later another American East Face expedition reached the top. The climbers were substantially the same as in 1981 and success on this difficult route was in no small measure due to our first attempt on the great face. I was not with them this time: the summer of 1983 saw Julie Tullis and me on K2. We were following another dream. But in 1985 we were able to visit the Karma Chu and the old base camp site just in front of the East Face. Shartse, Lhotse and Everest looked down on us while I told Julie how the camera rolled into Tibet, and of all my adventures in this rare place.

Doug Scott

Lightweights on Kangchenjunga

The darkest hour is definitely just before the dawn, and this was the wildest I'd ever known, with chips of ice flying into my face and raining down from above, blasting my nylon suit.

RIGHT: *The Everest group, seen from the North Col of Kangchenjunga, with (left to right) Makalu, Lhotse and Everest, its northeast ridge prominent.*

In the spring of 1979, Georges Bettembourg, Peter Boardman, Joe Tasker and I went to Kangchenjunga to attempt a new route up the West Face to the North Col, and then up the West Ridge to the summit. There was a day when Peter, Georges and myself went to our own particular 'summit' – out on a limb – 10,000 feet above Base Camp, feeling a million miles from home, five miles from Joe and the Sherpas.

It was 4 May. We were up in the westerly jet stream that had battered our mountain for weeks. With every step across the Great Terrace we had to brace against ice axe or ski pole. The wind was strong: 100 mph? Well, it was strong enough to blow flaky bits of rock uphill. During the worst gusts we had to huddle together until a slight lull allowed us to jump up, stumble and trip on over the boulders until the next blast. Then we cowered again, backs to the wind, holding on to our down and windproof suits. At least we were cocooned against the cold. I tried to rationalize the wind's impact on myself by reasoning 'so what, it's only air particles, only wind moving around the globe – get with it lad, you're not freezing yet.' But always the thought that I might freeze up – might not get it right. And we would be off, staggering on another few paces. The nearer we got to the ridge, the stronger and noisier the wind became – roaring west into Sikkim. And there we were on the ridge-crest, one after the other, part of the first obstruction the Westerlies had met since Everest. We dived over the ridge with the wind,

BIOGRAPHY

Born in 1941, Doug Scott is one of the world's leading high-altitude and big-wall climbers who has pioneered new routes on many of the world's most difficult mountains. He began climbing at the age of 12 and led his first expeditions in the mid-1960s to the mountains of the Sahara, southeast Turkey and the Hindu Kush. His historic ascent with Dougal Haston of the Southwest Face of Everest in 1975 brought him to the forefront of Himalayan climbing. This was a climb in more or less traditional siege style; but his ascents of such peaks as Shisha Pangma, Shivling, Kusum Kangguru, Nuptse and, most notably, Kangchenjunga, described here, favoured the rapid, lightweight approach by a small team, without the use of supplementary oxygen.

He has twice attempted the unclimbed, eight-mile long Mazeno Ridge of Nanga Parbat; there are few mountain ranges around the world that Doug Scott has not visited. He is married to the Indian climber Sharu Prabhu, who joins him on many expeditions, including ascents of Jitchu Drake in Bhutan, Kanjiroba South Ridge, two peaks in the Fansky Mountains of Tadzhikistan, and in Antarctica. Doug Scott's book Himalayan Climber, *records a remarkable climbing career.*

looking for shelter, and as I crossed over I felt the most incredible electric charge in my back, like a hundred needles jabbing into my spine, like the marrow was being addled, making me wriggle and squirm, trying to avoid it. The only way out was down and through the static of hundreds of flying particles, down to the relative calm of Sikkim.

About 50 feet down we started the laborious job of hacking out a tent platform from the steepening slope that dropped away 6,500 feet to the Zemu Glacier. Three hours later, we had the tent up. There was enough room, but not enough oxygen at 26,000 feet with the doors shut and the fumes overwhelming me as I leant over the stove, melting ice for tea and biscuits. Georges, finding himself on the side of the tent, pressed against the slope, staggeringly demanded a hot water bottle

for his cold feet, and that was after watching me struggle with a stove which seemed to be going out every few minutes! Still, not one to disappoint, I passed him his hot water bottle, admittedly with a mumble or two.

I took a headache pill and slept well, until Peter woke me at 1.30 a.m. to help with the tent, which was being hammered by the wind. He yelled that the wind had changed direction, as if I didn't know; it had now broken the centre fibreglass hoop. By 2.30 a.m. the wind was extreme, as was our position, blown like washing hung out on a line on that snowy slope. We panicked our way into oversuits, boots

and gaiters, working in shifts as Peter and I took turns to hold the broken ends of the hoop, hoping to prevent it from tearing the fabric. Our gloved hands were wet and cold, the finger-gloves soaking up condensation. Then, horror of horrors, every climber's nightmare – the whole tent was blown two feet along the ledge towards the edge. In one bound I tore the zip open from the stitching and was outside, heels dug into the ledge, holding on to the tent, trying to prevent it, Peter and Georges from plunging down to the Zemu Glacier 10,000 feet below.

The darkest hour is definitely just before the dawn, and this was the wildest I'd ever

known, with chips of ice flying into my face and raining down from above, blasting my nylon suit. I grabbed an ice axe and rammed it through the tent fabric, where the ties had ripped off. I stamped it down but the wind simply ripped the tent away another few inches, and I was back holding on with both hands, as poles snapped and bits of fabric tore off. It was like wrestling with a giant wind-surfer. Georges yelled for his crampons and I flung them in, yelling to pack everything in our rucksacks – 'Don't abandon anything!' No rout this, I thought. The outer sheet of the tent stripped off into the cold night, black against the eastern horizon,

pale orange seen through the turbulent mist and snow.

And all the time I clung on, wrestling with the surviving hoop, but finally twisting it down and breaking it to lower the tent's resistance, yet feeling I was losing out, with my frozen hands and failing strength, scared I was going to lose the gear, and my friends and me as well, all tumbling down to the Zemu. 'Surely this isn't the way I'm going – blown off a bloody mountain, sliding down into an unknown valley – come on, get a grip.' And I shouted for them to get out quick, but it all took time. First a Karrimat came through the entrance, followed by rucksacks and Peter. Georges was last, cutting his way out of the back with his Swiss penknife. He was still drowsy from having taken too many sleepers. As he emerged, we let go of the tent and it flew off, yet another black shape, fast disappearing, to become a dot in the distance – then it was gone from view.

It was now 4.30 a.m., with us squatting on that icy ledge, 6 feet long by 4 feet wide, at over 26,250 feet (8,000 metres), in the strongest wind any of us had ever experienced. Summit thoughts were non-existent, but we still had to climb up to survive this ordeal and get ourselves down. For the first hour we clung on to each other, going into a stupor of cold and utter misery. Peter wasn't saying anything, he seemed to be getting hyperthermia. I thought myself that this time I had gone and taken a step too far, and pushed myself beyond my limit. For the first time in my life I thought I was going to die. Our situation was deteriorating fast. Georges realized this first and, in a burst of energy, dashed off up the ropes we had tied off to a dead man belay plate 10 feet above us. From this, he made a bold attempt to reach the col 40 feet away, but the rope was wind-tangled and pulled him up short. He had two more goes before reversing back to our ledge. It was my turn. But as I stood up, I felt so unstable that I dipped back down, with my head

bunched into my chest, hiding from the flying ice and snow. 'Got to do something,' I concluded after five minutes rest and mind-race. I took my sack off, grabbed two ice axes and pulled up to the dead man plate. Then, with frozen fingers, bit by bit, I untangled the flailing rope. Georges joined me and payed out the rope as I took off and reached a point just below the col. I came to a halt, blasted by the winds from the west, crouching upon crampon points and ice picks – my face pressed against the ice, trying to find some relief from the turbulence.

Georges shouted: 'Doug, go for *eet*, go for *eet*,' but I missed a slight lull. 'Go for *eet*, Doug,' yelled Georges again. '*Go for*

eet!' he yelled again and again into the hurricane wind, raging across our mountain. I went for it, scampering up on blunt crampons, scraping and scratching at the hard green ice, all in a continuous flailing of limbs, trying to reach the top before the next onslaught – which I did. I threw myself over the ridge and squirmed down on my stomach back into Nepal, literally clawing my way down slope, pulling myself downhill with ice picks to some rocks where I tied off. Without goggles and glasses, my face was covered in ice – a cascade of frozen snot and sputum in my beard and hair. I was now out of immediate danger. I paused and noticed irrelevant thoughts, like getting my hair cut at a

certain hairdressers in Kathmandu: the first alien idea had arrived after hours of total concentration centred on that ledge and 50 feet of snow above.

Eventually, with rope tied off, Georges squirmed over the ledge. 'Doug, my sack, eet has gone down the Zemu Glacier.' 'Don't worry kid, we'll get it all together,' I yelled, as we both pulled Pete over to join us at the Rock Island. Later Georges told me how he'd untied his sack, and left it nestling in the brew hollow and the wind had just taken it, like a screwed up bit of paper. We were now back in Nepal and I could sense our joint relief, though it was hard to see each other through the ice encrustations upon our frozen features.

ABOVE: *Georges
Bettembourg leads an
ice pitch on the face
below Kangchenjunga's
North Col.*

RIGHT: *Joe Tasker, a
thousand feet below the
summit.*

We began to stagger and shuffle down to the cave bivouac at 25,500 feet, and arrived there at 10.00 a.m. We climbed on down to the col for 1.00 p.m. and on down the north face to the glacier camp for 3.00 p.m., and finally Joe. He couldn't stop talking – the Sherpa don't talk very much, and with all the worry of waiting, he fussed around like a mother hen, plying us with brews and food. We had now descended 10,000 feet vertically, and covered five miles of the mountain, all in the day, but then we had got off to an early start!

This first attempt at Kangchenjunga had been the closest call I had ever had, the finest line I'd drawn between being here and not being here. With all my being I had hung on to take what comes to those of us caught out so high in such conditions. I will never forget it, because I was there 100 per cent, oblivious to all else but surviving the wind and the cold, and for a few moments climbing *beyond* the wind and the cold, when, at Georges' insistence, I 'went for eet', to face the unknown with adrenalin running high, exhilarated, euphoric, detached, free and climbing beyond ego, going for it.

During the next few days I lay on the grass under my flysheet, just letting it all come in, dreamlike, watching animated scenes of home behind my eyelids. I wondered if I had learned anything. If I had now the right to comment on anything of world-shattering importance. I decided I hadn't. I couldn't be bothered with any of that or bothered with thinking of anything. I just felt so much at peace, so relaxed with myself and my friends. I will always feel warmth towards them both from having shared that particular ordeal together, and also Joe, who contained his disappointment at not being up there with us, but who then took care of us. I sat on the grass at Base Camp, my bottom all bony and my body all skinny, nursing my frostbitten finger-ends, stinging from strong anti-biotic cream, wrapped up in Joe's white silk gloves. I knew that my hands could be a passport home, like some wounded soldier exiting out with honour from the Flanders mud bath. I had taken it to the limit, why push my luck a second time? Yet, although I had excuses to leave, there was Kangchenjunga, still smoking snow and mist. What a mountain it turned out to be. I now knew many of its secret places – at least to 26,200 feet on the northwestern flank – but I did not know about that last 2,000 feet. I had returned humble but strong, feeling for this earth and full of wonder that I am here at all, able to continue living on it. What more had this mirror mountain got to show me?

After a second abortive attempt, thwarted by yet another storm, Joe, Peter and I reached the summit on a glorious day later in May, above the clouds and all our earthly worries. I came down to find that such worries had not gone away but now I returned to view them from a different perspective and to tackle them with renewed strength and objectivity – one justification for what we do, if one were needed.

BELOW: That's it! Peter Boardman, Joe Tasker and Doug Scott a few minutes short of Kangchenjunga's untrodden summit – that is kept sacred for the gods.

Kitty Calhoun Grissom

Makalu's West Pillar

We made steady headway and I became confident and exhilarated by the feeling of being so high, like being on a tenth floor balcony of a skyscraper.

My heart was pounding from lack of oxygen and excitement as I scrambled up the last talus slope and reached the abandoned stone walls that would become our Base Camp. Above, wispy clouds raced across a crystal sky and plumes of snow swept over the summit of Makalu. I stood motionless, in awe of the majestic peak before me. Our route, the West Pillar, was an elegant rock buttress that bounded the immense granite West Face of Makalu. It was first climbed by the French in 1971 and since then only one other climber, John Roskelley in 1980, had reached the summit by this route. I was eager to climb, full of nervous energy – like a drug addict anticipating a fix.

On March 26, 1990 we established Base Camp at 17,500 feet at the foot of the west pillar. My team-mates – John Schutt, Mark Houston, Kathy Cosley, John Culberson, my husband Colin Grissom – were as keen as I to start climbing. The 100-mile trek from Hille to Makalu had brought us through the most remote area of Nepal I had yet seen. For the last seven days we post-holed through knee-deep snow as we crossed three 14,000-foot passes and then descended into the isolated Barun valley.

After a day of sorting gear, we set out with the first loads. Three hours' scrambling brought us up a huge talus slope to the site of Camp I, tucked in the rocks on the south side of the ridge. A dozen tent platforms were lined with baling wire, tin cans and gas cartridges from previous expeditions. Panting like a dog from the altitude, I found temporary shelter from

RIGHT: *Makalu, with Chomolonzo behind, seen from the Northeast Ridge of Mount Everest.*

BIOGRAPHY

Kitty Calhoun Grissom began climbing at the age of eighteen on the crags of her native South Carolina. Later, at college in Vermont, she added ice climbing to her skills, and in 1984 ventured abroad, to the Cordillera Blanca in Peru. Soon afterwards she turned her attention to the Himalaya. A two-person attempt on Thalay Sagar in the Garhwal was defeated by hunger and exhaustion after an eight-day storm, which pinned the climbers on portaledges high on the face, with almost constant avalanches and only one-and-half days' rations. But in 1987 she successfully climbed Dhaulagiri alpine-style with John Culberson and Colin Grissom; and three years later led the Makalu expedition, which she tells about here. She was the first woman to climb this eight-thousander, which at 27,766 feet, is the fifth highest mountain in the world. Grissom has been a guide for the American Alpine Institute since 1985 and has taken an MBA at the University of Washington.

the wind behind a large boulder and marvelled at the tremendous views of the Barun valley and Baruntse to the west, and Lhotse and Everest to the northwest. I felt great respect for the French team and imagined how exciting it must have been on the first ascent. For the next five days we ferried the rest of our supplies and equipment up to the camp, and on April 4 Mark Houston and Kathy Cosley moved up.

Above Camp I, 60° slopes led to a mile-long knife-edged ridge. We worked in pairs, alternating the leading after two days so that no one would have to be a support member and carry loads for more than four days at a time. I waited my turn

186

but hounded my companions. 'You mean you've already fixed 2,000 feet of rope?' I asked John Culberson in obvious disappointment. I had hoped we wouldn't have to start fixing until above Camp II. I enjoy the freedom that comes with climbing fast and light. Besides, I didn't relish carrying the loads that would be necessary to fix the entire route.

'Yeah,' John replied. 'Just wait till it's your turn and you'll see.' Colin and I started climbing to John and Schutt's highpoint to lead the remaining few hundred feet to Camp II. The ridge dipped and rose and I felt as if I were on a roller-coaster ride. To my left, a rock wall dropped 2,000 feet to the glacier, and to my right 70° slopes fell to unseen terrain below. The route led down a rock band, around overhanging cornices, up a giant bump and down to a windy plateau. Adding to the thrill was a powerful wind that would have blown me away, had I not been clipped into fixed lines. At the crest of the bump we fixed more lines and fought increasing winds before dropping down onto the plateau

RIGHT: Camp at dawn, on the lower Barun Glacier, with Makalu behind.

and anchoring the rope. I returned to Camp I, humbled. I had not anticipated this much work so low on the route. We placed Camp II at 21,000 feet in a large cave formed by a crevasse, where we could escape the howling wind. By mid-April, after many gruelling six-hour round-trips from Camp I, Camp II was stocked and Colin and I moved in.

Above Camp II, 2,700 feet of mixed rock-and-ice bands, interspersed with patches of snow, guarded the pillar above. Colin and I climbed easily up steep snow and blocky rock faces until we were pushed out onto the South Face by overhanging rock on the ridge above us. A narrow ramp of verglas-covered rock slabs with downward-sloping holds led across the steep South Face. Terrible Traverse, the French had named it, because of the terrific exposure. I started across with butterflies in my stomach, but encountered few problems.

After fixing this section we descended to Base again, excited by the stimulating climbing and our progress. Mark and Kathy took over in front and over the next two days fixed another thousand feet of rope up increasingly difficult rock bands. John and Schutt

replaced them, but a nagging cough forced John down to recuperate after only a day of fixing. The mountain was taking its toll. Unfortunately, the high altitude at Base Camp made it difficult to recover fully from exhaustion or illness. Hacking coughs continued to plague several members.

Colin and I went back up to Camp II with Schutt, hoping to reach III in a day or two. We climbed the icy slopes, over the blocky rock bands, across the Terrible Traverse and up seemingly endless mixed rock and ice slabs. I was amazed at how sustained the route was and distressed that it took us hours to reach the highpoint. We ascended the fixed lines, moving as efficiently as possible to conserve time and energy to lead several pitches before rappelling over a thousand feet to Camp II by dark. Over the next four days, we finished fixing the route to the site of Camp III at 24,200 feet. On April 29, the three of us moved up and dug a small cave in the leeward side of the narrow ridge to protect us from the relentless wind. The camp was cold and cramped and I was glad to bail out of our little cell once morning came.

Above Camp III, the rock pillar soared upward and our most challenging climbing began. While Colin, Schutt and I approached the wall, I looked up at the cold granite, silently praying that the route would not be too difficult for me. Snow-filled cracks snaked up through steep rock slabs as far as I could see. Soon I was leading and all my anxiety disappeared as I focused on piecing together the moves, brushing off the snow in search of holds, gingerly placing my crampon points on crystals and pressing hard on the rock as I mantleshelfed up.

We made steady headway and I became confident and exhilarated by the feeling of being so high, like being on a tenth floor balcony of a skyscraper. Yet, after three days of climbing above 24,000 feet, the excitement was soon replaced by fatigue. We descended for a much-needed rest while Mark, Kathy and John moved up to Camp III to take the lead. That night, however, was a nightmare for Mark. Aggravated by the increasingly cold dry air, his bad cough worsened, resulting in an injured rib. Next morning, bent with pain, he descended to Base Camp to begin a slow recovery.

Colin, Schutt and I rejoined the others at Camp II on May 6. The following day, with support from John and Kathy, Colin and I climbed back to Camp III. After carrying an extremely heavy load, John wished us good luck and said he could not climb higher because of his persistent cough and lack of appetite, which kept him from recovering from each day's work. He then headed for Base Camp. Meanwhile, Colin and I fixed 300 feet of rope above our highpoint before returning to Camp II for another rest.

We were relieved by Kathy and Schutt, who managed to fix an additional 200 feet of rope up a steep dihedral where a frayed cable ladder dangled. By now, each additional pitch became a major accomplishment, for the slabs had given way to strenuous off-width cracks and dihedrals. Technical climbing at this extreme altitude required incredible effort.

After a day of recuperation, Colin and I headed back to Camp III, passing Kathy on her way down. Apologetically, she told us she was descending to Base Camp in a state of exhaustion. I could empathize as I felt myself becoming weaker by the day. I had long ago lost my voice due to a throat infection and my

OVER EVEREST

FIRST PICTURES OF THE HOUSTON MOUNT EVEREST FLIGHT

SPECIAL ILLUSTRATED SECTION

AN AERIAL CONQUEST—THE PEAK FROM ABOVE

One of the many remarkable photographs secured on April 3 during the historic flight over Mount Everest by members of the Houston Everest Expedition. It was taken by Colonel L. V. S. Blacker, the observer and photographer in the aeroplane piloted by Lord Clydesdale, and gives a vivid impression of the awe-inspiring summit of Everest as seen slightly from the north-west.

body, in search of energy, had used up my fat and was now fuelled by muscle tissue. Above 18,000 feet the body does not digest food efficiently, and it was simply a matter of time before I too would be forced to retreat. Each of us had given so much to this mountain. I fervently hoped that between Colin, Schutt and myself we would have enough strength to finish this draining route.

At Camp III, we rejoined Schutt and, the following day, the three of us reached the most difficult section of climbing on the route, at 25,000 feet. The choices before us left me filled with doubt. To our left was an overhanging, flaring crack and to the right, a smooth vertical wall with a useless, broken ladder at its base. Colin, armed with a rack of large Friends, a pair of étriers, and blind determination, began the struggle up the forbidding crack. Once he crested the overhanging rock, he disappeared from sight and we could only guess at the climbing above as the rope inched upward. Two hours later he arrived at a belay stance, having overcome the last 20 feet of a steep, blank face.

Above the crux 500 feet of lower angle slopes separated us from Camp IV. It was late in the day so we returned to Camp III. 'I'm getting tired of this,' I exclaimed, imagining yet another day spent fixing rope on the route. It was wearing on the others, too; I could see it in their faces. 'Yeah, maybe we could pack enough food for five days and try to make Camp IV tomorrow,' Schutt suggested.

LEFT: Kitty Calhoun Grissom negotiating the Terrible Traverse above Camp II, so called by the French team who first reached the top.

RIGHT: Makalu's West Pillar, seen through a notch between Lhotse and Nuptse.

ABOVE: The fantastic West Pillar of Makalu, photographed in 1933 by the first aviators to fly over the roof of the world. So impressive did it seem, that the shot was misidentified in The Times as 'the awe-inspiring summit of Everest'.

LEFT: *Makalu wears a plume of blown snow as a climber approaches along the snowy crest.*

experiences with Colin flashed before me. Although I knew he'd made the right decision, it was difficult to accept. Secretly I hoped that somehow he might get a second chance. Schutt and I planned another attempt the following day, but when we awoke just before midnight, still feeling weak, we thought it wisest to opt for a rest day instead.

It was snowing lightly and visibility was poor when Schutt and I left Camp IV on May 18 at 1.15 in the morning. We were desperately hoping to make the summit. We had only one day's food left and were fast losing strength after four nights at 25,500 feet. I felt I was sleep-walking, following the faint silhouette of my companion up the hard, wind-packed slopes. Falling snowflakes danced in the breeze and shreds of ancient rope rapped against the rock.

At dawn, we reached the junction of the West Pillar and the southeast ridge at 27,100 feet. I was shocked awake by blasts of

No one argued and the next day we moved like turtles under our heavy loads. Finally, on May 14, after a long, hard day, we arrived at dusk at the site of our last camp, at 25,500 feet. We had to chop a platform for our three-person tent, an exhausting effort that took two hours in the relentless wind. It was nearly midnight by the time we settled in and finished dinner. The next day we rested, but on the following morning, May 16, we set out for the top at 2.20 a.m. It was a perfect morning, clear and still.

The summit, at last, seemed attainable. Yet, after climbing up 45° mixed snow and rock gullies for six hours, we were driven back by ferocious winds that rose quickly out of the southeast. To those watching through binoculars from Base Camp, retreat must have seemed inevitable as clouds of snow rose up over the entire summit ridge in billowing plumes.

Back in Camp IV, Colin, Schutt and I collapsed in the tent, thoroughly exhausted and disheartened from our forced retreat. Each of us, intensely focused on reaching the goal, had withdrawn into our own little worlds; and so it was a shock to me when that afternoon, Colin told us that he had to go down. His bronchitis had sapped what strength remained. I looked at him in dismay. Memories of pure pleasure as well as some near-death wind from the southeast and distressed because my feet were beginning to freeze. A layer of rock, barely visible through the clouds, became my goal. If we weren't out of the wind by then, I would have to go down. A wave of joy swept through me as we reached the rock band and I recognized it from the pictures I had seen. We were near the summit. Miraculously, the wind had died and with renewed determination, I tied into the 5 millimetre cord we carried with us.

We ascended the last rock barrier to gain the gentle, corniced snow ridge. Loosely packed snow and lack of oxygen slowed progress to an agonizing crawl.

In the clouds, the corniced ridge seemed to go on forever. For two hours we endured this suspended state. Then, at long last, after weeks of extraordinary climbing, Schutt and I finally reached the pointed summit. It was 11.45 a.m. The sky was clear above us; a sea of clouds below obscured all but the distant tops of Everest and Lhotse to the northwest. We embraced, relieved that all we had to do now was get down safely.

After fifteen minutes on the summit, we began the descent and arrived back at Camp IV at 4.45 in the afternoon, utterly spent. The next day we packed up and staggered out of camp like zombies, laden with gear, anxious to begin the 10,000-foot descent to rejoin our companions.

By the time Colin, Schutt and I arrived at Base Camp, Mark, Kathy and John were already ferrying loads down from our high camps and removing much of the fixed rope, a process that took five days. I was grateful to all my team-mates, for without the combined effort of each individual, our success would not have been possible. We finally left Base Camp on May 24, having spent 60 days on that incredible route.

As I looked back towards Makalu and its west pillar for the last time, it stood shrouded in a massive layer of dull grey clouds. I would soon enjoy the well-earned pleasures of a shower and ice cream, but I was hesitant to go on. I wanted to savour the sweet feelings that come with such achievement. I knew they would be replaced with emptiness as I searched for a new focus.

LEFT: Makalu from Chamlang, with the West Ridge seen in the centre of the picture.

The Sherpa View

As a boy I remember the wonderful stories told by the old Sherpas and thinking: 'How is it possible to climb up into the sky where only the gods and goddesses can live?'

For most Sherpas, working with expeditions is purely a way of earning money, and a hard and dangerous one at that. We come under a lot of pressure from our families not to go to high altitudes. They do not like us climbing and worry a lot. Many of my friends have been killed. In the early 1970s there were several big accidents costing many Sherpas' lives. Every household in the Solu Khumbu (the Everest region of Nepal) has been affected. I kept on mountaineering because I enjoy it, but also it was the only way I knew to make a living. However, after my third climb of Everest I decided to listen to my family and friends and to stop. Since then, I have not been above Base Camp, though I have been back twice. I think in the next generation we'll see far fewer climbers amongst Sherpas. Education brings more options. Maybe they will think we were stupid to work so hard in such cold and dangerous conditions. No-one else in Nepal wants to do this work. The fact is most of us don't have any choice. Our farms are high and small, and we need extra income to support our families.

I am one of the few who enjoy the challenge and don't regret the hard work; I am proud to have done my best, caring for my clients, and I respect the people I climb with. Wonderful friendships are forged on the mountain and although I may not be wealthy or well-educated, I have friends all over the world. I have travelled widely and am treated so well wherever I go that I worry I can never return such hospitality.

This climbing relationship is very important for us Sherpas. We call every leader a *Bara Sahib*, literally 'Big Boss', but obviously not all are the same. It is only after two or three expeditions with the same leader that the real friendships are made.

BIOGRAPHY

Pertemba Sherpa, P.T. to his many friends, is a small and deceptively slender man with a huge, open smile. He is one of Nepal's finest climbers and has a rare talent for organisation and expedition logistics. Nine times on Everest, he has made it to the summit on three occasions, and helped many others attain the highest goal in the world. He tells us here, in an interview conducted through Lisa Choegyal, of his life and how he and Nepal's climbing sherpas feel about mountaineering in the Himalaya.

Then we become not just friends but brothers, part of the same family, tied with a strong bond based on trust and loyalty. The only person universally respected as *Bara Sahib* in Solu Khumbu is Sir Edmund Hillary. Every-body, from young children to old men, refers to Sir Ed as *Bara Sahib*. He is honoured not only because he climbed Everest, but for what he has done for the Sherpa people. He visits us twice a year and his Himalayan Trust sets up schools, clinics and projects to help us. He was the first to donate money for the rebuilding of Thyangboche Monastery when it burned to the ground in 1989. He is like the father of the Solu Khumbu Sherpas and there is no-one like him.

We have a strong sense of hierarchy on expeditions and it is our job to treat every leader with the same respect. In return, he must be a good organizer. I would say he also needs to be a nice man, friendly, easy to talk to and able to explain things clearly. I then brief my Sherpa staff in advance so they know what is expected. I must also check how they are feeling and ensure that they stay healthy and strong. A Sirdar is the middleman between the foreign expedition members, Sherpas and porters, and must listen to all sides. It can be a difficult position. If the leader does not know his team, or have the right skills and personality, it is very dangerous for us all. Sometimes the leader pushes too hard. He literally can hold our lives in his hands. On the Nepal side of Everest almost half of those killed have been Sherpas: 34 Sherpas and 78 foreigners. When I climb with Chris Bonington we carefully plan the coming days and check constantly with each other. Some leaders will ask for my ideas and opinions, some will not.

LEFT: Sherpas picking their way through the shifting Khumbu Icefall. It is so dangerous most climbers try to limit the number of times they pass this way, but porters have to carry loads here day after day. Half those killed on Everest are Sherpas.

BELOW: Pertemba climbing the South Summit Couloir on Everest in 1975. That year he made the first of his three ascents of Everest with Peter Boardman.

If weather conditions are very bad we might refuse to go. I might politely say to the leader, 'Let's try tomorrow as it is not good to go today.' I might insist we move through the Khumbu Icefall in the early morning and not in the afternoon when it is dangerous. Most Sherpas prefer not to go high or to take unnecessary risks just for money.

The early expeditions used to pay a fixed wage per day. An advance was given at the beginning and the balance at the end. Now most expeditions use a bonus system and pay extra for every trip above Camp 4 to the South Col, or for every carry from Camp 1 to Camp 3. It works better as the Sherpas have an incentive to try harder. But there have been instances when bonuses are promised and not paid by unscrupulous leaders. I keep daily records, counting how many carries each Sherpa has done. At the end I total it up and tell the leader. In my day it was much less, but today above Base Camp, Sherpas earn between 200 and 500 rupees extra per day (£2-£5/$3.50-$8), depending on the altitude and the expedition's budget. They may get a few thousand rupees tip on top of this. Those prepared to go to the summit get a lump sum of perhaps 10,000 rupees (£110/$180).

The older Sherpas who worked with early explorers before the 1950s really established the fame of the Solu Khumbu men as being trustworthy, loyal, extremely hard-working and very friendly. We have benefited from their reputation and now everyone knows and wants Sherpas on expeditions. But apart from Tenzing Norgay, who is known all over the world, few people knew those old Sherpa climbers' names. I feel sorry that they worked so hard for little reward or recognition.

These days there are a lot of expeditions. In autumn 1991 there were over 80 expeditions, most of which used climbing Sherpas. It is not surprising that we hear stories that Sherpas and sahibs sometimes have relationship problems. There are good and bad Sherpas, just as there are good and bad leaders.

The younger generation of Sherpas is better educated. They are also better climbers as they have had training. They communicate well and are invited to visit friends outside Nepal. They read the many books and articles about Himalayan expeditions and I hear them complain that there are not enough mentions of Sherpa climbers. They co-operate, work hard, do their duty, support their members, and all for what? We were born in the wrong time and place to be on the inside of today's published stories. I keep my happiness and pride within me, and though I cannot read well I enjoy looking at the pictures and reminiscing with my friends.

I was born in 1949 in Solu Khumbu. My father was a farmer in Khumjung, with about 40 yaks. He and my mother were very religious and she made many pilgrimages before they had children. It must have worked. They then had so many that when I was about five I was sent to live with my paternal grandparents who were yak-herders up in the Gokyo Valley, near Cho Oyu. When they got too old, I went with them to live with my two aunts who were nuns at Debuche, below Thyangboche Monastery. I studied with the monks and learned *pejha*, the Tibetan Buddhist books. At eight years old I became very ill and nearly died. In those days there was no hospital or school.

In 1960 I was lucky to be in the first class of Sir Edmund Hillary's school at Khumjung. My classmates included Ang Phu (the first person to climb Everest by two separate routes, killed on the West Ridge in 1979), Ang Rita (the Himalayan Trust officer), Mingma Norbu (a wildlife warden trained in the United States) and Lhakpa Norbu (successful Sirdar with Mountain Travel, Nepal). At first, the school building wasn't finished and we sat on the rocks outside with our teacher. Sir Ed and his climbing friends would often stop by and tell us stories. One of the most exciting times was a games competition including volleyball and football with the climbers. One, Jim Wilson, was so tall he could touch the roof and we named him *Rahkegatwa*, which means 'Langur Monkey'. He was very fast and we loved trying to catch him. Many older Sherpas and expedition climbers came to help Sir Ed build the school and they showed us basic climbing, rope techniques and rappelling. We thought it very exciting and I remember thinking, even at that early age, 'One day, I want to do this'.

During my five years at Khumjung we had plenty of fun and I learned a lot. Many of my friends went on to further studies but I wasn't clever enough for one of the scholarships offered by

Desmond Doig and others. My elder brother, Ang Tsering worked for the Himalayan Trust and got me a job building the airstrip at Lukla. Whenever a plane landed we liked to rush over to see who was in it. I got friendly with Captain Emil Wick who flew the Pilatus Porter. One day, Colonel Jimmy Roberts came in on a helicopter sightseeing flight with some friends. He asked me some questions and I was able to answer in English which I'd learnt in school. He knew my brothers, as the eldest, Pasang Tendi, had been on Everest in 1963 and 1965. Before flying off he asked if I would like to work in Kathmandu.

Several weeks later Captain Wick arrived and asked me to come with him to Kathmandu. It would cost nothing, he told me, Colonel Jimmy had made all the arrangements. I ran to find my brother who gave me permission to go and some money, 25 rupees I think, so I left the same afternoon. I was 16 years old and had never been out of Solu Khumbu. I figured that if anything went wrong I had a couple of relatives in Kathmandu who would look after me Phu Dorje (who'd climbed Everest in 1965) and Tashi (Nuptse summiteer). But Colonel Jimmy was there to meet me at the airport.

I worked for two years in his house, cooking, cleaning and looking after his dogs. I started taking people trekking when Colonel Jimmy set up the first trekking company, Mountain Travel. He is a famous adventure-man and did lots of mountaineering and exploring in the Himalaya. Soon I was able to gain experience on small peaks. I always watched and listened carefully, but it took many years to learn as in those days there

LEFT: Sherpas prepare to evacuate a victim of altitude sickness from a high camp.

RIGHT: A rescued Sherpa is given comfort and medical attention at Base Camp.

ABOVE: A column of
Sherpa porters in the
Western Cwm of Everest
during the 1975 climb
of the Southwest Face.
This was the first
expedition on which
Pertemba was Sirdar.
He was 26 years old.

was no climbing school in Nepal. In 1970 I joined the successful British and Nepalese Army expedition to Annapurna, led by Major Bruce Niven, my first expedition leader. I tried my hardest, and made it to the last camp. This was also the first time that I got to know Chris Bonington, who was on Annapurna South Face with Dougal Haston and Don Whillans. We stayed together in Pokhara, then met again after the expedition.

In 1971 I was selected as a high altitude Sherpa on the International Expedition to Everest. I was very young and thought myself extremely lucky. With Norman Dyhrenfurth and Colonel Jimmy, the leaders, I met the King of Nepal. I had been ill with an ulcer and worried that I was not strong enough, but I climbed a lot with Dougal Haston and went to the highest point reached on all the different routes.

At the start of the 1971 Expedition I'd been sent to Raxaul to meet Major Harsh Bahaguna and to bring equipment from India. At Base Camp we were split into two groups. Mingma Tsering (from Phortse village) and I helped set up Camp 3, then we returned to Camp 2, leaving Harsh and Wolfgang Axt there. They were to establish the route higher, but a big storm came. They waited a day, which was a mistake, then without waiting for the bad weather to clear, tried to come down. They did not stay together, which was another mistake, and Wolfgang arrived alone at Camp 2 very late in the afternoon, just before dark.

He said he'd heard Bahaguna shouting and so had others. A search party of 10 or 12 people went up that evening and found Harsh hanging on the fixed rope, but he was dead. It was very late and all of us got lost getting back. Don Whillans and I had luckily grabbed a few ski poles to mark the trail in the snow. We

all nearly died. After much discussion, the expedition decided to abandon the West Ridge and try the South Col route. The other Sherpas and I were asked to set up Camp 3 at the bottom of the Lhotse Face, so we broke trail, made the route and erected two tents. Then the expedition again switched plans and decided to try the South Face. They asked me to go up and bring the equipment down. I got really angry and said, 'No way, I'm not going up there again.' I had been on all the routes and why should they keep changing their minds? But I am a Sherpa and I had to continue to work and carry loads.

Five of us went up as far as Camp 6 on the South Face – Don Whillans, Dougal Haston, two Japanese and myself. I was eating some tsampa with chilli and Naomi Uemura, my tent mate, wanted to try some. He liked my food and ate a lot but the next day his stomach was very upset and he had to go down with his friend, so there were only three of us left. Dougal decided it was too risky, so we came down. By the time we reached Base Camp there was almost no one left as the members had gone. We cleaned Base Camp and walked back. The team did not work well together and failed, but everyone noticed I could climb and I never had any difficulty getting a job after that.

I went to Everest in 1972 with Chris Bonington and learned a lot from him and Dougal Haston. I really wanted to reach the summit. I enjoyed climbing with my old and new friends, although we failed due to very strong winds. In 1974 I was invited to Holland, then went to Switzerland for further technical training. We did some climbing in Chamonix, the Pyrenees and the English Lake District. In 1973 I went to the Hindu Kush with a team led by Max Eiselin.

To be chosen in 1975, at the age of 26, as Sirdar of Bonington's Southwest Face Everest expedition was very exciting, but I was secretly worried about managing such a big responsibility. I had been a trekking sirdar but never in charge of even a small expedition. It was my third attempt on Everest, I knew the route

ABOVE: *Sherpas at work, maintaining a safe route through the Khumbu Icefall.*

LEFT: *Thyangboche, spiritual centre for the Sherpa people. The old monastery was swept away by fire in January 1989 and contributions came from all over the world to help the Sherpas rebuild it.*

and was determined to get to the top. Assisting older expedition sirdars like Sonam Girme and Lhakpa Tsering who could not read and write had given me some experience. Despite mixed feelings, I decided to give it a try. The most important task was to put together a strong team of Sherpas. So many friends and relatives needed a job, but I was the one who had to judge and decide. Ang Phu was second Sirdar and Mike Cheney of Mountain Travel helped a lot. We carefully selected the best team of 60 strong, friendly and honest Sherpas. We had a great time, worked very hard, took care of each other, cracked lots of jokes and successfully climbed the mountain.

It was my first time to the summit of Sagamartha, the Nepalese name for Everest. When Peter Boardman and I reached the Chinese tripod on top, there was no view at all due to bad weather, but I felt great. I felt this was everything I had ever wanted, and I had done it! Peter asked me to talk into his tape recorder. I found it so difficult to speak, the words would not come. All I said was: 'Hurry up, we must go down!' Most of all, I worried about the deteriorating weather, so I tied the Nepalese

flag to the tripod, we shook hands, took photos and started back down. We met Mick Burke coming up alone just below the summit. Martin Boysen had turned back after losing a crampon. Mick apologized for not keeping up with us and was excited to be so close to the summit. I lent him my Olympus camera, having taken the last photograph of him and rewound the film. Peter and I agreed to wait for him at the south summit.

The weather changed very fast. We waited for two and a half hours but he never came. We left some food and a gas stove, hoping he would find them, and started down in the storm. It was a complete white-out and our footsteps had been covered, so we got lost. The slope was too steep and we knew we had missed the way so we returned to the south summit. Still Mick was not there. On the way down again, I lost a crampon. Peter and I were roped together, but with no protection as we had no time to belay. We were lucky to avoid two small avalanches. We found ourselves above the rock band but were lost again and could not find the fixed rope. The wind had dropped and there was only a little snow but we had no idea where to go, so we stopped.

Suddenly the clouds cleared and we saw the black rock above us. We knew we were too low so climbed up and then found the rope. Peter said, 'Now we are home.' I smiled, 'You are right.' It was dark and we followed the fixed rope down. Peter was much faster than me as I was very tired.

Martin Boysen was waiting for us in Camp 6. I was completely snow-blind for the next 24 hours and Peter had frostbitten feet. Martin looked after us for the next two days. He saved our lives. The weather did not clear so we could not go back up to look for Mick. His body has never been found but it is probable that he fell down the Kangshung Face from the Hillary Step. I am absolutely sure he went to the summit.

We ran out of oxygen and food, but on the third day the blizzard cleared. It was one of the hardest days because by now all of us had lost our crampons but we descended 5,000 feet to Camp 2. Some Sherpas had waited at Camp 5 and we had to rappel down on our arms in some places. It took a week for our arm muscles to recover. We had achieved our goal but we were deeply sad about losing our friend.

I went back to Everest in 1979 with the Germans, 1983 with the Americans and again in 1984, but not above Base Camp. With Al Read, I co-led the first successful expedition to Gauri-shankar in early 1985. While leading treks with Mountain Travel, I got the chance to guide many interesting people including Prince Charles and Prince Dhirendra, World Bank President Robert Macnamara and film actor Robert Redford. I have met Queen Elizabeth, Prince Philip and the King of Norway.

Since climbing Everest with Chris Bonington in autumn 1985, I have only been back twice and never above Base Camp. I was a joint leader on the 1988 China-Japan-Nepal Friendship Expedition and in 1989 a non-climbing Sirdar for the Japanese on the South Col route. My friend, Toichiro Mitani, had to turn back at 8,000 metres (26,240) feet on three expeditions and I was beginning to think he was just an unlucky man, but he made it on the fourth attempt. I knew how he felt.

My childhood dream came true in 1975 when I first climbed Sagarmatha. As a boy I remember the wonderful stories told by the old Sherpas and thinking: 'How is it possible to climb up into the sky where only the gods and goddesses can live?' It took me many years to learn, as there were no climbing schools. One thing we all seem to have forgotten is to take care of the world for future generations. We have shared our mountains and fresh air with explorers, climbers and tourists. It is important for everyone to help keep the environment clean and respect wildlife and nature. I think the only hope is for us all to cooperate to save the Himalayan range.

Now I have a small trekking company, Nepal Himal, and work in Kathmandu. I only take two or three treks a year with old friends. Last year we had a fire in the little house I rent in Kathmandu and I lost all my mountaineering mementoes, many books, letters from friends, my summit photographs and the Key of San Francisco. All that I saved from the fire was my passport and the decoration medals I had received from Nepal and China. Though I am a poor man, I have been to the United States four times and to Europe three times. I was excited to be invited for the 40th Everest anniversary celebrations in London. It was a great honour and the chance to see many of my friends. To me, friendship is more important than any achievement.

BELOW: Looking to a rosier future for Sherpas. Pertemba on Island Peak, or Imja Tse, in the Khumbu Himal.

Voytek Kurtyka

The Polish Syndrome

A tenacious individualism – in spite of a system bent on levelling people

– contributed to the emergence of some singular personalities whose

alpinism bore a very individual mark and style.

Mountaineering is a complex and unique way of life, interweaving elements of sport, art and mysticism. Success or failure depends on the ebb and flow of immense inspiration and energy. Detecting a single rule governing this energy is difficult – it arises and vanishes like the urge to dance, and remains as mysterious as the phenomenon of life itself. Undoubtedly, it was one such enormous wave of energy that nourished several generations of Polish climbers over the last two decades. How else can one explain the succession of brilliant Himalayan achievements by the Poles, especially considering the material deprivation of the period known as the PRL or Polish People's Republic? It was a time of limited freedoms and administrative restrictions, not to say actual poverty. Expeditions involved thousands of dollars but, as Sherpas like to say, 'No problem'. From 1975 onwards Polish successes were astonishing, and their way of achieving them no less so.

*

In the field of exploratory Himalayan alpinism, Poles have established 23 new routes on 8,000-metre peaks. Japan, in second position, boasts 15; Austria 13; the former Yugoslavia 9; and Great Britain and Italy 8 routes each. Polish mountaineers also initiated the winter era in Himalayan climbing, making the first eight winter ascents on eight-thousanders Most of the new alpine-style ascents on these high peaks were theirs – 9 out of 14 – and Poles have also contributed to the latest Himalayan fashion for flashed one-day ascents of eight-thousanders.

BIOGRAPHY

When, at the age of ten, Voytek Kurtyka moved to the city from the mountainous region where he had been born, it was like a bereavement. He missed the wildness of nature and the freedom to roam within it, so that when he discovered rock climbing at the age of 21, it felt like coming home. He knew at once that he had found what he loved to do. That was in 1969. Within three years he had made his first high altitude climbs in the Afghan Hindu Kush, when he forged the partnership with the British mountaineer Alex MacIntyre that was to last through four expeditions until Alex's death. In this important essay, Kurtyka postulates reasons for the phenomenon of Polish success in the highest mountains of the world and celebrates a golden age which is now, sadly, slipping into history.

I believe that the austere mountain world has always struck a chord in the Polish psyche. For centuries, Poles have lived between the devil and the deep blue sea. For almost all her history, Poland has been harassed by superior powers and by her neighbours. She's been invaded by Mongols, Tartars, Turks, and Cossacks, Russians, Germans, Austrians, Swedes, and the French. Willing or not, Poles have served as Europe's buffer against the worst invasions and suffered severely in the process. The Mongols stopped here in the 13th century, and several times the Ottoman Empire retreated from Poland's eastern steppes. Only 70 years ago, the new Soviet power, pressing against Europe, was defeated at Warsaw. The country endured the opening and closing events of World War Two. And, here again, communism fell to pieces.

Centuries of suffering and danger have bred an appreciation for such qualities as fortitude and tenacity, have taught Poles to cope in desperate circumstances. Wars and continual political chaos have forged an individualism, an inclination towards insubordination, an irreverence for norms and regulations. Having their broad steppes over-run by Turks and Tartars fostered a sense of adventure and a fascination with space. When, in the eighteenth century, European culture turned towards mountains and their conquest, Poles were among the first to embrace this special art. Similarly, Poles were sensitive to the fascination of unexplored territory, their most interesting accomplishments in this area occurring, paradoxically, not

RIGHT: Dhaulagiri. Polish climbers made the first winter ascent of this peak in 1985. In 1990, when this picture was taken, Krystof Wielicki soloed an impressive new route on the East Face in only 16 hours.

during 'illustrious' chapters of national history – as did those in Britain's golden age of the Royal Geographical Society – but rather in periods of Polish Diaspora and collapse of statehood.

After successive failed uprisings, waves of deportation and emigration, Polish names appeared in the farthest unexplored corners of the world. In 1850, Pavel Strzelecki discovered the highest peak of Australia, naming it for the insurrectionist commander, General Kosciuszko. In 1850, J. Chodzko climbed Mount Ararat (5,156 metres) in Turkey. Around the same time I. Domyko carried out the first explorations of the Chilean Cordilleras. Two major ranges of eastern Siberia were named the Czerski and Czekanowski mountains, after Polish political expatriates who, following the national uprising in 1863, turned their exile into an opportunity for geographic discoveries.

Another fascinating figure was Captain Gronbczewski, who in the Czar's service was one of the chief figures of the Great Game conducted between the British and Russian empires. His greatest achievements included exploration of the Kashgar Mountains in the years 1885-89 and, independently of the British, discovering K2 from the Shaksgam side. Gronbczewski was one of the forerunners of winter Himalayan activity, climbing in January and February of 1890 the high passes of the Kun Lun Mountains – col Hindu Tash (5,515 metres) and Col Kilian (5,459 metres).

At the beginning of the current century a group of Tatra climbers formed a Himalaya Club, but it was not until 1939, the eve of the Second World War, that the first Polish climbing expedition went to the Himalaya. A bold four-man team claimed the first ascent of Nanda Devi East (7,434 metres), the seventh highest peak ever to be climbed, and undoubtedly one of the most difficult Himalayan routes of its day.

After the Second World War – which ravaged the country, and cost the lives of some six million citizens – Poland fell under Soviet influence and suffered a period of isolation from the world. In an alien political system, alpinism was regarded as the frivolous activity of decadents and throughout the 1950s even access to the frontier peaks was forbidden. Soon, however, all those terrible Polish traits, which led to chaos and disintegration in times of peace, worked in a similarly destructive way on the communist system. Deep-seated recalcitrance and a long experience of subversion forced departures from typical Eastern European constraints. First, Poles regained their travelling rights and – deftly and openly – 'managed' foreign currencies. The country's official economy, run on the threadbare zloty, slowly developed a second monetary system based on the all-powerful dollar. International travel swiftly familiarized Poles with the intricacies of petty smuggling and this became a way of life and livelihood for many. The most exotic smuggling routes were developed by alpinists to fund their expeditions.

Within that strange, relatively tolerant Polish version of communism, a great breakthrough in Tatra climbing took place in the 1950s and 1960s, first by the generation of J. Dlugosz and S. Biel, and then, immediately afterwards, by that of E. Chrobak, Z. Heinrich, J. Kurczab, R. Szafirski and others. Naturally, the longing for bigger mountains revived. 1959 saw the start of a very productive period of expeditions to the Afghan Hindu Kush, which lasted until the Soviet invasion of that country in 1978. Activity here, above all, taught Poles the complex art of organizing expeditions, and familiarized a large group of climbers with high altitude. That initial 1959 expedition, led by B. Chcwascinski, climbed Noshaq (7,492 metres) within days of its first, Japanese ascent. Numerous six- and seven-thousand-metre peaks fell to later expeditions.

Some interesting and little-known climbs which took place in the Hindu Kush in the 1970s represented the early application of 'alpine-style' in high mountains. Judged on their sporting value, they could even be said to surpass alpine-style achievements in the Himalaya, although the same would probably also be true of some ascents in the Soviet Pamirs. One of the first and finest

199

finest and most forbidding walls of the Hindu Kush. It was here, too, on February 13 1973, that Zawada and T. Piotrowski, with their ascent of Noshaq, were the first to climb a seven-thousander in winter, effectively initiating the discipline of Himalayan winter climbing.

Modern Polish Himalayan alpinism began in 1971 with the first ascent of Kunyang Kish (7,852 metres), then the highest virgin summit in the world. Andrzej Zawada, the expedition's energetic and charismatic leader, had secured the support and friendship of a Swiss millionaire of Polish descent and, by stressing the national character of the expedition, he also won over the authorities. Zawada is an extraordinarily bold and creative man who readily challenges accepted practices and rules. His expeditions showed a dash and extravagence uncharacteristic of Poles. He cared deeply about their image in the mass media, even if such considerations were always subordinated to the principal goal. Andrzej combined typical Polish stamina – physical and mental – with a vivid imagination. From his Tatra days he retained his great fascination with winter climbing.

Some of the leading figures in Polish mountaineering (reading left to right, line by line): Antoni Malciewski; Pavel Strzelecki; Jan Dlugosz (seen here with Don Whillans, left); Andrzej Zawada leaving Lhotse Base Camp, December 1974; Tadeusz Piotrowski; (left to right in group shot) E Chrobak, A Packzkowki, W. Wroz, Z. Kowaleski; Maciej Berbeka; Maciej Pawlikowski; Alexander Lwow; J. Kurczab; Krystof Wielicki and Jerzy Kukuczka, exhausted after their winter ascent of Kangchenjunga in 1986; Kukuczka on top of Nanga Parbat, his ninth eight-thousander; A. Czok.

In 1974 Zawada threw himself into organizing the first Polish expedition to an eight-thousander. He would have preferred Everest or K2, but the permit, when it came, offered only Lhotse. Organizational delays turned the expedition from a post-monsoon into a winter attempt. On Christmas Day Heinrich and Zawada became the first to press above 8,000 metres in winter. They failed to gain the summit, reaching 8,250 metres, but engaged public interest in the climb and its rigorous demands. The poignant death of one of the members, a well-known actor named S. Latallo, was perceived as a national tragedy. This new high profile forced the authorities to extend broader assistance to climbing endeavours and Polish alpinism entered its most fruitful period. Despite poverty and limited freedom, climbers were overtaken by a tremendous inspiration which overcomes all barriers. The Himalaya offered an exciting escape from the drab system and grey stability of the PRL, and a rare opportunity for creative communication with the outside world.

In the same way that Polish alpinism has been shaped by the Polish mentality and penchant for exploration, so it is also characterized by an inclination for winter mountaineering – uncommon to such an extent in other nationalities. This Art of Suffering was an outlet for the traditional Polish values of

such climbs was the first ascent of the 1,800-metre north wall of Akher Caq (7,071 metres) by J. Jasinski, M. Kowalczyk, V. Kurtyka and J. Rusiecki in a 25-day climb.

In 1977, A. Lwow, J. Pietkiewicz and K. Wielicki took five days to achieve the first ascent of the 2,500-metre northeast pillar of Kohe Skhawr (7,116 metres). The same year, Jasinski, Kowalczyk, Zawada and T. King, made the first climb of the fine and very demanding north pillar of Kohe Mandaras (6,628 metres). Meanwhile, Kurtyka, MacIntyre and Porter, in a highly dramatic six-day climb, grabbed the first ascent of the 2,500-metre east face of Kohe Bandaka (6,843 metres), one of the

bravery and endurance. A tenacious individualism – in spite of a system bent on levelling people – contributed to the emergence of some singular personalities whose alpinism bore a very individual mark and style. Besides Zawada, there was Wanda Rutkiewicz, the first lady of international high-altitude mountaineering; Jerzy (Jurek) Kukuczka, challenger in the race to be first to all the eight-thousanders; and me – Wojtek (Voytek) Kurtyka – treading my own untried paths.

Equally unconventional were the methods employed to get us to the Himalaya. Organizing and financing expeditions in the PRL has to be the fishiest story ever told in world alpinism, not least because our alpine community was almost utterly anti-communist. You'd be hard pressed to find a single climber who was a party member. Many, indeed, would become active in the underground movement, such as J. Onyskiewicz, later to become Minister of Defence, and Lech Walesa's secretary, J. Milewski. No wonder that mountain activity was viewed so acidly by the government.

Mountaineering clubs, like all social bodies, were controlled by a system of privileges, formalities and regulations. Nobody had the right to die in the mountains on his own account. The flock was always responsible for the insanity of its own sheep. However, in Poland the system essentially never functioned – so much so that the chairman of the Alpinist Union for most of the PRL period, A. Paczkowski, was a man openly sympathetic to the political underground. The delicate process of getting financial support from the authorities was made easier when spectacular Himalayan achievements prompted more understanding from a political system attuned to revelling in the glory of success. The winter expedition to Lhotse in 1974 was unquestionably one

ABOVE: Kunyang Kish from the southwest, showing the long and complex South Ridge, climbed by the Poles in 1971.

RIGHT: The South Face of Lhotse, which claimed the life of Kukuzcka in 1989.

LEFT: Camp 3 on Himalchuli in 1978. Janusz Onyskiewicz (left) is seen in this picture with the British climber Iain Allen.

turning point, as was Wanda Rutkiewicz's unexpected ascent of Everest in 1978, and, in the 1980s, the 'race' between Kukuczka and Reinhold Messner.

With a monthly income of only $25, climbers had to work hard to get funds. One fruitful source, common throughout Eastern Europe, was the system of state subsidies and tax and customs exemptions. Then there were the carefully devised smuggling channels. Finally, came contributions of Western currency from foreign partners who willingly joined Polish expeditions. The most ambitious projects could count on a grant from the state budget ranging from several hundred to two or

three thousand dollars – unless it was led by Zawada. He regularly put in for $100,000 and would get around $30,000. Separate grants were made in Polish currency which, in that curious system, were partly used for buying our dollars. Less spectacular local expeditions got their money through so-called 'height-works' – roped access work – whose profits went untaxed. Earnings from these jobs were very high, the daily income of a climber often exceeding the monthly salary of an average citizen. Despite such opportunities, the zlotys acquired were worth hardly anything due to the exorbitant black market price of the dollar – not to mention the fact that black market purchases were illegal. That is why Polish expeditions so anxiously sought the participation of western members who, in return for Polish kit, contributed hard currency.

Soon a method was devised to increase the value of the zloty several times over. We found eager customers in all Asian countries for our ridiculously low-priced Polish goods. So instead of taking expensive dollars, a team would bring several hundred 'items for the porters' needs' – especially glass crystal, Russian-made cameras and whisky! These were sold at good profit, in New Delhi or Kathmandu, where in the 1980s the bazaars were often full of Polish goods. In some quarters you'd even hear Polish spoken. Between Poland and India a regular 'Himalayan connection' was forged, servicing Polish expeditions with lorries. Coming home, the whole nervous process was reversed, except that In thls case profits found their way into private pockets. Poles were a major 'customer' for Istanbul jeans, sheepskin coats from Kabul, cottons and silks from New Delhi. With the transition to a free-market economy, thousands of Poles engaged in this illegal importing went public, giving themselves names like India Market or Nepal Shop or, in my case, Orient Express.But while alpinists had opened up the best smuggling routes for clothing, they lost out to professional gangs in the more lucrative electronic and gold route betweeen Singapore and India.

Such were the circumstances under which the great phase of Himalayan exploration by Polish climbers occurred. Once all the barriers and bribes were successfully negoitated, the actual ascent of another eight-thousander was a picnic by comparison!

Building on the 1971 Kunyang Kish success, Poles made first ascents of such attractive summits as Shispare, Broad Peak Middle, Peak 29, Manaslu East and many more. An important figure in this development was Piotr Mlotecki, who as the leader carried out the first ascents of the three virgin summits of Kangchenjunga – South, Middle and Kangbachen. The Kunyang Kish generation became the living legends of Polish alpinism. They had created modern Tatra climbing in the 1960s and raised Polish accomplishments in the Alps to a world standard. They remained at the forefront of Himalayan mountaineering, inspiring successive generations of alpinists, until 1989 when Heinrich and Chrobak died in an avalanche on Everest. At the same time, the number of Polish routes on 8,000-metre peaks rapidly increased. Some mountains, like Kangchenjunga or Cho Oyu, now boast no less than three Polish lines. Many have two: K2, Makalu, Manaslu, Annapurna, Broad Peak, Gasherbrum II, Shisha Pangma. Kukuczka and Kurtyka were especially active in this field.

The second half of the 1970s saw the ascendancy of the great star Wanda Rutkiewicz. In 1975, she led the expedition which made a new route on Gasherbrum II, besides claiming the first ascent of Gasherbrum III. Three years later she was the first Pole to stand on top of Everest, on the same momentous day that Cardinal Wojtyla became Pope. Overnight she became a national heroine, alongside Kristina Chojnacka-Liskiewicz, who in the same year was the first woman to sail around the world alone. Wanda was a fervent supporter of women's alpinism and her first expeditions were organized under this banner; a successful women's expedition to Nanga Parbat followed the Gasherbrum triumph. Eventually, however, the mountains proved to be so littered with men that Wanda gave up the idea of purity, and in 1982 Kukuczka and Kurtyka joined her team of twelve women attempting K2. Her enthusiasm infected a large group of eminent women mountaineers. A. Czerwinska, H. Kruger-Syrokomska, D. Miodowicz-Wolf, A. Okopinksa and K. Palmowska all owe much to Wanda's inspiration. In 1983, Czerwinska and Palmowska achieved – on a two-person expedition – a female-ascent of Broad Peak, believed to be the only undertaking of its kind so far.

Latterly, Wanda accepted mixed expeditions, while stubbornly maintaining her position as first lady of Himalayan climbing In some ways her career resembled that of Messner, particularly in the extent of her popularity and her preoccupation with publicity. She, too, determined to climb all fourteen eight-thousanders, although in the event, she managed only eight. However, they included Everest and K2. Though her ascents followed traditional routes and methods, she was one of very few women to make a career out of Himalayan climbing. Wilfully, and with great charm, she argued that a woman's place was at 8,000 metres. Her fierce determination led to considerable personal damage. In 1981, despite a broken leg, she set out for K2 on crutches. Only when she reached Broad Peak base camp on the backs of Kukuczka and Kurtyka did she realize she had come too far. That doggedness cost her another operation and the waste of a whole year. Her last medical examination revealed a serious condition of the liver and kidneys. Nevertheless, she left for Kangchenjunga with her usual determination, and there – in May 1992 – was seen for the last time at 8,200 metres.

During the years 1977-78, my own alpine-style acitivity struggled to find a niche in Polish mountaineering. Undeniably high-risk, it provoked negative reactions from other climbers who were being forced to take collective responsibility for each other. Worse still, individual activity attracted no sponsorship. The Alpinist Union made no exceptions to its grant policy. I see now that I was committed to alpine-style from my very first contact with high mountains, although I don't think it existed as a notion in my mind then. Climbing the north wall of Akher Caq in a single push in 1972 was a natural and spontaneous act, transferring the technique of the Tatras and Alps to higher mountains. When that was followed by adverse experiences within two big and unsuccessful expeditions – to Lhotse in the winter of 1974 and K2 in 1976 – I resolved not to go on any more large ventures with their numerous limitations and chance partnerships. It became clear to me that alpine-style is a higher form of the mountaineering art, not only in its sporting aspect, but also in human terms, because through it you can experience the mountain world more intimately and deeply. Eliminating accidental partnerships makes for closer bonds.

Since then, for me, every expedition has involved a careful choice of both the objectives and the partners I climb with.

Thanks to Zawada's tolerance, in 1977 I successfully split from the main group of the Polish-English partnership and, with Alex MacIntyre and John Porter, was able to realize the ascent of the east wall of Kohe Bandaka. I still consider that one of my finest mountain experiences – the wall demanded special technical skills, intuition and a psychological strength. No wonder it forged such a felicitous Polish-English bond, yielding in subsequent years magnificent ascents of the south face of Changabang (eight days on the wall) and the east face of Dhaulagiri (three days and a storm on that one). For Alex and me, alpine-style meant a way of life and a state of consciousness that allowed us to fall in love with the mountain and, in consequence, trust our destiny to it – unconditionally. Later I would call that the 'State of Nakedness', by which I meant lightness, defencelessness and confidence. This moment of entrusting was usually preceded by a torment of doubt and fear. But even this gave an enriching experience and insight.

The need to climb in this manner enhanced the relationship between partners, their sensitivity to each other and to the character of the mountain. Pehaps this is why, paradoxically, alpine-style in the Himalaya entails comparatively few mishaps. Throughout my period of extremely high-risk activity, neither I nor any of my partners have lost a single proverbial hair from our heads during our common undertakings. In Kukuczka's extremely tragic career, our joint four-year cooperation was for him the only period free from disasters. It is worth noting that none of the fourteen or so alpine-style routes opened up on eight-thousanders has involved the death of a single person.

1980 was an important year in Polish mountaineering. Zawada achieved his life's ambition as expedition leader with a double success on the world's highest peak. On February 17, L. Cichy and K. Wielicki completed the first winter ascent of Everest, initiating winter mountaineering on 8,000-metre peaks.

After the climb, Zawada did not bother to dismantle base camp as the following spring Kukuczka and A. Czok set their

RIGHT: Alex MacIntyre on Day 8 of the Polish-English climb on the South Face of Changabang.

feet on Everest again, opening a new route up the south pillar. These events had distinguished a group of excellent mountaineers with a remarkable capacity for high-altitude climbing. Czok went on to climb Makalu solo in 1982, spending three consecutive nights at 8,000 metres, and completing a new route up the west face. Heinrich, Chrobak, Wroz and Piotrowski, outstanding big mountain climbers of an earlier generation, supplemented the group and soon they were joined by a younger wave: M. Berbeka, M. Pawlikowski, P. Piasecki, A. Lwow, R. Gajewski, L. Wilczynski, A. Hajzer and others.

Before long, Wielicki had become a champion of Himalayan winter climbing. After Everest, he made the first winter ascent of Kangchenjunga with Kukuckzka in 1986, and in 1989 soloed Lhotse in winter, wearing a surgical corset to hold his spine together after it was damaged in a stone avalanche on a previous expedition. A striking feature of Wielicki's ascents is his exceptional speed. He was the first to achieve a one-day ascent of an 8,000er when, in 1984, he scaled Broad Peak in 17 hours, thus launching the trend for rapid ascents. In 1990 he performed a similar feat on the more difficult English-Polish route on the east face of Dhaulagiri. The trend was zestfully taken up by Chamoux and Batard of France, Loretan and Troillet of Switzerland, as well as myself. So far, Wielicki has climbed eight eight-thousanders, including four high ones, and Manaslu by a new route. He seems to be heading towards completing them all.

Throughout the 1980s Poles pursued their quest for first winter ascents with exceptional dedication. After Everest came Manaslu, Dhaulagiri, Cho Oyu, Kangchenjunga, Annapurna and Lhotse. Besides Wielicki, Kukuczka too scored notable success in the Art of Suffering – three first ascents and a repetition on Cho Oyu – as did Berbeka with two firsts and one of the minor summits of Broad Peak. So far, all first winter ascents of eight-thousanders (achieved in the recognized winter season) are the work of Poles. The Japanese were first on Dhaulagiri, but they climbed outside the 'official' season, at the start of December. I can't believe the Polish propensity for this peculiarly masochistic art is any accident.

Jurek Kukuczka came late to the era of Polish-English collaboration when he joined our team for the west face of Makalu. The following year Alex MacIntyre died on the south wall of Annapurna, and I began my four-year partnership with Jurek. We continued making new pure alpine ascents on eight-thousanders. On Makalu, Jurek had already displayed those qualities which would make him the most efficient Himalayan climber in the world. After disappointment on the west wall, Alex and I both felt further sacrifices would be pointless, but Jurek remained game. After Alex left base camp, Jurek – supported only by my gaze and in the teeth of fierce winds – accomplished one of the finest solo ascents of an eight-thousander, climbing Makalu by a new route on the northwest ridge. In so doing, he revealed his most remarkable trait – an uncanny mental stamina.

Jurek was the greatest psychological rhinoceros I've ever met among alpinists, unequalled in his ability to suffer and in his lack of responsiveness to danger. At the same time, he possessed that quality most characteristic of anyone born under Aries – a blind inner compulsion to press ahead. Characters like that, when they meet an obstacle, strike against it until they either crush it or break their own necks. Recognizing these twin beasts inhabiting Kukuczka goes a long way towards explaining his successes and the tragic events that dogged him and, ultimately, his own death.

In 1983 we succeeded in establishing two new routes on Gasherbrums I and II in one expedition, and in 1984 carried through our most stylish joint enterprise by traversing all three summits of the Broad Peak massif. After that, our paths gradually diverged until eventually we took up opposite positions in Polish alpinism. My propensity for falling in love with certain mountains was alien to Jurek, particularly as some of the objects of my desire were less than 8,000 metres. Nor did he share my fascination with technical difficulties – rather, he shunned them. His passion was surviving in the death zone, at the highest altitude. Difficulties and style were only incidental in the game.

Jurek frankly admitted that alpinism was a sport for him, by which he meant an arena for competition. Consequently, he openly sought a form of alpinism in which he could compete with others, and win. Amazingly, despite this attitude, he was devoid of egocentricity and vanity, and on attaining international fame lost none of his endearing naturalness. For this I candidly

admired and loved him. On the other hand, his unreflecting readiness for blind charging annoyed me.

Three times duing our active partnership, I had to call a halt in the face of enormous risk. That threw him completely, provoking his anger, in the same way that I was angered at being so obstinately pressurized into playing Russian roulette. As the years passed and Jurek-the-Ram stormed from success to success amid many tragic occurrences, the rift between us deepened. Four of his partners died, not to mention some others on his expeditions. But it should be remembered that the careers of Rutkiewicz and Wielicki proceeded equally tragically.

After our double success on the Gasherbrums in 1983, Jurek decided to challenge Messner for the fourteen eight-thousanders. By then he had six to Messner's nine. Thus, was seen the first really public contest in the Himalaya. Jurek completed all fourteen in 1987, but he lost the race by one year. Still, his tally is imposing: nine new routes on eight-thousanders, including one solo; five others climbed in alpine-style, or similar. He climbed four eight-thousanders in winter, three of them as first winter ascents. Jurek died in 1989 on the south face of Lhotse. At an altitude of 8,200 metres he was attempting the crux, which barred the way to the summit. In loose snow and with poor protection, he relentlessly pushed his way into a blind corner – from which a charging ram knows no retreat. Jurek fell, and, after his rope snapped, plunged more than a thousand metres.

My entire energy, since parting with Jurek in 1984, has been absorbed by just three mountains: Gasherbrum 4, Trango Tower and K2. Seeking an appropriate partner for those very difficult and risky climbs, I teamed up first with the Austrian, Robert Schauer, and later with two Swiss – Erhard Loretan and Jean Troillet. Robert and I pulled off a highly dramatic eight-day first ascent of the west face of Gasherbrum 4, during which we had to face every one of the nightmares that menace alpine-style climbers – poor protection, dangerously heavy snow conditions, inability to descend, then an awful deterioration in the weather which trapped us in the death zone for three days without food or drink. We descended at last in an exhausted condition down an unknown ridge. No wonder that after arriving on top of our wall we abandoned the more or less horizontal traverse to the summit itself.

Friendship with the Swiss – great masters of space with their parapentes, skiing prowess and rapid ascents – brought me a fine new route on Trango Tower with Loretan, as well as non-stop 24-hour ascents of two new routes on the Tibetan eight-thousanders, Cho Oyu and Shisha Pangma. Although we operated as a three-person team, these latter climbs were done solo. None of our three attempts on the west face of K2 proved successful.

The Shisha Pangma climb was my twelfth new alpine-style route in the Himalaya. Six were on eight-thousanders, but the best have been ascents on the shining walls of lower peaks like Changabang, Trango Tower and Gasherbrum 4. K2 remains my constant failure, but, goddammit, there must be a way to reach a harmonious tolerance of failure. On the last attempt, we had barely approached the wall before Loretan decided we couldn't manage it. I tried to quell his pessimism, but after a ghastly nightmare in base camp, when it seemed that a dark thick mass was attempting to strangle me, I too gave up.

By quoting all the statistics I do here, I highlight the sharp conflict between sport, served by these numbers, and art, which figures kill. Unfortunately, I know it is an eternal conflict between vanity and the absolute, and simply the fact that after twenty years of climbing the struggle still rages within me is basically my only defeat. Following the recent tragic years, Polish Himalayan climbing has died down. Horrifyingly, the majority of inspired alpinists who devoted their lives to the mountains have been killed.

Many of them, like Heinrich, Chrobak, Piotrowski, Rutkiewicz and Wroz, died around the age of fity, after following for years the voice they could not resist. If only one could be certain it is the voice of truth and not illusion! My head is full of wandering, fearful dreams of mountains and I feel caught in a trap. Almost physically I sense in Poland the subsiding of the great mountain inspiration. I believe it is being replaced by the onerous awareness of a new era and the necessity of meeting its demands. For the first time in almost 200 years, the Poles seem to have hardly anything to fight. I am concerned for this nation.

LEFT: The Braldu river issuing from the Baltoro Glacier with Trango and Cathedral groups behind. Voytek Kurtyka put up a fine new route on Trango Tower with Swiss climber Erhard Loretan.

Valery Khrischaty

The Cold Breath of a Mountain

My feet get no warmer. The night is dragging on forever. Then, at last, I start to feel my toes. The pain is unbearable, but welcome. . . .

Pik Pobeda – Mount Victory – rises 7,439 metres (24,410 feet) above sea level. It is the highest summit in the Tien Shan range, otherwise known as the Celestial Mountains, the central part of which lies under vast tracts of ice. Glaciers here are spread over ten thousand square kilometres. Pobeda's summit is not clearly accentuated, topping as it does a gigantic monolith of a mountain. At the 7,000-metre level, the structure measures a good ten kilometres across, and its surmounting central plateau is a powerful 7,400 metres. It is from this lofty pediment that the summit nudges a mere 39 metres higher.

The mountain is the farthest north of any of the 'seven-thousanders', rendering it the harshest and cruellest of peaks. I have visited it several times over the twenty years I have been climbing, yet Pik Pobeda remains for me a mountain of mystery. It has its own climate and an extremly fussy character. The story of its exploration is an epic of heroism, joys of success and painful losses. With the greatest respect and admiration I salute those who, more than 60 years ago, were bold and brave enough to take up its challenge.

Between the years 1939 and 1961 the numbers of those who reached the top and those who found death on its slopes were sadly almost in balance: 25 people climbed it, 27 perished. Now that climbers have more sophisticated equipment, the score is more in favour of those who successfully tread the summit. Nevertheless, each year it harvests its toll.

I tend to think there were not many in our group who really expected we'd

BIOGRAPHY

Born in 1951 and killed in 1993 by a sérac fall on Khan Tengri, Valery Khrischaty from Kazakhstan was one of the world's strongest mountaineers and a fierce advocate of 'alpine style' climbing. He had made more than forty ascents above 7,000 metres (23,000 feet), including a string of hard winter firsts in the Pamirs and Tien Shan. He climbed Everest by a new south pillar route, Kangchenjunga without oxygen and with only one bivouac, and a new route on the west side of Dhaulagiri (8,172 metres).

Here we reproduce his diary account of the first winter ascent of the ferocious Pik Pobeda on the borders of Kirghizia and China.

succeed when we decided to tackle the mountain in winter. In early January 1990, Russia's national team undertook a reconnaissance of the central Tien Shian where Khan Tengri and Pik Pobeda are located. V. Nepomnyashy led a group whose main task was to assess the chances for a possible winter ascent. They were to be followed in by our team of 14 from Kazakhstan. In addition, we had invited five participants from Leningrad and two from Saratov. All were anxious to get to grips with the problem.

We met the Russian group at Przhevalsk

BELOW: *Pik Pobeda (or Mount Victory) seen from base camp on the Inylichek Glacier.*

airport, eager to learn its conclusion. They were categoric: it would be extremely difficult to reach the top of Pobeda in winter. And in the conditions witnessed in the preceding ten days, absolutely out of the question.

On 19 January the southern Inylichek Glacier greeted us with good weather. We set up a base on the right hand slope. It was noon. The bright sun was almost blinding. Fifteen kilometres away were the mountains, crowned by Pik Pobeda, but covered in a veneer of clouds. A heavy, grey pall of cold hung over its great slopes.

*

19 January Of the 25 people in our expedition team, 20 are ready to climb. We split into four groups of five and work out a siege campaign. First we must prepare the route, fix ropes and excavate snowholes while we acclimatize. Then will come the assault itself. Two groups, each comprising two teams, will operate one after the other, my team with that of Valery Balyberdin to have first crack. Balyberdin's men are all from Leningrad, mine are a mixed bunch. The other two teams are exclusively Kazakhi. In an emergency, one group of ten will support the safe retreat of the other from the route.

Balyberdin and I leave base camp with our teams on 21 January. We cross the Southern Inylichek glacier and, hugging the right bank, head for the northern slopes of our mountain. At 4,500 metres we set up Camp 1 by erecting two tents and digging a snowhole, and as we do so, the clouds evaporate. In the incredible purity and transparency of the air, distances immediately seem to shrink, and it feels as if you could almost touch the summit. At this time of year the sun is usually hidden behind the main peak so that Pobeda's northern slopes lie almost constantly in deep shadow. It is 6 p.m. and the thermometer registers -43° C (-45° F). While we have the petrol Primus going inside the double-layer tent, we are warm enough, but as soon as it is extinguished, all the inside walls, the clothes and food are covered with an icy crust of hard hoar. So, you have to tuck yourself deep into a sleeping bag, putting heavy down jackets on top. In the morning a thick furry frost overlays everything. One clumsy move and it drops off the tent onto you, giving you a foretaste of what's outside.

This severe frost prevents us from getting stuck into the route before 11 a.m. (In the end we spend only the first and last nights in tents, the rest in snow caves.)

23 January, 9 a.m. After gaining the snowy plateau we climb along a steep and narrow snow and ice-covered crest. Huge snowdrifts demand the utmost caution. After lunch a cold westerly wind blows up, and the temperature plunges to -45° C (-49° F). You don't feel the full strength of the cold when you're moving, but as soon as you stop your limbs begin to freeze. We dig out a snow cave at 5,500 metres. The other two teams, who left base two days ago and are following the route we have prepared, dig their own cave at 5,200 metres in which to spend the night.

The next day a cloudy mist envelops the surrounding mountains and the visibility is down to four or five hundred metres. The strong icy wind often reaches hurricane force. It is impossible to leave the cave without double-layered clothing, wool and fur gloves, and a facemask. But the others, barely 300 metres below us, are experiencing only moderate gusts of wind.

The ice, scoured by the cold wind, has become like bottle glass. Our sharp crampon-points keep skidding off it. Trying to insert our ice screws throws up chips of ice like lenses; it is difficult to get them to bite into such a hard surface in order to organize safe belays.

The wind is stronger now, and we can only see a hundred metres' distance. At 6,050 metres we dig two small snowholes. This is the fourth night of our climb. Our sleeping bags are damp. The temperature is almost 50° below (-58° F).

25 January All four teams have descended to base for a three-day rest.

29 January Not a cloud in sight! And it is warm . . . only minus 14 (7° F)! At 10 a.m. the teams – again led by Balyberdin and myself – climb to Camp 2 at 4,900 metres, leapfrogging Camp l. Even when you are standing on the sunlit slopes of the glacier, you can feel the icy breath emanating from the shadowy flank of this northern giant.

We have good equipment, which gives us confidence. But however good your outfit, your experience and skills, an element of luck is still required when attempting this mountain. If you are fortunate with weather, and have the very best gear, you can expect to reach the summit even in the fiercest cold.

30 January The sun generously floods all the summits around with light. It even feels a little warmer in our shadow. But the thermometer still shows more than 30° below (-22° F). It is easy to ascend. Without straining ourselves very hard, we reach the cave at 5,950 metres and spend the night there. Over the radio we learn that the other two teams are not far behind us.

The last day of January At last the crest gradually begins to widen and somewhere at around 6,500 metres blends into the slope of the mountain. Here we come against ice drifts and decide to dig two more caves. Tomorrow we must set up our high assault camp – the higher the better.

1 February It is 9 a.m. when we leave the caves. Balyberdin will follow two hours behind us. We pass the ice drifts, to their left, and start climbing along an icy slope as steep as 50°. The weather is marvellous.

BELOW: The North Face of Pobeda, from base camp on the Inylichek Glacier.

And this is the fourth day running it has held up, very rare here.

By 3 p.m. we call it a day at 6,950 metres. Balyberdin's team, worrying that it will be unable to find a suitable place for a cave on the windsept slopes, decides to spend the night in an icy crack at 6,800 metres.

2 February, 5 a.m. I cook breakfast. Then at 6 o'clock we start getting ready, although the severe cold prevents us setting out before 8.30. The thermometer shows that it is lower than 50° below. We reach 7,000 metres. The skies are clear now. Windy. Our hands quickly grow numb if we take off our fur gloves to leave only our woollen ones. I'm glad I put on my mask before leaving the cave. We have been on the go now for over an hour: it's almost time to make radio contact, as arranged. I hold the ice-axe with one hand, then the other, but still cannot coax any warmth into my fingers. As we approach the higher crest, the gusts of wind slap us more strongly and more often. Some clouds come in from the west. It warms up to minus 44 (-47° F).

This is my thirtieth climbing expedition to a seven-thousander. But on no other mountain have I experienced such sudden and unexpected changes of weather.

Balyberdin told me, over the radio, that his team had reached 7,150 metres, but he'd decided to go back down to 7,000 and dig a cave there. Without enough daylight left, he would postpone his summit push until tomorrow. They are joined there by the two rearguard teams.

We had thought the top not far off, but it turns out to be just a curve of a slope and the main crest is still 150 metres away. All of us are very tired and there is little daylight left. We have to hurry.

On the final crest, the cold southwesterly wind rises to hurricane force. And still the summit must be 500 metres away. Visibility is poor. We veer to the left a bit, hoping to spot the summit. It almost seems that we will have to abandon our hope of collecting a stone from the top

today, but then, at 2.15 p.m., we find the rocky outcrop on the summit. The highest point of the Tien Shan has thus been reached by the following men: Valery Khrischaty (leader of the expedition), Gennady Mikhailov and Sergei Ovcharenko from Alma-Ata, and Gennady and Sergei Bogomolov from Saratov.

On the descent a crampon of one of our party works free. In this wind and cold it is very hard to put it back on – these are the times you could get frostbitten. There is nowhere to shelter from the wind. Only 200 metres separate us from the cave at 6,950 metres, but the onset of night plunges us into total darkness. If the lads from the other teams had not signalled the right direction with their torches, I don't know long we might have fumbled about in the ice looking for the cave – and this after eleven cold toilsome hours above 7,000 metres. Carefully avoiding crevasses and icy drifts, we reach the cave at around 9 p.m.

3 February The weather turns very nasty in the morning. Hurricane winds. No one from the other three teams dares chance a summit bid. It would be madness in these conditions. With the gale still blowing we start down, leaving the other three groups in the caves to await better weather.

It takes three and a half hours to descend only 500 metres. Cold to the bone, we dive into our cave at 6,500 metres. The wet sleeping bags have frozen solid; we have to thaw them out before they do the same to us. There is just enough petrol to melt a little over a litre of water from the snow. Despite the cold, we are all parched with thirst. I spend half the night rubbing my frozen feet inside the cold sleeping bag. All the others are doing the same. At times I get almost desperate, fearing I will never unfreeze my limbs. Worn out with warming my feet, I have barely fallen asleep before I am woken immediately because of the cold, and have to rub, rub and rub some more. Then I repeat it all over again, sitting in the cold sleeping bag against the frozen wall of the cave. The nerves and muscles in my neck have started to ache from hypothermia. I can barely turn my head. And still the morning doesn't come! My feet get no warmer. The night is dragging on forever. Then, at last, I start to feel my toes. The pain is unbearable, but welcome. . . .

Dawn is breaking. Will the lads up the mountain dare to storm the summit today? In my mind I imagine a situation that would require us going back up there, and I realize that after this night in the cave, even if the wind drops by half, I would not make it alive up to the others, or, if I did, I wouldn't be much help to them. The mountain has sunk its teeth into us and won't let us go. Even retreating down takes considerable effort. But the lower we go, the weaker the wind. At 5,500 metres I take off my mask and, when we get to the cave at 5,200 metres, I am able to discard all the fur clothing.

*

High above us, six of the fifteen did try to storm the summit. But the wind and cold turned them back at 7,200 metres. They had a hard descent to base camp and almost everyone got frostbitten; some even had to have amputations later.

On 7 February, all the members of the expedition gathered in base camp.

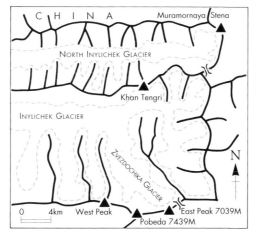

RIGHT: The Tien Shan mountains lie on the borders of Kirghizia and Kazakhstan with China. Pobeda is the highest summit at 24,410 ft (7,439 m).

CHINA
Muramornaya Stena
NORTH INYLICHEK GLACIER
Khan Tengri
INYLICHEK GLACIER
ZVEZDOCHIKA GLACIER
N
0   4km   West Peak   East Peak 7039M
Pobeda 7439M

Michael Thompson

Climbing Well, Treading Softly

. . . mountaineering is a self-organizing activity, at the heart of which is the aesthetic principle of 'doing more with less'.

The Himalayas are growing faster than the forces of nature can wear them down. That is why they stick up so far. It also explains why their river valleys are so tremendously V-shaped, and why bits (sometimes as large as 10 cubic kilometres) keep on falling down into those valleys, eventually ending up, ground to a fine powder, somewhere in the vicinity of Bangladesh. The Himalayas are not a state; they are a process. The whole region is one huge conveyor-belt, and the challenge for those who live there is to do something useful with all the stuff before it disappears out into the Bay of Bengal.

Climbers, you might think, are only giving a tiny helping hand to this awesome process – charging pig-headedly up the down escalator, as it were. But it is what they are doing lower down – among the people, the animals and the plants that have colonized the flow – that they need to worry about. Trees felled for firewood, buffaloes converted into burgers, bright young lads killed in heroic antics before they can make any contribution to their communities, and local economies distorted in ways that may not be ecologically sustainable, are actions that have consequences far beyond setting the odd rock on its downhill way a little ahead of time, or fouling the Khumbu Glacier, or leaving an oxygen cylinder on the South Col.

The defilement of the pristine realm that Lionel Terray always spoke of as existing 'high above the lives of men' can get mountaineers very excited, but it has negligible physical connection with the alterations they may have set in train on their way up to (and down from) the Terraysphere. That there is a helicopter incorporated into the ice of the western cwm of Everest (not to mention a fair few climbers) is neither here nor there, so far as

BIOGRAPHY

Michael Thompson is a social anthropologist. He divides his time between Geneva (where he is Senior Fellow at the International Academy of the Environment) and London (where he is Director of the Musgrave Institute). He was a member of the Annapurna south face expedition in 1970 and of the Everest southwest face expedition in 1975.

the environmental health of Nepal is concerned. But it is not quite that simple.

To leave a helicopter in the Terraysphere you have first to leave some pretty messy footprints lower down, among the villages, paddy fields and forests of the approach march. Conversely, if two of you set off from Europe without any excess baggage, and a few weeks later are standing on the top of Everest, then the most you can leave in the Terraysphere is yourselves and the contents of your rucksacks, so your impact on the Nepalese countryside and its inhabitants will be correspondingly slight. In other words, there is a close connection between the *way* we behave up there and the impacts we have down below. It is this connection that I want to focus on. Rather than repeating all those worthy but boring exhortations about leaving nothing but footprints, taking nothing but photographs and so on, I am going to try to relate the environmental impact of mountaineers directly to the theme of this volume: the essence, excitement and ethos of climbing. My argument will be that mountaineering is a self-organizing activity, at the heart of which is the aesthetic principle of 'doing more with less'. And if mountaineers stay loyal to this essential principle then that will do more to minimize their impact on the world of men (that, like it or not, they have to pass through on their way to and from their beloved Terraysphere) than anything else.

Extracting the Essence There is a theory of risk that is based on the idea that everyone has a 'risk thermostat'. Different people will have their thermostats set at different temperatures, but they will all try to respond to changes in their situations so as to bring the levels of risk they perceive themselves as taking back into line with the settings on their thermostats. This explains why we find

ourselves climbing a grade harder, once we've equipped ourselves with some new technological device: nylon ropes instead of hemp, or Friends instead of drilled-out nuts. It also explains the unease people feel when they perceive themselves to be subject to risks (nuclear power is a favourite example) that are not within their personal control. In distinguishing between situations in which the thermostat is able to function and those in which it is not, this risk compensation hypothesis corresponds nicely with the everyday distinction most people draw between two kinds of risk: voluntary and involuntary.

Mountaineering is usually seen as the exemplar of a voluntary risk: something that people should not be forced to take, nor forcibly restrained from taking. But it is never that simple, and mountaineering has often been threatened by external regulation. Queen Victoria wanted it banned after the deaths that accompanied Whymper's first ascent of the Matterhorn, and in recent years there has been a hard-fought struggle between the 'anarchists' and the 'organizers': the former seeing themselves as the defenders of the true spirit of mountaineering, the latter wishing to bring it within the ambit of the Sports Council and the Outdoor Pursuits wing of the education system. Those who see it as part of education would like the

ABOVE: Chandrakot, Nepal. This charming village lies on the popular trekking route to Annapurna. A conservation project engages local support for long-term, environmentally-sound development.

BELOW AND LEFT: Rubbish abandoned by climbers on expeditions to Everest: in a crevasse below the Southwest Face, 1975 (below) and by an American team at the Nepalese Base Camp in autumn 1976 (left).

thermostat set so low that only a major act of God could remove one of their students from their care; those who see themselves as Conquistadors of the Useless want to be free to set it as high as they dare.

Some of the more perceptive of these Conquistadors are well aware that it is through the gradations of these voluntary settings of the thermostats that their seemingly unstructured activity gains its coherence and direction. Respect in mountaineering ends up focused on that informal elite who, in consistently doing more with less, and in staying alive in the process, are busy breaking the new ground (or, as test-pilots say, 'pushing out the envelope'). Thus, those who perform most aesthetically on the mountain define what the aesthetics of mountaineering are, all without any committees or officers or rule-books or examinations or certificates or badges. Of course, it will be objected that this structuring mechanism (whereby those who perform best define the criteria by which the quality of performance is to be judged) is completely circular – and so it is until we add the *essence*.

The essential point is that mountaineering would not exist without a direction, and it would not have a direction if it did not somehow generate a definition of achievement that united personal skill with personal risk-taking. To focus on skill without risk-taking would by-pass the whole business of risk compensation which, as every mountaineer knows, is what makes it all exciting enough but not too terrifying. Conversely, focusing on risk-taking without skill would lead the activity into a death-or-glory cul-de-sac. In other words, the relaxing of one or other criterion results in the demise of the activity of mountaineering: from boredom in one direction and from death in the other. Only when both criteria are applied is it possible for the activity to continue in existence. That is how mountaineering self-organizes itself, and why the aesthetic of 'doing more with less' is its essence: without it mountaineering would cease to be mountaineering.

This essence, of course, is always under threat: from outside, by commercial interest and by bureaucracy and, from inside, by those mountaineers who want to be up there with the elite without quite accepting the risks that entitle them to be up there.

So the essence has all the time to be defended, and nowhere is this defence more needed than in the Himalayas. 'Giving the mountain a chance' is not a sentiment that comes easily to commercial sponsors, and the whole business of selling places on expeditions guarantees that their members will do much less with much more than did Reinhold Messner before them. If the tide is running this strongly in the wrong direction, what can turn it? My answer is: the environment. The argument is wonderfully simple. Those who consistently aim at doing more with less will not only be defending the essence of mountaineering, but they will be having less impact on the environment than any of the back-sliders.

But Is this Enough? No matter how hard they try to de-materialize Himalayan mountaineering, these paragons will still be having an impact, and some will always argue that the whole business of flying half-way round the world to disport yourself in the Terraysphere is inherently unsustainable. The real test, it seems to me, is not whether the mountaineer is having an impact but the scale of that impact relative to the impact she would have had if she'd

stayed at home, like the proverbial couch-potato, with the television blaring, the central heating up full, the Volvo poised in the driveway in anticipation of the trip into town for a newspaper or a takeaway and so on. This is not an easy calculation to make, but it is possible to get some idea of the swings and roundabouts that are involved.

Once in Nepal, and living in the Nepalese manner, the Westerner's energy consumption falls to about one hundredth of what it was. This, of course, is offset by all the fuel she has used in flying there and back: about 80 gallons per passenger if the plane is fairly full. This is about quarter of a year's worth of driving, but very much less if you take all energy use (and not just driving) into account. So, surprisingly, she's actually in credit at the Carbon Bank after only a month or so in the Himalayas. She could, of course, go into the red again if she started whizzing around in helicopters and demanding meat and two veg every dinnertime, but I'll assume she's come to Nepal in order to mingle with its mountains and its people. And provided she stays long enough, walks to and from her chosen mountain, scatters small sums of money at grassroots level, and generally approves of and emulates (in some small way) the achievement of the local people – bringing up a family on a few square yards of hillside and the odd portering job – then I think neither the world nor the Himalayas will be any the worse for it.

Chris Bonington

Postscript

'**D**oing more with less', goes to the core of the meaning of adventure. It means applying the minimum of resources and numbers to any particular mountain challenge. The ultimate is to climb solo, one person totally alone on a high mountain. But most of us prefer to hedge our bets, to have others in support, to be linked by a rope, both to help our chances of survival and also to succeed. Ethical arguments represent the struggle to resolve these two conflicting aims of playing the ultimate risk game and surviving to enjoy it.

There are parallels in a wider field, for this goes to the centre of what we need to do in everyday life if we are to avoid depleting the natural resources of our planet. Both John Hunt and Mike Thompson refer to the title of Lionel Terray's magnificent autobiography, *La Conquête de l'Inutile*, translated for an English readership as *Conquistadors of the Useless*. We climbers might well be 'Useless Conquistadors' venturing into the 'Terraysphere', but in writing about it we can have a positive role that is not just vicarious entertainment but also a model for a broader approach to the way we carry out our lives on the surface of the Earth. Climbing becomes a tiny, all-embracing yet dramatic cosmos, a mirror for life. And hopefully, like life, it can also be a lot of fun, a mixture of humour and tragedy, of passion and angst, of idealism and ambition.

We have seen much of this in the prose of our contributors and the background history written by Audrey Salkeld and Stephen Venables. Here, as John Hunt wrote in his foreword, are the clues to why we climb.

But where do we stand today?

The mountains have sustained considerable pressure in the last hundred and fifty years, the duration of this young sport. Seen from a distance, the peaks appear to be just the same as they were two hundred or even two thousand years ago. Everest might be a little higher, thrust upwards by the collision of two continental shelves, the valleys a little deeper, the sides scoured of top soil by erosion. It is only when you come closer that the broad scars, caused by thousands of feet tramping up them, can be seen on so many of the lower mountains; on Sca Fell and Snowdon in the United Kingdom or Fujiyama in Japan; or rock faces bare of vegetation, scoured by climbers wanting pristine, clean, sterile rock for their sport. Or, on the sides of the higher peaks of the Alps, the mechanized paraphernalia of a ski industry, Alpine huts allowing climbers to penetrate the furthest reaches of the mountains in civilized comfort, or helicopters flitting among their spires, ready to rescue the unwary.

The area around Everest and so many other mountain regions, which just a few years ago were places of mystery, are now on the tourist trail. It is no longer a question of exploratory climbing but rather a form of super alpinism, with the Everest Base Camp, and many others, resembling the camp sites scattered around the Alps. Access is easy, there are tea shops or hotels near the foot of the mountain and there are any number of people. In the spring of 1993 there were twenty expeditions camped below the Khumbu Ice Fall of Everest, thirty-three people reached the summit in a single day, and it has become a guided tour no different in principle from Mont Blanc or the Matterhorn, although the price – at the moment anything up to $45,000 – is as superlative as its height.

Looking into the future, the majority will probably continue to flock to the 8,000 metre peaks in the Himalaya and the highest peaks in the world's other continents, the best climbers split between seeking out a rapidly decreasing selection of possible new lines and trying to climb existing ones faster or in better style. The vast majority, however, appear happy to repeat existing routes – a development of the cycle of climbing that has been present in the Alps for years.

But there is still exploration to be carried out in the Himalaya and other ranges in the world, on the smaller, lesser known mountains, often on peaks that do not even have a name but are just spot heights on a map. To me, this is climbing at its best, and there are enough unknown corners left to satisfy another generation or so of mountaineers, but it is a finite quantity and in the not-too-distant future an unclimbed peak could be rarer than the finest emerald. The moral is to get out there while there are still plenty left just waiting to be climbed.

But in doing so how can we try to preserve a feeling of unspoilt, untouched wild country? The starting point is to avoid leaving our traces, to carry our litter away with us. This is something that more and more climbers are becoming aware of. In 1990, together with Charles Houston and Sigi Hupfauer, I walked to the foot of the Diamir Face of Nanga Parbat. Base Camp is situated on a little grassy meadow to the side of the glacier. It's an idyllic site. As we got closer we saw it was littered with rubbish, part hidden in the long grass, under boulders and in the wreckage of a base tent that some group hadn't even bothered to take with them. There had been several expeditions there that season; you could tell their origin from the writing on the tins and packages. One expedition had even left a page from their application form almost as if it were a visiting card. We cleared up what we could, burning the rubbish, crushing the tins and then burying them in a deep hole. One could argue that the mess was little more than cosmetic, that it didn't actually damage the environment and that there are many more important issues. But at least meticulously clearing our own rubbish is something that we climbers can do, and if we can do this, then perhaps we can start trying to influence the wider, more intractable problems as well. If we made such efforts for the regions we explore, then we would certainly be better qualified to judge.

I went to Nepal in 1993 and visited the Everest Base Camp on the 40th anniversary of the first ascent. I was pleasantly surprised, for there was none of the piled rubbish I had been led to expect.

ABOVE: The Rupal Face of Nanga Parbat – the tallest mountain wall in the world at around 5,000 m. A truly imposing prospect.

brings the visitor in the first place. In Sola Khumbu it was encouraging to see fuel-efficient stoves with back boilers for hot water being installed in the Sherpa hotels. In addition several hydroelectric schemes are being developed.

Returning to mountaineering ethics, Messner has examined the development of alpinism within the framework of his own ascent of Mont Aiguille, arguably the first ever technical climb. He pines for the simplicity of an earlier age and the skill of Dibona, ' . . . he never took a fall, he never destroyed any myths. He did leave a few behind.' At the same time Messner questions, by implication, the way alpinism has developed, with its multi-day, multi-discipline ascents, linking climbs by parapente or ski. Many other climbing commentators have been more forceful. Indeed, Catherine Destivelle was criticized for her 'media circus' in the way her solo ascent of the Southwest Pillar of the Petit Dru was filmed by helicopter. But there is nothing new in this. Walter Bonatti's original ascent in 1955 was closely followed by the media, as indeed were the prewar attempts on the North Wall of the Eiger. Climbers have recorded their climbs for the benefit of the public from the very inception of our sport. Albert Smith lectured to packed audiences on his ascent of Mont Blanc in 1851, Mallory toured the country after his attempts on Everest in 1921 and '22, while Captain Noel brought back a troupe of Tibetan monks to provide background music and dancing for his magic lantern show after the 1924 expedition. The motive, surely, is a combination of a need for recognition as well as earning an income, combined with the creative satisfaction of telling a story well.

Some of the magic of alpinism has perhaps departed, but it is not so much because modern climbers' aspirations have changed but rather that most of the great lines have now been sought out. Therefore, to explore new frontiers, the climber has used new disciplines – the ski, snow-board, parapente, all of which demand a high level of skill and an even greater level of risk. Once again there has been criticism that the ascents are a form of commercially motivated media circus. Maybe they are, but imagine the sensation of gliding from the summit of the Fou, past the serrated tops of the Aiguilles, down the line of the Mer de Glace, to land at the base of the Drus. What a cocktail of experience, of extreme climbing, flight, mobility and speed.

And there are still lines hidden away, traditional adventures to be had. Marc Twight found his on the dark walls of the Pèlerins in winter, Bouchard on the great North Face of Temple in Canada, Sean Smith, on the soaring granite of the Central Tower of Paine in Patagonia. In the Himalaya, where the contrast is even greater, with the crowds around the 8,000 metre peaks, the possibility of exploration still exists in so many little-known valleys far away from the spotlight of competition.

The story of Polish climbing in the Himalaya is particularly rich, and Kurtyka's account not only gives a fascinating background in which to set the achievement but also captures the strength, yet tolerance, of his own personal commitment to alpine-style climbing on such an amazingly wide variety of objectives. His six 8,000 metre peaks are coupled with those smaller gems of Changabang South Face, the Trango Tower and the West Face of Gasherbrum IV, a mere shave below that magic height of 8,000 metres. In exploring his own motivation and that of his friend and climbing partner Kukuczka, he comes to terms with

I discovered that the Sherpas had set up a committee and had organized their own rubbish disposal system. It was encouraging to see this initiative coming from the local people rather than central government. But, as Thompson observed, the mess we leave behind us is just one small part of the problem. It is the wood we consume, the impact we have on the people living in the area, that has a much more profound effect on the environment.

In this respect I'd question Mike Thompson's observation that climbing in a more adventurous style, with smaller teams would, in reality, diminish the mountaineers' impact on the environment, since the volume of trekkers and the growth of tourism, with its accompanying glut of tea shops or hotels, has a far greater impact than any number of large expeditions. However, the example set by a climber changing his style of climbing to lessen his impact on the environment is important. Tourism, particularly when it is the local people who have exploited it with their own hotels and businesses, has undoubtedly raised the standard of living in many mountain communities. The challenge is to do this in a sustainable way, without denuding forests or ruining the appearance of the valleys – the very attraction that

Kukuczka's competitive drive, seeing in it not so much a fierce ego or need for fame but rather the motivation of any athlete who revels in competition. He also senses the conflict within himself, and I suspect most of us, summing up, 'I know it is an eternal conflict between vanity and the absolute, and simply the fact that after twenty years of climbing the struggle still rages within me is basically my only defeat.'

It is interesting to compare this with Messner's yearning for the ideals of his hero, Dibona, and his own motivation as he found himself caught up in (or did he seek) the glare of publicity in becoming the first man to climb all fourteen 8,000 metre peaks, only just in front of Jerzy Kukuczka.

But to date, the hardest and most impressive climb ever to be made is Tomo Cesen's claimed solo ascent of the huge South Face of Lhotse which had defeated some of the world's finest mountaineers – Messner, Christophe Profit, Marc Batard, Pierre Béghin and Krysztof Wieliki in a total of thirteen separate attempts, many of them by large siege-style expeditions. Cesen has set new standards, but only if he did indeed complete the climb, for there is a huge question mark not only over Cesen's claim on the South Face, but on all his other solo climbs as well. No one saw him on any of the summits he claimed to have climbed solo; there are no photographs to prove he went there and, more disturbing, one of the few photographs he used to show he was very close to the top of Lhotse turned out to have been taken by someone else. Cesen has stuck to his claim; some believe him and others don't. Messner, who presented him with his Snow Lions Award for his ascent of the North Face of Jannu, now questions his achievements.

Is Cesen the introspective, private individual who just wants to go out and push the limits further than any one has ever done before, without troubling to ensure he has solid evidence of what he has achieved, or has he fabricated a whole series of climbs for fame and gain? If he did indeed climb the South Face of Lhotse, how sad it is to deny such a huge achievement, and if he has lied about the ascent, what a terrible thing for him to have to live with for the rest of his days, a burden hardly compensated for by a few, or even many, material advantages gained in the shape of sponsorship or book and film contracts. As for myself, my heart wants to believe him, but my head can't help asking questions. There are a lot of discrepancies.

The whole sad business highlights the contradiction between ego, the need for

ABOVE: Lhotse South Face, which Reinhold Messner had predicted would be a route for the year 2000. Tomo Cesen claims to have sooled it in 1990 but Messner, for one, doubts that.

LEFT: An evening view of the Northwest Face of Jannu, photographed by Doug Scott on his way to Kangchenjunga.

recognition and the desire for the inner quest of self-fulfilment. Ego can be discerned as much in the motives of some detractors as it is in the claimants. There is nothing new in challenged ascents. The first ascent of Mount McKinley by the American climber Cooke in 1906 was discredited, and Maestri's claimed first ascent of Cerro Torre in 1958 is still contested. The Chinese claim to have made the first ascent of Everest from the north in 1960 was disputed because it was felt there was a lack of evidence and, more to the point, their account was disparaged because of the political rhetoric which struck a discordant note in Western minds. Today, however, with fresh evidence there seems little doubt that they did indeed reach the summit as they maintained.

The most fundamental development of all in climbing is closer to home. It is the growth of what has come to be known as sport climbing – the use of pre-placed bolts for protection instead of an array of alloy wedges and camming devises that can be placed in cracks or fissures in the rock. It's all about the level of risk we want to take in climbing and how important we perceive this risk element to be. To understand the arguments it is necessary to examine how methods of protection have evolved over the years. In Britain, because the crags are so small and also because of the way rock climbing developed almost as a sport in its own right, a set of ethics evolved that were very different from those observed

in most of the rest of Europe. The use of pitons in Britain was always abhorred. The sport emerged as an end in itself rather than just being training for the higher peaks of the Alps. The extensive use of pitons would have removed much of the fundamental challenge of cragging, shrinking our small rocks to an even greater degree. The prewar climber had his hemp rope and carried a sling or two which he draped over spikes of rock or around chock stones to use as running belays. In the Alps, on the other hand, because the scale was so much greater, the challenge bigger, pitons were used from an early stage, not only on the big North Walls but also on the smaller crags which were regarded as little more than training grounds for the real mountains. The only exception was on the sandstone of Saxony, described here by Dietrich Hasse. Because of the soft nature of the rock, which would have been destroyed by pitons, climbers evolved a strict code of ethics from an early stage in the region's mountaineering history, using jammed knots for protection.

Back in Britain, with the inevitable increase in climbing standards and the consequent greater chance of falling, the climber wanted to increase his chances of survival and therefore developed more sophisticated techniques. The inserted chock stone was first replaced by nuts with the threads drilled out and then these were refined into variously shaped alloy wedges. The

RIGHT: Collective effort – Chinese mountaineers tackle the North Col of Everest, head on, in 1975.

biggest development of all was the invention of the Friend, a camming device that could be slotted into different sized cracks. Placing protection is an art form in itself. You need to find the right shaped crack and select the appropriate device. There is always that level of uncertainty, of whether it will hold in the event of a fall and, when your second follows up the pitch, everything is removed and there is little or no trace of your passage. The climber, essentially, is accepting the natural form of the rock, and becoming attuned to it rather than forcing his will upon it. This style of climbing was never fully adopted in the rest of Europe although it enjoyed a brief popularity. It did, however, travel across the Atlantic and indeed was refined in the States, firstly by Yvon Chouinard who produced a series of carefully thought-out wedges and Hexcentric shapes, and finally, and most importantly, by Ray Jardine, who invented the Friend.

Another style of climbing was also being developed. Expansion bolts were adopted from building and civil engineering. They had the opportunistic advantage that the climber was no longer dependent on a line of cracks or the natural terrain but could go anywhere, drilling a line of bolts up a blank wall, and if there were no holds, simply pulling up from bolt to bolt. A number of routes were made in the Dolomites in the mid-fifties using this technique. But there were soon cries of protest from the purists. It negated so many of the reasons why we climb. Not only was the risk element removed but also much of the magic of exploration. You could go anywhere. You no longer had to interpret the rock. As a result this style of bolted big wall climbing died out in the sixties, to be replaced much more recently by a different approach to the use of bolts. The standard of free rock climbing was getting steadily higher throughout Europe. Ed Douglas has explored its development in Britain. On the sun baked limestone walls of the Verdon and other areas in France and Italy, there was a paucity of cracks for protection and yet plenty of tiny pockets for hand and foot holds. Bolt protection offered the solution.

This is really how sport climbing was born. The name comes from a number of contributory sources. The approach to climbing was becoming more athletic as standards increased and therefore a higher level of strength and agility was needed. People began to train. In Britain, Pete Livesey was one of the first. He found that man-made walls provided handy training areas. A logical development in this country, with its unreliable weather and short days in winter, was the indoor climbing wall, the first of which appeared in the early seventies, but which have steadily been improved to come closer to natural climbing.

With this increase in standards the climber was pushing himself to the level where falls were inevitable and, at the same time, the holds were so exiguous, the ground so steep, often overhanging, that it was impossible to place conventional protection. It seemed irrelevant anyway, since the challenge was essentially gymnastic, that of pushing the body to its absolute limits, as would any athlete.

In parallel came formal competition climbing. This was first developed in the Soviet Union and was initially ridiculed by Western climbers, but in the eighties it was adopted on the Continent, the first big competition being held in Italy. Whereas the Russians had tended to opt for speed climbing protected by top ropes, the Western version was more akin to the bolt protected climbing already popular on limestone. The climbs were led with the competitors, for safety sake, compelled to clip into all the bolts, on the way up.

British climbers had already been introduced to bolt protected climbing on the Continent and it was inevitable that competition climbing would be introduced into Britain. It happened in 1988 when John Dunn organized an event at Malham Cove. It was to be televised for BBC's Saturday sports programme, 'Grandstand'. Traditional climbers were aghast and the British Mountaineering Council mobilized its forces to put a stop to it. Was the fuss justified? I think so. It helped to define the role of competition climbing, steering it away from the natural crags and onto man-made structures, since the BMC then went on to help organize the first indoor international grand prix competition to be held in Britain, which was staged in Leeds in 1989. Interestingly, almost all competitions throughout the world are now held on man-made walls since these, in most respects apart from aesthetics, are better than the natural crags.

The conflict within the climbing world is not so much about competition climbing but is about territory, a question of which, if any, crags can be bolted. On the Continent there has been very little controversy. Pitons had always been used for protection and, although British free climbing had a brief vogue with the

introduction of metal wedges and Friends, it never really caught hold. As sport climbing began to use bolts for protection – which the French call 'free climbing' – the custom has spread, with almost every route on the Continent now being bolted. Doug Scott had a recent visit to Spain and was appalled by the number of bolts he found in routes that had originally been climbed using traditional protection. He wrote an article in *Mountain Review*, entitled, 'Bolts from the Blue', deploring the trend not only in Spain but in Britain as well.

I recently went to St Bees Head, a magnificent cliff of red sandstone on the west coast of Cumbria. I had last been there some thirty years ago when we had made a first ascent up steep, crumbling sandstone, past obstreperous sea birds and through piles of bird droppings. I never returned, although others put up a few routes. Then in the last couple of years some local climbers, armed with bolt guns, began putting sports climbs up the lower, firmer tier of the cliff. You could climb the first twenty metres or so and then lower off. I went with an open mind and was surprised to find how many people were there, many of them familiar faces from the past. Martin Berzens and Neil Foster, two traditional climbers with a whole list of outstanding new routes on Yorkshire grit and limestone, were there sampling the E3s and 4s. John Adams, who had made the first ascent of 'Lord of the Rings', that magnificent girdle traverse of the East Buttress of Scafell, had put up many of the routes on St Bees, while Andy Hyslop, proprietor of a climbing shop in Ambleside, owned the battery operated bolt gun. The conversation was of the different merits of various brands of bolts. The gun itself operated with a quiet whirr, barely discernible above the squawk of sea birds and the lapping of waves.

There were natural lines with cracks for protection. Doug Scott had been there some months earlier but refused to have anything to do with bolts and had battled up an overhanging crack using traditional protection. There were indeed places you could have put in wires or Friends, but most of the lines are bolted and it is seductively easy to carry a few quick draws and just clip in on the way up. It made for an enjoyable afternoon by the sea, pushing yourself that little bit harder than you would have dared without the bolts. I'll go back but I, as I'm sure is the case with most who were climbing there that afternoon, will always prefer the high mountain crags with their traditional climbing. I quickly tire of the sameness of these bolted routes – they have none of the individual character that each and every naturally protected climb has, none of the very particular, unexpected challenges.

Is this development in climbing such a dangerous threat to everything we hold dear? Quite a few climbers think it is. Doug wrote in his article:

'For a hundred years the British tradition existed, and now in the last ten years the holes are being drilled into the rock, and faster still as new petrol driven drills become available. . . . The old order changeth, but it doesn't always change for the better, not if the past is scrapped out of hand.'

And the argument will go on. It is important that it does, for it is through this continuing dialogue that our sport can develop in a way that will maintain the quality of our traditional 'adventure' climbing values at the same time as allowing the development of sport climbing. There is a continuous cross-over between the two styles as was very obvious that afternoon on St Bees. It is difficult to predict how the balance will develop in the future as more and more climbers are introduced to the sport through indoor climbing walls. There is already pressure to develop more areas for sports climbing, or even to start placing bolts on belay points in the name of safety. Just recently in Britain, the National Trust, which owns many of our finest crags, have become aware of the number of cliffs that have been bolted. They have objected on aesthetic and environmental grounds. The case is the same in the United States where several national parks have banned all bolting for similar reasons. It is ironic, and I think regrettable, that the strongest upholders of traditional climbing might end up being institutions that are the custodians of the land and not the climbers themselves. It is up to the climbing body as a whole to argue the issue through, to come up with a policy that can be agreed by both schools of thought and then, most important of all, for people to stick to those decisions. I sincerely hope for the sake of the enjoyment and fulfilment of future generations of climbers, that the crags with features that yield natural lines will always be free of bolts, that they also will be able to enjoy the romance of exploration with that vital piquancy of risk – in essence, 'doing more with less'.

Another interesting development in the last few years is the way women have caught up with men in climbing ability. They have taken an active part from the very beginning – Lucy Walker and Miss Brevoort in the 1860s, Lily Bristow, whose letters from Chamonix opened this anthology, right through to the present day. But even when I started climbing some forty years ago, relatively few women actually took the lead when rock climbing, and those who did were climbing at a very much lower standard than men. It was all too easy to take the view that women not only were not as strong, but also that they didn't have the same appetite for risk taking – that the man was the hunter and the woman the home maker – a facile stereotype or could there be some truth in the observation?

The big breakthrough in women's climbing seems to have come about in the wake of the development of sport climbing. The risk is undoubtedly lower, there is less equipment to carry and none of the business of fiddling with nuts and Friends to get the right fit. Very quickly women were getting close to the best male performance in competition climbing. For example, Lynn Hill, an outstanding competition climber, in effect came third over-all in

ABOVE: Catherine Destivelle, danseuse de roc; bold and, for some, a controversial figure.

the World Championships at Lyon in 1990. Whereas in the eighties the best women climbers were leading at only E3 or 4 in standard, today there are plenty climbing at E5 or 6.

Catherine Destivelle, in her remarkable solo ascent on the Southwest Pillar of the Petit Dru, took it a step further, committing herself to a sustained artificial route on a big mountain. She did this after a successful spell in competition climbing – yet another sign of the crossover between the two aspects of our sport. Britain's best woman mountaineer is undoubtedly Alison Hargreaves, who made a remarkable series of solo ascents in the Alps in the summer of 1993, culminating with the North Face of the Croz. In 1993 also, Lynn Hill was the first person to climb the Nose of El Capitan completely free – a major innovative step by any standards. There is no reason why women climbers shouldn't equal men in their performance in an even wider sphere in the mountains. On rock, their power-to-weight ratio is often as good, if not better, and they also tend to be more supple. On higher mountains, as demonstrated by Wanda Rutkiewicz and Kitty Calhoun Grissom, they can participate fully in any expedition. It's refreshing to see an increasing number of mixed groups on rock or on expeditions, taking an equal part in their climbs.

The majority of the contributors to this collection have essentially been in the classic mould of exploratory climbers, although even here there is a wide spectrum of personal motivation, conditioned by the period of time at which they ventured into the hills, their background and their own psyche. The differences in emphasis really reflect the particular level and style of competitiveness that the individuals possess.

Reinhold Messner and Jerzy Kukuczka are both outstanding, indeed unique, exploratory climbers, but they were equally captivated by the competitive drive of being first to climb all fourteen 8,000 metres peaks, a race which Messner won whilst strenuously denying that he was undertaking a race at all. Voytek Kurtyka and Doug Scott, on the other hand, have consistently followed a path of exploratory climbing on peaks of both over and under 8,000 metres. Rob Collister, at another extreme, captured the delight of climbing a classic traverse of Mont Pelvoux in the Dauphiné, while Ed Douglas explored the ramifications of modern extreme rock climbing.

Kurtyka is so right when he states: 'Detecting a single rule governing this energy is difficult – it arises and vanishes like the urge to dance, and remains as mysterious as the phenomenon of life itself'.

Glossary and Reference

ABSEILING Method of descending steep terrain by sliding down a rope. Coloquially: 'abbing off'. The same as rappelling.

ACCLIMATIZATION Process of physiological adaptation to living and climbing at high altitude where the thin air has less oxygen and is at lower pressure.

AID Direct use of inserted devices (pitons or other artificial means) for further progress on a climb.

ALPENSTOCK A stout stick with an iron tip. A nineteenth-century term, from the German, 'Alps stick'.

ALPINE-STYLE Method of climbing large mountains without previously stocking fixed camps; this usually means going without additional oxygen or sherpa support. There are degrees at which one can dispense with equipment, assistance and companions for ultra-lightweight alpine-style ascents.

ANCHOR The point to which a fixed belay rope is anchored. Either a natural rock feature, a piton in a rock crack or ice, or a deadman in snow.

ANGLE A folded steel piton.

ARÊTE A sharp rock or snow ridge.

BELAYING Tying oneself to a firm anchor in order to safeguard the other climbers in a roped group and to prevent oneself being pulled off.

BERGSCHRUND The gap, or crevasse, between the glacier proper and the upper snows of the face of a mountain.

BIVOUAC (Bivvy) Temporary overnight stop without a proper tent.

BRACHIATE Swinging from one hold to another by the arms.

BRÈCHE A deep notch in the skyline, a gap in a ridge.

CAMMING DEVICE A tool used in protected rock climbing to supply a secure fixture for a rope.

CHIMNEY A very narrow gully.

CLIMBING ROPED Where there is no fixed rope and climbers rope together to safeguard each other over difficult or dangerous ground. They can either move together or one moves at a time with the other(s) belaying him or her.

CLIMBING SOLO Climbing alone.

COL A dip in a ridge, usually between two peaks. The same as a saddle, or pass.

CORNICE An overhanging mass of wind-sculpted snow projecting beyond the crest of a ridge. A potentially dangerous feature.

CORRIE A deep rounded hollow or basin at the head or side of a valley. The same feature as a coire, cirque or Cwm.

COULOIR An open gully.

CRAMPONS Frames of metal spikes which can be fitted to boots to give a grip on ice and firm snow slopes.

CREVASSE A crack in a glacier surface, which can be wide and very deep, made by the movement of the glacier over irregularities in its bed, or by bends in its course.

DEADMAN An alloy fluke or plate which is dug into the snow to provide an anchor. The harder it is pulled, the deeper it digs itself in.

DIHEDRAL/DIÈDRE The terms for a wide-angled or 'open book' crack or corner.

ENCHAINEMENTS The stringing together of two or more hard routes as a single enterprise, made possible usually by speeding up the descents in between – by skiing perhaps, or paragliding.

ÉTRIERS Portable steps or foot slings used in aid climbing, usually of a light alloy or nylon webbing.

FACE (or wall) The steep aspect of a mountain between two ridges.

FIXED ROPE On the steep ground of prolonged climbs, the lead climber – having run out the full length of rope – attaches it to anchors, so that all those following can use it as a safety line by clipping into it. It remains in place for the whole expedition.

FREE CLIMBING Climbing without recourse to artificial aids, such as pegs and étriers, although protective runners are allowed.

FRIENDS Revolutionary camming devices invented in the 1970s for protecting rock climbs. They offer flexibility in their application.

FRONT POINTING Climbing straight up steep snow or ice by means of digging in the forward-projecting points of crampons and supporting a balance with hand-held tools.

GENDARME A sharp pinnacle of rock on a ridge.

GLISSADE A controlled slide down hard snow as a speedy means of descent. The ice axe is employed as a brake.

HEXENTRIC A form of nut, used in rock climbing.

ICE FALL Where a glacier falls steeply and creates a series of cre-vasses and pinnacles of ice. Because of its constant movement, an ice fall is one of the most dangerous mountain features, yet it can rarely be avoided as a route of access to the upper slopes.

ICE SCREW Literally that, a threaded piton which can be screwed into ice (or hammered in and screwed out) as a protective belay.

JAMMING Wedging parts of the body or aids into or against a rock face during a climb, as in hand-jam, leg-jam and so on.

JUMARING A method of climbing fixed rope with jumar clamps or other ascenders. Fitted with a handle, a jumar can be slid up a rope but locks onto it to support weight when subjected to a downward force. (See also Prusiking)

KARABINERS Oval, or D-shaped metal snap-links, offering a universal means of attachment: climber to rope, ropes to belays, as runners, for abseiling etc. Can be shortened to Krabs. In North America is usually spelt Carabiner.

KLETTERGARTEN A rocky training ground.

MORAINE Accumulation of stones and debris carried down by a glacier.

NÉVÉ Permanent snow above the head of a glacier. (Same as firn.)

NUT A metal chockstone carrying a wire loop, for insertion into a crack as a running belay to protect a falling leader.

OFFWIDTHS Cracks too wide for a fist jam and too narrow for more than an arm or leg. Awkward and strenuous to climb, as they are to descend. Can be difficult to protect.

PENDULUM To swing across from one position to another on a rope.

OUTLIER An outcrop of rocks, surrounded by older rocks.

PITCH A section of climbing between two stances or belay points.

PITON A metal peg hammered into a crack to support a belay. There is a wide variety of these for every possible contingency, bearing such names as Angles, Leepers, Bongs, Bugaboos and Rurps.

PROTECTION The number and quality of running belays used to make a pitch safer and psychologically easier to lead.

PRUSIKING Originally a method of directly ascending a rope with the aid of sliding prusik knots, or friction hitches, with foot loops. These days various mechanical devices have replaced the rope knot for easier prusiking.

RACK The assortment of ironmongery a climber takes with him on a climb. Can be carried on loops on the climbing harness, or on a bandolier across the shoulder. Racking gear so that you can retrieve the right piece in a hurry is a personal art.

RAPPELLING *see* Abseiling

RIME Frost on solid surfaces, formed from frozen water droplets.

ROTTEN ROCK Unreliable, friable rock.

RUNNER (or running belay) An intermediate anchor point between the lead climber and the main belay, where the climbing rope runs through a karabiner attached to this anchor. This increases security by reducing the distance that a leader could fall.

SASTRUGI Ridges and other raised formations on a snow surface caused by wind action.

SÉRAC A pinnacle or tower of ice, usually unstable and dangerous.

SHERPAS Properly, an ethnic group of Tibetan stock, living below Everest in the Sola Khumbu area (female: Sherpanis). From the Sherpas' effective monopoly of high altitude portering in Nepal, the name has come to be applied to all those who work in that profession, even those from different ethnic groups such as Tamangs.

SIRDAR The head Sherpa on an expedition. He acts as the middleman between foreign expedition leaders and the porters.

SPINDRIFT Loose powder snow carried by wind or a small avalanche.

SPUR A rock or snow rib on the side of a mountain.

STANCE The place where climber makes a belay, ideally somewhere comfortable to stand or sit.

TALUS (or scree) An accumulation of rock fragments that have fallen from a crag. This can build up as steeply-sloping fans, suitable for 'scree-running'.

TERRODACTYL A special type of ice-climbing implement – the first angled pick on an ice tool, designed by Hamish MacInnes.

TOP ROPE Rope secured from above.

TORQUE To twist an artificial aid into position to give a secure hold.

VERGLAS A thin coating of ice on rocks, making the going dangerous.

WINDSLAB A type of avalanche that can occur when a snow layer compacted by wind settles insecurely on top of old snow. It falls as enormous blocks or slabs.

A COMPARATIVE TABLE OF INTERNATIONAL ROCK-CLIMBING GRADES

UIAA	F	USA	GB	AUS
I	1	5.2	moderate	
II	2	5.3	difficult	11
III	3	5.4	very difficult	12
IV	4	5.5	4a	
V-		5.6		13
V	5	5.7	4b	14
V+			4c	15
VI-		5.8	5a	16 / 17
VI	6a	5.9	E1	18
VI+	6a+	5.10a	5b	19
VII-	6b	5.10b		20
		5.10c	E2	21
VII	6b+	5.10d	5c	22
VII+	6c	5.11a		
	6c+	5.11b		23
VIII-	7a	5.11c	E3	24
VIII	7a+	5.11d	6a	25
VIII+	7b	5.12a	E4	
	7b+	5.12b	6b	26
IX-	7c	5.12c	E5	
IX	7c+	5.12d / 5.13a		27
				28
IX+	8a	5.13b	6c	29
X-	8a+	5.13c	E6	30
				31
X	8b	5.13d	7a	32
X+	8b+	5.14a		
XI-	8c	5.14b	7b E7	33

CONVERSIONS METRES TO FEET

metres	feet
3,300	10,827
3,400	11,155
3,500	11,483
3,600	11,811
3,700	12,139
3,800	12,467
3,900	12,795
4,000	13,124
4,100	13,452
4,200	13,780
4,300	14,108
4,400	14,436
4,500	14,764
4,600	15,092
4,700	15,420
4,800	15,748
4,900	16,076
5,000	16,404
5,100	16,733
5,200	17,061
5,300	17,389
5,400	17,717
5,500	18,045
5,600	18,373
5,700	18,701
5,800	19,029
5,900	19,357
6,000	19,685
6,100	20,013
6,200	20,342
6,300	20,670
6,400	20,998
6,500	21,326
6,600	21,654
6,700	21,982
6,800	22,310
6,900	22,638
7,000	22,966
7,100	23,294
7,200	23,622
7,300	23,951
7,400	24,279
7,500	24,607
7,600	24,935
7,700	25,263
7,800	25,591
7,900	25,919
8,000	26,247
8,100	26,575
8,200	26,903
8,300	27,231
8,400	27,560
8,500	27,888
8,600	28,216
8,700	28,544
8,800	28,872

Index

Acknowledgements

So many mountain friends have helped in the production of this book. The editors and publishers wish to place on record their gratitude for the generosity and patience of all contributors. A special thank-you, too, must go to translators of that material which was not originally in English: to Ingeborga Doubrawa-Cochlin for the writings of Wanda Rutkiewicz and Irena Kesa; to Adam Czarniecki for Voytek Kurtyka; Angela Kalisch for Reinhold Messner; Alexander Luty for Valery Khrischaty, and to the late Jill Neate for Peter Habeler and Dietrich Hasse. We also acknowledge the assistance given to Tony Streather by Ralph Barker, and to Pertemba by Lisa Choegyal.

Additionally, we are indebted to Michael Westmacott and other officers of the Alpine Club, Shane Winser at the Royal Geographical Society, H. Adams Carter of the American Alpine Journal, and to the British Mountaineering Council.

Chris Bonington and Audrey Salkeld

The publishers would like to thank Audrey Salkeld for her invaluable help in researching the often very elusive illustrations for this book. Special thanks are also due to Ingeborga Doubrawa-Cochlin, Jozef Nyka, Zbigniew Kowalewski and Mikolaj Blaszkiewicz for their work on the Polish sections of the book, to Frances Daltrey of the Chris Bonington Library, to the staff of the Libraries and Map Room of the Royal Geographical Society, and in particular to the ever-patient Jayne Dunlop, and to Bob Lawford of the Alpine Club. Every effort has been made to trace copyright-holders but if errors or omissions are brought to our attention we shall be pleased to correct them in future editions of the book.

(Abbreviations: B=Bottom, C=Centre, L=Left, R=Right, T=Top.
Pictures on page 200 are credited alphabetically from left to right.)

Alpine Club endpapers, 17B, 18TL, 18TR, 18C, 19T, 80R; Alpine Museum, Zermatt 14C; *Alpinismus* 45; Aquarius Picture Library 67TR; Beloeil/Twight 38; Eric Bjornstad 82T; Barry Blanchard 97-101 (all eight); Chris Bonington and Library 17T, 30C, 42, 63B, 73B, 111T, 142-3, 144T, 155B, 186-7, 192, 193T, 195, 196B, 197, 217, Hilary Boardman 113, Peter Boardman 193B, 211B, Brian Hall 18B, Alan Hinkes 216T, John Porter 203, 204B; British Library/Oriental and India Office Collections (WD 350) 148C; Adrian Burgess 124-5; Adams Carter 156R; Sylvie Chappaz 34 (both), 37R; Jonathan Chester/Extreme Images 136-7, 138-41 (all eleven); Chrobak 202T; Leszek Cichy/Archiv Kurt Diemberger 168-9; John Cleare/Mountain Camera 2-3, 5, 6-7, 24R, 38-9, 44-5, 51 (all three), 64L, 68-9, 82-3, 83, 153, 155T, 157, 159, 164, 170-1, 171, 172-3, 187, 194T, 196T, 201TR, 201B, 211C; Rob Collister 24L, 24-5; Ed Cooper 82B; Mike Covington 180; Cowboyography/Valdez 102; Noel Craine 128BL; Rainer Dick/Archiv Hasse 61B; Leo Dickinson 168T, 194B; Mandy Dickinson 76R; Kurt Diemberger 174, 176, 177R, 178T, 178C; Mark Diggins 77; Ingeborga Doubrawa-Cochlin 200i; Glenn Dunmire/Mountain Imagery 90; John Earle 116, 117B, 118R, 119, 120, 121T; Fell and Rock Climbing Club 50; Mick Fowler 10, 68, 70-1; Peter Gillman 163B, 189T; Kitty Calhoun Grissom Collection 186, 188, 190; S. Gutiev 52-3, 54; Brian Hall 124 (all three), 125; Dietrich Hasse 56T, 56-7, 58, 59L, 60-1, Archiv Hasse 56B, 59R; Bill Hatcher 103-7 (all nine); Andrzej Heinrich 200l; Bruce Herrod 115, 213; Robin Hodgkin 53B, 55; Steve Hong/Mountain Imagery 94R; Charles Houston 156L (all seven); Hulton-Deutsch Collection 163T; Lord Hunt 20-3 (all seven), 49T; Michael Kennedy 145T; Mrs Valery Khrischaty/Kazakh Alpine Federation 206; Troy Kirwan 96; Bob Koates 62; Jerzy Kukuczka 200m; Voytek Kurtyka 198, 200d; Hamish MacInnes 67TL; Roger Mear 130-1, 132-5 (all four); Reinhold Messner 172B; Czeslaw Momatiuk 200c; Ben Moon 75T; Pat Morrow/Mountain Camera 112B; Greg Mortimer 136; Bernard Newman 76L; Josef Nyka 30L, 30R, 200a-b, e-h; Bill O'Connor 26, 29L, 64R; Popperfoto/Look/Wiesmeier 75B; Paul Ramsay 72; Reebok/Karol Marketing 122; Reed International Books Ltd 81B, 109TR, 109B; Rex Features/Sipa Press 219; Kev Reynolds 49C, 49B; Royal Geographical Society 13B, 78, 80L, 109TL, 109C, 146-7, 148BL, 149C, 149B, 150 (both), 160, 161C, 161B, 162, Chris Caldicott 13T, 211T, David Constantine 212-13, G. Dainelli 152, Dr Filippo di Filippi 149T, Paul Harris 212T, 212C, Eric Lawrie 111B, Roger Mear 15B, 26-7, V. Sella 81T, Eric Shipton 117T, 118L, 121B, Bill Tilman 151T; Wanda Rutkiewicz Collection 28, 29R, 31 (both); Salkeld Collection 14L, 14R, 15T, 15C, 16, 19B, 43, 46-7 (all four), 52, 110, 148T, 148BR, 151B, 154, 158 (all three); 161T; Victor Saunders 70, 71, 73T, 73C; Doug Scott 180-1, 182-5 (all five), 189B, 190-1, 216B; Rudolf Seifert/Archiv Hasse 59C; Sean Smith 11 (all three), 126-7 (all three), 128T, 128BR, 129 (both), 174-5, 202B, 205, 206-7, 208-9, 215; Frank Spooner\Gamma Sport 32, 33, 35L, 36 (both), 37L, Gerard Kosicki 35R; Gordon Stainforth 63T, 65, 66, 67B; Tony Streather 165-7 (all five); Mike Stroud 130; Heinz Lothar Stutte/Archiv Hasse 61T; Geoffrey Tabin 142, 144B, 145B; Anne Thompson 210; Judy Todd 123; Marc Twight 40-1 (all four); Stephen Venables 1, 8, 177L, 178-9, 201TL; Bradford Washburn 78-9, 84-9 (all ten); Ed Webster/Mountain Imagery 91-3 (all five), 94L, 95; Wielicki Collection 199, 200k; K. J. Wilson Collection 112TL, 112TR, 200j, Alison Chadwick 168B, 170, 172C; Andrej Zawada 204T.